choice
and
change

choice
and
change

the psychology of adjustment, growth, and creativity

revised edition

April O'Connell
Santa Fe Community College

Vincent F. O'Connell
Consulting Psychologist

Prentice-Hall, Inc. Englewood Cliffs, N.J. 07632

5894285

-90

Library of Congress Cataloging in Publication Data

O'CONNELL, APRIL.
   Choice and change.

Edition of 1974 by V. O'Connell and A. O'Connell.
Includes bibliographical references and index.
   1. Personality.   2. Maturation (Psychology)
I. O'Connell, Vincent,   joint author.
II. Title.
BF698.027 1980   155.2'5   79-27582
ISBN 0-13-133066-7

CHOICE AND CHANGE: THE PSYCHOLOGY OF ADJUSTMENT,
   GROWTH, AND CREATIVITY, REVISED EDITION.
APRIL O'CONNELL
VINCENT O'CONNELL

Printed in the United States of America

10 9 8 7 6 5 4 3 2 1

Editorial/Production Supervision by Joyce Turner
Interior Design by Cathie Mick
Cover Design by RL Communications
Manufacturing Buyer: Ed Leone
Drawings by Heidi Klier
Photographs by Wyatt Saxon

Prentice-Hall International, Inc., *London*
Prentice-Hall of Australia Pty. Limited, *Sydney*
Prentice-Hall of Canada, Ltd., *Toronto*
Prentice-Hall of India Private Limited, *New Delhi*
Prentice-Hall of Japan, Inc., *Tokyo*
Prentice-Hall of Southeast Asia Pte. Ltd., *Singapore*
Whitehall Books Limited, *Wellington, New Zealand*

Dedicated to
Florence and Charles Libby
and
Bernard and Ida O'Connell
Good Family
Good Friends

contents

Part Three   THE EMOTIONAL SELF:
AND THE FORCES OF SOCIETY

preface

When the original edition of *Choice and Change* was written, we had not foreseen the need for a revised edition. *Choice and Change* was our modest attempt to bring together the various and multi-faceted aspects of personality theory and research. Specifically, we wanted the readers to get an historical view for the advances of personal psychology as it exists today; to understand some of the determinants of personality patterning as it applies to their own lives, and to explore a few of the burgeoning techniques and methods for furthering their creative potential. That was our first objective. Our second objective was to bring this material together in a way that would combine a high interest level with literary style so that the students would have a book they like to read and, in fact, would enjoy reading. We wanted to share with them some of the excitement and fascination that all of us who work in psychology (in one way or another) find in the areas of personal and interpersonal theory, research, and application.

The heart-warming response from students and instructors alike have confirmed that we met the second objective, and that *Choice and Change*, first edition, was a highly readable book. The first objective was successful only to the extent of our inclusions. We have been besieged with requests to include other kinds of materials. The problem in writing the revised edition has been to include the most desired material but, at the same time, to keep the book from becoming an overly long compendium that might result in the encyclopedia style of so many text books; that is, to lose the very readability that students and instructors have appreciated.

This revised edition, then, is (in large measure) the result of your suggestions and ideas. The result is a total reorganization of the book that a glance at the Table of Contents will quickly reveal. For example, the chapter on the highly creative person (formerly Chapter 2) has been moved to the end of the book to serve as a kind of capstone for rest of the chapters. In addition, other chapters have been combined in order to make way for four new chapters dealing with:

individual differences and personal life-style;

love, sex, and marriage;

language and communication;

death and dying, divorce, survival, and remarriage.

Furthermore, we have added much new material to previous chapters including, for example, the following:

the extension of life-span development and tasks
by vanGennep, Levinson, and Sheehy;

the intellectual and moral development of the child
by Jean Piaget and Lawrence Kohlberg;

the life-style emphasis of Alfred Adler;

other therapeutic approaches such as Rational-Emotive therapy, Reality therapy, Implosive therapy, Behavior therapy, and an actual transcript of a Gestalt session with Fritz Perls.

One of the most perplexing criticisms of *Choice and Change*, first edition, was that the students found the book so interesting that they did not know how to take notes or study for tests. To answer that problem, we have completely revamped the Student Guide Book and the Instructor's Manual. The Student Guidebook now has a "Points to Remember" section for each chapter as well as several other types of study aides which, we believe, you will find more academically rigorous, but that the students will find challenging and innovating.

We have also kept the best of the line-drawings from the first edition, but we have added some thirty photographs we believe clarify the text material.

Finally, and in direct response to your requests, we have added an Applications to the end of every chapter. The original edition of *Choice and Change* presented the theory and problems of personality integration in the first half of the book and the applications and therapeutic methods were not introduced until the second half (Part II) of the book. In this edition, every theoretical discussion is followed by a practical discussion on how the material presented may be applied not only in personal lives, but also in professional roles including education, nursing, and the various psychology-related fields.

If you like the revised edition of *Choice and Change*, you have only yourself to credit. If you find something amiss or missing, won't you let us know?

We would like particularly to thank all those consultants who have contributed in one way or another to the manuscript.

Thomas T. Hewett, Drexel University
Maurice Cadwalder, San Jacinto College
Ernest J. Doleys, DePaul University
Mildred Treumann, Moorhead State University
Charles B. Dawson, Brevard Community College
Gerald Corey, California State University, Fullerton
Ralph C. Wiggins, Jr., Virginia Commonwealth University
Vergie Lee Behrens, Phoenix, Arizona
Russell Lee, Bemidji State University
Wayne Weiten, College of DuPage
Ronald N. Tietbohl, Wesley College
Norma Lee K. Mittenthal, Hillsborough Community College

April O'Connell/Vincent O'Connell
Gainesville, Florida
Winter, 1979

to know thyself:

a look at the process

ONE

personality integration: the ever-new, the never-ending process

Joy, sadness, anger, indifference, depression—even occasional maladjustment—are all part of the growth process.

some tenets of growth psychology

A New Direction: Humanistic Psychology

There is an ebb and flow in all things and so it is also in psychological theory.

The Adjustment Approach to Personality

Thirty, forty, and fifty years ago, books on personality theory used concepts and terms no longer considered useful for the science of human behavior and the reality of today. *Mental health* and *mental illness, normal* and *abnormal behavior,* and *good* or *poor adjustment* were the prevailing constructs.[1] Then, many persons, like Candide,* viewed their society as "the best of all possible worlds," and anyone who could not fit into that world—someone who was awkwardly out of step or who had not grasped the American drive for achievement and success—somehow must be badly adjusted, unadjusted, or maladjusted. It was the job of our American psychologists to "adjust" these people. Adjustment seemed that simple—then! *Industrial* psychologists helped men and women to adjust to their jobs; *school* psychologists helped children adjust to school; *clinical* psychologists helped families adjust to each other, and so on. Though we did not realize it then, this was leading toward a Procrustean mentality** and this attitude even began to appear in American politics, business, and foreign policy. It was the kind of thinking which led a General Motors executive to declare "What's good for General Motors is good for the country!"

That kind of belief system and theory eventually produced a kind of patriotic chauvinism preventing us from seeing our faults and our

*Candide, a fictional character invented by the French satirist, Voltaire, was so limited in his thinking and outlook that no matter what outrage or disaster befell him, he continued to think that it was "the best of all possible worlds."

**Procrustes is a mythical Greek personality who forced his victims to sleep in his iron bed. If they were too large for the bed he cut their legs off. If they were too short, he stretched them.

limitations. We had come to perceive everything American as the best that there is. The American way of life was advocated from the pulpits of our churches, from the desks of our public officials, and even in our school systems to the point that we became blind to what we had become as a nation and as a people.

Society Under Indictment

To be sure, there always were some with clearer vision. Our near-sighted patriotism was satirized by Sinclair Lewis in his novel, *Main Street*.[2] Our WASPish culture was indicted by other books such as Laura Hobson's *Gentleman's Agreement*,[3] which dealt with the anti-Semitism of our society, and sociologists like Vance Packard whacked away at corporation executives whom he called *The Status Seekers* and *The Pyramid Climbers*.[4] John Steinbeck revealed the ugliness of our impoverished migrants in *Grapes of Wrath*.[5] David Riesman called us *A Lonely Crowd*.[6]

In the late sixties and early seventies, a series of traumatic events shook this nation. Black resentment and rage flared up in the ghettos. Violence killed first a president, then his brother running for office, as well as a nonviolent spokesman and leader for the black population of our country. Students rose up all over the country to protest our military engagements, burning their draft cards and leaving their country to avoid participating in what they called an unjust and imperialistic war. Several unarmed students were killed by the state's National Guard on the campus of a midwestern university. The televised events of Watergate and its aftermath revealed the extent to which our personal and private liberties—all those rights ordained by our founding fathers through the Constitution and first ten amendments—had been corrupted by political, business, and military interests. No matter that we were made gullible by our "innocence." We can no longer afford to be innocent.

It is not surprising that psychologists and other social scientists have become increasingly embarrassed by the word *adjustment*, especially when some say that it is our society which is sick[7] and needs to be treated.[8] They argue that terms such as *adjustment, mental health*, and *mental illness* are not only meaningless, arbitrary, and fallacious but are downright dangerous.[9]

We have been blind, for example, to the ugliness in our country,[10] and we have been deaf to our critics. In a country where all people are supposed to be created equal, we have ignored the existence of class and caste.[11] In a land of abundance we have ignored the existence of

We wanted our immigrants to lose their ethnic qualities; we wanted our black citizens to act "white;" and we wanted our lower socioeconomic classes to model themselves after the middle class. We are now learning to appreciate those characteristics that distinguish one group from another.

the poor, the ignorant,[12] and the American Indians. In this age of social welfare and medicine, we have allowed the aged to live out their lives in misery and humiliation.[13] We urged our immigrants to become Americanized, our black citizens to become more "white," and our lower classes to model themselves after the middle class.

This is not to say that there are not values in our culture and in our way of life that are good. No one else can raise a hog so lean and big on an acre of corn as can the Iowa farmer. The Imperial Valley in California, once a desert, now produces fruits and vegetables, thanks to American engineering and imagination. American products are still among the best and least expensive manufactured goods. Moreover, more than any other country in the world, American education still is attempting to achieve the most good for the most people. And we still open our portals to the tired, the poor, the homeless, and the wretched of the world.

The Growth Approach to Personality

We have been deaf and blind to many things about ourselves, but there have been some changes. The eruptions of the ghettos, the clamor for equal rights by blacks, Indians, Spanish-Americans, students, and women, and the shocking national and international events have not been in vain. We are beginning to listen to what our critics have been trying to tell us all along. Part of this awareness is leading to a different kind of psychology, one that emphasizes *growth*, not adjustment; the *unique*, not the normal; and the *creative*, not the average.

This approach to personality has many names: humanistic psychology, "third force" psychology, existential psychology. Whatever it is called, it emphasizes the growth of the individual toward his or her highest creative potential. For that reason, we shall call it *growth psychology*. This approach works toward freeing those untapped resources and abilities within each person that can lead to fuller, more thoughtful, more rewarding ways of living. This approach asserts that "adjusting" the person to society is no longer the ultimate goal for either the person or society. The growth approach puts the *person* first before the *job*, before the *institution*, even before *psychological theory*.

Growth psychologists are *humanistic*. They are interested in the clinical research findings of those who study "sick" individuals, but they also are interested in the "farther reaches" of human personality[14] and seek also to study extremely creative and gifted people. Humanistic psychologists study the experimental findings of animal research but are inclined to be cautious about applying these findings to human beings without corroborative evidence. Humanistic psychologists welcome statistical data on normative behavior, but they recognize that the "creative" individual cannot be confined within the same psychological categories as the average person. Humanistic psychologists emphasize that the breathing, living, sensing, loving, multifaceted human being is more than a statistic, more than a laboratory rat, more than a patient "lying sick in a hospital."

EMPHASIS ON INDIVIDUALITY. Growth psychologists recognize, too, that there is a commonality in human behavior; indeed, that there needs to be a commonality in behavior to avoid social chaos. Growth psychology chooses to emphasize the variations and essential differences distinguishing each person. We are coming to value those differences once again. We no longer want to "homogenize" our various ethnic minorities. "Black *is* beautiful" and so is brown, red, yellow, and white. Wider ranges of behavior and dress now are acceptable. Long hair is accepted, short hair, or no hair. Women's liberation groups have enabled many to feel worthy whether they be plain, fat, tall, short, or intellectual. There is more acceptance of many kinds of love. There is growing recognition that the truly integrated person is one who can resist *enculturation* (that is, who refuses to become "a face in the crowd")[15] and who is able to deviate from others in our society in significant and constructive ways. Research studies of persons who have been identified as creative human beings (remarkable for their ability to integrate the higher functions of love and service to others) have found them to be somewhat out of step with their culture, even "deviant." This is not to say that they make loud protests or commit acts of destructive rebellion, but they all seem to hold beliefs independent of prevailing opinions. These persons are able to think and act autonomously. They resist being molded by their present circumstances. They see themselves being *of* their culture but also *apart* from it. Abraham Maslow, who studied what he called the "healthy" personality, saw them as

not well adjusted (in the naive sense of approval and identification with the culture). They get along with the culture in various ways, but of all of them it may be said that in a certain profound and meaningful sense, they resist enculturation and maintain a certain inner detachment from the culture in which they are immersed. . . . they select from American culture what is good in it by their lights and reject what they think bad in it.[16]

Keep in mind, however, that when Maslow talked about being "less enculturated" and "rejecting what is bad" in our culture, it is not to be understood that "self-actualizing" persons are rebels for the sake of being rebels. They do not reject everything in the culture and they do not alienate themselves *from* the culture. Rather, they keep struggling to see what is wrong and to correct it.

ON NOT WANTING TO BE ADJUSTED, SHAPED, FOLDED, OR OTHERWISE MUTILATED.   Where has all our talking led us so far? First, we do not want to be "adjusted" to a society which in itself needs revision. All free societies have always had courageous reformers who kept on pointing out what they believed to be basic problems within those societies. They are persons who do not intend to become adjusted to standards they do not accept as viable and good. Particularly now, as we face the ecological crises of the eighties, we need persons who can imagine a world different from the one we live in and who are willing to share their visions with the rest of us.[17] Such a need does not rest on an adjustment model—that model is "worn out," so to speak— but on a model that fosters growth, individuality, and creativity, and particularly one that fosters the understanding that we must live peacefully together on this planet. One of the best known humanistic psychologists in the world, Carl Rogers, wrote the following in the sixties, and it seems more true today than when he wrote it:

If the human species is to survive at all on this globe, the human being must become more readily adaptive to new problems and situations, must be able to select that which is valuable for development and survival out of new and complex situations, must be accurate in his appreciation of reality if he is to make such selections. The psychologically mature person as I have described him has, I believe, the qualities which would cause him to value those experiences which would make for survival of the human race. He would be a worthy participant of human evolution.[18]

THE GROWTH MODEL MAY NOT BE "RIGHT" FOR EVERYONE. There *are* "sick people" who are so crippled by their emotional conflicts and so divorced from their inner controls and from their growth "center," that they indeed may need to be hospitalized or be given special therapy. The growth model is *not* suited to these people, since they are at the basic level of learning how to cope with their inner chaos and their outer confusions. The growth model *is* appropriate to those persons who currently maintain an adequate life style but who are motivated to pursue more creative lives and expressions according to their individual needs, drives, motivations, behavioral dispositions, talents, and dreams. This has been the task of the "psychonaut" ever since the Greeks enjoined us, twenty-five hundred years ago, to "know thyself."

IT IS SOMETIMES APPROPRIATE TO BE UNADJUSTED, MALADJUSTED, UNHAPPY, DEPRESSED, OR ALIENATED. This is also part of the growth process. According to the growth model, we all are going to experience pain, sorrow, moments of failure, feelings of inadequacy, inferiority, and helplessness from time to time. In fact, these all are part of the growing process. It is the person who has closed off suffering that is more likely to be closed off from further growth. "Growing" persons have not achieved a magic formula for life that ensures success and happiness or makes them invulnerable to pain or injustice. On the contrary, growing persons do suffer humiliation, misfortune, hurt, fear, and anxiety. It is appropriate even to "die." That is part of life too, as Dr. Elisabeth Kubler-Ross teaches us in her book, *Death: The Final Stage of Growth.*[19] Throughout this book we shall emphasize that any person from time to time can experience feelings of depression, contemplate suicide, suffer from anxiety, use "defense mechanisms," or engage in behaviors that can be labeled "neurotic," just as most of us also can be "unadjusted" to new situations or can experience "transient states of unreality." We would prefer not to label someone "emotionally sick" just because these very human experiences happen to that person now and then. Sometimes the appropriate response to a situation is to be anxious, depressed, — even "maladjusted." The point is not that one is labeled *this* or *that*, but what this anxiousness or depression or "maladjustment" says about one's current living situation, and what one can do for oneself to get through that stressful situation and its crisis.

The Fallacy of Mental Health

A few years ago, Thomas Szasz, a psychiatrist tired of the labels which make people think of themselves as "patients" and angry at the way society labeled people as "sick," nailed his "ninety-five theses" on the walls° of the medical society.[20] Szasz declared: "There is no such thing as mental illness. We invent it! The majority of the people who are called mentally ill are mostly those who are too poor or too ignorant to defend themselves from such accusations." "Furthermore," says Ronald Laing, "they have been hindered, not helped, by our treatment of them."[21]

In like manner, we have invented a fallacy called *mental health*. Because we have invented it, we tend to think that it really exists. Sometimes, it is even discussed in the social science literature as if it were something one achieves, like a diploma, or is awarded, like a medal. We are beginning to realize that it is none of these things. "Mental health" is a *concept*, an abstraction that has little to do with who we are and how we live in the *here-and-now*°° of the everyday world. There are no mortal beings who are so enlightened, so integrated, or so evolved that they could call themselves "mentally healthy." If perfect mental health were possible for *one* person, for *one* moment, in *one* situation, in the very next moment and in the next situation, that person would be confronted with new situations, new emotions, and new confusions.

The fallacy of mental health is dangerous in that it creates an ideal that we never can achieve. In that respect it is similar to another abstraction, "success," which William James, a pioneering American psychologist, once called the "bitch goddess." James characterized her as an eternal seductress, for no matter how close you get to her, she always recedes farther into the distance. She is only a mirage, after all.[22] "Mental health" is our modern "bitch goddess," a "false god" to

---

°An allusion to Martin Luther, a religious reformer, who nailed a series of indictments on the door of a medieval church.

°°Here-and-now, is a term used by existential philosophers and psychologists to indicate practical, concrete reality as opposed to ideal possibilities.

"Mental health" (like the abstraction "success") is a concept none of us can live up to.

whom we pay homage but who is just as impotent as was the biblical golden calf.

If we cling to the abstraction "mental health," most of us will find our emotions to be very different from that concept, and this gap between the myth and the reality will lead to a gnawing suspicion that we must be mentally "unhealthy." Many of us actually entertain the thought that there really are "mentally healthy" people who do not have fears, anxieties, confusions, depressions, or all those other negative qualities that have come to be associated with "mental illness." And, of course, that is all nonsense.

The Limitations and Traps of the Humanistic Growth Model

Just as there are traps to the "adjustment" model of personality functioning, so too are there traps in the model proposed by the humanistic psychologists. The adjustment approach emphasizes the necessity for individuals to aspire to a model of living based on the expectations and demands of others in "society." The trap in that approach is that it stressed a kind of de-personalized conformity to group standards which by and large ignored the necessity of acknowledging individuality in personality development.

The trap in the growth model is that it can begin to degenerate into selfishness—the impulse to "do your own thing" first, last, and always. Thus, if it is to work, the growth model of personality has to confront and ultimately resolve the problem of the kind of unbridled hedonism in which the person adjusts largely to his or her own self-interests, without regard for those other persons who share his or her living space. Actually, to adopt or recommend this kind of overweening selfishness is to misunderstand the growth model. As we shall see in chapter 13, "highly integrated" personalities seek not only their own growth but also the growth of others who share and participate in their lives. That they value their own liberty to grow does not mean that they have a license to do whatever they want. Here, as elsewhere, the distinction between *liberty* and *license* is crucial. License lacks the essential ingredient of responsibility, whereas liberty assumes self-governance.

If we no longer can consider "achievement of adjustment" as a viable model for living, is there another model? There is, one which is not new but which is emerging from the many trends of growth psychology. Let us call it a "process" model.

life as process

Process Defined

As with the term *mental health*, the word *process* is also an abstraction but an abstraction rooted in very real events going on within us at any given moment. Life consists of many processes. There are the biological processes of breathing, digesting, metabolizing, eliminating, and the like. There are the developmental processes of learning how to crawl, to grasp, to speak, to walk, and to develop into a physically adult human being. And there are the psychological processes of thinking, feeling, perceiving, behaving, and so forth. The *process* we are discussing is the sum total (and more) of all of these processes, the larger one that subsumes all the others, which we call *living*. *Process* is the way we coordinate our internal drives with external reality. It is the means by which we integrate our biological, emotional, social, and intellectual experiences into purposeful action and further growth. It sometimes has been called personality integration.*

One cannot properly speak of having "achieved" this process of

---

*integration, n. 1: the act or process or an instance of integrating . . .
integrate, vb. 1: to form into a whole; unite; 2*a* to unite with something else . . .
Webster's Collegiate Dictionary

Personality integration is the means by which we integrate our biological, emotional, social, and intellectual experiences toward purposeful action and further growth.

personality integration anymore than one can achieve mental health. It is a continuing, always-new process enabling survival. It is how we attempt to put together all the millions of bits and pieces of information and experiences making up our waking life.

Some persons seem more involved in their personality integration than the rest of us do. In a sense, they have reached what we might call a "highly integrated" level of personality functioning. These persons have reached a level of being-in-the-world* which allows them to view the process of living as a joyful adventure, and, despite the setbacks, and discouragements to which we all are subject, they still are able to experience excitement, hope, love, and compassion. We

*A phrase formulated by the German existential philosophers, Ludwig Binswanger and Martin Heidegger.

hope you will understand that these persons differ from the rest of us only in degree, not in kind. The process is the same. Perhaps they are more conscious of their process, which allows them greater inner adaptation, choice, and change. They have the ability to bounce back after setbacks and tragedies. They have what psychologists call "ego strength."

In this book we shall study the various aspects of the process of personality integration. We do not aim for "mental health" or "success." We do not promise you a rose garden.* We do hope that by deeper insight into some of the aspects of personality integration, you will be able to manage the crisis points and the twists and turnings of the human adventure with more insight, ease, and grace.

developmental psychology: an overview

In the remainder of this chapter, we will take a sweeping look at what happens to those of us who live in the West in the twentieth century. We will define this process in terms of our time and geography, for we must not forget that our processes do not always coincide with other eras and other cultures.

It has been said that four persons changed the course of twentieth-century thinking. Charles Darwin changed our understanding of our biological inheritance, Albert Einstein changed our understanding of the physical universe, Karl Marx influenced our understanding of how the wealth and power of the earth may be distributed among humankind, and Sigmund Freud transformed our beliefs about human psychology. It is appropriate to begin with Freud's work, not only because of his profound insights into human personality but because he was a pioneer in developmental psychology, particularly the psychosexual development of the child.

Sigmund Freud: The Psychosexual Development of the Child

When Sigmund Freud proposed his revolutionary theories of depth psychology, nothing (probably) was quite as shocking to the society of his times as his insistence that the infant is born a highly sexual being. Moreover, he insisted that this sexual drive was a necessary part of the child's psychic development. If the sexual drive (which he called the

---

*Again, we allude to the title of a fictionalized autobiography, *I Never Promised You a Rose-Garden*, by Hannah Green.[23]

libidinal instinct or *libido*) was overly restricted or repressed, the child could become psychologically warped, resulting in neurosis or even psychosis. The reader must remember that Freud was speaking to the Victorian society of his time, a time when, for example, childhood masturbation was threatened with dire consequences; "If you don't leave your 'Peter' alone, I will cut it off!"[24]

Freud viewed the person as a maelstrom of instinctual and often opposing drives. One such instinct is that of *self-preservation*. The sexual instinct (the libidinal drive) is almost as powerful and energetic as the instinct for self-preservation. The sexual instinct, however, had become so complicated by commandments, rules, excessive modesty, guilt, shame, denial, and so on, that pent-up libidinal energy was doing psychic damage to members of that civilized society. Yet, Freud said, some taming of this powerful and aggressive force by society is necessary to transform the basically savage, primitive, lusting, incestuous, narcissistic infant into a civilized adult. In this process of "taming" and "socializing," the basic raw instinctual drives would be sublimated into other forms of expression such as work, art, poetry, and scientific achievement.[25]

The socializing process of the child resulted, according to Freud, in two separate but interrelated psychosexual developments. The first centers on the child's sexual development; the second deals with the child's psychic development.[26]

HUMAN SEXUAL DEVELOPMENT: PSYCHOSEXUAL STAGES. As posited by Freud, the child goes through several developmental phases before reaching full adult sexuality. The first two stages Freud called the oral stage and the anal stage of infant sexuality.

The Oral Stage. In the first year of life, the energy of the libidinal drive is organized around the pleasurable activities of the mouth. The breast is not only life giving, it also is a source of sexual excitation, sensation, and pleasure. Eventually, anything that is associated with the mouth, such as the thumb, pacifier, or any inanimate object, becomes a source of sexual pleasure. The infant, at this stage of development, is passive and *autoerotic*, that is, sexual pleasure is centered on its own body. If the adult continued to gratify his or her sexual instincts through oral means, it was considered perverse. But even in the fully heterosexual adult, traces of the oral stage can be discerned in nail biting, pencil chewing, smoking, and drinking to excess.

Today we are much more able to accept the idea of infant sexuality. We witness the infant's delight in finding things to put into its mouth, for this is one of the ways the infant discovers the world, namely, that *this* thing is edible and *that* thing is not; that *this* thing is soft and chewy and good to eat while *that* thing tastes terrible. Later, we observe the child hugging a blanket and sucking on it. In fact, the idea of a "security blanket" has passed into popular language.

The Anal Stage.   With the development of teeth, the child leaves the *passive* stage and shifts to an *active* orientation to the environment. The child can now chew its own food. This also is the beginning of toilet training. Not only is the control of bladder and bowels a source of parental love and approval (or conversely, parental anger and disapproval if the child should not control them), but the child also discovers the pleasure associated with control of bodily functions. Urination and defecation have a decidedly pleasurable aspect, and Freud considered this pleasure as having a strong sexual element. The libidinal instinct now is centered at the anal orifice (where it formerly had focused on the oral orifice).

If the child overlearns the control of bladder and sphincter, remaining *fixated* at this level of sexual development, he or she is in danger of becoming what Freud called an *anal personality:* one who cannot "let go" of the feces easily and who holds on to the point of constipation. A constipated (anal) personality overvalues money (symbolic of feces), hangs on to it for dear life (is a miser), is excessively clean and tidy (harboring a secret fear of being dirty and overcompensating for it), and displays great obstinacy (refusal to let go or give in).

The Phallic Stage.   By the fourth year of the child's life, a new phase of libidinal development is reached, in which his or her genital organs begin to play a more dominant role. The child discovers that manipulation of the genitals is a source of pleasurable sensations. But parental disapproval puts an end to this activity (or it becomes more secretive).

The Latency Period.   At this point, the child enters what Freud called the *latency* period, from about age six to the onset of puberty. This is the stage at which sexual activity in the child becomes less dominant. Freud assumed that the libidinal drive had become somewhat dormant, but he also believed that parental disapproval of childhood masturbation also was part of this seemingly quiescent period of the sexual drive. At any rate, the sexual drive reemerges at puberty with greater force than ever before.

The Genital Stage.   With the onset of puberty, the adolescent is ready to enter into adult sexuality, which Freud identified as full genital coitus with a person of the opposite sex. But before the young man can become a fully genital person, he must give up his attachment to his mother, which Freud called the Oedipus complex (See Box A). Similarly, the young girl must give up her attachment to her father, which Freud called the Electra complex.

Box A
Freud's Stages of Psychosexual Development

AGE SPAN	LIBIDINAL (SEXUAL) DEVELOPMENT	PSYCHOLOGICAL DEVELOPMENT	LEVEL OF CONSCIOUSNESS
Birth to about 2 years	Oral stage Libidinal drive focused on mouth area. Passive-dependence on world for needs.	Child is born an id, ruled by "pleasure principle."	Baby is an "unconscious" being, unaware of being a separate entity from mother or mother's breast—the source of "all good"
About 2 to 3 yrs.	Anal stage Libidinal drive diverted to toilet training activities. Active-aggressive development.	Super-ego develops as the result of toilet training and other prohibitions. Beginning of *socialization* period	Freud equated the super-ego with conscience. The super-ego is more accessible than the "unconscious" is and thus is "preconscious material"
About 3 to 4 or 5 years	Phallic stage Sexual curiosity; discovery of masturbation.	Ego is developing, and *reality* principles now guide the child.	Child becomes a conscious being aware of self and others
Between 4 and 6 years	Oedipus complex comes to fore Libidinal drive now focused on parent of opposite sex.	Parent of same sex is seen as rival.	Child becoming aware of its own sexual identity
Between 6 and 11 yrs.	Latency period Libidinal drive dormant as a "developmental phase," or repressed as part of "socialization" and "reality" principle.	Child gives up attachment to parent of opposite sex, becoming identified with parent of same sex.	Child is identifying with its own psychosexual role
Puberty	Full genital stage Libidinal drive now fully phallic.	Person is able to engage in sexual activity with opposite sex.	Person experiences self as fully heterosexual being

20

The tragic outcome and suffering of Oedipus may represent the guilt and shame we feel for unacceptable and unconscious wishes.

During his research into the meaning of dreams, Freud believed he had discovered a basic theme in the deep attachment of sons to their mothers and of daughters to their fathers. As he studied how these attachments developed in the psychosexual evolution of the child, Freud began to notice that certain themes in the family's inter-personal relations already had been discussed in the world's great myths. Freud noticed particularly how the ancient Greek story of Oedipus described what he saw happening in the family life in his own time. Oedipus was the Theban king who had (unknowingly) violated the most sacred taboos of society, that of killing his father (patricide) and having intercourse with his mother (incest). (See Box B).

Box B

The Story of Oedipus
The Oedipus myth begins before the birth of Oedipus, when a certain King Laius of Thebes received a message from the gods that he would sire a son who ultimately would kill his father (Laius) and marry his mother (Laius' wife, Jocasta). That possibility was just as horrifying to a king in ancient Greece as it is to us today. So to prevent such an eventuality, as well as to save his own

life, Laius gave the infant to a shepherd with orders to leave the child outside so that it would die from exposure or starvation or be killed by wild beasts.

The shepherd, however, took pity on the baby and, instead of leaving the child to die, carried him to the neighboring city-state of Corinth, where the child was adopted by King Polybus, and brought up as a prince. When Oedipus learned he was not the true son of Polybus, he went to Delphi to consult the priestess of the god Apollo. The message he received was cryptic (as oracles tended to be): Oedipus was told simply not to return to his own land, for if he did, he was fated to kill his own father and to marry his mother. He therefore set out for Thebes, completely unaware that he was doing exactly what the oracle has warned him not to do!

On the road to Thebes, he met an older man who rudely told him to give way so that he may pass on the narrow road. Oedipus had been reared as a prince and was not used to such treatment. In the ensuing fight over the right of way, the older man was killed. But what Oedipus did not know is that the man he has killed was Laius, King of Thebes — his own father!

When Oedipus arrived at the outskirts of Thebes, he learned that the city was being devastated by the Sphinx, a lionness with the head of a woman. The Sphinx killed anyone who could not answer her riddle: "What has one voice and yet becomes four-footed, two-footed, and three-footed?" Oedipus correctly answered "Man, for he crawls on all fours as a baby, walks upright on two legs in adulthood, and needs the use of a cane in old age to walk, which makes him three-footed." The Sphinx thus was outwitted and destroyed, and Oedipus entered Thebes as a hero.

In the meantime, news had come to Thebes that the king had been killed by persons unknown. There is grieving for the death of Laius, but the citizens of Thebes were too overjoyed at the death of the Sphinx to mourn for long, or even to determine how the king died. Instead, they turn to Oedipus, their hero, and asked him to become the new king of Thebes by marrying Queen Jocasta. The couple lived happily together and produced four children.

All went well for Thebes until the children of Oedipus and Jocasta approached adulthood, when a great plague descended on the city. An oracle again was consulted and a cryptic message again was delivered: the plague would cease only when the murderer of Laius was discovered and was driven from the city! When Oedipus began to investigate the killing, he discovered that he, himself, was the murderer of his own father, Laius, and that he had married his own mother! In his grief and guilt, Oedipus blinded himself and, chased by winged furies, went into exile. Jocasta hanged herself. Their two sons killed each other in their fight for the throne, and their two daughters died in terrible ways. The violation of a societal taboo is suffering and death.

Freud believed the story of Oedipus did indeed represent aspects of human relationships that often are hidden from conscious awareness. He surmised that other abiding truths about the history of civilization and human psychosexual development might be revealed in other mythological tales. With regard to the Oedipus myth, for example, he said that when a boy is born into a family the mother and the child develop a natural, close attachment. This attachment or bond is cemented in the love, caring, fondling, nursing, and comforting the mother gives the child. A child who receives that kind of attention from his mother in babyhood grows up psychically strong and stable.

Freud believed that the young boy would like to get rid of his father, as did Oedipus in the legend, for then he could keep his mother all to himself—she would be his alone. Before you dismiss this idea out of hand, we ask you to remember how children very easily play "kill" with their playmates. Children have a somewhat different concept of death than do adults. In their fantasy play, children very often kill each other ("Bang-bang—you're dead"), and they see their playmates fall and "die," and then everyone gets up to play some more. Death as a finality has little meaning for children until some real death of a friend or relative hits home.

Moreover, anyone who has been around family life long enough has witnessed a little boy saying to his mother (or a girl to her father), "I'm going to marry you when I grow up." But when the little boy begins to show a preference for his mother and makes demands on her time and attention, he soon begins to realize that the giant (his father) receives the mother's first attention when he is around. Furthermore, if the child interrupts at certain times, he can be spanked or pushed away and soon learns that he should keep such power demands to himself.

We do not intend to overlook girls here, for the girl soon enough begins to show a preference for her father. In turn she is his "pet," his "darling," his love-in-miniature. Freud called this relationship the Electra complex, after another Greek legend. (For a modern version of that myth, you might want to read or see the play by the American playwright Eugene O'Neill, *Mourning Becomes Electra*.) Freud observed that the Oedipus theme is revealed throughout the literature and mythology of Western culture—for example, in Henrik Ibsen's *Rosmersholm* and in William Shakespeare's *Hamlet*. Hamlet, as you will recall, killed his stepfather and simultaneously loved and hated his mother. Freud believed the play reflected Hamlet's own confused Oedipal feelings toward his mother. For example, the fact that Hamlet killed his stepfather (also his uncle) instead of his father is simply the psyche's way of making the truth of patricide more palatable.

FREUD'S TOPOLOGY OF HUMAN PERSONALITY: THE ID, THE EGO, AND THE SUPEREGO.   Early in Freud's career, he posited two aspects of human mentality: a *conscious* and an *unconscious* part of the mind. The idea of an "unconscious mind" was not totally new; for a hundred years and more, philosophers had been discussing the possibility of an unconscious mind. But it took Freud's research into hypnosis and *free association* to give substance to this hypothesis. Under hypnosis Freud found that a person was able to remember events long forgotten or "repressed." Later, he discovered that repressed material could be elicited under the conditions of free association, the technique of encouraging the patient to say whatever came into his or her mind without fear of being considered "bad," "naughty," or "sick". Freud's further work on the unconscious led him to formulate three aspects of human personality: the *id*, the *ego*, and the *super-ego*.

The Id.   A newborn baby has no sense of "I." Since the infant still lacks a sense of separateness from the environment, it is largely an "unconscious" being. *Freud called this baby-unconsciousness an "id" (the Latin word for "it"). The id can be thought of as an organism of undifferentiated energy which strives only for growth and pleasure.* Far from possessing anything that approaches the rationality of adulthood, the infant, according to Freud, is a cauldron of primitive emotions and instincts. Thus, by its very nature the *id* is impulsive, blind, irrational, and pleasure-seeking. Very simply, the baby cries when frustrated and responds with delight to attention. The *id* stage of personality is essentially self-centered, oriented only toward its own pleasure and the avoidance of pain.

The Super-Ego.   This life of having every wish indulged cannot continue forever, since eventually children must realize that there are other persons in the world. For example, as they crawl around they discover that they are not allowed to touch certain objects unless they want their hands slapped. They are taught also, when the time comes, that they may not urinate or defecate whenever and wherever they feel the need to do so. They discover also, sometimes to their surprise and displeasure, that they may not hit their little brother or sister without running the risk of getting hit in return. In other words, they are initiated into the *socialization* process. More often than not, they rail against the limitations imposed on them. They sulk, pout, whine, and engage in any kind of maneuver which will enable them to continue to get their own way.

According to Freud, these early confrontations or encounters with the "outside world" (the parents and other members of the family) result in the development of the super-ego. In other words, *the super-ego emerges as the result of socialization.* Children learn that *this* is the right thing to do and that *that* is the wrong thing to do. According to Freud, *the super-ego is the basis of our conscience* and is one of the enduring aspects of personality.

The Ego.   At the level of the "blind," instinctual *id* we simply say, "I will do what I want to do," while the *super-ego* is the power of parents and society which says, "You may do this; you may *not* do that." It is from compromising between the directives from the id ("I will . . . ") and the super-ego ("You may not . . . ") that children's sense of "self" eventually comes into being. It is through these experiences that children begin to understand and to acknowledge that they are an "I," an individual entity who is indeed separate from their mothers and their physical surroundings. This beginning sense of self Freud called the *ego* (Latin for "I"). *The ego is therefore the conscious level of personality,* that part of ourselves of which we are aware and which we identify as the seat of reason, intelligence, self-knowledge, and so forth.

   Freud saw the ego as a kind of battlefield between the id and the superego, which could be caught in the conflicts between the two. Freud called these conflicts *neuroses.*

According to Freud, the ego is a battleground between the id and the superego.

Freud said that much of the fate of each individual life is often decided in these early childhood years. If the socialization process in the family is essentially a real caring of the child and if it is relatively consistent, the ego of the child becomes relatively healthy and aware of reality, and the person learns how to function according to the *reality* principle rather than to the *pleasure* principle.

FREUD'S THEORY OF FIXATION.   If children however, are not cared for, if they are neglected or treated inconsistently in these early years (indulged too often, frustrated too often, or both at various times), their "egos" can then become fixated at certain "crisis" points. These crisis points, according to Freud, may occur during the oral and anal developmental stages. If a personality is fixated at the oral level, even as adults they will lack those societal standards by which one recognizes that other people also have feelings, rights, and needs. Such persons remain *passive-dependent* personalities who wish to be taken care of all of their lives, or perhaps become *psychopaths* or *sociopaths* who have little feeling for others and calmly set out to "do them in" for their own benefit.

If children have been overdisciplined (instead of overindulged), then they may grow up constantly concerned about not doing the "right" thing. The danger of overdisciplining occurs at the anal stage, when children learn to "do their duty" in the "potty" instead of in their pants. It is also during this stage that one is asked to give up the pleasure principle—not to hit one's sister when one wants to, not to throw food on the floor, and so forth. A certain amount of discipline develops character; too much instills endless guilt, remorse, and feelings of inferiority—in other words, the "neurotic anxieties" of our times.

An Example of Fixation.   People may be able to operate in many (even most) areas of everyday life in an integrated manner, yet "have fixations" in other areas in which they function less well because of conflicts and unfinished situations stemming from early life. We recognize a "fixated" behavior *by its highly repetitive nature*.[27] Fixated people respond in essentially the same stereotyped manner to a given stimulus every time. They seem to lack a wide repertory of emotional responses to a certain category of situations. They just keep doing or saying the same kinds of things over and over again. Their behavior is simply uncreative, monotonous, and predictable. An example will illustrate this.

A man we know is highly creative in his work and job, gets along well with his associates, has an apparently satisfying relationship with his wife and children, yet he has an unreasoning, irrational, and highly prejudicial emotional reaction to policemen, lawyers, judges, administrators—anyone distinctly representative of authority. His behavior toward "them" (and he often talks about "the Establishment") is highly stereotyped; he reacts to "them" in more or less the same way, with fear, hatred, resentment, and feelings of persecution. Any mention of the "law" or the police provokes in him verbal abuse, harangues about "corruption" or "the government"—just as if someone had "pushed his button." At these moments, his co-workers, friends, and relatives brace themselves for a sermon (which they have heard many times before) or quietly excuse themselves.

Carl Jung and the Second Half of Life

Freud's work on the psychosexual development of the child was monumental, but he said very little about the development of the person past the stage of puberty. It was Freud's student, Carl Jung, who directed our attention to the stages of adult life. When reading Freud's works, adulthood seems to be not much more than the reenactment and resolution of childhood conflict, strivings, trauma, rivalry, and so on. Freud had concluded simply that the adult was able to perform two acts: the ability *to work* and the ability to engage in complete and satisfying heterosexual activity, *to love*. But we must remember who Freud's patients were. They were men so emotionally warped that they were unable to carry out their jobs and women unable to carry out their duties as wife, mother, and lady of the house. Both men and women often were confined to their beds and who could not sleep at night but did during the day, who remained in their rooms while the rest of the family enjoyed each other's company. Jung, on the other hand, saw many persons who were not neurotically disabled but who were out in the world, often famous personalities. They were not emotionally crippled people but instead, extremely intelligent, vital, energetic persons who sought Jung's help only at a particularly critical time in their lives.[28] If Freud gave us an insight into our childhood, Jung gave us an insight into the second half of our lives. From his work with people in their maturity, Jung concluded that the second half of adult life was a vastly different experience than was the first half of life *with its own special developmental crises and tasks.*

JUNG'S FOUR DEVELOPMENTAL STAGES.   Jung divided the person's life into four developmental stages: childhood, youth, maturity, and old age. *Childhood* is roughly that stage from birth to puberty. It is a time, said Jung, of learning how to make meaning out of the chaotic state of internal and external experience. The second stage is *youth*, which extends from puberty into the middle of life, somewhere between the thirty-fifth and fortieth year. We might think this rather old to be entitled youth, but Jung saw these years as having two specific

tasks: to develop an ego complex and to accumulate various possessions (education, job, status, spouse, family, house, material comforts,
and fame). The third stage, *maturity*, begins where youth leaves off, in
the years around thirty-five to forty. At this age, people become aware
of how one-sided their lives have been. They have stressed all the
material aspects of existence and have neglected the other side, which
Jung called the *spiritual* aspect. Suddenly all the attainments of
youth—achievement, money, success—seem to have less value, and
they go in pursuit of something else. The object of that pursuit Jung
calls the "soul," the other side of oneself. Aware of how one-sided
their lives have been, people frequently become quite different in the
second half of their lives. If he has been a chaste husband, he may
now become a *roué*. If she has been docile and domestic, she may now
become quite aggressive and pursue a career. Finally, there is *old age*,
whose crisis is to recognize that life is not mounting and unfolding any more but that "an inexorable inner process forces the contraction of life." It is the task of old age to focus on itself, to attain an illumination of its own. If the morning of life, said Jung, is significant in
terms of a person's achievement in the outer world, the afternoon of
life must focus on the facts on one's death and one's relationship with
things of the Spirit. The old person becomes *submerged* once again in
unconscious psychic happenings, a reversal of the task of childhood in
which the child *emerges* from the unconscious state (Freud would
have called it the *id* state) into (self) consciousness.[29] We cannot help
but reflect how similar Jung's stages of life are to the four stages of life
as laid down by the Indian philosophy of Yoga developed over two
thousand years ago (see Box C).

Box C

The four stages of Yogic life include:
1. *brahmachari,* the celibate student life;

2. *grihastha,* the householder with worldly responsibilities;

3. *vanaorastha,* the hermit who seeks spiritual truth;

4. *sannyasi,* the forest dweller or wanderer, free from all earthly considerations
   and concerns.
—Paramahansa Yogananda, *Autobiography of a Yogi* (Los Angeles: Self-
Realization Fellowship, 1972), p. 288.

Europeans tend to have a comprehensive view of life, at least that
is how it seems to us when we compare their writings with those of the

"youth culture" of the United States. At any rate, their writings reflect a better understanding of the life process from birth to death. For this understanding we now will look at the work of two men, native to northern Europe: Arnold vanGennep of Belgium and Erik Erikson, who was born in Denmark but who emigrated to the United States fairly early in his professional life.

Arnold vanGennep and the Rites of Passage

VanGennep wrote *Les Rites de Passage* in 1908. We mention this fact to underscore his far-reaching vision. He was not a sociologist, an anthropoligist, or even a "social scientist." He simply thought deeply about life, and his meditations took him to study how societies throughout the world and throughout time have responded to life, death, marriage, growing up, parenthood, and other changes of status. vanGennep noted that in both tribal and civilized life, these transits and passages are marked by what he called *rites of passage* which allowed the person to celebrate this transit and to enable others in the person's environment to make note of it. These observable rites of passage are characterized by designated behaviors by the person con-

Today, one of the Rites of Passage for young people is obtaining their driver's license.

cerned, and by festivities, feasts, and holidays in which the whole group takes part. These external behaviors and activities enable all the members of that society to integrate the person's change of status. Thus we have the rites of baptism and circumcision, the rites of first communion (marking the transition from infancy to childhood), the rites of puberty, and the end of childhood (confirmation in Protestant and Catholic churches, and bar mitzvah in the Jewish community), and every society, no matter how primitive, has a public rite of passage from the single to the married state.

Box D

The life of an individual in any society is a series of passages from one age to another and from one occupation to another. . . . Transitions from group to group and from one social situation to the next are looked on as implicit in the very fact of existence, so that a man's life comes to be made up of a succession of stages with similar ends and beginnings; birth, social puberty, marriage, fatherhood, advancement to a higher class, occupational specialization, and death. . . . In this respect, man's life resembles nature, from which neither the individual nor the society stands independent. The universe itself is governed by a periodicity which has repercussions on human life, with stages and transitions, movements forward, and periods of relative inactivity.

Arnold vanGennep, *The Rites of Passage*,
(Chicago: University of Chicago Press, 1960)

Especially important are the evolved funeral rites of each group or society, for those rites are meant to accomplish several purposes. First, the funeral rite helps the person reach the "other side;" second, the rite ensures that the deceased does not remain as a malevolent ghost; third, it enables the tribe to demonstrate their grief by weeping, wailing, and decking themselves in "sackcloth and ashes;" and finally, the rite allows the members to resume group life, thus mending the gap left by the departed person.

There also is the rite that marks the transit from the *profane* life to the *sacred* life: the initiation of the person into holy orders. We are somewhat familiar with these rites through the Catholic and Protestant rites of priesthood and the rites connected with monastic life. But all societies across cultures and over time have celebrated publicly the transformation of the person from a mundane to a holy state, including the anointment with oil of the ancient Hebrew priests; the investiture of the Roman vestal virgins; or the sacrifice of the Green God (reconstructed in Mary Renault's novel, *The King Must Die*).[30]

Erik Erikson's Psychosocial Development

VanGennep's work was not published in English until 1961, but his work had tremendous influence on European thinking and on European psychologists. One of these psychologists was a man who called himself Erik Erikson.[*] Erikson elaborated on the work of Freud and his psychosexual stages and on vanGennep's significant passages and transits. As Erikson formulated it, the human life span is divided into eight life stages, each with its own particular life crisis and its own particular life task. If the person accomplished the life task and lived through the crisis, growth to the next stage would be easy. If the life task were not accomplished, the person would remain mentally and emotionally crippled. American psychologists have found Erikson's work very useful as a model of the human life span, which has led to interest in adult development, not just as an extension of childhood but as a phase of life with its significant aspects and which emphasizes the importance of society in the development of the individual.[31]

STAGE I: BASIC TRUST VERSUS BASIC MISTRUST. The task to be accomplished in infancy, said Erikson, is *trust*. The infant is virtually helpless. The baby is completely dependent on others to take care of it: feed it, bathe it, protect it from the elements and give it that kind of physical and emotional mothering which will give it the will to live and to accept the world as a kind and loving place. If, by some chance, the infant is neglected, abused, or rejected by a mothering figure, it may never learn to trust the world sufficiently to "grow in grace,"—physically or emotionally strong. We know from innumerable studies of children who have not had this kind of mothering,—that if they survive at all, they are physically, intellectually, and emotionally stunted. Research has piled up evidence that babies left too long in day-care centers, orphanages, or hospitals tend to be more sickly, more "neurotic" in their behavior, academically retarded in school, and may even suffer mental illness then or later on in life.[32] Because they were thrown into a world not sufficiently loving, kind, and supportive, they do not achieve stability out of the "blooming, booming confusion of sights and sounds" that William James called the infant consciousness.[33] A sense of order or stability constitutes what is called a strong *ego structure*, and through it we make sense out of the thousands of stimuli received every moment. Without this thread of continuity, a person lives in a torment of confused, unconnected, and meaningless events. The world seems to go on throughout life, "doing things to one," without rhyme or reason. In extreme cases, the lack of ego

[*]Erik Erikson was not his "given" name; he adopted it as a part of his own identification process.

The infant needs psychological and physical mothering to develop basic trust *and a strong ego* structure.

structure is so extreme that there is little logical continuity in moment-to-moment awareness, and one's waking life is a continuous night-mare, which we call "schizophrenia."

STAGE II. AUTONOMY VERSUS SHAME AND DOUBT. Erikson himself specified this only as that time when we begin to stand on our own two feet, to do things "by ourselves" and "for ourselves." As infants, all had to be done *for* us, all was done *to* us; we had no choices. At this age, but then somewhere between ten months and two years, we begin to move around under our own locomotion, to feed ourselves, to get control of our bodily functions, and to have some control over our life. Through the beginning of language we can let the world know our needs and even our desires. "Cookie" or "bye-bye baby" may get us something to eat or lifted into the air. We can say "no" now, so we have choices available to us that were not available to us in infancy. All of these events, which give us some control over ourselves and our environment, enable us to meet the next life crisis and task, that of *autonomy*.

In addition to learning what they can do for themselves, children also learn what they may *not* do. They may not "mess" in their pants anymore; they may not hit their baby brothers or throw food on the floor. Thus they learn the "I may do's" and the "I may not do's" that enable them to get along in the world.

If these life tasks are not accomplished, children may remain obedient but passive and dependent on others on the one hand; or aggressive and rebellious on the other. If they do not learn that they can say "no" if they want to, then they always will need permission from someone else to do things and will remain dependent all their lives. (We all know adults who seem to need constant attention from others, and who borrow money, clothes, cigarettes from others with no intention of returning them.) On the other hand, if they do not learn that the *world* can say "no" as well, then they may never get through the egocentric and narcissistic stage of development. They may remain determinedly defiant and self-seeking, forever resisting the conventional rules of society—the kind of adult who always is just a little "shady" and who gains satisfaction from outwitting the law, "suckering" other persons by winning over them. This is the stage, then, at which children learn both yes and no. The yes allows children to be spontaneous and self-expressive, and the no is so that they do not always have to test their legal or moral limits, ending as juvenile delinquents as youngsters or as adults remaining just outside the law.

STAGE III: INITIATIVE VERSUS GUILT.   Somewhere in the age range of three to six, children make another step. They have learned how to take care of their immediate needs; now they learn how to plan ahead, to think in terms of yesterday and tomorrow. They are beginning to have a sense of time, a memory of the past and a concept of the future.

Initiative includes learning how to play with others, how to get two or three friends together and to organize what they will do. They even may plan exactly what they are going to do before they do it. "Let's play house and I'll be the Daddy and you can be the Mommy and Petey can be the Baby. And I'll get up and go to work and you'll take care of the baby till I come home . . . and . . . and. . . ." This kind of "let's pretend" may go on for a long time; in fact, by the time the children finish planning, they may not play it out at all but go on to jump rope or some other kind of activity. In that case, the *planning has been the play itself*. Play enables children to integrate their perceptions of family life into some kind of order.

Children also are not confined to their immediate environment. They are beginning to develop a sense of geography. They learn where their house is and where their friends are, how far they may go and still be able to find their way home. Besides learning the basic elements of geography, they are learning some sense of time. They may not be able to read the clock, but they can sense that it is just about time to go home and turn on a favorite TV program.

They also are getting a sense of themselves. They have learned that there are others in the world and are more willing to share with them, to *cooperate* with the world. If they do not learn to cooperate with others in their society, they tend to be overly competitive which, as an adult, takes the form of always "being on the make," wanting to conquer, to take over, or to be always in control. As they learn to initiate and to cooperate, they become the kinds of individuals who are morally responsible and who seek to find niches for themselves in the world, ready to contribute and to do their share for others. If they do not, they remain defiant, not outside the law but constantly sticking their necks out, pitting their physical and mental energies against others, seeking to conquer the opposite sex and to win out over others competitively.

STAGE IV: INDUSTRY VERSUS INFERIORITY.   In primitive societies, this passage takes the form of learning the "how to's" of the tribe: if one is an Eskimo, how to catch a seal; if one is a Polynesian, how to spear a fish; if one is an African, how to follow an animal spoor. These tasks prepare children to become industrious members of their society. Through mastering these tasks, children gain a sense of *competence*. If they cannot do what the other members of their tribe can do, they fall prey, Erikson said, to feelings of inferiority.

What are the tasks that children in our society must learn to do to become a functioning member? Erikson said that it is learning the "three R's," how to read and write and manipulate numbers. These skills are necessary to get and keep a job, to take care of household accounts, to pay one's income tax, to keep abreast of the news, to vote, and the like. It is not just the tools of basic literacy that people need. They need the "widest possible basic education" for the greatest number of possible careers.

Besides the obvious mastery of skills necessary to one's self-support, there is another outcome to the long, arduous passage we call education in this society. It is *a sense of competence as a person.* For every skill that we learn, we gain additional self-worth at the psychological level as well as at the productive level. It matters little what kind of skill it is, that adds to our feeling that we can deal adequately with our world; skills may range from auto mechanics to typewriting, from creative carpentry to creative writing. Every competence we acquire adds to our overall sense of personhood — we are a person who can do this and this and this. It is no wonder that Erikson said that if

BOX E
Implications of Erik Erikson's Eight Life Stages

STAGE	AGE (approx.)	TASK	ASPECTS OF TASKS	IF NOT ACCOMPLISHED	LASTING ACCOMPLISHMENT OF SUCCESSFUL OUTCOME
I	Infancy (0 to 1 yr.)	*Basic trust*	Physical and emotional "mothering." A sense of order and stability in the events it experiences; feelings of being wanted and loved and cared for.	*Basic Mistrust* Life remains chaotic, unconnected. Child is sickly, physically, & psychologically disabled. High infant mortality; childhood autism; academic retardation.	*Drive and Hope*
II	"Toddler" (1 to 3 yrs.)	*Autonomy*	Learns to stand on own two feet; feed self, etc. Controls bodily functions. Makes basic needs known through language. Discovers *choices*: learns to say no and yes. Accepts no as well as yes. Learns rules of society: "may do" and "may not do."	*Shame and Doubt* Lack of autonomy produces passive dependence on others; unable to assert own will results in *overobedience*; unable to accept "no" results in personality constantly rebellious; perhaps "delinquent"	*Self-Control* and *Will Power*
III	Preschool (about 4 to 5 yrs.)	*Initiative*	Learns geography and; time can go and come back, can think in terms of future, has developed memory, learns beginning adult roles. More loving, cooperative, secure in family. Good chance of becoming a "moral" person.	*Guilt* Wants always "to be in control." Sense of competition drives person to be "overcompetitive." May be always outside law.	*Direction* and *Purpose*

Implications of Erik Erikson's Eight Life Stages — continued

STAGE	AGE (approx.)	TASK	ASPECTS OF TASKS	IF NOT ACCOMPLISHED	LASTING ACCOMPLISHMENT OF SUCCESSFUL OUTCOME
IV	School (about 6 to 12 yrs.)	*Industry*	Learns the "how to's" of society; in Western society masters "3 R's"; begins to understand matrices of society. Learns to feel worthy and competent.	*Inferiority* If person fails to learn industry, begins to feel inferior compared to others. If overlearns industry, may become too "task-oriented" and overconform to society.	*Method* and *Competence*
V	Adolescence 12 to late teens or early adulthood	*Identity*	Sexual maturation and sexual identity. Discovers *role* in life; ponders question "who am I?" as distinct from family. Develops social friendships; rejects family.	*Role Confusion* May not achieve a personal identity separate from family. May not become socially adult or sexually stable.	*Devotion and Fidelity*
VI	Early Adulthood	*Intimacy*	Learns to share passions, interests, problems with another individual. Learns to think of "we," "our," "us" instead of "I," "me," "mine." Affiliates with others: family, place of work, community. Achieves stability.	*Isolation* Inability to be intimate with others. Becomes fixated at adolescent level of sensation-seeking and self-pleasure. Avoids responsibility. Lacks "roots" & stability.	*Affiliation and Love*

VII	Middle Adulthood	*Generativity* Transition to transpersonal values. Fosters creativity and growth in others younger than self; provides leadership; seeks to contribute to community, next generation, world. May be most creative period of life.	*Stagnation* Becomes "cog-in-wheel," automated. Growth limited remains rooted in past. May experience breakdown of zest for life. Feels life is passing by him or her.	*Production* and *Care*
VIII	Old Age	*Ego Integrity* Recognizes and accepts diminished faculties; realizes one's mortality. Feeling of having lived good life and paved the way for future generations. Luminosity of truly "wise" person.	*Despair* Reaps bitter fruits of what one has or has not sown earlier. Fears death. An old age of misery, anxiety, and despair.	*Renunciation* and *Wisdom*

(Adapted from Erikson)

37

we do not learn industry, we may acquire a sense of inferiority that will hamper us all our lives.

There is also a danger at this period that people will become so task-oriented that they may consider themselves worthy only if they achieve, or they may conform so completely to the demands of their technological society that they do not question how they are exploited by that society. Thus they need to gain a sense of themselves *as independent of what they can do.*

STAGE V: IDENTITY VERSUS ROLE CONFUSION. The passage through adolescence is another long one, and, indeed, for some it never ends since those individuals never reach psychological adulthood. They live and die an adolescent. We are concerned here, however, with the narrower interpretation of adolescence, which starts somewhere after ten or eleven years of age and continues to early adulthood. The task of the adolescent, according to Erikson, is *identity.* By identity, Erikson meant sexual identity, but he also meant our larger identity as well—who one is as a person, what one stands for, and what place one will carve for oneself in society. It is in this adolescent period that the young person begins to ask himself or herself some of those universal questions as, "Who am I," and "What do I stand for?"

Elsewhere we have described adolescence as the "Big Crisis" because it is at the adolescent period that many previous unresolved life crises erupt again in all their demonic and primitive force but now with all the additional thrust and strength of the physically and emotionally powerful adult. It is as if one has the power of the adult but the emotions still of the child. If the process is carried through successfully, however, if parent can weather the "storm and thunder" that accompanies adolescence, one frequently is able to resolve some of the uncompleted tasks of earlier stages.

In the hunt for their own identity, adolescents reject their families and frequently all their families' institutions. But they cannot stand alone, so they cling to their peer groups in groups, adopting each other's styles, clothes, language, walk, and the like. In the struggle to find an identity outside the family, they try many roles, imitate many persons, and wander through a complex of ideas until they find those that seem best suited to their temperaments and personalities. The next stage is adulthood.

STAGE VI: INTIMACY VERSUS ISOLATION. The adolescent is concerned with "I," "my," and "me." The world centers on *their* needs, *their* wants, and *their* confusions. It is hard for them to consider the needs of other people. This is the task that the young adult needs to accomplish: the ability to think of "us."

Erikson called the life task associated with this stage *intimacy*, by which he meant not only sexual intimacy and emotional intimacy but also psychological intimacy. One is able to allow other persons within one's world, to think of their needs, desires, hopes, aspirations, and fears, as well as one's own. It is the age at which the person can say "we" instead of "I," "our" instead of "mine." They share their lives, house, belongings with others; with a spouse, with children and with parents if they need their support. Later, the "we" can be extended to one's colleagues, one's community, and one's world.

If adults retreat from this task, they are subject to *isolation*, the inability to be intimate with others. They see the world as different from themselves. They develop protective devices to keep others away; they remain disengaged with the world and thus are subject to feelings of loneliness within themselves, prejudice toward others, or alienation from the world.

STAGE VII: GENERATIVITY VERSUS STAGNATION.   Middle adulthood is marked by the cessation of those pleasures which brought satisfaction as young adults: the acquisition of possessions, status, home, family, children, recognition, and so forth. At this time, the acquisitive motive is no longer dominant. Middle-aged adults have advanced in their jobs as far as they want or will be able to; they have raised their children, who are one by one leaving the nest; they have obtained enough security to satisfy their wants and needs; and they have achieved enough to satisfy their sense of accomplishment.

It is at this point that the individual needs to recognize that another level has been reached. Carl Jung had already noted that it is the time of life when, having taken care of our physical and emotional needs, we must satisfy our spiritual needs. Erikson expressed it differently, but the meaning is similar. He said that at this age, the person needs to know that his or her life is being lived and lived well, not just for himself or herself but in relationship to the whole psychological-social-historical development of humankind. They need to feel that they have contributed to the course of human existence on earth. Sometimes this need is satisfied by parenting.

On a less ordinary level, this need is frequently satisfied by becoming a leader in one's community or organization, one who enables others to take their place in the community or to make that community a better place in which to live. The middle adult learns to generate the growth and creativity of younger persons. Thus, Erikson called the life task at this stage *generativity*. Its opposite is stagnation.

STAGE VIII: EGO INTEGRITY VERSUS DESPAIR.   The task of old age is the recognition and acceptance of one's diminished faculties, the waning of the life force, and the nearness and reality of death, not with despair, not with bitterness, but with the peace of a life well lived and with a sense of having bequeathed something of significance to other generations.

In this country we do not know very much about this passage. Other, more primitive societies have handled this stage better than we do. Their old people are the keepers of the tribal history, the wise who are the storehouse of the tribal wisdom or the elders to consult when the tribe or a member is in a crisis. Americans, though, reject the idea of age and we send our old people to hospitals or homes for the aged, thus denying them a valid place in our civilization.

In order for us to accomplish the task of old age, we need to have led a full, rich, productive, and creative life. The task of old age, like that of infancy, is not achieved in that time span. It needs to have been done before. By old age it is too late. If by that time people have not met all the preceding life crises, and lived and worked through their associated life tasks, then they can only live out their lives with regret or enfeebled in body and mind. The task of old age is, ironically, the reaping of what one has earlier sown. If one has lived life well and with meaning, then one may live out the end peacefully and with the knowledge that one's life has been a significant contribution in the (unfolding of generations.)

A Final Note on Erikson's Life Stages: A Favorable Ratio

Erikson warned us that his developmental stages were somewhat misunderstood by social scientists as *achievement status;* that is, when the person has developed trust in the stage of infancy, it has been securely obtained once and for all. Not at all. These life tasks, he said, must not be thought of as "a goodness," which is "impervious to changing conditions." The life tasks are a continual process of integration as the "personality engages with the hazards of existence," even as we must continue to cope physically with the various processes of metabolism. At every turning point, there are moments at which the personality first progresses and then regresses in its struggle to maintain equilibrium.

What Erikson suggested is to think in terms of a "favorable ratio" of (say) basic trust over basic mistrust. Although this task should be accomplished in infancy, there will be times when the person even at a later stage may very well lose this favorable ratio and have to learn to integrate that task once more, relative to the new life crisis and life stage. There will be times when all of us suffer from feelings of mistrust, dependence, guilt, shame, or doubt. Furthermore, none of us can or should feel completely autonomous, trusting, industrious, or intimate. We will vary from person to person in our completion of these tasks, as well as from culture to culture. What is important is that enough of these tasks are learned at the critical stage so that when we do suffer setbacks we can draw from the reservoir of that competence to sustain us until the favorable ratio is again accomplished.

Seasons and Passages of Our Lives: Daniel Levinson and Gail Sheehy

We come now to two other works on our life cycle development. The first is by a group of researchers at Yale University, led by Daniel Levinson.[34] Levinson and his associates studied intensively forty men over a period of ten years: their problems, their concerns, their life changes, their aspirations, their disappointments, and their gratifications. What they discovered, it seemed to them, was a confirmation of the developmental process throughout a man's life, related not to socioeconomic level, not to profession, not to experiences, not even to intelligence, but to *age*-related factors. These forty men represented widely differing backgrounds, from author to engineer to blue-collar worker. Yet, the life crises of these men, although varying with each person, seemed to demonstrate that there is a common, underlying ebb and flow to the fundamental life process.

The second study was done by a journalist, Gail Sheehy,[35] who found herself making significant changes at her own mid-life period and who set out to find if other men and women were experiencing the same kinds of life-shattering crises. Because Sheehy drew so largely from Levinson's work and because Levinson's work is so much more scientifically precise, we shall devote most of our discussion to the Yale University research results.

The Four Great Eras

Like Jung, Levinson divided up the life span into four great eras, which correspond roughly to Jung's great developmental divisions. Levinson compared these eras to the acts of a play or the chapter divisions of a novel in which the writer divides the life of the characters. The sequence of development is defined as follows:

1. Childhood and Adolescence: roughly from birth to twenty-two years;
2. Early Adulthood: roughly from seventeen years to around forty-five years;
3. Middle Adulthood: roughly from age forty to about sixty-five years (or retirement);
4. Late Adulthood: from about sixty years to end of life.

The reader will notice that these four great age segments are of twenty to twenty-five years each. Furthermore (and this is of great significance), each age overlaps with the others over a span of four or five years. It is during these overlapping transitional years (late adolescence, age forty to forty-five, and retirement) that the person experiences his or her *major* life changes and which are characterized by sweeping de-structuring and restructuring of physical, emotional, intellectual, and spiritual existence. Levinson called these great structural changes the *cross-era* transitions, and they are punctuated, so to speak, by what he called *marker events:* separation from family, marriage, divorce, sickness, and death, rather like vanGennep's "rites of passage." Finally, within each of the great eras, there are minor cycles, phases, and transitions. All in all, Levinson concluded living is a constant process of structuring, de-structuring, and restructuring of life style to meet our changing needs, values, and aspirations.

In combining all these major eras, cross-era transitions and other subdivisions, Levinson formulated a developmental model for human life as seen in Box F. Now let us take a closer look at what all these eras, cross-era transitions, and other subperiods entail in terms of life events and developmental tasks.

THE EARLY ADULT TRANSITION.   This is, in essence, terminating one's childhood and moving into the early adult era. Up until this time, the person has been harbored and supported by his or her family. At about seventeen to twenty-two years, the person begins the separation and transformation process necessary to become an adult. The route this separation takes varies according to the individual and his/her socioeconomic background: he or she may leave the home by running away, going to college (or even to a reform school), or entering the armed services. He may even transfer his home to another quasi-home structure with parent surrogates. She may continue living in the parental home until the early twenties or later and still accomplish this developmental task by becoming more socially, economically, and psychologically independent.

This physical separation should lead to the second developmental task, that of gaining a more realistic understanding of the world, the people in it, and of his or her own abilities and values.

THE ADULT ERA.   Having made the painful transition from childhood to adulthood, the person enters the early adult period in which he or she begins the tasks of structuring his or her first *realistic* life choices (many of his or her choices at ages seventeen to twenty-two often are unrealistic and are based more on fantasy than on experience). Most persons now begin to find a vocational niche for themselves, contemplate and enter the marriage and family state, and become independent adults, financially, socially, and psychologically.

(BOX F)
The Anatomy of the Life Cycle (Research on forty men of various walks of life)

ERA	MAJOR PERIODS	QUALITY	SOME OF THE DEVELOPMENTAL TASKS	SOME ASPECTS OF PERIOD
PreAdult Years (0–22)	Early childhood (0 to 3 years)	Conflicts between self-drive and society.	Distinguishes between the "me" and "not me."	Center of attention. Harbored and protected by family.
	Transition to middle childhood (5 to 6 years)	Readjustments necessary to larger world.	Recognizes validity of other family members. Expands awareness of neighborhood, school, peers.	No longer center of attention in family or school.
	Middle childhood (7 to 11 years)	Period of relative stability.	Becomes disciplined, industrious; learns basic skills.	Has resolved early emotional struggles (family and transition to school, etc.). Conflicts with family.
	Puberty (12 to 13 years)	Sweeping physical and emotional changes.	Withdraws emotionally from family attachments.	
	Adolescence (12 to 17 years)		Culminates preadult era.	Beginning of "dreams" about future and self-in-society.
Cross-Era transition	Early adult transition (17 to 22 years)	Separation from family. Feelings of loss and anxiety about future.	Terminates and moves away from childhood, tests some initial life choices (rarely realistic, much fantasy).	Establishes new home site: college, military, training school, running away, even voluntary foster home. Initial choices involving much movement: job to job, college to college, place to place.

The Anatomy of the Life Cycle (Research on forty men of various walks of life) — Continued

ERA	MAJOR PERIODS	QUALITY	SOME OF THE DEVELOPMENTAL TASKS	SOME ASPECTS OF PERIOD
Early Adult (17 or 18 years to 40 or 45 years)		A "novice adult."	Forms a "life dream/scheme," and makes provisional life structure.	Takes on responsibilities.
	Entrance into adult world (22 to 28 years)	Creation of first stable, realistic life structure.	Forms mentor relationships. Forming an occupation.	Has learned much from unrealistic choices and experiences of 17 to 22 age period. Establishes home base.
			Forms love relationships, marriage, and family.	
	Age 30 transition (28 to 30 years)	Some modification of first life structure.	Works out flaws of 22 to 28-year period, revises life dream/scheme.	"Marker events" may have changed sense of self, "death" of one or two parents, love affair, divorce, change of job."
			Creates more satisfactory life structure.	
	Settling down period (33 to 40 years)	Beginning of new stability.	Renews commitments to work, family, friends, and community. Redefines dream/scheme as a "personal enterprise."	Begins to think "If I'm to make something of myself, I'd better do it now." Career ladder becomes important. Now a "junior" executive.
		Becoming "one's own person."		
		Voice of authority; may now be senior member of work organization.	Culmination of early adulthood.	"Quality of life" becomes important: home, family, friends.
Cross-Era transition	Mid-life transition (40 to 50 years)	De-structuring process and upheavals.	Reappraises life and goals.	"What have I done with my life?"

Era	Period			
		Moderate to serve crises.	Provides a bridge to middle adulthood. Begins to flail against established conventions and structures.	"What do I really want from job, family, wife, children, life?" May appear to others as "sick" or "irrational."
M i d d l e	Entrance into middle adulthood (45 to 50 years)	Beginning of new stability but marked by events which influence life: drastic job change, divorce, love affair, serious illness, death of loved ones.	Violent upheavals of mid-life transition cease. Builds a new life structure.	Some make viable adjustments to world but not to self so that inner life has no meaning. They resign, decline, and fail to make adequate new life structure.
A d u l t h o o d			Begins tasks of individuation.	
	Age 50 transition (50 to 55 years)	Moderate readjustments (similar to age 30 transitions).	Modifies 45–50 year life structure work later in mid-life transition.	May be a crisis time for those who changed too little at mid-life transition.
(40 or 45 years to 60 or 65 years)	Culmination of middle adulthood (50 to 60 years)	Stable period (analogous to "settling down", period of late thirties).	Builds a second middle-adult structure; rejuvenates self.	For those who can "individuate" successfully, this period may be beginning of great fulfillment.
Cross-Era transition	Late adult transition (60 to 65 years)	Major turning point of one's life.	Terminates middle adulthood; creates basis for late adulthood. Must release authority and "center stage." Infirmity increases.	Because no longer "center stage", capable now of illumined wisdom. Increasing frequency of death and serious illness of loved ones' friends, colleagues.

(Adapted from Daniel J. Levinson and others, Seasons of a Man's Life (New York: Alfred A. Knopf, Inc., 1978).

THE AGE THIRTY TRANSITION.   Levinson warned that no life-structure is ever permanent. Even if this structure from ages twenty-two to twenty-eight seems, to all intents and purposes, to be success-ful and "happy," there comes a mid-era transition, at about age thirty, in which the person begins to feel hemmed in by the very successful structure he or she has created. Sheehy called this transition "Catch-30," meaning that the person feels trapped in a tight life structure, the very structure that he or she has spent a decade creating. Some per-sons may get a divorce at this time; others may decide to find a new job; and still others may go back to school. It is a time of de-structure and restructure. Although this particular life crisis is moderate for most persons, some may even hit "rock bottom." How the de-structur-ing process occurs varies with each person. This person may de-struc-ture intentionally and thoughtfully, while another person's whole life structure may seem "to come apart at the seams," but both Levinson and Sheehy believed that it will, to some extent, become dismantled.

AGE THIRTY TO FORTY: SETTLING DOWN AGAIN.   After the age-thirty crisis, most persons seem to settle down into one of their most productive and satisfying new life structures. This age period is assso-ciated with career and all its associated values: social status, good sala-ry, esteem as a member of the community, creativity, and a family life that seems to have "quality," that is, to be rewarding and satisfying. Somewhere toward the end of this period (from thirty-five to forty years), most persons are coming into their own at their place of employment; beginning to be accepted as a "voice of authority," and taking on more and more responsibilities at work and in the com-munity.

THE MID-LIFE CRISIS: AGE FORTY.   Toward the end of the thir-ties, according to Levinson and Sheehy, there comes another crisis, even more sweeping than the age-thirty transition. Because this tran-sition is such a major one in our society, we shall discuss it more fully. For many years, psychologists and social workers have discussed the "menopausal depression" of women that comes about this time. At this time, many women seem to experience severe depressions that may be tied to hormonal changes or to a feeling that they are losing their youth and sexual attractiveness, or that their job as mother and wife seems to be coming to an end with nothing to take its place. Men, too, seem to undergo a psychological crisis which may take the form of uprooting themselves from family through divorce or psychological separation. They may even change their entire life style and appear to others to have become mentally and emotionally deranged.

What is happening, said Levinson, is that these persons are begin-ning to discover how much of their lives have been based on illusion (what the Indians call *maya*). They are suffering from dis-illusion-ment. Suddenly all the values that they have esteemed seem empty and meaningless. Furthermore, they must solve four *polarities* that now exist in their lives, the kinds of polarities that Carl Jung stressed so often.[36]

RESOLVING THE MID-LIFE POLARITIES. The first polarity the person must solve is the *young/old polarity*. Although the man, at forty, feels himself to be still young and is not ready to join the "middle-aged" generation, he finds that younger persons are beginning to address him more respectfully and to consider him as one of the older generation. The second polarity pertains to the *destruction-creation polarity*, which seems to include the awareness of his own death. At about age forty, he may be experiencing the deaths of one or more of his parents, grandparents, relatives, and close friends, all of which brings the imminence of his own mortality a little closer. Such awareness makes him suddenly and acutely conscious of what he has done to hurt others (parents, children, spouse, colleagues, friends), and he wonders how to make amends. He becomes aware of love and the richness or lack of it in his own life. He wonders also how to be more creative, to participate in human welfare, and to give of himself to the world. The third polarity is that of *femininity-masculinity*. For much of his life, a man may have denied much of his "feminine" side (his tender, loving, emotional feelings), preferring to put his psychic energies into work and achievement. Now he may begin to allow himself to do more nurturing things or to express the artistic and creative aspects that have heretofore been suppressed. Finally, he resolves the polarity of *attachment-separateness*, which Carl Jung called the search for the soul and things of the spirit. Material and worldly success becomes less of a motivation, and the person seeks to relate to transcendent values. If he has been estranged from relatives and friends, he may now seek a rapprochement. If he has been tyrannized by personal ambition, he now may devote himself to supra-personal concerns and projects, to community projects, to charitable organizations, or to worldwide causes.

THE CONTINUING PROCESS. Levinson described what happens after the forty to forty-five transition. There is again another "settling down" period during the fifties. Then yet another transition and so on (see Box F). So it goes throughout our lives, said Levinson and Sheehy, it is a matter of "changing seasons" and "passages," life cycles and stages. We build what we think is a good, viable, and permanent life structure. But no life structure that we make can ever be either perfect or permanent. We are part of a constant process of examining what is faulty and out of proportion in our current life structure, of de-structuring what is no longer valuable or significant, and of exploring ways to restructure our lives so that we can live our next years more creatively. It is not easy. Transitions frequently involve feelings of being uprooted and alienated. Change is never easy, but the alternative is stagnation.

BOX G
Passages of Adult Life

AGE	STAGE	QUESTIONS	CRISIS	SUCCESSFUL RESOLUTION
Late Adolescence (18 to 22 yrs)	"Pulling Up Roots"	"Who am I?" "How can I establish my own identity distinct from my family?"	The grass is greener elsewhere. (I have to get away from family/ high school/hometown to college/service/ "see the world"/anywhere but here.)	May have many false starts but begins to feel self-supportive and a person in one's own right.
Early Adulthood	"The Trying Twenties"	"How do I put my aspirations into effect?"	Faces enormous tasks of mastering life-work, getting a family started, and establishing self in community.	If successful, person has sense of stability, putting down roots.
Age 30	"Catch 30"	"What kind of a trap have I gotten myself into?"	A feeling of "rock-barren" and a general tearing down of life choices built in twenties.	Can be a time of new vision, life partnership, aspirations.
34 to 45	"The Deadline Decade"*	"Why am I doing all this?"	Experience the waning of youth, failure of physical powers, attractiveness.	Person can arrive at a new authenticity of self.
After 45	"Renewal or Resignation"	"What can I do with the rest of my life?"	Parents may have died; children have grown up and left home; job is not "a dream of possibility" but just a job.	New wisdom and understanding. Parents are forgiven their inadequacies, children their selfishnesses, and friends are more important.
After 50	More Critical Leanings	"What have I done with my life?"	Sense of desolation.	More objectivity about life, more willingness to be oneself—"less facade."

Adapted from Gail Sheehy, Passages *(New York: E. D. Dutton & Co., Inc., 1976).*
*Sheehy believed this deadline came earlier for women (age 35) than for men (40 to 45 yrs).

There also is the rewarding aspect of these changes and choices in our lives. When we are willing to face the realities in our life, unpleasant as they may be, and when we are willing to struggle through the transitions that need to be made, we come out on the other side, said Levinson, a more integrated, a more individuated, a more "whole" person. We become our singular selves, able to express what we really are. Besides giving up what is stagnant and dead, we are making ready, as well, to reap the harvest of the new seasons. That means letting go of the old. Nothing new can come unless we are able to let go of what is dead or dying. Birth, growth, stagnation, death, and rebirth. It is a constant process.

applications and coping techniques

Now that we have come to the end of this rather lengthy chapter, what have we discovered that can be applied to our own living? How can we use these theoretical discussions in our own personal living space? Each person, of course, will have discovered something different, something that is especially applicable to him or her, but there are also some general principles to which all of us can relate, which we present below.

1. Consider Life as a Constant Process of Discovery

The main theme of this chapter is that life is not a "solid state" or an objective to be achieved, but a continuing, challenging developmental process from birth to death. Every age, era, and period has its special life crises to be confronted and worked through, its tasks to be mastered, and its competencies to be added "unto oneself." Let us compare the life process to a river's journey, which has its source, its tributaries, its directional flow and currents, its twists and turnings, its rapids and smooth places, and its outflow into larger waters. No place on that river's journey is ever like another, and we cannot know what lies ahead until we get there. From birth to death, we always are in the process of discovering and rediscovering where we are on that journey. This point of view will help us to sustain the difficulties of the journey, for we know that no matter how stressful or traumatic our situation currently is, we can eventually work through most difficulties and eventually, will reach a smoother part of the river's journey. Similarly, when we are in a time of easy flow, we will not be disappointed when we again experience the rapids and shoals of existence. We can never "rest on our laurels," so to speak. We need to formulate a creative philosophy of life, one that emphasizes the ebb and flow of existence and that views living as an ongoing, never-ending process.

2. Remain Open to the Growth and Change of that Process

As we travel on our life journey and create our life structures, we need to remember that no life structure can ever be perfect or permanent. Life is neither perfect nor permanent.

Take, for example, two persons who marry. In their first life structure, they both may be in school, or one may be working while the other finishes his or her education. This life structure with its college activities, its goal of educational achievement, its quality of student life has its own special values and excitement and also problems (particularly the ever-present problems of financial pressure). When this process is completed, the couple may move on to create their next life structure of permanent residence, the beginning of a family, and the social milieu of other young parents. It is a time of putting down roots. Life with young children has its special delights and also its special problems. The relationship between the two persons changes as they make the passage from lovers to parents, and there are new choices to confront: shall they move to a larger residence? Shall they move to a new location for job advancement? The forms of entertainment so relished in the college experience give way to other interests which pertain to family-based activities.

As the children grow up, the quality of family life also changes. The constellation of the family is no longer that of children needing and wanting the nurturing of their parents. Adolescents begin to form their own identities and to pull away from parental authority. Family process now is a matter of physical and emotional separation by both parents and children. These stresses and strains may necessitate a destructuring of the couple's values and needs.

When the children have left the house, the parents may have to cross that especially trying age-forty passage. Whatever this entails, it restructures and prepares for the "second half of life." And so it goes, requiring our adaption to the choices and changes in our lives.

3. Remember that the Most Difficult Times of Our Lives Occur at the Times of Passage and Transition

The human organization is essentially conservative. Change does not come easily to us. The passage from the prenatal existence to an independent one is, in all likelihood, not welcomed by the infant. That momentous rite of passage, the "first day of school," may have been eagerly anticipated by the young child, but it is not without its fearsome aspects, and the first year of school is a process of learning to relate to a world which is unlike the safer harbor of family life. Ultimately, the child's peer group will become more important than the child's parents, but the six-year-old cannot see that now. The transition to school requires a new psychological reorganization and time to integrate the many events that the child is processing.

The big transitions that we make throughout our life generally will be experienced as our most stressful moments. We will, from time to time, wonder if we are able to cope. We may feel that we "are coming apart at the seams." At these times, we need to remember that it is natural to experience confusion, depression, anxiety, alienation—all of this is part of the growth process and may even be necessary to it, if we are to make the passage to the next stage.

Adults, like children, are fearful of what lies beyond the bend. It is well to remember at these times that if we can successfully process the emotional turmoils and physical de-structuring, there is generally a calm flow up ahead and a landscape which is more creative and richer than the one we have left behind. In our present youth-oriented society we tend to emphasize the joys and values of early life; yet each age has its own harvest of joys and rewards, which we can know fully only when we get there. Parent life with small children is certainly a lovely time, but it has its problems: health concerns and doctors' bills, balancing love with discipline, the increasing expectations of school work and "conferences" when Johnny is not learning or is "acting up." The joys of grandparenthood, on the other hand, can include loving the children, even spoiling them, without the concerns and responsibilities of living with them every day. Thus, one can participate in the joys of family life but also be able to retreat to the peaceful privacy of one's own life again.

4. Staying With the Process Requires Letting Go of the Past, Remaining Rooted in the Present, and Welcoming the Future

Some persons remain fixated at some past level of their lives. You may know such persons, as, for example, the man who "replays" his war experiences over and over again. Somehow that seems to him to have been his "finest hour." Or take the woman who bemoans her current existence with adolescent children and looks back at those happier times when the children were so young and needed her. They are trapped in their own pasts.

Other persons are fixated not in the past but in the future. They always are planning to do the things they want to do when . . . he or she is out of school, when the children are grown up, or when "we retire." Living in the future prevents us from experiencing what life has to offer here and now. Furthermore, that future that is being planned for, saved for, and toiled for seems somehow never to happen. Their psychological farsightedness prevents them from seeing what is at hand.

We need to learn to let go of the past, to remain rooted in the present, and to welcome the future. The ancient Greeks had a saying: you can never step in the same river twice. What is gone is gone, and the future can never be fully foreseen. This is not to say that we cut off all our past ties, and it is not to say that we do not make goals for the future. On the contrary, friends become more important, not less so, as we get older. Without setting goals for ourselves, we can hardly achieve them. We value the past for it helps us see our own history, from where we have come and where we are now. Memory helps to bind all our experiences together and is a vital part of the integrative process. The ability to see ahead (imagination) enables us to create and plan for a better and more creative future life. What is essential to remember, however, is that we *live* not in the past, nor in the future, but in our moment-by-moment experiencing and awareness of *the process*.

There is a new approach today in psychology . . .

discovering and owning our individual differences

2

Part of the process of personality integration is the recognition and appreciation of our individual differences.

I. Introduction: Learning to Value Our Individual Differences

   A. *Values defined: Abraham Maslow*
      1. *Hierarchy of needs*
      2. *Physiological needs*
      3. *Safety needs*
      4. *Belonging and love needs*
      5. *Esteem needs*
      6. *Needs for self-actualization*
      7. *The mechanistic model of human personality*
      8. *The emergence of the humanistic model*
   B. *Life style defined: Alfred Adler*
      1. *Constructive and destructive life styles*
   C. *Some theoretical life styles: Eduard Spranger's six types of men*
   D. *Gordon Allport's becoming*
   E. *Carl Jung's "type" psychology*
      1. *The extraverted type*
      2. *The introverted type*
      3. *Psychological type as innate and inborn*
      4. *Jung's four functions: thinking versus feeling; sensing versus intuition*
         a. *The sensing function*
         b. *The intuitional function*
         c. *The thinking function*
         d. *The feeling function*
         e. *Use of the functions*

II. Becoming Aware of Our Particular Differences

   A. *Physical make-up*
      1. *Sheldon's physical types*
      2. *The biological approach to the study of personality*
      3. *Physical characteristics and social learning*
      4. *Self-fulfilling prophecies*
      5. *The late-maturing boy and the early-maturing girl*
   B. *Becoming aware of our emotional differences*
      The nature-nurture controversy
   C. *Effects of sex and birth order*
      1. *Sibling rivalry*
      2. *Effect of birth order*
      3. *First-born versus later-born*
      4. *First-borns and achievement*
      5. *The only child*
      6. *Sexual differences*

introduction: learning to value our individual differences

The thesis of chapter 1 was simply that the process of personality integration is continuing introspection (questioning and examining where we are in our current life situation), de-structuring what is false or outmoded, redetermining values and goals more personally rewarding to ourselves, and restructuring a life style that, while more consistent with our inner needs, also is viable with "external" reality. This seems to be as valid for those in their thirties, forties, and fifties as it is for the person just coming into early adulthood. Even when we have experienced great satisfaction and achievement in one phase of our lives, the transition to the next era seems to bring new crises, new needs, and new values. As bewildering as this process may seem to us at times, it is, nevertheless, a source of renewal: it maintains our will to live, provides new purposes and meanings to replace outmoded ones, and revitalizes our energies.

Knowing what is worthwhile for each of us is to become aware of our individual differences; that is, learning *to appreciate how each of us is different,* one from the other, and *valuing our differences.* It also is the willingness of each person to determine his or her own life style, based on those differences.

We are discussing two very abstract concepts: *values* and *life style.* Before we go any further, we need to understand these two terms. For that we shall turn to the work of two men: Abraham Maslow, who saw the evolution of personality as an evolution of needs and values, and Alfred Adler, who popularized the term *life style.*

Values Defined: Abraham Maslow

Abraham Maslow was one of the great pioneer humanistic psychologists. It was his genius to see a now obvious truth, that the way to learn about truly integrated and creative people is to study integrated and creative people.[1] This point of view, although it may seem rather commonplace to us now, was original in the study of human personality in the forties and fifties. Until then, most of what we knew about human functioning was based largely 1) on studies of sick and highly neurotic persons, 2) on statistical studies of the *average* individual, and 3) on laboratory experiments on animals. Maslow directed the attention of American psychologists toward another dimension, toward that person he called *self-actualizing*. What Maslow described are those persons who seem to have a clear idea of their life goals, who can mobilize their energies for their life goals in relatively efficient ways, but who are also sensitive to the needs of others. Not only do self-actualizing persons pursue and achieve their own goals, they also enable their society to evolve. Maslow called them the "shining lights" of civilization.

HIERARCHY OF NEEDS. In his study of how people live and grow, Maslow came to a significant conclusion: that human beings have a definite *hierarchy of needs;* that is, that certain needs and values must come first and be satisfied before other "higher needs" and values can come to the fore. Before human beings can lift their gaze to the stars, they must satisfy their bodily and earthly needs: air, food, water, shelter, freedom from pain and danger, and so forth. When once these needs are satisfied, then they can come to value other "higher" elements of life, such as love, self-respect, esteem, and the expansion of consciousness.

These "higher" needs and values are peculiarly human; they distinguish us from other life forms. We will discuss this hierarchy of needs, but we ask the reader to remember that these needs are not as discrete as shown in Box A but continually overlap, ebb, and flow with different intensities throughout our lives.

PHYSIOLOGICAL NEEDS. The first needs that must be taken care of pertain to survival, or what social and biological scientists have called the instinct for self-preservation. These basic needs are to maintain the body in homeostatic condition: general and specific hungers, sex, water, air, and shelter. The person who is deprived of these will seek to reduce those needs by any possible means, including working for slave wages, begging, stealing, or accepting charity or welfare. We are mistaken if we think the hobo or the panhandler suffers unduly from pride when he begs for a quarter for a "cup of coffee." What he values is the food or the drink he will buy with that quarter.

SAFETY NEEDS. People need to feel safe. They need to feel secure in their jobs and to have a certain stability in their lives. They need to feel some structure and order in their everyday living so that they are not overwhelmed by chaos. They need to have a safe place to rest their heads, a "territorial" place of their own. All this may sound obvious but many of you may not go home always to a peaceful place free from anxiety. Many persons have found themselves living in tension because the people they live with make it so! Each person must find his or her own place, no matter how small and how humble, that is that person's own sanctuary, that person's castle, where he or she may feel "safe" and quiet, to replenish body and spirit.

BELONGING AND LOVE NEEDS.   Presumably, many of the belonging and love needs have been satisfied by a close and caring family, by our friends, and by others we hold dear. But these needs emerge over and over again in our lives in varying ways. The need for love and belonging becomes particularly dominant during adolescence when this need cannot be satisfied by our families. We need then a different kind of love and belonging—the kind that comes from our peers.

Sometimes young people come to college not yet having found a group with which to identify and to which to belong. Intellectually advanced and emotionally sensitive high school students often find themselves out-of-step with the prevailing personality type considered "popular." For these kinds of students, college provides a welcome harbor: it is here that such students can find others like themselves and where they can begin to "belong" to a group with real conviction and identity.

In increasing numbers, older people are coming back to college. They feel somewhat awkward and out of place in a classroom full of younger persons, particularly at first, even though elsewhere they have their needs of belonging well satisfied. Eventually, however, they too will find they are accepted and "belong."

ESTEEM NEEDS.   If all we had to do was to feel safe, have enough to eat and clothes on our body, and people that love and accept us, then we might be as happy as South Sea islanders are purported to be. Most human beings need to feel not just loved but *needed* by others. We need to know that we are esteemed for what we contribute to the general welfare, to feel that we contribute something unique, something that others can respect. We need to feel that our existence makes a difference and that our offering to society, however great or small, is valuable. For some, this will come through great achievement and honors such as the ability to express themselves in great works of art or through scientific discovery. Others may find those needs satisfied through improving our planet and by making it a better place to be.

NEEDS FOR SELF-ACTUALIZATION.   Finally, there is the need for self-actualization. It can be described as *the need to be and to express the highest potential that one is capable of achieving.* When we have achieved all the other needs, there remains the human urge to explore our individual differences and to actualize our own talents

Maslow's Hierarchy of Needs*

```
NEED FOR SELF-ACTUALIZATION

Self-mastery, desire to help others,
ability to direct one's own life,
rich emotional experiences, a sense
of meaning to one's life.
```

```
ESTEEM NEEDS

Self-esteem, esteem of others, achievement,
recognition, dignity, appreciation,
self-confidence, mastery of oneself and one's
environment.
```

```
BELONGINGNESS AND LOVE NEEDS

Love, affection, belongingness need for
family, friends, group, clan, territorial imperative;
community.
```

```
SAFETY NEEDS

Security, stability, dependency, protection; freedom from
fear, anxiety, chaos; need for structure, order, limits, etc.
```

```
PHYSIOLOGICAL NEEDS

Homeostasis; specific hungers  sex, food, water; air, shelter,
and general survival.
```

and gifts, a desire to become that which we truly are: our most expressive, creative, dynamic selves, with freedom to master our fate and go beyond our current state. This need takes many forms, from a sense of freedom to be utterly oneself to that overwhelming and mystical sense of being in perfect harmony and at one with the universe.

Where once psychologists talked mainly of homeostatic needs and tension reduction, we now speak also of those other motives which we sense but which we cannot always name, the human yearning to go beyond the known, to understand something now only dimly perceived, or to achieve a new level of consciousness for oneself or for humankind. There is in humankind a potential, which once it can begin to be expressed, urges us to reach for something just beyond our grasp, sometimes just beyond our awareness. This was Maslow's contribution to the understanding of human personality.

*Adapted from Abraham Maslow, *Motivation and Personality*(New York: Harper & Row, 1954).

THE MECHANISTIC MODEL OF HUMAN PERSONALITY. This viewpoint seems rather self-evident now, but until Maslow's research was published, certain social scientists tended to view human personality as a gyro-mechanism. Their approach to personality viewed the human being as being like any other living organism and as having certain bodily needs (air, food, water, sex, etc.). When our bodies lack enough of one of these we suffer a tension that results in a *drive* to restore the body to its proper homeostasis (a state of bodily biochemical balance). To put it more simply: When we are hungry, we seek food; when we are cold, we look for shelter or other ways to warm ourselves.[2] In satisfying (or not satisfying) our homeostatic imbalance, humankind "happens" upon better ways of doing things: building houses instead of living in caves, raising animals instead of hunting them, and weaving and sewing clothes instead of donning animal hides. According to the mechanistic model, once a person has achieved a homeostatic state, that person is no longer motivated to achieve and must await more bodily tension in order to initiate any other activity.[3] This model of humans has led one contemporary anthropologist, Desmond Morris, to view the person as not much more than a naked ape in clothing, and human society as a kind of civilized zoo.[4]

THE EMERGENCE OF THE HUMANISTIC MODEL. There is more to organismic life than the mere reduction of bodily needs or drive states. We know, from the lives of many famous men and women, that even though they were rich and could have had a life of luxury and ease (all their bodily needs satisfied), they exhibited an urge toward something more, to explore the unknown regions of their physical world and to expand their knowledge of human existence.[5]

One model of humankind asserts that we are nothing more than "naked apes" who live in "human zoos."

The humanistic model of psychology asserts that a person is more than an intelligent laboratory rat, more than a gregarious naked ape, and more than a sophisticated computer. The human personality strives for challenging and creative self-expression and evolution, a transcendence of ordinary personal limitations toward higher states of consciousness.

Life Style Defined: Alfred Adler

We have defined values in terms of human needs. The second term we need to define is life style. To understand this concept, we turn to the work of Alfred Adler, one of those great personality theorists who was first a student of Freud but who, like many others, broke away from Freud's narrowly sexualistic theory of human functioning to pursue his own insights into human personality.

The term "life style" has become familiar to us in recent decades and has come to mean our financial status or the way in which we live, whether we live moderately, frugally, or luxuriously. But as Alfred Adler devised this term, life style has a much larger connotation. It means the whole flow, pattern, and direction of a person's life. Adler considered our individual life styles as "acts of creation" involving our goals, our values, our aspirations, the sum and substance of what is known as our "personality," our attitudes, and our achievements.[6] No two styles can be alike. Our life styles are so individualistic that Adler called his approach to personality "individual psychology." Adler wrote that one's life style is more than the sum of a person's minute, day-by-day behaviors. To understand a person's life style, one must study the person's whole existence from its source to its ultimate direction. One must be able to see its flow, harmony, and poetry and to discover the person's great underlying themes and rhythms. Life style is exactly what novelists try to describe in character portrayals. It is what students mean when they say, "I like psychology because I like to know what makes people tick and why they do the things they do!"

CONSTRUCTIVE AND DESTRUCTIVE LIFE STYLES.   Although we may not fully comprehend the whys and wherefores of a person's life style, we often are able to discern whether this person seems to have a destructive or constructive life style, whether this person has no direction or that person is "getting somewhere." Some life styles seem to have purpose, to be active and dynamic while others seem stagnant and confused. Still others seem to be picking their way cautiously toward their life aims while others seem bent toward alcoholic or barbiturate suicide. Some life styles seem to be a frantic circular chase for sensation and excitement, while others may seem limited and dull. Furthermore, one's life style may be in direct contradiction to one's aspirations and intent. Consider, for example, an acquaintance of ours who has stated many times that his chief goal in life is "to do some serious research and writing—to make a significant contribution to science." His behavior, however, belies his expressed intentions. Although he has been married only a few years, one of his chief pastimes seems to be to demonstrate his masculine attractiveness. He wears see-through shirts, rides a powerful motorcycle, has many conferences with his female students, discusses sexual games with his office mates, and generally gives the rest of us the impression that his interest in women has less to do with their charms than with his conquest of them. His life style, as we have known him, has been so consistently the same year after year that we can make some fairly good guesses about his future as it unfolds. As he gets older he will continue to act as the office Lothario until, as a middle-aged man, he will exasperate his wife by continuing to tell off-color jokes at parties. He also will embarrass his daughter as he tests his fading charms on her high school and college friends. Even his son will not be safe from his intent to prove his "masculinity," since he will challenge his physical and sexual vigor against that of his son and his son's friends. The tragedy of this man's life style is not so much in what he is doing, but what he is *not* doing. Despite his professed aspiration to make a significant contribution to science, his energies and the time needed for scientific endeavor are going elsewhere.

Some Theoretical Life Styles: Eduard Spranger's Six Types of Men.[7]

We cannot be certain, but we can guess that Alfred Adler derived some of his concepts of life style from Eduard Spranger, an early twentieth-century German philosopher—psychologist not well known in this country but very well regarded in Europe. Spranger spent a lifetime observing the affairs of the great and near-great of Europe and concluded that Western civilization had produced certain "types" of men. These types have vastly differing orientations toward life and what makes it significant. We shall look briefly at these six types, since they seem to exemplify some of Adler's ideas of life style.

Although there are few pure types of men, Spranger felt reasonably comfortable that there were at least six basic motivations toward life: the *aesthetic*, the *political*, the *economic*, the *religious*, the *social*, and the *theoretical*. The aesthetic values life for its beauty or for the beauty he can make from it. If he himself is not an artist, writer, sculptor, he at least delights in works of art and attempts to surround

Box B
Types of Men[7]

	THEORETICAL TYPE	ECONOMIC TYPE	POLITICAL TYPE	SOCIAL TYPE	AESTHETIC TYPE	RELIGIOUS TYPE
1. Motivation	TRUTH Objective knowledge; intellectual understanding.	UTILITY Self-preservation; desire for security and the "good life."	POWER Desire to influence others; to be a force in the world. To effect change.	LOVE Service to others; to nurture, to love, and to be loved.	BEAUTY To create art; to make of one's life a work of art.	MEANING To understand the significance of life; to relate oneself to the universe.
2. Guided By	Principles, logic, reason; classifies, analyzes, systematizes experience. Seeks to understand *what has taken place*, i.e., to grasp laws of universe. Is observer, not participator, in human affairs.	Acts on instinct; keen judgment; can make quick decisions; pragmatic; makes the most of *what is*; opportunistic; what is useful is valued. Values self first, then family, etc.	Self-autonomy; freedom from instinctual desires; desires to bring about *what could be*; plans for future; has initiative; is good executive. Prides himself on "realism" and understanding of men.	Feelings are dominant; understanding of others and their needs: to encourage in them their highest potential: *what can be*. Warm and sympathetic. Self-sacrifice is self-enriching.	Value judgments of like/dislike, ugly/beautiful; dominant; open to all life has to offer, pain as well as joy; open to all experiences; to create a masterpiece.	Strives for self-perfection, to relate self to universe and highest good. Cosmic consciousness, knows *what ought to be*. All experiences mediated by "still small voice." Finds no pleasure in this world, longs for other world.
3. Highest Value	To break through ignorance, to discover.	To enjoy security, comfort, and luxury.	To influence the lives of others; effect social change.	To love and to be loved.	To express self and individuality.	To receive spiritual gifts and "grace of God."
4. Political Leanings	Tends to be radical or ignorant (apolitical).	Conservative or reactionary. Firm belief in "law and order," social and legal contracts.	Consuming *raison d'être*. All other interests take second place.	Perfect love leads to socialism or perfect Christian communism.	Liberal political beliefs but is not active.	"Render unto Caesar what is Caesar's." Political indifference, since this world is (even at best) a prison.

5. Attitude toward Beauty	Only truth is beautiful.	Beautiful objects valued for their "net worth" and for enjoyment of the good life.	Music and art as background for political themes, as in posters, marching bands, etc.	People are the ultimate beauty as part of God's creation.	The highest good: no meaning without beauty.	This world is not beautiful. Art can be seductive; leads away from purpose of life.
6. Attitude toward Truth	Ultimate good, only good. Truth at any price.	Truth is what is functional and "operable."	To avoid chaos and panic, truth may have to be withheld.	Truth can be a sword to hurt or destroy.	"Beauty is truth; truth, beauty."	Mortal beings cannot grasp truth, which is the Divine; all we can know are fragments of the whole.
7. Attitude toward Religion	Abhors "mystic" elements, views religion as primitive science; if religious at all, it is metaphysical. *God is truth.*	May operate at a "psychic level," believes in "chance," or in "luck" or in gambling, may feel "hot." *God is giver of gifts.*	Believes in a patriarchal form of religion with self as chief minister. *God is all-powerful ruler of world.*	May be very religious; views earth as creation of God and people as "children of God." *God is love.* "Love ye one another."	Sees divine in manifestation of forms; sees God in nature; pantheistic. *God is beauty.* Identifies with mythological elements.	All earthly experiences to be in service to ultimate meaning. *God is spirit.* Seeks ultimate religious experience: mystic understanding.
8. Attitude toward Knowledge	Progress comes through knowledge. Values education.	Values practical and technological knowledge.	Especially interested in psychology and social science, since they allow person to know what motivates people.	Knowledge applied in service to others as in "helping professions."	Values the humanistic arts.	Understanding does not come by cognition but by revelation.

Types of Men[7] – Continued

	THEORETICAL TYPE	ECONOMIC TYPE	POLITICAL TYPE	SOCIAL TYPE	AESTHETIC TYPE	RELIGIOUS TYPE
9. Attitude toward Money	May be helpless to cope with practical financial affairs.	Able to use, invest, multiply resources. Enjoys what money can bring. Everything has "a net worth." Everyone "has a price."	Money to be used toward political ambitions, therefore is useful. In own life, may be austere and frugal.	"Give all ye have to the poor." Material possessions are useful to bring happiness or health to others.	Willing to starve for art; aesthetic orientation antagonistic to economic orientation. Finding a "use" for something may even destroy its value.	Has little use for riches of this world. Money brings neither happiness nor goodness.
10. Attitude toward Social Interaction	Is asocial. Does not value ancestors or class distinctions, so is cosmopolitan. Likes quiet life; values professional colleagues; work is life.	Many social relationships: business, home, and family, friends. "Public relations is good business."	Is keen student of human nature; charismatic to others; able leader; generally has low view of human motivation. Enjoys groups of people.	All life is sacred. "As much as ye do it for the least of these, my brothers, ye do it unto me."	Persons not valued in themselves but for what they can add to beauty or excitement. A person may be anything except boring.	Treats all persons kindly, but earthly friends take second place. Primary relationship is that between self and God.
11. Attitude toward Emotions and Feelings	Distrusts feeling; has minimal affective behaviors. Little concern for people; what is important is truth, not life.	Feelings are mainly focused on what is *useful* and what can *benefit*. Life of luxury bring satisfaction.	Tries to free himself of physical passions so as to be "one-sighted," and there is no personal life.	Love is the greatest gift; is guided by feelings, which border on the religious. "Mother Love."	Passionate engagement with the world; all feelings and experiences are welcome: sadness and suffering as well as joy and beauty.	Operates from deep *psychic center of self*; all other human passions are mortified.

	Philosopher, scientist, scholar, researcher. PLATO, ARISTOTLE, EINSTEIN	Executive, accountant, banker, salesman, most business persons. ALEXANDER HAMILTON, ANDREW CARNEGIE	Statesman, diplomat, college president, executive. THOMAS JEFFERSON, FRANKLIN ROOSEVELT	Physician, nurse, counselor, psychologist. TOLSTOY, FRANCIS OF ASSISI, ABRAHAM LINCOLN	Artist, playwright, dancer, musician. GEORGE SAND, MOZART, SHAKESPEARE	Genuine "men of the cloth"; the mystic saints. WILLIAM BLAKE, FRANCIS OF ASSISI, ALBERT SCHWEITZER
12. Highest Type	Philosopher, scientist, scholar, researcher. PLATO, ARISTOTLE, EINSTEIN	Executive, accountant, banker, salesman, most business persons. ALEXANDER HAMILTON, ANDREW CARNEGIE	Statesman, diplomat, college president, executive. THOMAS JEFFERSON, FRANKLIN ROOSEVELT	Physician, nurse, counselor, psychologist. TOLSTOY, FRANCIS OF ASSISI, ABRAHAM LINCOLN	Artist, playwright, dancer, musician. GEORGE SAND, MOZART, SHAKESPEARE	Genuine "men of the cloth"; the mystic saints. WILLIAM BLAKE, FRANCIS OF ASSISI, ALBERT SCHWEITZER
13. Perversion	Becomes pedantic, concerned with trivia; unable to relate to persons and ongoing events of world.	May become a robber-baron, ruthless; J. P. Morgan, the Mafia, "wheeler-dealers."	Desire to dominate the world: Hitler or Machiavelli.	Love may turn to hatred. Medea destroys her own children to spite her husband.	Dilletantism (Nero) or decadence; or sensuously selfish, as Hedda Gabbler.	Could become a black magician, like Faust: sell soul to the devil (Charles Manson). Or be a narrow-minded dogmatist or over-zealous reformer (Cotton Mather).

Adapted from Eduard Spranger, Types of Men: The Psychology and Ethics of Personality (*New York: Johnson Reprint Corp., 1928*). Note: Some of the names listed for types are Spranger's; others are ours. We would be interested in the readers' nominations for categories 12 and 13.

himself with them. His motivation in life is to derive beauty from it. The economic person values not what is beautiful, but what is *useful,* practical, materialistic. He understands the needs for self-survival and the survival of his society and derives his *raison d 'être* from the concerns of business and the acquisition of wealth. The religious person is oriented toward understanding the *meaning of life.* The religious person is less interested in how the world is than in how it *should* be The religious man needs to believe that life has some ultimate purpose and good. The political man values power and influence over other qualities. At his lowest level, he can dominate his family; at his highest, he can be an outstanding statesman in international affairs. The theoretical man values the discovery of truth rather than beauty or goodness. His is the motivation of the scientist or philosopher, and his role is that of observer and discoverer of the universal laws rather than of participant in the affairs of men. Finally, there is the social man who is oriented toward service to other people because of his great compassion for others' sufferings and helplessness. There is no such thing as a "pure" type. We all are probably a mixture of two or more or even all. But some orientations seem to dominate over others. Albert Schweitzer (philosopher, writer, musician, physician, theologian) undoubtedly, was one of the strongest mixtures of several of these orientations, but was (by his own admission) primarily motivated by a religious orientation.

A group of psychologists found this classification so useful that they derived a psychological test from it to enable persons to become more aware of their personal value system which might help them in their vocational-educational decision making.[8] Presumably, if one's highest values are economic and political, one ought not to go into a social service vocation such as the health-related fields but ought rather to consider some aspect of business or government.

Gordon Allport's Becoming

Gordon Allport, one of America's most distinguished theoretical psychologists believed, like Adler, that to understand people's life styles it is necessary to see them as more than the sum of their day-to-day, minute-by-minute behaviors, as these sometimes may seem contradictory or even chaotic. Therefore, one must view people in terms of their *propriate strivings,* motives of a higher order than those of tension reduction or self-preservation. These higher order motivations lead people to accomplishments hitherto unknown. He cited the life of Raoul Amundsen, as an example, who from the age of fifteen determined to be an explorer. Nothing could keep him from this central commitment, not obstacles, discouragement, fatigue, hunger, ridicule, or danger, and he became the first man to reach the South Pole. Allport compared this systematic approach to the life style of the mental patient who seems unable to maintain long-term goals and who has difficulty maintaining a life style of expectation, planning, problem solving and intention. It was Allport's notion that the healthy, creative person with a constructive life style is always in a state of *becoming* — evolving, as it were, into something beyond what he or she has been.[9]

Carl Jung's "Type" Psychology

It may seem surprising that Sigmund Freud, who changed the very way we think about human nature, did not investigate individual differences among people. But Freud was interested in discovering the common themes of human motivation; how we are alike rather than how we are different. He was looking for a kind of field theory of human nature.

It was Carl Jung, one of Freud's students and later famous in his own right, who called our attention to the fact that there really might be different types of personality. Jung believed that a person's behaviors, interests, drives, and motivations cannot be entirely accounted for by one's early experiences (as Freud believed) or by our conditioning in early life (proposed by Ivan Pavlov and later by B. F. Skinner). On the contrary, Jung believed that we are *born* with certain, innate psychological differences that determine who we are and what we can become. In other words, we fall into certain personality "types."[10]

Two of these theoretical types have become so accepted that they are a part of our everyday language: the *introverted* personality type and the *extraverted* personality type. Jung's usage of these terms differs from the popular usage.

THE EXTRAVERTED TYPE. The consciousness of the extraverted person looks out onto the external world for meaning and value. Extraverted types are immensely interested in persons who come their way, in the events of their immediate environment and also of the larger social scene. Generally, the orientations of extraverted persons are compatible with societal values which make them rather easy to be around. Extraverted persons seem to accommodate to others relatively easily and manage the economic and practical areas of living with relative efficiency. At their best, extraverted persons are affable, adaptable, and can get projects and tasks accomplished. They make skillful executives, know how to run meetings, and are able to calm an atmosphere when a discussion gets prickly and people are "at each other's throats." At their worst, extraverts do not seem to have a sense of themselves, and thus, they pursue "popularity" and lack self-direction.

THE INTROVERTED TYPE. In contrast to the extraverted type, the introverted type focuses on his or her internal feelings, thoughts, ideas, and fantasies. Since introverted types are more motivated by their subjective experiences, they are less interested in the pragmatic tasks to be accomplished than in the stimulation they experience from new ideas and theories. The introvert is less outgoing than the extravert is, more solitary, more independent of thought, and able to take firm stands on issues regardless of public approbation or disapproval. The introvert is harder to understand and get along with, and less able to express emotions. Finally, the introverted type does not value status or economic achievement as much as the pursuit and understanding of underlying and universal meanings of life not readily apparent or understood in everyday living. The introvert makes a good scientist, scholar, accountant, and political theorist. Of course, none of us are pure introverts or pure extraverts. This designation is a matter of degree, and most of us fall somewhere in the middle.

The two types are different even in the psychological disturbances they exhibit. The extraverted type is prone to be over suggestible and therefore prone to hysterical and other physical ailments. The introvert's most frequent neurosis is morbid fantasy, depression, and can become an isolated recluse. The extravert suffers by a loss of selfhood; the introvert suffers from agonies of the spirit. It has become axiomatic that Americans have developed an essentially extraverted philosophy and mode of life with their emphasis on participatory democracy, group membership, peer acceptance, and the importance of popularity," physical attractiveness, and youth. The introvert in our society may be so disregarded as to become a "born loser." Nevertheless, one can find highly successful introverts in the United States in the universities, in the scientific laboratories, in art studios, and in any place human endeavor relies more on highly individualistic emotional and intellectual insights than on group cooperation.

PSYCHOLOGICAL TYPE AS INNATE AND INBORN. Jung emphasized repeatedly that these two different orientations stem from *biological* differences. These are basic characteristics that the person exhibits immediately at birth. It seemed to Jung that all children display these differences from earliest childhood, even in infancy, despite the similarity of environmental conditions. Children can be forced to act against their basic type by one or the other of the parents, just as children can be forced to switch from using their left hand to using their right hand. Some forms of stuttering have been attributed to this switching of hands since (presumably) it forces the neurological system to act in reverse. In just such a way, people acting contrary to their basic personality type eventually must become neurotic since they are falsifying their own basic mode of existence. Therapy consists in having people find their basic orientation and restructure their living to accord with it. Jung made an interesting statement about the differences between himself and Freud, concerning psychological type.

Box A
Freud as Extravert; Jung as Introvert[11]

An interesting aspect of Jung's psychological type theory was his observations of himself and Sigmund Freud, his teacher, as representing the two basic types of introvert and extravert. Of all Freud's students, Carl Jung was the youngest and considered by many as the most brilliant. Jung and Freud developed a sort of father-son relationship, and it was known among the psychoanalytic group that gathered around Freud, that Freud considered Jung as the "crown prince" who would take over the work of the psychoanalytic school of psychiatry. But Freud and Jung had serious disagreements and eventually Jung broke away to form his own school, which he called analytic psychology. In his autobiography, Jung explained that part of their difference was that Freud was essentially an extravert, while he (Jung) had always been introverted. It was easy, said Jung, for Freud to preside over a group of extremely able, intellectual physicians, thinkers, and theoreticians. Jung said that he, himself, was incapable of such a position and, true to his own "type", retired to his home in Switzerland and ventured, thereafter, very little into the social or political world.

JUNG'S FOUR FUNCTIONS: THINKING VERSUS FEELING; SENSING VERSUS INTUITION.   Jung's work on introversion-extraversion was followed by his work on what he called the *four functions* of human personality. Jung concluded that human experiencing can be divided into four distinct functions: thinking, feeling, sensing, and intuition. According to Jung, thinking and feeling (like introversion-extraversion) are polar functions and so are the sensing-intuitive functions. Of course, we all have all four functions to some degree; otherwise, we could not survive. But in most of us, said Jung, one or two tend to predominate, one is auxiliary, and one tends to be a bit atrophied. Together these four functions comprise how we take in and perceive the world, and how we act and react to it.

The Sensing Function.   There are two ways of receiving information and making sense of the world: *sensing* and *intuition.* Sensing is what we do when we systematically apprehend our surroundings through the physical senses. We observe the size and shape of a room, estimate a person's weight, get a "map" in our head when we walk or drive somewhere, observe how someone is dressed and that person's physical features. Persons who are good sensers appreciate neatness and orderliness, are able to remember names and faces, and generally have an appreciation for how things work and operate. They have good apperception of the physical world. They make good engineers, builders, carpenters, accountants, office managers, and whatever needs accurate perception of one's physical surroundings.

The Intuitional Function.   The intuitional function is something like a hunch or an "extra sense." It enables us to know not only what is there, but what is *not* there. It allows us to imagine possibilities and to grasp for the intangible. People who have a strong intuitive sense may not be able to tell you how they have come to a conclusion, but they seem to do it quickly. The sensing person will take out slide rule or calculator and is very good with it; the intuitive one prefers to make a hypothetical guess first and then to corroborate it. Although the intuitive person may arrive at some completely wrong guesses, that person sometimes will provide an answer or solution that astonishes others. Highly intuitive persons are not as steady and sure-footed in the physical world as are the persons with a strong sensing function. They can be very absent-minded, lose tangible objects, not.be sure what day it is, or even realize that a friend has shaved his beard for weeks or months. But if intuitive persons do not have a good grasp of external reality, they seem to be able to grasp the internal aspects of situations or even of people. When a problem seems to have no logical, rational, easily found solution, the intuitive may be able to cut through the impasse with a new idea.

The Thinking Function.   We have said that the intuition-sensing polarity is the way we perceive the world. The other polar functions pertain to how we compute this information, how we react to it and what we conclude about it. We do so generally in one of two ways: we *think* it through, step by step, rationally and logically, or we come to an emotional appraisal of the situation. Persons who have a strong thinking function weigh the pros and cons of a situation and the advantages or disadvantages of one or several solutions and come to what we would call a logical conclusion. The person who has a strong thinking function does well in those situations which need objective analysis and precise decision making and to which the necessary raw data can be supplied.

The Feeling Function.   The feeling function is the valuative experience. It is not only whether we like or dislike someone or something, but whether that someone or something will have a positive or a negative outcome for us. Not all situations can be properly apprehended in a disinterested and logical way, since we do not have all the facts at all times. The person with a strong feeling function can, in a sense, fill in the missing data by picking up the "mood" or "feeling" that does not show up in a set of figures or specifications. For example, although the thinker can respond to what a person says, the "feeler" can assess what another is feeling but is unable to express. It goes without saying that feeling types make excellent elementary teachers, nurses, and counselors.

Use of the Functions.   Each of us uses all four functions even if we rely predominantly on just one or two. When we need to come to logical conclusions using facts and figures or when we need to make a rational analysis of current conditions, that is the time to use our thinking function. When we need to decide the value of something to us, or whether this or that course of action would be *better* for us, that is the time to use our feeling function. When we need to get around in our physical or social world, that is the time to use our sensing function. When we need to determine a future goal or bring something into being which is not there now, that is the time to use our intuition. To think, to feel, to sense, and to intuit: these are the four aspects that Jung considered the basic functioning of human personality.

When we do not understand other persons, it is probably because their way of functioning in the world differs significantly from ours. Some people "feel" their way around the world and are comfortable with the emotional self; laughter, tears, pain, and joy all are experienced naturally and easily. These people understand their emotions and the emotions of others. "Feelers" may not understand people who seem to "think" everything through, who are "cool" emotionally, and whose actions are based on logic. In fact, if you ask a "thinker" what his or her feelings are on a certain topic, he or she may very well be *unable* to tell you and wonder privately what feelings have to do with it. Marriage can be difficult when one partner is predominantly a

A schematic representation of Jung's theory of personality "types."

"feeler" and the other is predominantly a "thinker." In a like manner, the strong intuitive type may be irritated by the strong senser type, since the senser seems to stay too close to the surface or to "facts."[12]

becoming aware of our particular differences

Up until this point, we have discussed the various theoretical approaches to the differences in human personality which make people so fascinating. Perhaps you have already gained some insight into *your* orientation to life, what Adler called your life style, that is different from those of others that you know. It is a valuable insight, for surely this will help determine what you want to do with your self, what you want to do professionally, and how you want to live your personal life. We live in a time of great freedom and choice. Our life style is no longer solely determined (as it was in previous societies), or by the circumstances of our family's wealth, rank, and profession.

On the other hand, how we emerge as human personalities also is determined by factors other than free will and choice. Our personalities are influenced by many variables over which we have had no control, our genetic inheritance and behavioral dispositions, our early interactions with our family and how we are conditioned by our culture, our peer groups, and our society. To become more self-governing, we need to become aware of how these factors have influenced our thinking, attitudes and behaviors. We need to know, in other words, why we are the way we are. In order to understand the present, we need to consider the past. Once we have this kind of historical perspective, we are in a better position to analyze those aspects of ourselves we value and want to keep, and those aspects we would like to change so that our future will become a more creative expression of ourselves. Let us examine some of these factors.

Physical Make-up

There is a kind of literary tradition that one's physical characteristics indicate one's emotional temperament. For example, we see "jolly old St. Nick" as fat and good natured, but Ebenezer Scrooge, that old skin-flint of literature, is portrayed as thin and bony, miserable not only in physique but in temperament. Shakespeare characterized that lover of women and wine, Falstaff, as large and portly, but Cassius (the man who plots the assasination of Julius Caesar) as having a "lean and hungry look" and asserted that "such men are dangerous."

Can you identify these persons according to Sheldon's physical classifications?

That is the literary tradition. Is there, psychologists have wondered from time to time, any truth to this in real life? Is there a correlation between a corpulent frame and a love of "the good life?" Are thin persons misanthropic and discontent? One psychologist, William Sheldon, set out to investigate this possibility.[13]

SHELDON'S PHYSICAL TYPES. Sheldon undertook his investigations by trying to correlate physical constitution and mental-emotional attributes. He photographed four thousand young college men in the nude; compared their likes, dislikes, interests, hobbies, recreations, and values; and concluded his research by suggesting that there are three basic body types: the *endomorph,* the *ectomorph,* and the *mesomorph,* each of which is correlated with three basic temperaments. Sheldon based his three types on embryonic development. The mesomorph is mostly muscle, bone, and connective tissue which gives the person's body a hard, firm, strong, and rectangular shape. These persons, with their concentration of muscle have athletic, active, temperaments and constantly use their motor apparatus. The endomorph, by contrast, has proportionately more of his body given over to the visceral organs and to those areas of the body connected to the digestive tract. Such body types tend to be rounder, physically softer, and possess an emotionally "easy temperament." They prefer spectator sports, like to eat, enjoy the "good things" of life, and are generally affable in disposition. The ectomorph, on the other hand, is thin, poorly muscled, "all skin and nerves." The ectomorph prefers quiet, intellectual activities and is quite a bit more introverted than the other two types are. Many college professors seem to fit the physical and emotional characteristics of the ectomorph.

One should not get the impression that there is any such thing as a pure type. Most of us will be a combination of types and have mixed characteristics. Sheldon's research has been highly criticized, but we are left with the inescapable fact that Sheldon and his associates did discover that certain physical and emotional characteristics seem to correlate. If that is the case, then even the body type we are born with may influence our personality.

THE BIOLOGICAL APPROACH TO THE STUDY OF PERSONALITY. Although Sheldon's work was received by a storm of criticism, there has been steadily accumulating evidence in recent years, that babies are born with vast biological differences in the skeletal system, the digestive tract, the muscular system, the circulatory system, the respiratory system, the endocrine system and even in the microscopic level of the blood. These variations among human beings have been taken seriously by those researchers who specialize in the field of "individual differences."[14] The biological differences of the neonate, said Roger J. Williams, himself a biochemist, must have far-reaching effects on the individual's distinctive patterns of likes and dislikes and on the person's whole value system and personality.[15] Researchers have observed differences in even the number of "pain, touch, and temperature receptors," from individual to individual, a difference which suggests that each of us experiences "the world" in different ways. Our nervous system presents wide variations. In human beings, for example, there are eight different patterns of branching for the facial nerve. Williams considered these differences in bodily equipment at birth so enormous as to have inevitable consequences upon personality.

PHYSICAL CHARACTERISTICS AND SOCIAL LEARNING. Whether or not we are born with different body "types," it is surely true that the physical characteristics with which we are born will affect the way we experience the world. Physically, each of us represents a set of physical structures quite different from those of any other man or woman. It is important to realize that even these physical differences will cause the world to be slightly different for each person and thus affect that person's functioning. For example, a person who is color blind perceives the world quite differently from how a color-discriminating person does. So also, a farsighted child has more difficulty in learning to read than other children do, since learning to read requires fixation at *near* point. A lefthanded person makes constant adjustments in a world designed for righthanded people.

It is also true that we are all born with innate bodily weaknesses as well as with strengths. Some children already are quite myopic early in life and will have difficulty playing ball or engaging in other games requiring good vision. Others may be physically excellent specimens except for teeth that will cause them trouble all their lives. In any first-grade class of thirty children, one can expect to find at least two or three with speech or hearing difficulties; another several who are unusually awkward and uncoordinated; perhaps a child with petit-mal epilespy that will not be discovered for several years; and maybe several others who suffer from some sort of respiratory ailment. The whole area of exceptional children and special education has taught us that every child is exceptional in some way. None of us is born as a perfect physical specimen. The effects of being born "different" from other children will have profound psychological effects on the growing child. Probably all of us have grown up in some way feeling "stigmatized," as one psychologist put it, by some physical characteristic.[16] One child may have childhood diabetes which puts him or her under a set of special conditions which inhibit certain activities; another may be somewhat crippled; this person has a "stuttering" problem, that one feels "fat" and so on. An interesting exercise is to go around a classroom of college students or adults and ask them to name at least one thing about them that was a cause of suffering. One college student, dark and handsome, confessed to something he had never told anyone. He had grown up in a family of blue-eyed, fair-haired people and was always made to feel somehow peculiar. Yet, he was lively and spirited and the person who led interaction among the class members.

All of these differences, which may be the cause of much suffering in childhood, frequently turn out to be occasions by which the person learns to develop an inner resource for later satisfaction and reward. Not being able to play ball as well as others may cause the young boy to hang back and take the spectator's part. If he is called "sissy" or other such derogatory terms, he may well compensate in other ways such as reading voraciously to fill up his free time. The artist of this book told us that she took up art when she was in high school because she was not accepted by her high school peers as being "too different" from them. She looks back at that situation with a sense of happy irony—the outcome of that alienation from others in her peer group has resulted in a good deal of adult satisfaction in her art. History is full of biographies of men and women who were limited as children but who became (partially because of these limitations) very exceptional adults. Alfred Adler, who himself had been a physically weak child and who strove for superiority in other areas called this phenomenon *compensation.*

SELF-FULFILLING PROPHECIES.   Another way that our physical characteristics may affect our personality is how other persons view us. If we are born looking "just like so-and-so," people may expect those characteristics of us and encourage that particular set of behaviors in us. The fact of being born a redhead in our world may indeed have a relationship with being "hot tempered," a relationship that is the result of a *self-fulfilling prophecy:* the redhead may allow his or her anger to show more openly simply because that is what is expected!

The concept of the self-fulfilling prophecy has been researched by Robert Rosenthal and Lenore Jackson. They reported the results of their research in a book called *Pygmalion* in the Classroom.*[17] The experimenters, Rosenthal and Jackson, told teachers of an elementary school that certain of their students would probably show "unusual intellectual gains in the following year," a potential that had been discovered through testing. Actually, there was no known difference between these children and others on test performance as the target children were selected at random. At the end of the year, the children were retested, and the target children did indeed show significant gains on achievement and also, surprisingly enough, on intelligence scores as well. Rosenthal and Jackson concluded that these gains resulted from the fact that the teachers expected and therefore demanded more from the target students.

The experimental results have not been so dramatically reproduced in other attempts.[18] Nevertheless, it seems very likely that children will learn to behave in ways that they perceive to be expected of them. In fact, speech pathologists and therapists have been saying for many years that what we call "stuttering" often is brought on by parents' overconcern when their child is normally non-fluent around the time of four years of age.[19]

Our own experience in public schools verifies that our own school systems tend to reinforce the good students for what they do well rather than to assist the poorer students to become more competent. Who gets to do the homework arithmetic problems on the blackboard? Probably the good students because the teachers can count on them to have the correct answers. Who gets to do oral reading in the small

---

*Pygmalion is the mythical Greek sculptor who carved a statue so beautiful that he fell in love with it. In answer to his prayer, the goddess of Love, Aphrodite, transformed the statue into a beautiful woman. G. B. Shaw, the Irish playwright, turned this myth into a masterpiece of English literature, and it was then turned into a musical comedy, called *My Fair Lady.* Shaw's story is of a young flower girl who is made into a lady by a Professor Higgins by changing her cockney accent into upper class speech.

reading groups in the early grades? Surely not the one who hesitates at every other word but, rather, the one who can read fluently and with expression. And who gets chosen for the school football, baseball, and basketball teams? The one who is already skilled and competent, more skilled and competent than the average student.

THE LATE-MATURING BOY AND THE EARLY-MATURING GIRL. If we develop our physical maturity early in life, people will tend to treat us as being more mature, and we will feel more competent, more able to handle things, and take ourselves more seriously. If we are small and develop our adult physique later than average, we will be more apt to be treated as a child for a longer period of time, both by our families and by our classmates. This is especially true for the "late-maturing boy" and the "early-maturing girl." Studies of these two types of children have revealed this.[20] Late-maturing boys are not only less competent and skilled on the athletic fields, they also tend to be socially immature in other situations.[21] Early-maturing girls are not only big for their age, they also are more mature in handling social interactions.

Becoming Aware of Our Emotional Differences

There also seem to be some innate, perhaps genetic, factors in regard to "how we are" as people. There is evidence accumulating that we come into the world with what psychologists call *behavioral predispositions;* that is, we are born predisposed toward certain general patterns of emotional behavior. All of us have observed that some children are eager, spontaneous, physically energetic, outgoing, and aggressive, whereas other children seem to be quiet and prefer to play by themselves. Still other children seem to be "fretful" and generally reside in an "unhappy state." These behavioral predispositions are evident very early in life, and seem to manifest themselves throughout the life of the individual—to constitute an "emotional set."

THE NATURE-NURTURE CONTROVERSY. Before Freud, people's adult characters were thought to be the result of hereditary make-up—those traits inherited from parents and grandparents. People of "dubious" character were thought to have come from "bad blood." For example, a boy might turn out to be a renegade "just like his father." A favorite theme in nineteenth-century literature was the sudden surfacing of a hitherto hidden "trait"—such as "madness"—which was supposedly passed on from father to son as, for example, in Henrik Ibsen's play, *The Wild Duck.*

Once Freud's theory of personality development began to gain acceptance, the pendulum swung the other way. Personality theorists

Studies of neonates reveal innate physical and psychological characteristics that have proven to be predictive of adult personality.

then began to emphasize the effects of early environmental experiences, and the child's conflicts with the family became the focus of personality theory. The controversy between advocates of the "hereditary" school of intelligence and personality and the advocates of the "environmental" approach to human growth continues. The geneticists maintain that "nature" is the decisive factor in what "personality" can become, and the environmentalists contend that personality is primarily a social phenomenon (nurture). As is often the case in such arguments, both sides in the "nature-nurture" discussion have "a piece of the truth," but American psychologists have placed considerably more emphasis on environmental factors in the development of personality. Perhaps this point of view is the result of the American desire to believe that all persons are created equal. However, we now are being forced to listen to what the European psychologists have been saying all along, that there are definite genetic factors in personality. Recent research evidence has tended to substantiate this opinion. Identical twins, who are genetically similar but who have been raised in different home environments, tend to have closer resemblance to their natural parents in significant variables (including intelligence, emotional stability, and in physical characteristics) than to their foster parents.[22]

Longitudinal studies of children affirm that some preschool children tend to avoid dangerous activities and physical and verbal aggression, conform to adult standards, and are somewhat timid in social situations. They seem actually to be small, shy, intellectual adults and, indeed, when these children grow up they tend to choose intellectual careers in music, physics, biology, and psychology; others tend to be active and aggressive in the preschool period and as adults become football coaches, salesmen, and engineers.[23]

Such studies support the "type" theories of Jung and Spranger. It is not *all* how you and your parents got along, evidently. For some characteristics, anyway, you just seem to "be born that way." Psychologists today seem to be discovering what most mothers have been saying about their children for many years, that this baby was "happy from the moment he (or she) was born" while that baby was always "fussy and colicky," seemingly from the day that he or she was born.

Still, even as we write this, we must insert yet another argument for the environmental proponents who insist on the *social learning* between the child and the parents. For example, consider the effects of such behavioral dispositions on the parent-child relationship. An athletically inclined father will interact quite differently with a strong, robust son with whom he can play ball than with a boy who seems passive, less energetic, or less interested in sports. Or consider the mother who is herself emotionally subdued and passive. How does she react to an aggressive and extremely husky baby who begins to demand all her attention almost from the day of birth? The mother may soon become physically exhausted from the demands of such a child, whereas she will feel more comfortable and loving toward a child who is more subdued, more like herself. Such emotional interactions will inevitably have their effects on the rearing of that child.

Effects of Sex and Birth Order

In addition to our relationship with our parents (particularly our mother or mother-surrogate), our early emotional reactions are determined and shaped in relation to our siblings.

SIBLING RIVALRY.   Freud believed that sibling rivalry is one of the basic conflicts of childhood.[24] The newborn male baby, he postulated, is the crown prince of his family. He feels himself to be the center of the world (which he sometimes is). When a second child is born, the first child now finds it difficult to move over and allow the new baby to share the spotlight and attention. Venting his childish emotions, he rages and pouts. He feels rejected and jealous. But these feelings and actions are directed not so much against the parents (who have withdrawn some of their attention from him) as toward the new addition to the family who is threatening his place. He secretly hopes that the new baby will disappear and may even have fantasies of helping it to some dire end (flushing it down the toilet along with his feces). He may even hit the baby or otherwise try to do it some harm. Parents these days are less concerned about this type of behavior since they now know that most children can suddenly "regress" in behavior after the birth of a new baby. For example, they may take the baby's bottle for their own, revert to thumb sucking, or demand to be held in Mommy's lap more often (only for a while in most cases).

But they may also react against their "infantile" wish to be the baby by trying to be a "mother" or "father" figure to the new child; that is, according to Freud, if they cannot regain their central role by regressing, they may seek approval by acts of caring, by becoming a second "little mother" or "little father."

Central to Freud's concept of rivalry in our early sibling relationships is that these jealousies and conflicts are reflected and repeated in our adult relationships with peers and working associates. For example, children who never feel quite secure in their family may later not know how to compete successfully in the adult world, and children who gain attention from parents by crowding out their brothers and sisters may, as an adult, be fiercely competitive and jealous of any honor or promotion that comes to a co-worker.

EFFECTS OF BIRTH ORDER. There has been some interesting research on the personality characteristics of only children, older children, younger children, and children who come from large families, summarized in a little book, *The Sibling*.[25] We can mention here only a few of these findings; the interested reader is urged to consult the book itself, as well as other research data.

FIRST-BORN VERSUS LATER-BORN. It is not surprising to find that first-born children are perceived as more bossy, more verbally aggressive, generally more able to use their authority, and that they use their "oldest" status as a means to secure their ends, but they also try more to use reason, logic, and other forms of intellectual persuasion. Younger children, on the other hand, have learned to use a low-powered technique to get what they want: crying, pouting, tattling, even threatening. But younger children also learn to be more conciliatory and to rely more on strategy techniques: compromise, flattery, pleading, and giving in. Younger children also learn to switch among many roles to get what they want. (In the view of I. D. Harris, first-born children see their function in the family as authoritative, even messianic, while the later-born view themselves as agitators who harass and challenge the "established authority."[26]

Another point the authors of *The Sibling* made is that although first-born children (of either sex) are highly influenced by their parents, younger children are much influenced by their older siblings. Adler suggested that later-born children become power seekers as a result of their long years of subjugation.[27]

FIRST-BORNS AND ACHIEVEMENT. In terms of achievement, first-borns seem to have the advantage. Studies of highly gifted children reveal a predominance of first-born children. National Merit Scholars, for example, show a significant predominance of first-born children. First-borns dominate *Who's Who*, and even our astronauts seem to be mostly first-born children.[28]

The reasons behind the eminence of first-born children probably are not so much related to biology (inherited superiority) as they are to the "sociological" structure of the family. The family generally gives to the first-born a degree of exclusive time and attention impossible for subsequent children. The first-born generally also has greater access to family resources; he or she, for example, is more likely to receive a college education. As many a parent can testify, by the time the younger children come along, they have become more relaxed in their "parenting," and they also can be somewhat weary. Thus, standards (both academic and behavior) are often more lenient. Older children are frequently heard to say, "Boy, I wasn't allowed to get away with that when I was his (or her) age." Furthermore, with one or more children already in college, the later-born children may not be pushed as hard in the same direction, if only because of a smaller family bank account.

THE ONLY CHILD. An only child mostly resembles the oldest child. Like the oldest child, he or she is more highly verbal and seems to adopt the standards of the "adult" society more readily than do children with siblings. This may be because the parents take the child to more places, include him or her in more of their activities, and talk to him or her more frequently. It is easier to include one child in the parents' activities than it is to include two, three, or more. At the same time, both the oldest child and the only child can be more dependent on the approval of the adults in their society. Since they more readily identify with the adult world than with their peer group, they will conform more to adult standards and accept them as their own more readily and at an earlier age. They also tend to use their brains more than their brawn, show more anxiety in the face of threat, evince more need for nurturance and reinforcement from others, and are more conscientious and reliable in carrying out their duties, which probably accounts for their tendency to take positions of responsibility and authority later on in life.[29]

SEXUAL DIFFERENCES. The fact that sex has a determining influence on personality and life style is almost axiomatic. Throughout traditional civilization, women have been kept in a secondary and subordinate position. Although there have been societies which have allowed women more freedom and equality, these have been the exception rather than the rule. Most civilizations have tended to divide their societies into sex "roles"; that is, certain behaviors and traits are encouraged and permitted for one sex and denied to the other. By and large, boys have been reinforced for aggressiveness, physical and social independence of thought and action, adventurousness, worldly achievement, and family leadership. Historically, they have been seen as the "breadwinner," the one who provides the income and financial support of the family. Girls, on the other hand, have been encouraged to be submissive, yielding, nurturing, receptive, enduring, and meek. The Bible calls the female a "helpmeet," one who assists her husband. Simone de Beauvoir called her "the second sex."[30]

BIOLOGICAL DIFFERENCES. We all are aware that our sexual roles have been conditioned early in our lives by our cultural norms and standards. But whether there is any basis for these role differences in the biological differences of males and females is quite another matter and one that deserves to be investigated. Current scientific controversy is so emotionally charged that no opinion now can be accepted unequivocally. There are certainly some basic biological differences between men and women. Some are statistically beyond doubt: more males are born than females, and males are born larger, heavier, and have a higher basic metabolism. At puberty, males develop different sexual characteristics which also seem to be related to certain emotional characteristics. These facts are undeniable. There also seems to be some indication that men and women differ significantly in certain intellectual capacities. For example, men tend to excel in spatial relationships and mathematical skills while women have been found to be superior in verbal skills.[31]

But the minute we begin to investigate psychological differences we are treading on shakier ground. Is the fact, for example, that men are found to be more dominant psychologically in our society a matter of biology or the result of age-old social learning? We simply do not know. Are men truly stronger than women? If we are considering physical strength, then, yes. But there is another aspect of this called *constitutional strength,* and on this women are found to be stronger in almost every measure. Although more males are born, more males die in infancy. Women live longer than men do. Women are better able to stand pain than men are. Three times as many boys as girls are stutterers. And many more boys than girls are judged to be emotionally disturbed, have learning problems, and are disposed to have certain, sex-linked characteristics such as color blindness and hemophilia.[32]

LEARNED SEX DIFFERENCES.   Learned sexual differences begin early in life. Mothers tend to respond to boy babies differently from how they respond to girl babies. To the former they are more physical; they caress their sons and play with them more energetically; in contrast, they are gentler with their daughters and tend to make more verbal baby-talk.[33] Is this the basis for girls being more language-oriented than boys are, and for boys being more physically aggressive than girls are? Freud thought so! "Anatomy," said Freud, "is destiny."

For many years, though the custom is beginning to fade away now, a baby was marked as boy or girl by the very colors of the clothing. Boys were more often allowed to accompany their fathers than girls were. Household chores usually were designated by sex. Traditionally, in the American home anyway, boys were expected to mow the lawn and take out the garbage, while the girls were expected "to help mother" with the cooking and house chores. Even our schools encourage girl-only sports and activities, while certain sports and activities are for "boys and men only." Although girls receive better grades in school than boys do and tend to show earlier academic aptitude, it is still the boy who is encouraged and pushed to go to college and "make something" of himself in the professions or in business. A woman, even in today's changing attitudes toward women, is still the oddball in the engineering or medical class. Thus our family, our schools, and our culture all have helped to mold the life style characteristics associated with our sexual roles.

MIXED VERSUS SINGLE-SEX SIBLING EFFECTS.   A boy who has only brothers tends, on the average, to have more "masculine" interests than does a boy with a sister. Similar findings apply to families with two girls—such girls were found to have distinctly more "feminine" interests than girls with brothers. It seems natural enough that a boy or girl with an opposite-sex sibling would have a wider spread of interests, since they play together, talk together, and take an interest in what the other is doing. Thus, a boy with a sister tends to show fewer strictly athletic interests and a greater interest in "strategy" games such as chess and puzzles. A girl with a brother is more interested in "heterosexual" activities and is more aggressive. In other words, it appears that a family with a sister *and* brother has the effect of cross-fertilizing interests and activities. This finding is of even more interest when we discover that *studies of highly creative men show that they are more open to their feminine aspects and thus are more imaginative* than their less creative counterparts are.[34]

Another interesting finding is that a single male child with two sisters shows a *counteractive* behavior; that is, he seems to show more "masculine" behavior (in terms of interests and playmates) than does a boy with only one sister. Evidently, a single boy with more than one sister may feel in danger of being overwhelmed by the feminine side of the home environment and escapes (or is encouraged to escape by his parents) into a world of masculine interests.[35]

cultural and subcultural differences

Societies differ drastically in their models and expectations of behavior. An eight-year-old Polynesian girl thinks nothing of suddenly being given the care of her three- or four-year-old sibling to tote around all day, bathe, feed, and mother. A child in our society might be expected to play with a sibling for a while, but the all-day care of one's little brother or sister would be viewed as persecution by an American eight-year-old.[36]

Our Western societies are more complex than are the isolated societies that most anthropologists study, and there are wider emotional reactions and models from which to choose. Nevertheless, even nationalities within the Western world show definite cultural differences. The French have been found to be more like other French than they are like the English. Even if we erase the stereotyped traits associated with certain nationalities, the French do seem more emotionally expressive! The English do seem more "reserved" in extending friendship, although they usually extend cordiality very easily. Germans, on the other hand, do seem to be more patriarchal and masculine-oriented, whereas the Irish do tend to produce strong women who become matriarchs in their particular families.[37]

These cultural differences have had an effect on all of us, and they have had an effect on you and your emotional behavior. For example, if you have an emotionally reserved father and an Italian mother who openly displays emotions and affection, you will tend to model yourself after the parent for whom you have greater regard. It may be that as a boy you came to feel that emotion is feminine and thus identified yourself with your masculine father. Of course, if your father was so reserved that no relationship at all was possible with him, then very likely you favored your mother's warmth and affection, and her effect became your model of emotional behavior.

Likewise, if you are a second- or even third-generation American in an affluent milieu, but your parents or grandparents came from, say, Scotland, then you may still carry forward the frugal tendencies of your forebears who became acquainted with reality in the Scottish Highlands, where only "oats, peas, beans, and barley" grow.

On the other hand, if you are of Italian ancestry, you still may need to use your hands to express the complexity of life and the feeling of being a human with others. Anyone who has ever seen a French shrug or observed the fluidity with which Italian-Americans express themselves with their hands knows what we are attempting to state in words.

North America has been peopled by almost every conceivable nationality, and the process is continuing. We are, as a continent, still receiving immigrants, even as we realize that we may be running out of living space and want to close our doors to those who want to come and live with us. We are not merely a melting pot, nor are we a single nation. Rather, we are a curious mixture of Scandinavian, French, German, Armenian, Spanish, African, Italian, Russian, Chinese, Japanese, and Dutch cultures, not to mention the English, Irish, Jews, and those others who have brought their heritage to our shores and stayed to become citizens of our country.

We are experiencing a wide variety of behaviors among our friends, peers, and associates. It is as though there were, now, no "right" way to behave or be, and it is this that makes us still a melting pot, a place and an occasion for growth and evolution.

Let us not be overawed or impressed by the phenomenon of personality in our own culture. We are only one nation, attempting to discover for ourselves where we are going, what kinds of emotional responses we can try out in safety, and how these responses will determine what the next generation may be and what coming generations will have to contend with as a result of our mistakes in child rearing, socialization, and emotional development.

applications and coping techniques

1. Become Aware and Appreciative of Your Individual Differences

Although we share many commonalities, we vary from each other in significant ways, and it is these variations that make us unique persons. Part of the college experience is to provide you with an awareness and appreciation of these differences.

By the time we leave high school, we have gained a fairly good idea of how we differ from our parents and our siblings. That is the task of adolescence. Having rejected the authority and values of our parents, we identified so strongly with our adolescent peer group that we wore the same clothes, cut our hair the same way, used the same slang, listened to the same music, and the like. To be different was to be ostracized. As a consequence, the high school experience tends to constrict individuality. Because of the pressure to conform, the high school years, in our society, are a *leveler* of personality.

College, fortunately, is the place where we can begin to understand and to express our individuality. The "straitjacket" of conformity can be loosened. In high school one had few arenas from which to choose: team sports, cheerleading, band, for example, on the one hand, or the antiestablishment crowd who used drugs and alcohol, on the other. It was a dichotomized society. In college, no matter what your interests are (and they may range from photography, journalism, theater, and dance to scuba-diving, science, livestock, and farming), you will be able to find like-minded persons to share your enthusiasms. Politics, intellectual research, the arts, religious pursuits — it is all here and valid. College is multi-experiential. Now, as never before, you can investigate and express your individuality.

2. Think of Yourself as a "Human Becoming"

We have frequently heard college students express the desire to know who they "really are." It is, perhaps, something you yourself have said or desired. This yearning is part of the need to discover and realize our fullest potential. But such a yearning rests on a mistaken notion; it implies that knowing who we really are is a permanent insight, like looking at ourselves in Snow White's "magic mirror." "Oh, magic mirror, on the wall, tell me 'who I am' once and for all."

Knowing who we really are is part of the process of self-discovery. Because the process of self-discovery is a lifelong event, so also is the process of knowing who we are. Allport discussed human personality as always "becoming" that which one truly is. We can think of ourselves, then, not as a human being, but as a *human becoming* — always becoming more of ourselves. Everything we learn, everything we master, every experience that we endure adds a little bit more to us in terms of human personality and functioning. We are not the same person we were at ten that we are at twenty, and we are not the same person at thirty that we become at forty. We are becoming something more . . . and more . . . and more.

A friend of ours had a most difficult childhood. She was orphaned at an early age and lived with relatives who both rejected and abused her. As she tells her story, "I was a freaky, gawky teenager who stuttered terribly and didn't know how to get along with others." Our acquaintance managed to go on to college and to graduate work, get a degree in speech pathology, and eventually win some notice for her work in that area. A childhood acquaintance of hers looked her up after many years and expressed surprise at the change in her: our friend now was poised, spoke easily, was liked by her students and colleagues, and seemed very different from how her acquaintance remembered her. Our friend listened to these comments and smiled. "You remember a person I hardly know any more," she said to her childhood acquaintance. "In fact, you know her much better than I do. It is true that this person (whom we both know) has my name, and we look something alike (although I am much older than she is), and we share many of the same memories. But besides these things, we do not have much in common. I do hope you are willing to get acquainted with me as I am now."

So it is for us all. You will, on occasion, have an opportunity to realize how much more you have become. You will meet someone whom you knew in a previous situation, and after you have talked a while and have run out of stories about what has happened to so and so whom you both knew, you will suddenly realize that your worlds have grown very far apart. You are no longer the person you were. You may say goodbye to the person and promise to "give a telephone call sometime," but you know, in your heart, that it will not be so. It is a somewhat sad insight, but also very self-revealing. It is a kind of measure of your growth and development. You are always "in process."

3. Become Aware and Appreciative of the Differences in Others

When we were young, we identified with *our* house, our family, and our dog. And what was ours, was right! Although this kind of identification phenomenon is good for the growing child, it is the basis, also, for our unconscious prejudice of the customs of others different from ourselves. We tend to grow up thinking that other persons should be how *we* are, act as *we* act, believe as *we* believe. It is insular thinking and part of the process of self-discovery is the discovery also that there is no "right way to be," at least not in our time. Personality today is an open-ended phenomenon. What is truly right and just for us may not be so for another.

Furthermore, as we have more interpersonal experiences and gain a wider perspective of human society, we will come to appreciate the vast differences in human motivation and interests. We will be able to understand and work with others who hold different values from ours, and whose life styles differ significantly from ours. It is just these broad understandings that give us the large picture and fit us for more advanced positions of responsibility and authority in our chosen fields of endeavor. It is the mark of the successful business executive, department head, and chairperson that he or she can relate to and understand the needs and problems of many types of people. That kind of understanding is necessary for leadership and organizational skill.

4. Develop a Life Style that Fits Your Individuality

As you begin to discover your own interests, capabilities, body rhythms, emotional predispositions, psychological type, and so forth, think of ways of living and being that are in harmony with your self-development. In chapter 1 we said that the values of one generation cannot be applied unequivocally to the next generation, nor can we adopt another's life style completely without damaging ourselves. Constructing a creative life style requires thought. We need to study ourselves. We need to develop habits of introspection, self-study, and self-analysis. We need to ask ourselves: "Am I doing what I really want to do?" "Are my goals consistent with who and what I am as a person?" "Have I really thought out my values or am I doing the 'popular' or 'expected' thing?"

We live in a time of great variation of life style. It is more possible today than ever before to construct a life style for yourself. If the life style that you have constructed seems later to hold less value for you, you can restructure it in accordance with your further growth and further "becoming." Thousands of citizens are going back to college in their thirties and forties and even in their fifties and sixties, in order to bring more meaning and satisfaction into their lives. The overwhelming percentage of these older students have not only found it a useful vehicle for restructuring their lives, but they also are, often, some of the best students.

What is important, then, is to recognize that your life is in your hands and in no one else's. Whatever the circumstances of your past, the remainder of the journey is up to you. How you live your life, constructively or destructively, is of your choosing. That, as a matter of fact, is one of the lessons of existential philosophy.

We compared the process of living to a river. Erich Fromm described you as a painting that is being painted by you, the artist. Thus, you are both the subject and the object of your own life, and while we are about it, the verb as well. Your life style is your own creation. Let it be an authentic expression of your individuality.

In one sense, one's world view is simply a projection of one's personality.

defense mechanisms: necessary for survival: barriers to growth

3

Too frequently, it is not so much that we have emotions, as that our emotions "have" us; that is to say that we resort to nonproductive, or destructive, defense mechanisms.

I. In Defense of Defense Mechanisms

   A. Defense mechanisms as barriers to growth

   B. Why do we erect defense barriers?

II. Anxiety as an Underlying Theme of Modern Life

   A. Anxiety versus fear and worry

   B. Personal anxiety, social anxiety, global anxiety

III. How Can We Know When We Are Defending Ourselves?

   A. Defending by attack
      1. The pain-attack response
      2. Verbal aggression
      3. Sarcasm, ridicule, and wit
      4. Vandalism
   B. Defending by withdrawal
      1. Flight into failure
      2. "The born loser"
   C. Defending by physiological anesthesia: alcohol, narcotics, "pill popping"
   D. Defending by psychological anesthesia: denial, repression, amnesia, and "forgetting"
      1. Defending by rationalization
      2. Defending by insulation
   E. Defending by manipulative behaviors
      1. Eric Berne's games people play
      2. Perls's underdog
      3. Everett Shostrom's manipulative styles
   F. Defending by distortion
      1. Projection
      2. Scapegoating
      3. Reaction formation
   G. Defending by substitution: some "healthier" defenses
      1. Substitution
      2. Sublimation
      3. Compensation (or overcompensation)
      4. Fantasy

IV. Is There Any "Right" Way to Be?

V. Applications and Coping Techniques

in defense of defense mechanisms

We need not be ashamed of our defense mechanisms. They are a part of our nature; they are necessary to our survival; and there is no one who is completely free of them. We do not have to be "defensive" about our defense mechanisms. We all have them.

We stress this because, in some circles, it has become popular to confront someone with the statement,"you're being defensive!" That kind of confrontation implies that the speaker himself or herself is free of defenses. Do not let anyone play that game with you. We need our defense mechanisms until we can discover better ways to cope with the world and the problems that confront us. The real question is not whether we have defense mechanisms, but how well they are working for us and if we can find better ones.

Defense Mechanisms as Barriers to Growth

Although all our defense mechanisms are aimed at helping the organism survive, some defensive operations can become so dominating and self-perpetuating that they block further psychological growth. A certain defensive maneuver may have been a means of coping with frustrating and threatening situations when we were children, but when continued in adulthood it may create difficulties because the behavior is no longer appropriate to adult life. For example, children who have learned how to get their mother's attention by whining or having temper tantrums have found that that pattern of behavior is a fairly successful way to getting attention when they need it. If they continue to rely on whining, they prevent themselves from developing more mature ways of interacting with others. These people will be called "immature" or "childish" and will eventually discover that, rather than getting them what they want, this behavior is self-defeating.

Our defense mechanisms impose a barrier to personality integration in that they blur our vision of the world, deafen our ears to what others are saying to us, and generally distort or confuse our perceptions of everyday experiences. Two psychologists, John Dollard and Neal Miller, put it very bluntly. Our defense mechanisms make us "dumb" so that we do not demonstrate our intelligence.[1]

Defense mechanisms cloud our ability to view reality. We may spend unnecessary hours of pain and anxiety indulging in real or fanciful acts, hours that could have been put to more creative use.

Recognition of the major defense mechanisms and how and when we use them is useful in any search for self-knowledge and personality integration. This project can be extremely difficult for the beginning student of personality, particularly when we attempt to study and observe our own defenses. Just as color blind persons may never realize that they cannot see certain colors until this is pointed out to them, we may not be aware of our defense mechanisms until someone else brings them to our attention.

Why Do We Erect Defense Barriers?

Defense mechanisms are necessary because they help protect us from *pain*. Each of us can endure just so much pain. When *physical* pain becomes too intense, we lose consciousness and thereby effectively block out further painful stimuli. Physical pain is one such stimulus; anxiety or *mental* pain is another.

Each one of us can stand only just so much anxiety. When that point is reached, a kind of psychological "trigger point," we begin to defend ourselves against further painful stimulation. In short, we begin to use our defense mechanisms.

anxiety as an underlying theme of modern life

Anxiety versus Fear and Worry

Most readers will not need a definition of anxiety, since it has become a rather common event in our lives.

Anxiety resembles fear, but it is not as specific. For example, one may be afraid that one will fail a test—this is a specific fear. Once the test is met and passed through safely, the anxiety passes. That can be more properly regarded as an understandable and normal worry. The kind of anxiety we are discussing now is something over and beyond temporary worry. Anxiety is not specific. It is experienced as a vague sense of discomfort, a kind of nameless apprehension or dread that says that something is wrong somewhere but what it is is not known, or that something undefinable is about to happen that brings on a mood of uneasiness or chronic anxiety. The nagging worry of "never

When physical pain overwhelms us, we lose consciousness; when psychological pain threatens to overwhelm us, we escape via our defense mechanisms.

really feeling safe" beginning in childhood can lead to psychological breakdown, physical breakdown, and the kinds of personality disintegration not as easily understood or recognized.

Personal Anxiety, Social Anxiety, Global Anxiety

The anxiety and stress we have today come from several sources. The first is personal and includes our relationships with our parents, extended family and friends, children, business associates, and whether

We face another kind of anxiety today — global anxiety.

we will, for example, maintain good health, keep our jobs, make a decent living, and have a good marriage. These are the everyday problems of living that have always existed. We call this *personal* anxiety.

The second type of anxiety is *social* anxiety, which comes from trying to live up to society's expectations and values. David McClellan and others who have studied need achievement indicated that our nation is one of the most need-achieving societies in history.[2] In 1961, *Time* magazine devoted several pages of copy to *angst* or the kind of anxiety which built up after World War II. It placed much of the cause of our social anxiety on the American need to achieve or to be successful.[3] In the sixties, many Americans fled the cities and the pressures of societal life and went where they could find more time, more simplicity, and more solitude. Another factor that contributes to our social anxiety is our very concern to become a more *just* nation as we try to assist the poor, the uneducated, the immigrants to our country, those whose civil liberties have been trampled, and even our desire to help other less fortunate countries the world over.

The third source of anxiety is becoming increasingly common. We call this *global* anxiety. Global anxiety pertains to the existential questions of our survival and hangs like a shadow over all our functioning so that our personal anxieties become even more magnified.

Box A
Some of the Sources of Social and Global Anxiety[4]

1. *The pressure to be successful.*
   The need to achieve and to climb the social and vocational ladder.
   The need to be well informed and concerned.
   The need to stay young, slim, and beautiful.

2. *The shadow of World War III.*
   The constant concern with cold wars, territorial disputes, nuclear weapons, and the inability to maintain peace.
   Increasing international terrorism.

3. *Disillusionment with the "American dream."*
   The plight of our cities, dollar de-evaluation, increasing taxation, and inflation.
   The problems of the poor, the ghettos, the underpriviledged; our law and penal systems; concern for equal rights for all; and injustice at every level of our courts.
   The increasing concern with violence: political assassinations, increased vandalism, organized crime, and other criminal dominance.

4. *From the rape of the planet: guilt and fear of survival.*
   Recognition of how we have poisoned the soil we farm, the air we breathe, the seas we fish.
   Suspicion that pollution of our world may be irreversible.
   The desperate search to find new energy sources as our fossil fuels run out.

5. *The pace and alienation of modern life.*
   Our frantic pace of life.
   Our "rootlessness" as 20 percent of Americans move every year.
   The size of our country in which families live at great distances and lose contact with each other.

6. *The "organizational person" complex in the corporate and megacorporate structure.*
   The "plastic" society and its separation from woods, country, and water.
   The "assembly worker" cog-in-the-wheel experience.
   The meaningless work of blue collar laborers on the assembly line.

how can we know when we are defending ourselves?

Now that we understand that our defense mechanisms are a protection from the overwhelming pain of anxiety, we need to determine when they are operating. It is not easy to become aware of our defense mechanisms. With a little detective work, however, we can begin to discover them underneath their camouflage of rational and orderly behavior. The key is to catch ourselves when we are doing or saying something that does not fit the situation or the people involved.

Perhaps you have found yourself doing something not characteristic of your "usual self." Or perhaps you have heard other people make remarks such as: "I was so overwrought I didn't know what I was doing," "I knew I was saying the wrong things but I just couldn't

Defense mechanisms are ways of defending ourselves. Unfortunately, we sometimes resort to very primitive defenses.

help myself," or "He didn't seem to be himself." On occasion, one does not seem to be oneself and feels out of sorts or at one's wit's end.

This feeling of being out of control, not acting like oneself, not being able to make a decision, or being "tied up in knots" is one of the signals that there are forces at work within us of which we are only partially aware. Any one of a number of things may be happening. We may be experiencing so much anxiety that we feel helpless and confused, our self-esteem may be threatened, or we may simply be unclear about our own feelings. We may be temporarily under so much stress that our usual adaptiveness and energy are at a very low ebb. Finally, the choices confronting us may be conflicting, and we seem unable to make a constructive decision. Again, all of these explanations (anxiety, self-esteem, frustrations, conflicts, stress) are abstract and need to be defined. When we find ourselves in uncomfortable situations and when we sense discomfort and pain, we can be sure that our defense mechanisms are operating.

Defending By Attack

THE PAIN-ATTACK RESPONSE.   Attack is the most physical and primitive and aggressive form of defense—at least it is certainly the most uninhibited form of defense. The need to strike back has been studied under experimental conditions by Nathan Azrin,[5] who described this response as an instinctual reflex in animals. Azrin observed that when animals are shocked by electric current they will immediately attack another animal nearby. If there is no other animal to attack, a shocked animal will bite and attack an inanimate object, such as a ball. Should there be nothing else on which to vent its rage, the animal may even bite itself. Azrin concluded that this pain-attack response is a kind of "pushbutton" response with the same sequence, shock-pain-attack, following always in rapid order. Furthermore, there seemed to be no lessening of the attack response over time: the animal attacked every time. Many readers will recognize this response if they have ever had an injured dog. When the owner bends down to help it the dog may even bite its owner. Azrin's experiments suggested that any kind of intense pain is a total organismic sensation and that the organism—be it animal or person—tends to react to the intense stressor by striking back at the closest object.

VERBAL AGGRESSION.   We generally outgrow the childish or adolescent need to strike out physically at the human object we think is the cause of our pain, although this still happens, as is known by the police who are called to intervene in family fights. Even as we grow older, we still find ways to strike back at the person who has frustrated our desires. All of us have shouted, screamed, or said things that we wish later we had not said.

SARCASM, RIDICULE, AND WIT.   Adults' verbal aggression generally is more sophisticated and may even become habitual behavior. These persons have become so sensitive to actual or imagined insults that they adopt a kind of acid defense called sarcasm. In some groups, particularly among adolescents, verbal insult is used as a method to relate to others. For the high school student, sarcasm may even denote friendship for another person.

People who rely on acid remarks in later life as a way of relating and defending themselves are adopting a life style of verbal aggression. They may continue to feel as though they were winning battles with their associates. Indeed, their associates may adopt behaviors aimed at appeasing them, such as letting them have their own way to avoid the acid comment. They may even "cozy up" to them in the mistaken belief that appeasement is the way to avoid attack. Sarcastic people may seem to have a keen wit and may even consider themselves competent and successful in everyday living. What they do not realize is the extent of their loneliness and their lack of genuine friendship. They may sense that others do not trust them, that others may actually fear and dislike them. Yet they are caught in the vicious

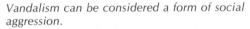

Vandalism can be considered a form of social aggression.

cycle of verbal aggression in which wit does not ease but causes uneasiness and distance. So the cycle spirals, culminating in the anecdote of the person who shouts at his therapist, "I said, I don't know why I don't have any friends. Why don't you listen, you blockhead!"

VANDALISM.   In the larger social context, acting-out behaviors can take the form of riots or vandalism. The adolescent who wants to get even for being picked up as a shoplifter may later come back and throw a brick through the store owner's window. The vandalism and race riots of the ghettos have been attributed to "black rage," the spilling over of frustration and anger at the white establishment.[6]

Defending by Withdrawal

Instead of aggressing against another, human beings can withdraw when the pain of anxiety or frustration is too much to bear and when they cannot cope with it assertively. This defense often is seen in children, who may turn away and pout, cry, or fantasize. *Withdrawal* is a kind of defeat in the face of an overwhelming environment.

Regression is reverting to an earlier behavior that relieved anxiety. When the baby is brought home from the hospital, the older sibling may suddenly begin thumb sucking or have "accidents," behaviors that may have been given up months before.

As children get older, they may simply withdraw from situations that elicit feelings of inferiority. The late-maturing adolescent boy may avoid any attempt to enter into sports or athletic competition. The adolescent girl who feels unpopular or ugly may become isolated and not attempt to make friends with others (finding it safer to stay in her shell). We recognize these persons as the shy child who hangs back in any social gathering or who prefers watching television to joining after-school clubs. The "milquetoast" personality is a fixture of the office; he stays by himself and never ventures his own opinion at the office or at home with his wife. Watching television seems to have become an American form of escape for the person who finds interpersonal situations too risky. It is not uncommon for a family to eat in front of a television as a way of avoiding dinner conversation. These are the relatively "mild" forms of withdrawal. Other forms are less benign.

FLIGHT INTO FAILURE.   A series of experiments several years ago studied the effects of failure on achievement. They revealed that when we fail in some task or project we tend to lower our goals.[7] These experiments confirm the observations of school psychologists that some students just seem to decide in advance to fail, apparently so they will not be disappointed when they do fail. Thus, avoiding success is yet another method of insulating ourselves against the fear of failure. We see this sort of behavior in students who avoid studying for a test. If they pass the test they can congratulate themselves for achieving a passing grade and for knowing that they could have gotten a higher grade if they had studied. If they fail, on the other hand, they can console themselves with the fantasy that they would have passed if they *had* studied.

Frequently truant juvenile delinquents may be really running from the school in which they experience failure and may feel that they do not measure up to others. Rather than make the effort to study, they find a boost to their self-esteem on the street with other, similar adolescents in showing their prowess in looting, shoplifting, getting drunk, and dealing in marijuana and other drugs.

"THE BORN LOSER."   The born loser is another example of flight into failure. Somehow this person always seems to miss the mark. This person is the employee who seems always to be passed over for promotion, the student who studied the wrong chapter for the test, the family member who always seems to be left out of things. We may find ourselves feeling sorry for this person, but after trying to help this individual, we begin to discover that the situation is more complex than we had thought. No matter what we do to "help" that person, he or she outwits our attempts, and we find ourselves mired down by the person's life style of helplessness and confusion. At last, we realize that there is a powerful self-sabotage going on.

One of the more subtle, and ultimately destructive, forms of the born loser's flight into failure is to choose a marriage partner, maybe even several in succession, who see to it that that person's goals are never achieved. Some men will deliberately select the kind of wife who will nag him, belittle him, compete fiercely with him, and point out his failures. A first marriage of that kind can be blamed on inexperience. But when such a man divorces and then marries a second wife just like his first, we can rightfully suspect that although the choice seems accidental, the goal (failure) is not.

Defending by Physiological Anesthesia: Alcohol, Narcotics, "Pill Popping"

Related to flight into failure are the defenses by which the person blocks out the pain of anxiety by a number of anesthetizing devices. Human beings can be amazingly resourceful and creative and can avoid reality by many routes. One may use alcohol to drown out anxiety to such an extent that one becomes an alcoholic, which ultimately alienates friends, spouse, children, and destroys one's career. One may choose drugs, a common form of flight today, or one may direct tensions and conflicts into psychosomatic illnesses, "psychosomatiz-ing" anxiety into chronic invalidism, thereby closing off and limiting capacities to deal with everyday life. (We will discuss this form of defense also in chapter 4.)

There also are the vast array of analgesics and other nonprescrip-tion drugs, by which one blocks any symptoms of anxiety — the headache, the upset stomach, or the general case of "the nerves," which we treat by "pill popping." All of these are effective ways to anesthetize the *symptom* of our distress and anxiety but only prolong our confrontation with the *causal* situations which have aroused them.

Defending by Psychological Anesthesia: Denial, Repression, Amnesia, and "Forgetting"

Children, who are told by their teachers to have a parent sign a failing test paper, may actually "forget" about it when they get home. As adults we are well aware that we may "forget" a dentist's appoint-

Some persons escape anxiety through pill-popping.

ment. Freud called this forgetting "repression." He considered it the basic defense mechanism and the goal of his form of therapeutic method, psychoanalysis, was to unlock the unconscious mind and release the repressed material.[8]

Since Freud, we have obtained other clinical evidence that events in our life may never really be forgotten, particularly the important ones. Wilder Penfield, a psychoneurologist, published a paper suggesting that under certain conditions, people can remember events long past and forgotten. Penfield's subjects were patients suffering from epilepsy, and the conditions under which Penfield observed these findings were extremely unusual—he was operating on the temporal lobes of their brains. The patients were awake and conscious, and could relate their experiences as he pressed a small electrical current against various parts of their brains. Depending on where he pressed the current, the patients reported seeing persons from their past, remembering events from early childhood, hearing melodies, and even smelling certain scents. Penfield concluded that we may never lose complete memory of anything.[9]

Repression is what occurs, as Freud explained, when there is an event that is so overwhelming and bewildering that we are just not able to face it, and we need to remove it from our consciousness and awareness. We can turn to repression, denial, amnesia, or "forgetting" as ways of protecting ourselves from unbearable overstimulation. When we use repression to reduce pain or other kinds of stimulation, we block out our awareness and refuse to see what is there. The result is that we are not conscious of the event. Let us consider an example in which a child is injured and dies in its mother's arms. If the mother at that moment cannot face the reality of the situation, she may insist for a time that her child is still alive and then rage at those around her for not doing something to help her child. She is saying, in effect, "I cannot, I will not believe this event is happening. This awful thing cannot be happening to me. I refuse to accept the truth."

Young children often resort to denial, and parents sometimes mistake this defense for lying. For example, if children are asked if they did something, they may reply, in all innocence, that they did not. They may be lying, for children do lie on occasion, but they also can be telling the parent (and themselves) that they "could not do such a thing!" Thus, the mere act of saying that they did not do something may make it the "truth" for them.

Amnesia is another form of denial, but here the "forgetting" (or repression) is used not just to cloud one's awareness of a specific event, but to keep anything associated with it out of consciousness. Soldiers in combat have been known to reach such a peak of fear, anxiety, and exhaustion, that they can no longer function, and they collapse suddenly with "battle fatigue." At such times, they can also become amnesic and block out of consciousness the events which led up to their physical breakdown. Likewise, a person who has killed someone may not remember the event, since recognizing himself as a murderer may be more than he can integrate into his conscious awareness of himself. So he "forgets" the killing; that is, he represses the knowledge of the homicide and the events leading up to it.

Freud cited many examples of "forgetting" (small repression) in everyday life. He helped us understand that these defenses are present not only in neurotic and psychotic people but also in persons who seem to be getting along fairly well in their everyday lives.[10] Any one of us can "forget" (repress or deny) as ways of blocking unpleasant experiences, as when we "forget" to pay a particularly large bill or to prepare for a test. Forgetting a person's name may be the psychological equivalent of wanting to forget the person. Some difficulties in bridging the so-called generation gap can arise when older persons repress memories of their own childhood experiences, particularly of things of which they might now be ashamed. Thus, when young people begin to experiment with similar behaviors, their elders condemn them as unusually "irresponsible" or "undisciplined" and wonder what is happening to the younger generation.

DEFENDING BY RATIONALIZATION. Rationalization about ourselves, our acts, or our motivations is another one of the more common defense mechanisms. Compared to other defensive mechanisms, rationalizing is a relatively mild way of protecting our identities from pain. To rationalize (in the sense we are using it here) means to give a logical but false and self-serving explanation for something. For example, students who get a failing grade on an exam, and cannot or will not acknowledge their own responsibility, may rationalize it by claiming that they and the teacher have a personality clash and that the teacher failed them out of spite, or that the exam did not cover the course material, or whatever. Rather than face up to their own (real) lack of preparation, they *rationalize*—attribute their failure to some other factor. This defense mechanism always resorts to spurious reasons, explanations, and excuses.

Although rationalization is less self-crippling than other defense mechanisms are, it is still a defensive maneuver that prevents us from seeing something of ourselves. We always need to be suspicious of our excuses, if we are honest in our desire to learn how to integrate our personality. Excuses, excuses, always excuses—this is the key to those who use rationalization as a major defense. Instead of doing a job, they give an excuse for why it has not been done.

The "sour grapes" form of rationalization is found in Aesop's fable about the fox and the grapes. The fox tries unsuccessfully to reach the grapes on the vine. After many attempts, it finally gives up and, as it walks away, mutters to itself, "The grapes were probably sour anyway." A young man who fails to make the football team may rationalize his failure by telling himself that he did not really want to play on the team, that he would probably get injured anyway.

"Sweet lemon" form of rationalization, on the other hand, is when people extract a *positive* result from their frustration and disappointment. The wife whose husband is jealous may tell herself that his behavior is really proof of his love for her. A student who does not get the part she seeks in a play may comfort herself by saying that she now has more time to study. Sweet lemons is not the same as maintaining a cheerful, optimistic attitude toward life. Optimism and cheerfulness prevent one from becoming so cynical that one ignores the good this complex world does have to offer. "Sweet lemons" denies the pain altogether and twists any situation so that it is superficially a positive event. This is in direct contrast to highly integrated people who acknowledge all their feelings, even painful ones.

DEFENDING BY INSULATION.   Another way we defend ourselves against feelings of horror, shame, or guilt is to prevent ourselves from feeling anything at all. We turn off, so to say, the recognition that this event applies to us! We do not deny the experience, and we do not react to it. Instead, we build a zone of unfeeling into our understanding of the experience.[11]

Persons who work at predominantly intellectual (cognitive) pursuits seem to rely often on that kind of defense if they begin to discover that they are unable to manage the emotional situations and strains of the usual family life. Such a person might rely on insulation to defend against the stresses of being in direct contact with spouse and children; that is, he or she withdraws emotionally from family life. He or she is present physically, but his or her attention and interest are directed somewhere else. For example, this person may spend much time at the office "doing research" or may retreat into his or her study when at home to "get some work done." This person may also spend vast periods of time reading as another means of preventing interpersonal contact, and so on.

Defending by Manipulative Behaviors

We come now to the more sophisticated forms of defense. You may all know little boys or girls who try temper tantrums and other kinds of blackmail when they do not get their way. Adults, like children, discover manipulations to make others do what they want. Persons working in psychological and psychiatric clinics have written many books on the subject. Eric Berne, Everett Shostrom, and Fritz Perls are three who have written "best sellers" on manipulative defense mechanisms. Berne's *Games People Play* describes thirty or so ways that adults can tie each other up with manipulative devices. Shostrom described eight common manipulative styles which put other persons in defensive positions. Perls was an expert at unmasking the "power-play" of the weak, helpless "underdog." We can sketch only briefly some manipulative defense mechanisms by which people seek to gain their ends. We add, however, that many other kinds of manipulative styles (and ways to avoid them) will appear again and again in the pages of this book.

ERIC BERNE'S GAMES PEOPLE PLAY.[12]   One of the games that Berne described he entitled: "If It Weren't for You!" In this game, a woman marries a domineering man who is rather authoritarian and who prevents her from doing things she is afraid to do anyway. Neither he nor she is aware of what they are really doing. They both are convinced that he is keeping her from getting out into the world, having a career, or whatever. Now the twist of this life game is that she does not want to go out into the cold, cruel world. She married him to be protected and taken care of, but now she complains about how little liberty and freedom she has as compared to other women, "If it weren't for you, I could have . . ." thereby making her husband feel guilty about his demands on her. In order to salve his conscience, he ends up by giving in to her various small demands, like where they will go on vacation, what kind of a house they will live in, a maid to help her in the house, and so on.

PERLS'S UNDERDOG.   Similar to this life game of Berne's is Perls's "underdog." Instead of the more direct, aggressive concept of confronting another individual with anger or irritation, some of us take another tack which he called "underdog." In interpersonal friction, one person appears as the underdog, *the one who has been hurt, crushed or misunderstood by the other party* in the situation. This is a cat-and-mouse game in which the mouse becomes the winner! For if any of us really believes that we have hurt the underdog's feelings in some way, we may suddenly find ourselves apologizing to the underdog. Now *we* are on the defensive, and the underdog has the upper hand.[13]

What these manipulative mechanisms have in common is their "around behind" approach. The person frequently appears on the surface to be a "nice guy," a "weakling," or a "clinging vine" but these soft, kindly, helpless types seem to be able to get exactly what they want.

EVERETT SHOSTROM'S MANIPULATIVE STYLES.   Everett Shostrom classified eight manipulative styles. Although each form of manipulation has a distinct character, Shostrom's description emphasizes the element of power found in each case.

1. *The Dictator* is one who dominates others, or tries to, by giving orders, quoting authorities, or by pulling rank and age. He or she acts as a "Father Superior" or "Mother Superior," or "Junior God." He or she always is the Authority.
2. *The Weakling* seems to be the victim of the Dictator, but he or she has also developed great skill in sabotaging the Dictator's demands. He or she "forgets" to do what he or she is told, does not hear what is said to him or her, and becomes "mentally retarded" when confronted by the Dictator. Some of the role variations of this type are the Worrier, the Stupid-like-a-Fox, the Giver-Upper, and the Confused One.
3. The *Calculator* is the one who tries to use his or her wits to gain control over situations and people. He or she "plays it cool" and will lie, seduce, con, or blackmail others to get what he or she wants.
4. The *Clinging Vine* controls by being dependent on others. This person needs to be "taken care of" and protected. Actually, he or she is quite skillful at getting his or her own way (and getting others to do what he or she wants) by being the Parasite, the Crier, the Perpetual Child, the Hypochondriac, the Helpless One, or the Attention Demander.
5. The *Bully* controls and manipulates by aggressing against others with unkindness, cruelty, and sadism. If he or she is not actually cruel, there is nonetheless always a veiled threat in his or her mannerisms. Variations of this manipulative style are the Humiliator, the Hater, the Tough Guy, the Threatener, and in the case of women, the Bitch or the Nagger.
6. The *Nice Guy* controls by killing with kindness, caring, and love. Shostrom said that this is one of the most manipulative types of all and is the hardest to cope with, since it is difficult to fight a Nice Guy. He seems to want to please us, to be nonviolent, to be virtuous, and not to offend us. He is also the Noninvolved One, the Organization Man, and the Never-Ask-For-What-You-Want individual.
7. The *Judge* controls through criticism. He or she is out to make others feel stupid, guilty, or wrong. Variations of this form of manipulation are the Know-It-All, the Blamer, the Deacon, the Resentment Collector, the Vindicator, and the Convictor.
8. The *Protector* controls by being oversympathetic and overprotective. He or she prevents others from caring for themselves, taking care of themselves, or finding out things for themselves. Variations are the Mother Hen, the Defender, the Embarrassed-for-Others, the Fearful-for-Others, the Sufferer-for-Others, and the Unselfish One.[14]

Defending by Distortion

We come now to the more virulent defending mechanisms, the kind that can ultimately cause others to be victimized to a terrible degree.

PROJECTION.   Projection is one of the more frequent defense mechanisms. It is a powerful way of defending ourselves from insight into our own motivations. In its simplest meaning, projection means attributing the emotions, feelings, and motivations we experience to something else, particularly to other persons.

Projecting our feelings onto others is a natural way to understand other people. Because of this ability, it is possible to identify with another's joys and sorrows and to help that person grow. Because of their ability to project their feelings and insights, the novelist, poet, or playwright can create great works of art. It is only when projection becomes a barrier to growth that it becomes a negative rather than a positive force. An example is the husband who is secretly eager to have affairs with other women and may attribute his own motivations to his wife, even accusing her of seeking or actually having an affair with other men when she is simply being friendly toward them. He is not able to come to grips with his own desires, and thus he projects these impulses onto his wife, who in this instance is blameless. Projection may also explain the behavior of a mother who has not faced up to her own earlier promiscuity and now suspects her adolescent daughter of being promiscuous, when there is no reality in the mother's suspicion.

Projection as a form of defending the self against inadmissible impulses and desires is a powerful defense mechanism. Its power is that we deny that these very impulses and needs are part of our own personality. Yet the impulses and needs are there and may not be repressed with impunity. It is good for us to acknowledge their existence.

SCAPEGOATING. When projection becomes so powerful that it becomes a destructive force to others in society, we call it "scapegoating." The word itself comes from the biblical custom of symbolically heaping the sins of the community onto a goat which was then killed, thereby relieving the people of the burden of their anxieties. More recently, scapegoating has come to mean blaming a particular person or group for the misfortunes of oneself, one's group, or even one's entire nation or race. For example, Adolph Hitler, who had a good understanding of group psychology, directed his own sense of frustration and failure into anti-Semitism. No leader of a nation, whether an authoritarian dictator or a democratic prime minister or president, can carry out a major policy (for long) that the populace does not accept. In Hitler's case, he merely channeled and orchestrated the prevailing anti-Semitism.

Scapegoating takes many forms. In the United States, our own particular form has been the scapegoating of the black race by white society. We struggle and attempt now to amend these inequities through social legislation. This is a measure of our capacity to grow as a nation and as a community which still believes that certain truths are self-evident, or need to be. We are left with the residues of scapegoating in our language as evidenced by such words as nigger, wop, redneck, gook, kike, and spik. These words prevent us from seeing other persons as human beings because we label or categorize them as stereotypes. Not only do these labels retain the kinds of prejudicial attitudes that keep people from understanding each other, they also foster prejudicial attitudes in our children so that our sins are indeed "visited upon the third and fourth generations."

REACTION FORMATION. In reaction formation, we defend ourselves against feelings, thoughts, and wishes by repressing these impulses and then developing opposite or polar behaviors. For example, a child may have feelings of jealousy and hatred for a baby brother because he feels "displaced" by him as the object of the parents' affection. The child might directly express how he feels by fighting with his brother or finding various ways of making him miserable. Suppose, however, that the child begins to be frightened by the depth of his hatred and even wishes (unconsciously) that his brother would die. Let us suppose also that the parents do not realize how he feels, that they do not appreciate this inner conflict, and that they forbid him to hurt his brother. The child can deal with this complex of feelings and needs in many ways, but if he resorts to reaction formation to reduce the anxiety, he may repress his hatred and jealousy and become solicitous (perhaps overly so) of his brother's welfare. Outwardly he no longer feels hatred, but a concern for his brother's welfare. To that end, he may watch out for his brother and make sure "nothing bad" happens to him. But oversolicitous behavior is not the same as affection, and it has different results. No matter how "good" the older boy is to his little brother (seeming even sometimes to be a second father), the younger child's life is still a misery. When playing with his big brother, somehow the little boy gets hurt, or he gets lost when going somewhere with his big brother, and "accidents" seem to happen whenever the two children are together. The repressed hatred and jealousy emerge in subtle, almost unrecognizable forms, but emerge they do.

Other examples of reaction formation can be seen in the oversolicitous attention a man gives to his dominating mother in order to make up for his own wishes for her death, or in the seemingly loving care a man may give to an outrageously nagging wife, putting up with her nonsense or even bringing home flowers as a way to convince himself that he does not secretly want to get rid of her. But again, such attention only *resembles* love and affection. Actually, there is not the freedom and spontaneity of real love. There is too much politeness and too much pussy-footing in these relationships. One feels as if one were walking on eggs.

Defending by Substitution: Some "Healthier" Defenses

Are there any really "healthy" defense mechanisms? In a sense, all defense mechanisms are useful in that they help the person to survive, but in another sense no defense is healthy, since all defenses interfere with our vision and understanding of what is really occurring from moment to moment. But in the sense that they are more benign (less injurious), there are four ways of coping with anxiety that tend to have more positive than negative results: substitution, sublimation, overcompensation, and fantasy.

SUBSTITUTION. We are taking a path to the city, and our way is blocked; most of us will simply find another path and get around the obstacle if we can. This is a simple example of the process of substitution. If a young man cannot take one young woman to the movie, he finds another girl who can go. The boy who withdrew from sports may develop, instead, an interest in mechanics, piano, or reading. By substituting one constructive situation for another, we find a more creative way to manage our feelings of pain.

SUBLIMATION. Frequently this alternative behavior becomes autonomous; that is, it becomes a driving force of our personality, or so it seemed to Freud, as he thought about what makes a writer write, an artist paint, or a musician compose. Freud defined sublimation as the redirection of the *libido,* or sexual energy, into constructive channels. Freud believed that sublimation is one of the main defenses responsible for creative and artistic production and we continue to accept his definition though we no longer believe that great art comes into being *solely* because of rechanneling so-called neurotic drives and needs.

Sublimation can be important to personality integration: using this defense people attempt to redirect their frustrated or antisocial impulses into socially acceptable and constructive behaviors. Anna Freud, Sigmund Freud's daughter and an analyst in her own right, called sublimation the "normal" defense.[15] It is certainly a more creative defense.

You will understand how sublimation functions in your personality if you begin to notice the art forms, leisure activities or choice of vocations that appeal to you: how you attempt to express certain basic needs through poetry, storytelling, painting, or physical projects of any kind. A childless woman may adopt children or breed animals. A "bossy" individual may find satisfaction in executive management. A young man unrequited in love may turn that experience into a work of art. Sublimation is a "tidy" defense and one that deserves close examination if you want to allow for your dreams and yet are hemmed in with the compromises of reality.

COMPENSATION (OR OVERCOMPENSATION).   Sometimes people react to inadequacy or inferiority (imaginary or real) by refusing to admit defeat. Overcompensation sometimes can result in astonishingly productive results. Demosthenes was one of the greatest orators of Greek antiquity, yet it is said that he stammered as a child and even as a young man. How he overcame his infirmity, according to legend, was by speaking every day on the beach, where he would fill his mouth with pebbles and try to shout above the roar of the ocean. In this way, by overcompensating, he learned to speak not only clearly but well. Several speech pathologists of today have gone into that field because of their own early speech problems.

Biographers of great athletes sometimes note a similar kind of compensation. As children, these athletes may not have been well endowed physically—indeed, they may have been relatively puny in stature and musculature, and relatively small for their age. As "handicapped" persons in childhood, they learned to adapt early to their environment, but always with the acknowledged understanding that they had no intention of submitting to their fate. In fact, they reacted against their limitations by developing a degree of physical prowess and endurance that no one expected them to attain. Once weak, they became strong; once apparently incapable, they became models of capability, demonstrating what people can do once they set their mind to the task.

FANTASY.   The last defense mechanism we shall discuss in this chapter is fantasy, the psychological term for daydreaming. It is the substitution of thinking about an event for doing it. The adolescent who daydreams that he is an adventurer, the young girl who sees herself as a ballerina, the child who is playing airplane and is at the same time both the pilot and the airplane all are indulging in fantasy. Why do we list it as one of the more creative defense mechanisms? First, daydreaming harms no one else. Second, the person is not denying or distorting his or her secret drives and wishes—he or she is dealing with them if only on a wishful level. In his book, *Daydreaming*,[16] Jerome Singer stated that daydreaming may actually be the lode-star of our motivations and ambitions (See Box B).

Box B
David Krech on the Uses of Fantasy

When David Krech, one of America's noted research psychologists, was asked to discuss the relation between fantasy and the birth of an idea, he responded: There is no question that I do a lot of fantasizing and daydreaming about the research problems that I am working on, and in my fantasies and daydreams, I solve them all. And these solutions, in turn, lead to other and greater achievements! It's a real Walter Mitty routine. But I'm not sure that these fantasies or daydreams provide me with anything more than perhaps motivation or persistence. . . . Once I'm in a Walter Mitty daydream, challenges can be overcome at will. . . . I play with my ideas, I live with them, and fantasize about them. . . . In that way I keep them salient.

From Stanley Rosner and Lawrence E. Abt, eds., *The Creative Experience* (New York: Grossman Publishers, 1970), p. 61.

One of Singer's favorite daydreams was the desire to become a great scientist, and he has indeed gone a long way in the area of clinical research. Our daydreams to become a physician may at least point us in the right direction, to one of the health-related areas like pharmacy, perhaps. But even these defenses can become harmful. Daydreaming and fantasy can, if overindulged, become a substitute for action. The person may while away a whole life in wishful dreaming rather than in doing something about it. Like other defenses, daydreaming also has its negative aspects.

Overcompensation can also be a malignant defense mechanism. For example, it is very likely no accident that many of the dictators have been men of small stature. Napoleon Bonaparte was small in stature; yet he became a military genius who almost succeeded in imposing his will on all of Europe. Was it his small size that set him upon a path of proving his superiority? We cannot answer that, but we do know that the "tough guy" frequently overcompensates for small stature by "acting tough" and gaining a reputation as a "scrapper."

Even sublimation can have its less benign side if the person is expressing a neurotic need instead of creative talent. Jung described what he called an *artist manqué*, the person who decides to put his or her energy into artistic expression, not because of an inner driving force (as with great artists) but because of a sense of boredom or futility or simply because of hunting a *raison d'être* for a life that otherwise seems drab and banal. That person is wasting his or her time, for such a motivation, said Jung, is not the artistic spirit.

is there any right way to be?

We have spent an entire chapter on the forces at work that cause mental and emotional anxiety. We also looked at what anxiety and stress can do to us, as well as what we do to defend ourselves from the pain of that anxiety. We saw how we can "break down" psychically and emotionally if the pressure and anxiety become too great. We saw how our pattern of defenses can warp human personality, the twisting and turnings human personality can take, and the "knots"[17] we make of our lives, as Ronald Laing put it, that prevent our further growth and creative living.

The reader may well wonder if there is any "right" way to grow and how to recognize these "right" ways. The answer, unfortunately, is *no,* there is no model that we can copy to ensure our continued growth and successful living. Human personality changes from epoch to epoch and what was right for our forefathers can no longer be said to be right for us. Even what may have been right for our parents cannot be said to be right for us. Human personality is in a process of evolution. Today, as never before, we are witnessing a freedom and exploration of that process. Freedom, said Paul Tillich,° requires the courage to be.[18] Another social psychologist, Erich Fromm, pointed out that humankind "escapes from freedom."[19] In former ages with established traditions of behaviors for the individual, it was easier to know what to do and how to be. Depending on one's sex, status, and stage of life, there were definite and proscribed rules for behavior. Today, we are exploring a vast number of possibilities of human life style regardless of sex, status, and stage of life. In that sense, each of us is a pioneer of the frontier of personality development, what it is and what it can become. It is challenging to be a pioneer; it is also sometimes lonely and a bit frightening. It puts the responsibility and burden of our development squarely on our own shoulders.

If you feel rather bewildered and helpless at this point, it is not surprising. You may wonder if there is anything at all you can do to aid you in your self-exploration. Yes, there is, and in one sense, that is what this book is for: the various physical and cognitive methods and techniques developed by other pioneers to aid you in your self awareness and self-development. We would like to be able to give a simple list of do's and don'ts for growth, but that is just not possible in our day and age. Life is not simple, and human growth and development is very complex. It takes a lot of thoughtfulness, a lot of introspection, and a lot of determination to become a truly creative person. It is a lifelong task, a lifelong process of trial and error, of construction and reconstruction, of blocks and breakthroughs. "The proper study of mankind," said Alexander Pope, "is Man." There is surely no more worthier life engagement.

°Paul Tillich is considered one of the great theological leaders of the twentieth century.

applications and coping techniques

1. Accept Yourself as the Best That You are Able to be at this Moment

You have survived; you have grown to your present stage of development; and you are striving for greater awareness and further growth. No more can be expected of you than that. You are a person with limitations; yes, so are we all. You also have individual strengths and abilities, and you share with the rest of us the capacity to transcend your present stage of development. You will see, in chapter 13, how highly integrated and creative people accept every aspect of themselves, even their shortcomings, weaknesses, and defense mechanisms.

2. Recognize That the Responsibility for Yourself, Your Life, and Your Growth is Yours (and No One Else's)

One of the principal obstacles in the way of many a person's progress is fixating on past misfortunes. This particular difficulty comes up time and again in therapy. In seeking to blame some event or person in their childhood (one or both parents, one's teachers, or society) for the present mess in their lives, people fail to see that the "blaming game" is a dead end, a vicious circle that leads nowhere except to more of the same. More important, it prevents new actions and direction.

Studies of creative individuals reveal that they too can come from a difficult home situation, and many of them do not seem to have been close to their parents. This lack of closeness may have helped them establish their independence and self-support. Since they had no one to cling to and lean on, they learned to rely on themselves for direction. For example, Abraham Lincoln's mother died when he was eight, and it is said that his father was a rather shiftless person, as well as an indifferent father and provider. Charles Dickens, the English novelist who wrote many novels about children who suffered miserably at the hands of adults, was recalling aspects of his own childhood. When Ernest Hemingway was asked what it took to become a great writer, he once replied, "An unhappy childhood!"

One of the more radical "growth" approaches of our time is something called "EST," founded by a man who calls himself Gerhard Werner.[20] Men and women participants are put through several days of brutal training in order that they come to understand that they have put themselves in whatever "trap" they find themselves. Radical transformation of the personality in Werner's approach allows for no reasons, no justifications, and no excuses.

3. Proceed in Your Self-development and Striving for Growth at Your Own Speed and in Your Own Way

We all are unique. Each of us has our own destiny. We cannot be like any other. What is right and good for one person can be detrimental to another's growth.

As you proceed through this book, you will encounter many therapeutic methods for growth. They are as diverse and individual as the persons who developed them. Some of them will be more appropriate for you than others just as some of the ideas and concepts will be closer to your own philosophy and mode of being than others are.

4. Allow Yourself Moments of Anguish, Depression, Lethargy, even Failure

Karen Horney said that one of the most debilitating neuroses of our time is the desire to be perfect. Psychoanalyst Horney described that particular trap as the "tyranny of the should" and it involves the attempt to be perfect. This neurotic is convinced that he should exhibit

the utmost of honesty, justice, dignity, courage, unselfishness. He should be the perfect lover, husband, teacher. He should be able to endure everything, should like everybody, should love his parents, his wife, his country; or he should not be attached to anything or anybody, nothing should matter to him, he should never feel hurt, and should always be serene and unruffled. He should enjoy life; or he should be above pleasure and enjoyment. He should be spontaneous; he should always control his feelings. He should know, understand, and foresee everything. He should be able to solve every problem of his own, or of others, in no time. He should be able to overcome every difficulty of his as soon as he sees it. He should always be able to find a job. He should be able to do things in one hour which can only be done in two or three hours.[21]

The lesson to be learned from Horney's statement is simply this: that we all have moments when everything we do seems to go wrong, when our attempts to improve things seem like one step forward and two backward. We all make mistakes, want to give up, have moments of depression and lethargy, and lose our motivation. We all suffer pain and despondency and reach a point at which we could "just kick" ourselves. We want to stress that point: it is all right to cry, to shout, to be immature, to be silly, to be just plain stupid from time to time.

Many persons in this generation are eager to raise their consciousnesses, to become more spiritual, and to achieve certain life goals. Certainly it is good to have goals, but it is all right, too, just to mope around, to run away, or to wobble back and forth before coming to a new level of growth. When things go wrong or we discover we have made a mess of things, we simply "go back to the drawing board" and start again.

5. Maintain a Sense of Balance and Perspective as You Grow and Learn

The Chinese call it "the middle path" or the "middle way." It is an understanding that growth comes easier if we do not push ourselves unduly into any one direction, go all out, jump into something with both feet before we have had a chance to see what we are getting into. If we neglect everything else in our life for the sake of one single objective, we may lose hold of some other area. We all need to support ourselves financially, to take care of and nourish our interrelationships with others, to have moments of rest and relaxation, to give some time to our intellectual studies, to devote some attention to our spiritual renewal, to take care of material things like getting the plumbing fixed and making sure the garbage goes out.

We have known people to take such a radical approach to personality change that they have lost some perspective of their lives. It is well to meditate but choose an appropriate time and place. It seems hard to believe now, even for us, but we had to caution one young man about meditating while he was riding a bike on a busy thoroughfare. Fasting has been found by some to be a swift and effective way to "clean out" some of their physiological and psychological "garbage" but there is no sense to becoming emaciated or fall victim to kwashkior (a syndrome resulting from starvation).

6. Be Mindful of Others as You Grow

It may be good to become more assertive in your interactions with others or to change your life style, but it is not realistic to urge your parents, your business associates, or your friends to change theirs!

One of the outcomes of growth is the desire to help other people in their growth regardless of how *they* feel about it or its appropriateness to the situation. This kind of help will not be entirely appreciated by them. As we advise you to make choices and changes in accordance with your rate and development, we also urge you to allow others to proceed at their own rate of growth. Telling others what is wrong with them or advising them how to lead their lives will either be an exercise in futility or end with hurt feelings on both sides. Psychologists have learned one lesson: to listen rather than to advise. If and when a psychologist proposes something to a person, it comes out of long experience and much skill that this suggestion or that approach may be just the right thing to do at *this* time and for *that* person.

7. Develop a Sense of Humor

One of the great distinctions between ourselves as a species and other life forms is our ability to laugh at ourselves and our mistakes. It is one of the saving graces when all else fails. It is one of the marks, said Maslow, of the self-actualizing person. It is never the kind of humor, however, Maslow cautioned, that demeans and ridicules others but rather the kind that sees into the foibles of human nature but with great tenderness and compassion.

A sense of humor also keeps that sense of balance discussed above. When things are just not going well, and we look around at the messes that we can get into, we can do two things: we can cry or laugh. Both may be appropriate. Carl Rogers noted that persons who have undertaken therapy show a greater willingness to express both sides of the emotional spectrum, to experience and express all their feelings. Both expressions release our pent-up emotions. Humor, however, has one advantage over crying: crying can be self-generating and cause the situation to seem more tragic than it is. Laughing at our plight (if it is not the unrelated laughter of schizophrenia) seems to change our perspective of the situation so that suddenly we get a new viewpoint on "the human comedy." It gives us a sense of lightness, as well as a bit of breathing room, and the situation in which we thought we were trapped no longer seems quite so dismal or hellish. Humor, said Arthur Koestler, the great modern philosopher-writer, is related to the creative arts.[22] It certainly is related to sanity.

We have chosen these seven "coping" techniques. We could have chosen others, for these types of "common sense" suggestions are many. You may have your own self-guiding principles and if they work for you, by all means, continue to use them.

the physical self: the body as an ecological system

TWO

when the system is overloaded: persons under stress

What makes the Type A Personality more vulnerable to heart attack?

introduction: attitudes toward disease

It is easier now for people to accept the idea of psychosomatic illness than it was fifty years ago, when physicians, psychiatrists, and psychologists first began to discuss it. At that time, the idea that some of our major diseases could stem (at least in part) from emotional conflict or everyday situations was too difficult for many persons (especially physicians) to accept, reared as they had been in the "germ theory of disease." We could accept the fact that we might get a headache from the too bright lights and noise of a party, but the idea that we could get a "sick headache" because we did not want to go to the party in the first place, was too revolutionary to be accepted immediately. After all, it had taken scientists many years to convince us that disease was caused by germs, bacilla, and viruses; now, other scientists were saying that this was not the whole story. They were saying that the germ theory of disease was not an adequate explanation for why people get sick.

Primitive Beliefs about Disease

Before we begin to question the germ theory of disease, we must remember that, as an advance in the understanding of the etiology of disease, it was a giant step forward. Before that time, disease was thought to be revenge from the gods, the work of evil spirits, or punishment for our sins.

Box A

If thou wilt not observe to do all the words of this law that are written in this book, that thou mayest fear this glorious and fearful name, THE LORD THY GOD;

Then the LORD will make thy plagues wonderful, and the plagues of thy seed, even great plagues, and of long continuance, and sore sicknesses, and of long continuance.

Moreover He will bring upon thee all the diseases of Egypt which thou wast afraid of; and they shall cleave unto thee.

> Also every sickness, and every plague, which is not written in the book of this law, then will the LORD bring upon thee, until thou be destroyed.
>
> Deuteronomy 28:58–61

The Old Testament's attitude toward disease was that it was sent by Jehovah as a punishment for the wrongdoing of an individual or of a whole nation. A terrible plague was visited on the Egyptian people because of the Lord's vengeance, and this historical tradition was long remembered in the Hebrew tradition, a warning to keep God's commandments (see Box A). Another biblical explanation for disease was that it tested a person's faith; such is the message of the book of Job (see Box B).

Primitive societies still tend to believe that sickness comes from evil spirits who are out to do one harm, and frequently animal or human sacrifice is made to appease these spirits.

Box B

> And the Lord said unto Satan, Hast thou considered my servant Job, that there is none like him in the earth, a perfect and upright man, one that feareth God, and escheweth evil? And still he holdeth fast his integrity, although thou movedst me against him, to destroy him without cause.
>
> And Satan answered the Lord, and said, Skin for skin, yea, all that a man hath will he give for his life.
>
> But put forth thine hand now, and touch his bone and his flesh, and he will curse thee to thy face.
>
> And the Lord said unto Satan, Behold, he is in thine hand; but save his life.
>
> So went Satan forth from the presence of the Lord, and smote Job with sore boils from the sole of his foot unto his crown.
>
> Job 2:3–7

The people of the Middle Ages frequently ascribed disease to the work of the devil, or from persons who consorted with the devil. Another explanation was that disease was the result of "night air" or "swamp air."

It was not until the fifteenth century that a few scientists began to suspect that disease was caused not by evil spirits but by tiny, invisible particles of life now called germs. These early researchers called these germs "living seeds of disease" and even then believed that these germs could develop out of nothing, a kind of spontaneous generation in the blood streams of humans and animals.

The idea of *contagion*, that disease could be transmitted from one person to another did not occur until the fourteenth century when great waves of bubonic plague swept over Europe. In the seventeenth century bacteria and other minute life forms first were seen under the microscope. But the germ theory of disease was still not fully accepted until the late ninteenth century with the work of Robert Koch, Louis Pasteur, Robert Lister, and others. These scientists helped to disprove the idea that disease was caused by "evil spirits" or, rather, that these evil spirits turned out to be living organisms.[1]

The Doctrine of Specific Etiology

These scientists also discovered that each disease has a specific "causal" microorganism. In other words, tuberculosis is caused by the tubercle bacillus, and none other. Furthermore, the tubercle bacillus causes only tuberculosis and not mumps, chicken pox, or scarlet fever. That all seems elementary to us now, but it was a significant understanding in the history of medicine. It was such a breakthrough that it was difficult to see anything amiss with the theory of disease etiology.

It is an axiom in science that for a theory to be valid it ought to be *sufficient* to cover all the *necessary* conditions, to account for all the facts. When we apply this test to the germ theory, it seems to hold for most facts of disease, but it cannot account for some embarassing exceptions to the rule. How is it, for example, that if we all are in contact with a disease (such as when the flu runs through a city or place of work) that some of us may get it but not *all* of us? Why, if there are flu viruses in an area, do we *all* not contract the disease? To say that some of us are "immune" is not to *explain* these exceptions but only to *explain them away.*

Furthermore, as science began to uncover more of the facts of our biological environment, scientists came to acknowledge that the world is full of germs and microorganisms of all kinds. Indeed, the interior of our bodies is now known to be a virtual "hothouse" for bacteria. In fact, if our digestive tract did not teem with helpful bacteria, we would have a difficult time digesting the food we eat and eliminating what we no longer need.

It was when scientists began to pay attention to these exceptions that researchers began to look for a larger explanation for disease, one which could include the *facts* of germs and also the *exceptions* to those facts.

the beginnings of the psychosomatic approach to disease

One of the earliest hints that what we call disease may have a psychological component happened as far back as the mid-nineteenth century. A French physician, J. M. Charcot, was demonstrating the uses of hypnosis to medical students, among whom was a young man by the name of Sigmund Freud. Charcot was demonstrating that persons who were "crippled" or who stuttered could be "healed" instantly by a hypnotic suggestion but only as long as they were in the hypnotic state.[2]

We also should mention those other interesting persons who had "cured" people through "mesmerism" (named for Anton Mesmer) and who seemed to restore a person to health by what he called "magnetic powers." An American woman, Mary Baker Eddy, convinced that she had been cured of illness by acquiring the proper mental attitude, began a new religious sect, Christian Science, based on a positive mental health approach to perfect physical health.[3] But these phenomena, as interesting as they are, were not examined under the harsh light of scientific inquiry as were Charcot's hypnotized patients. One explanation for all these cures is that the patient was being treated for an hysteric symptom or hysterical conversion.

Hysterical Conversion

An hysterical conversion refers to that condition in which the person with severe, free-floating anxiety converts the anxiety to a localized physical problem such as paralysis, blindness, or deafness. We label this *hysterical* paralysis, *hysterical* blindness, or *hysterical* deafness. Freud described an hysterical condition known as *glove anesthesia* in which the person was unable to feel anything from the wrist down, a complete numbness of the hand. The neurological "wiring" of our body is such that our nerves run *lengthwise* from the end of the fingers up the arm to the spinal cord so that a condition in which the person can have sensation to the wrist *but not beyond is a neurological impossibility*. Therefore, it is said to be "psychological" or "hysterical" numbness or anesthesia. Even *amnesia* can be said to be an hysterical conversion if there is no physiological reason for the amnesia.

When Freud discussed the hysterical conversion symptom, he postulated two patterns of behavior: *suppression* and *repression*. Suppression and repression are often confused but they do not mean the same thing. Suppression means being aware that one wants to do something, such as hitting someone but not doing it, in other words, *suppressing* the act. Repression, on the other hand, means that the desire to hit someone may produce so much guilt that the person not only suppresses the action, but also the desire and impulse to do it are denied, "forgotten," *repressed*. It is also possible to confuse the word "hysteria" as used by clinicians with the popular usage of the word, in which a person who is called "hysterical" screams, laughs, and displays a generally "overwrought state." It is a pity that there is this confusion because in the psychological diagnosis of hysteria, the person seems to behave exactly the opposite, calm, resigned, even tranquil, *since all anxiety has been converted to the hysterical symptom.*

In Freud's time, hysterical reactions were quite common. We believe that this was so because the Viennese milieu (the society in which Freud grew up and whose customs he attempted to study) was heavily committed to defending itself against both sexuality and the emancipation of women. It is small wonder, then, that some women in that culture began to express—in symptoms—what the culture was doing to them . . . quite specifically! Part of the sickness of that society was the suppression and repression of sexuality—particularly feminine sexuality or sensuality. Men also experienced hysterical reactions but in more subtle forms. The authors, however, worked with a man who was suffering from what is an almost classic example of an hysterical reaction.

Mr. Smith, as we shall call him, was a man of "moral" fiber, and his conduct in business was ethical to an extreme. Mr. Smith treated his employees with unusual diplomacy and dignity, and they in turn were loyal to the firm and to him. He had many friends, and he was, as he himself admitted, a friendly and genial person. His home life seemed to him satisfying. He liked his wife, who happened to be intelligent, and his children who were doing well in school. But one day, before he came to see us and to his astonishment, he had awakened paralyzed in his right arm. He had already made the rounds of family physician, internist, and neurologist, all of whom concluded that there was nothing wrong with his arm neurologically or anatomically. They had suggested to him that his trouble might be "psychological" in nature and that maybe he should consider psychotherapy. The thought that there could be anything wrong with him psychologically obviously seemed somewhat amusing to him as he sat in our office on that first day of our acquaintance, but he was willing to try anything to get cured—even psychotherapy!

After a few therapy sessions, he gradually became aware that all was not as "ideal" in his life as he had supposed, particularly in his relationship with his wife. He began to realize that while he deeply respected his wife—who was intelligent, capable, and a good mother—she also was a source of irritation for him. He began to remember situations in which her nagging had got to him, and as he recalled those instances again, he began to feel and remember the headaches that resulted.

When he returned one week later, he was no longer paralyzed in his right arm.

Mr. Smith was also able to remember what had led to his paralysis. The night before his arm had become paralyzed, his wife had been (in his words) "giving him hell," and he had raised his arm to strike her. At the last moment he realized what he was doing, and he stopped himself and left the house. He had been horrified to realize that he could be capable of such violence. After suffering some moments of guilt and shame (gentlemen do not hit women!), he was able to return to the house, apologize to his wife for his behavior, and go to bed with a headache. The next morning his arm was paralyzed.

"The strange thing," he said with a smile of remembrance, "was that I had forgotten the incident of the previous night—both the disagreement with my wife and my impulsive urge to hit her."

Perceptual Defense

The fact of hysterical blindness or hysterical deafness may seem to us, at first, to be extraordinary situations that do not pertain to most of us. But they can be understood as extreme cases of something that all of us have experienced, which psychologists call *perceptual defense.*

Perceptual defending occurs in several small ways in our daily lives, but primarily as "selective (in) attention." Rather than blocking off whole sensory *modalities,*° as in hysterical blindness or deafness, we simply screen out the particular items or stimuli we do not wish to see, hear, or feel. For example, a child learns to screen out his mother's nagging if she suggests, for example, that he clean his room or mow the lawn. We all can remember the child who responds with "What?" every time he is asked to do something like that, as if he had some kind of hearing defect. But let the mother mention that a delicious dessert is waiting for him in the refrigerator, and the child then seems able to hear the message very well indeed.

By the time we enter school, most of us have become experts in perceptual defense. We hear the complaint among teachers, "He seems to let everything go in one ear and out the other."

In a lighter vein, young people in love commonly see their beloved through a veil of adoration. A boyfriend may have a wart on his face, or buck teeth, or a very large nose, but in the flush of romantic

°A sensory modality is a sense category such as vision or hearing.

love his girl knows only that he seems to appear good-looking to her, and she may even be unaware of his minor blemishes. Likewise, in the initial passion of romance one may avoid acknowledging—and not really see—that the loved one is in reality a mite stingy or a bit dominating. If he appears overly jealous and suspicious, that only proves the depth of his love and so to marriage. It is only after some months of marriage, when the fire of sexual hunger has somewhat abated, that one can "see" the wart on the beloved's nose, the slightly protruding teeth, or the stinginess, and become irritated by unreasonable and unwarranted jealousy. If love is blind, then marriage is an eye-opener!

Accident Proneness

By the 1920s, the clinical relationship between certain physical diseases and psychological tensions and strains was becoming more well known. People were talking now about "tension" headaches and "worry" ulcers. Early studies in industrial psychology began to reveal an interesting fact—that certain persons were more "accident prone" than others and that these persons seemed to have certain demographic personality characteristics. They seemed to come from broken homes and from larger families, and they appeared to be more aggressive, maladjusted, and to display more acting out behaviors than those who did not have this kind of accident frequency. There has been some reconsideration of the earlier studies on accident proneness, and the correlations do not tend to be as high. But even more recent investigators have not only sustained the implication that some people are simply more accident prone than others are, but there also is evidence now that all of us can be liable to accidents at certain times—those times when the pressures in our life become so intense that we are less aware of ourselves in the physical world.[4] At those times, we hit our head on a cabinet, or we underestimate the distance and we back our car into a tree, or we jab ourselves with an instrument we have been using for years.

Some investigators believe that this self-mutilation is actually an expression of hostility and anger toward an uncaring world—only that it is turned inward, against the self. At any rate, the evidence seems to suggest that there is more truth than poetry in the saying, "There goes an accident looking for a place to happen," when we see an automobile racing far above normal speeds.

Karl Menninger writes of an example of self-mutilation in a man who had become so angry with his brother

that he consciously contemplated killing him; he restrained himself, however, not only on account of the law and other such consequences but because, for his mother's sake, he felt a deep protective obligation to this brother. He became so remorseful that he made several attempts at suicide, all of which barely failed. For reasons not entirely clear to him, he then began to drive his car with a reckless abandon which seemed certain to result disastrously. But in spite of several serious accidents he was not killed. Next he conceived the notion of exposing himself to some disease that would kill him and deliberately tried to get syphilis by repeated exposures.[5]

Diseases of the Respiratory System

The earliest diseases to be identified with emotional problems *per se* were asthma and hay fever. By the late twenties and early thirties, clinical psychologists and psychiatrists were beginning to notice the close correspondence of persons suffering with these ailments and certain commonalities in their personality structure and family background, namely, a smothering relationship between the patient and the parents, particularly the mother.

ASTHMA.   Asthma is the psychosomatic response in which the person experiences an extreme degree of difficulty in breathing. In the asthma attack the person feels as if he or she may suffocate at any moment. Sometimes the attack may last for hours, and the wheezing and coughing can continue until the person feels exhausted. An asthma attack frequently ends with convulsive coughing, an experience no one wants to repeat once he or she has experienced it. Asthma attacks are now acknowledged to be intimately related to emotional upset. For example, asthma in children is found mostly in extremely anxious and insecure children who feel rejected or "smothered" by one or both of their parents. If the asthmatic child continues to grow up as an "asthmatic," his or her asthma attacks can become the principal method of expressing anger, hostility, resentment, and general unhappiness. When a person gets into a tight, emotional spot with which he or she feels unable to cope, a way to get out of it is by having an asthmatic attack right then and there. This response is calculated to bring on others' concern, guilt feelings, and eventually the physical attention he or she feels necessary to survive.[6]

HAY FEVER.   Another respiratory ailment that caught the attention of early psychosomatic clinicians is hay fever. Like asthma, hay fever is an allergy in which certain substances come in contact with the skin or skin receptors causing the mucous membranes of the nose, mouth and eyes to swell and produce a coldlike reaction that lasts for a certain period of time, when the pollen count, as they say, is high. Over and beyond the person's physical susceptibility to pollen, the case history of people who suffer from hay fever seems to indicate a certain common background, an overprotected childhood and one in which they were told they could not do this or that for fear of . . . and so forth. Under therapeutic treatment both the hay fever patient and asthma patient frequently have long periods (of years) when the vulnerability to this disease is decreased, and in fact, the hay fever or asthma does not occur even though the person is in the same environment as when the attacks did occur. They report also that this improvement can be correlated with the fact that their social and family life is at an even keel and that their social life is active.

THE COMMON COLD.   Once the psychosomatic elements of hay fever and asthma were identified, the common cold (another respiratory ailment) also came under suspicion. Clinicians had long noticed a peculiar relationship between the symptoms of the common cold and the external effects of crying. Therapists often have noticed that after some family blow-up or on-the-job "slight," the patient may say that it really did not have much effect but soon after he or she develops a cold. The person does not weep for one reason or another, but instead contracts a cold which has all the physical symptoms of weeping: watery eyes, sniffling, a red face, and puffy eyes. In this way, clinicians say, the body is able to do the weeping it needs to do even when the person denies that he or she feels hurt or wounded and does not permit himself or herself the needed release of weeping or crying.[7]

the flight-or-fight syndrome

At about the same time that these early clinical researchers in psychosomatic medicine were working, Walter B. Cannon, one of the early and great workers in psychosomatic research, stated his understandings of the body-mind interrelationship, in a book entitled *Wisdom of the Body*.[8] The body, he said, has to maintain a state of homeostasis in order to survive. When the body gets cold, we *shiver*, thereby warming us up; when we get too hot, we perspire, thereby reducing the temperature of our body. If we are not getting enough air, we may yawn and take in more oxygen. Thus the body has a kind of "inner wisdom" which produces various bodily responses. One of these responses is the *flight-or-fight syndrome*, which is precisely the opposite of the homeostatic state—it is an emergency state in which the body goes through many physiological changes in order to fight the threat in the environment or to flee from it. Suppose, for example, a cat scents a dog in the environment. It immediately freezes and its body responds with the flight-or-fight syndrome. Rate of respiration, heart

When confronted with a threat, the organism reacts with the "flight-or-fight" syndrome.

rate, and sugar production increase markedly, and thus, more energy becomes available so the animal can prepare itself to stand and fight the "enemy" or to take flight if that is more appropriate. The pupils of the eyes also dilate (improving vision), and the blood tends to withdraw from the body surface, thereby protecting the animal against bruising and bleeding of the skin and increasing the supply of blood to the vital organs. Blood clotting capacity also increases, as does also the tension in the striated muscles, providing for more rapid behavior response when needed.

These same physiological changes are also produced in us when we experience a threat or emergency in our environment. At these times, we may react with superhuman strength. Newspapers often carry stories of persons who have reacted with just this kind of strength in times of crisis. It may be no more than a six-line item describing how John Jones lifted the front end of his sports car to free a loved one pinned underneath, or someone may have jumped from the second-floor window of a burning building and landed unhurt. In such situations the body reacts to the emergency stress with a kind of total psychophysiological response clearly beyond our usual capacities. How the body and the mind were interrelated was explained further by the formulation of the *General Adaptation Syndrome,* described by Hans Selye, a physician researcher in the area of psychosomatic research.[9]

the general adaptation syndrome

THE GENERAL ADAPTATION SYNDROME.   This is the term Selye used to describe what happens when animals experience a dangerous amount of stress. Selye began his research with experimental animals.

136

The beginning of the *stress syndrome* always seemed to involve a primary period he called the *alarm reaction*. With further stress, the *stage of resistance* appeared. If stress at this level continued, the animal's abilities to cope diminished, and the final stage, the *stage of exhaustion*, would appear, and ultimately death would occur.

1. *The alarm reaction*. When an experimental animal first is subjected to physical or psychological stress (electrical shock, extreme cold, poison, etc.), the animal's body reacts by increasing the rate of production of certain hormones and the levels of certain sugars and salts. All of these secretions strengthen the body's defense systems against the oncoming stressors. Such a response is the body's normal method of meeting an emergency, since these increased levels of body chemicals (hormones, salts, sugars) increase one's strength and endurance. There is a certain similarity between Selye's alarm reaction and Cannon's flight-or-fight syndrome, but there also is this important difference. Cannon studied dramatic emergency situations. Selye studied less dramatic stressful situations that continue over time, or *prolonged* stress. In the alarm reaction the animal continues to secrete sugars, salts, and hormones (to defend itself against the emergency stressor) for so long that the animal's body functions begin to break down, as Selye's research showed, in the form of a withered thymus, diseased adrenal glands, bleeding ulcers, and the like.

2. *Stage of resistance*. If the stressor (physical or emotional) is not too severe and the animal does not die, the animal seems to be able to recover from the first-stage alarm reaction pattern. Its adrenal glands return to normal size, although they continue to function at abnormally high levels of secretion. The ulcerative condition also disappears, and the thymus returns to a normal state. In the *stage of resistance*, the animal's body thus *seems* to be adapting to the stressful condition by maintaining certain physiological defenses—for example, an increased production of white blood cells to defend against noxious germs and viruses. On the surface, everything appears to have returned to normal. Indeed, it was sometimes hard for Selye to tell the experimental animals (the animals under stress) from the control animals (the animals not subjected to the stressor). All seemed well . . . for a while.

3. *Stage of exhaustion*. The apparent adaptation of Selye's experimental animals did not last for more than a few weeks. After that the animals got progressively weaker, their internal organs became dangerously diseased again, sugar and chloride production fell again to dangerously low levels, and the animals began to die within a month. In other words, the organism can sustain the supercharged defense rate for only so long. Its defenses or resistances then collapse and life ceases. The *stage of exhaustion* is similar to the initial alarm reaction

in that the same sets of responses are present and the same syndrome can be seen.

In the stage of resistance, the body's defenses are marshaled only against the original stressor — for example, extreme cold. If the animal survives the alarm reaction stage and manages to achieve an adequate defense in the stage of resistance, it is a defense against only that one stressor condition. If the experimenters now add another stressor at the same time (say, electrical shock, which is considered an emotional stressor), the animal collapses immediately. *Selye thereby demonstrated conclusively that as the number of stressful conditions in the environment increases the organism is correspondingly less able to cope (or even survive).*

What does this mean for human existence? Let us take a theoretical application from the life of a young man who is doing his best to earn a living and provide for his wife and baby. He is having problems at his job which cause him some difficulty, but he manages to cope and live through this first stage of alarm. His body gears itself up to working under stressful conditions; as a result he is able to pass through the stage of alarm and is reacting to the stage of resistance. However, just as he thinks he is beginning to get on top of the mess at the job, his mother-in-law comes to visit and makes life hell for him at home as well. This additional stressor may very well be just enough to crack his stage of resistance, and he may then break down as revealed by some physical symptom — maybe a cold in the head or the flu.

Selye made it very clear that *stress* is simply part of the natural "wear and tear" of life on the tissues of organisms. We cannot escape natural stress even if we wanted to and who would want to lead such a dull life, if that were possible? Selye did point out that an excess of stress or prolonged stress of any kind can do more than the normal wear and tear — it can break down body tissue.

INTOXICATION BY STRESS. Selye concluded that stress is the everyday "wear and tear" of life; it is the "common feature of biological activities." Stress cannot be avoided, he said, for even excitement and enjoyable recreation produce wear and tear on our bodies. But by understanding that contracting disease is made more likely by exaggerated responses on the level of some hormone-producing glands, we can at least try to eliminate those stressful situations. Selye expanded Socrates' injunction to "know thyself" to apply not only to one's mind and emotions but also to one's body. We need to recognize when we are getting too "keyed up" (those jittery feelings and tingling sensations), to acknowledge when we are not getting enough rest, and to listen to our bodies when we begin to feel "on edge" or "all tensed up." Seyle believed that a man could become intoxicated by his own hormone production and that it was wise to be aware also of the signs of *overstimulation*. Even when the stimulation is enjoyable and exciting, long life and bodily health may require us to break off the interaction before it becomes stressful. To become aware of our critical stress level and to watch that it does not exceed the level we can safely handle are just as essential to good health as monitoring our intake of alcohol and food. *Intoxication by stress* is usually insidious simply because it may actually be enjoyable: we can become "addicted" to it. It is not always so easy to turn down the level of stimulation of one's body as it is to turn down the volume of the television. We can find that a stimulus, instead of being fun, is now a bother or even unpleasant, yet we are so tied to the stimulus that we are unable to prevent our bodies from reacting. Selye thought we therefore must provide for relaxation in our daily lives. Relaxation does not necessarily mean play, for play can be taken too seriously, we can become overexcited, and we again are trapped in overproduction of hormones.

the effects of life change and life crisis on health

Selye studied the stress syndrome as it appeared in experimental animals and then extrapolated from these findings to the effects of stress on humans. His work seems to us of fundamental importance to psychosomatic theory. More recently there have been some equally challenging studies of stress as it appears in the form of change. This work was done with humans, and the researchers discovered that *change alone*—even when it is seen as beneficial or "happy"—can have ill effects upon a person's psychosomatic balance, on health. Two researchers, T. H. Holmes, and R. H. Rahe, developed a "life change units scale," which measures how much change an individual has been subjected to over a given period of time. Some of the items in their scale note obviously hurtful and traumatic events—the death of a loved one, being fired from a job, a painful divorce, being flunked out of school, and so forth. What is thought provoking about their research findings is that even agreeable changes in one's situation—marriage, birth of a baby, promotion, a vacation—are considered emotionally stressful.* This was found to be the case not only with American subjects but also with Europeans and Japanese.

*These findings are not so surprising when we consider what is involved in a change—any change—in our situation. Consider, for example, the advent of a vacation traveling by car to a distant place for a couple and their two young children. Almost any parent will admit that many hours of driving are a lot easier on the nerves if the children are not along. We are reminded of their wanting to stop for frequent rest periods and complaints that they are hungry. Then think of the mother's attempts to keep the children from getting bored and from fighting, and we immediately understand how vacation trips sometimes can be less happy and more tiring than one originally hoped and fantasized.

Holmes and Rahe began to see that persons with many life changes—those with high *life crises units* (LCU) scores—were more likely to suffer from ill health than those with lower LCU scores. Moreover, there seemed to be a definite additive aspect to the scale: the higher the LCU score, the more likely the person was to come down with an abrupt and serious illness.

Of the crises rated by Holmes and Rahe, the death of a spouse is assigned the highest LCU score (100). This makes sense, for the death of a spouse involves not only the sense of personal loss and grief which follows, but also severe dislocations in personal habits (such as eating and sleeping) and the continued stress of learning to adapt to social relations as a single person rather than as a couple.

Any kind of externally imposed change in accustomed habit patterns can result in an increase in one's LCU score: going away to college, moving to another place, going into the army—all of these can be stressful because of the changes in eating, sleeping, relaxation, and recreation habits, not to mention giving up old friends and the effort in finding new ones.

There also is, in some cases, the pressure of adapting to new places, new smells, and new feelings. "Bumming around" the country can be a form of recreation for our youth, and it seems carefree and fun, at least on the surface. Frequent changes in eating, sleeping, and environment nonetheless can produce considerable stress.

Holmes and Rahe's early research showed there was a marked correlation—a definite relationship—between a high LCU score and an abrupt and serious change in a person's health. *Within eighteen months* of registering such a score, persons came down with major illnesses: tuberculosis, mononucleosis, cancer, leukemia, and the like. Further research revealed that even short-term periods (of two or three days) of high LCU scores resulted in minor aches, pains, colds, and other discomforts.[10] What this means is that the everyday minor illnesses we take for granted, such as the common cold, appear more often when we are stressed for even just a couple of days. Headaches are more frequent when there is tension in our environment; stomachaches, hay fever, and other allergies are more likely to reappear in difficult times or when there are major changes in our physical or psychological state.[11]

Stress factors are the obvious problems which we encounter repeatedly in our present working and living situations. They include all the kinds of adjustment difficulties in new situations, such as moving to another city, taking a new job, and going to college. They also may be family problems, unhappy work relationships, high-pressure jobs, continued worry about one's family and relatives—any and all of these can be the kind of *profound* stress that causes equally pro-

Table 4–1
Stress Ratings of Various Life Events*

EVENTS	SCALE OF IMPACT
Death of spouse	100
Divorce	73
Marital separation	65
Jail term	63
Death of close family member	63
Personal injury or illness	53
Marriage	50
Fired at work	47
Marital reconciliation	45
Retirement	45
Change in health of family member	44
Pregnancy	40
Sex difficulties	39
Gain of new family member	39
Business readjustment	39
Change in financial state	38
Death of close friend	37
Change to different line of work	36
Change in number of arguments with spouse	35
Mortgage over $10,000	31
Foreclosure of mortgage or loan	30
Change in responsibilities at work	29
Son or daughter leaving home	29
Trouble with in-laws	29
Outstanding personal achievement	28
Wife begins or stops work	26
Begin or end school	26
Change in living conditions	25
Revision of personal habits	24
Trouble with boss	23
Change in work hours or conditions	20
Change in residence	20
Change in schools	20
Change in recreation	19
Change in church activities	19
Change in social activities	18
Mortgage or loan less than $10,000	17
Change in sleeping habits	16
Change in number of family get-togethers	15
Change in eating habits	15
Vacation	13
Christmas	12
Minor violations of the law	11

*Adapted from Holmes, T. S., & Holmes, T. H. Short-term intrusions into life-style routine. Journal of Psychosomatic Research, 14, (1970), 121–32. Reprinted with permission of Pergamon Press, Ltd. Copyright © 1970 by Pergamon Press, Ltd.

Breakdown can occur just as easily in civilian life as it can in the stress and life-death situation of the battlefield.

nounced changes in the psychophysiological balance of the body.

There is evidence, also, that subtle pressures can create stress and anxiety and, in time, create equally profound changes in the body. For example, promotion of an executive to a higher position may be welcomed; yet it can cause ill health and instability, particularly among men with only a high school education as compared with men who have some college background. Research shows there is more frequent ill health among minority-group members in the United States, than among white middle-class Protestants, and there are more physical and nervous breakdowns among the unemployed than among those who are steadily employed. Tension regarding the security of one's social status and concern about being discriminated against can and do work as profound stressors. Let us not forget also that the anger and resentment a person may feel because of his or her insecurity in a supposedly egalitarian society also can cause psychosomatic reactions.[12]

ulcers: in the laboratory and office

Psychologists accept clinical data and assessment research for its heuristic value and observation of "real life," but they never are happy until they can confirm these kinds of data with laboratory evidence. Selye had produced diseases of the vital organs which seemed remarkably like those in human beings. But these stressors were physiological: starvation, electrical shock, and toxic substances. Wolfe, Rahe, and Holmes had correlated illness and emotional problems. Was it possible to produce these kinds of diseases in laboratory animals as the result of psychological stress? Joseph Brady, an American psychologist, decided to try.[13] He chose chimpanzees as his subjects, which he estimated to be about as close as he could get to humans.

Clinically, ulcer patients seem to be hard-driving, hard-working "worriers," and business executives seem to be particularly prone to this kind of psychosomatic reaction. They have to make decisions quickly under pressure, and if they make the wrong ones, they may lose their jobs.

Brady yoked two monkeys to an apparatus that generated electrical shocks. Both monkeys were subjected to the shock (which were not physiologically damaging) at twenty-second intervals, but one monkey, whom Brady called the "executive monkey" had a lever which would, by its learning to use it, prevent the shocks. The other monkey (the control monkey) had no such lever. Brady reasoned that the monkey that could prevent the shock was in the same psychological position as the high-powered executive; that is, it was in a position of constant pressure and vigilance. In one experimental situation after another, the control monkey who had nothing to do but receive the shocks survived with apparently no lasting effects. But the "executive monkeys," the ones under continual psychological pressure as well, all developed severe ulcers and eventually died.

The Case of the Air-Traffic Controllers

One of the significant observations from the Brady experiment was the observation that the monkey that had to do the "worrying" was significantly more emotionally pressured than the control monkey was. One

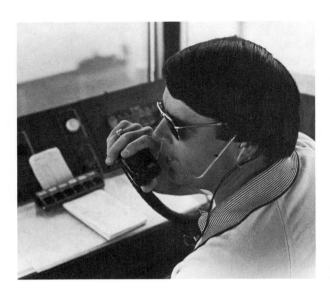

One of the most demanding and stressful jobs today is that of the air traffic controller.

of the most stressful jobs in this country is that of the air-traffic controller. The air-traffic controller is the person who uses radar, weather instruments, and communications equipment to guide airline landings and take-offs.

Sidney Cobb of the University of Michigan and Robert Rose of Boston University compared the health records of 8,435 pilots and 5,199 controllers. Both groups of subjects work in life-death situations, but air-traffic controllers are under greater psychological stress since they (like the "executive monkeys") must make the decisions. The air-traffic controllers were found to have a far greater frequency of high blood pressure, diabetes, peptic ulcers, and so on.[14]

cancer: reaction to loss

Even that most dreaded of all modern diseases, cancer, seems to have a strong psychosomatic component. A past president of the American Cancer Society has stated that many successfully treated cancer patients suddenly seem to develop cancer again after a serious emotional situation, such as the loss of a loved one or protracted unemployment.[15]

Another pioneering psychosomatic researcher, Harold G. Wolff, compared the records of survivors of prisoner-of-war camps and concentration camps six years after liberation with a similar population in terms of sex, age, and general socioeconomic level. He was not surprised to find that the exprisoners' physical resistance to diseases such as tuberculosis and intestinal disorders was lower than that of the nonprisoner population, that even after liberation they fell prey to these diseases; nor was he surprised that the liberated prisoners continued to commit suicide at a higher rate than normal. (The exprisoners had been psychologically "burned out" by their experiences.) What he had not expected to find was *twice the normal incidence of death from cancer* in the exprisoners.[16]

Another damning bit of evidence comes from a detailed analysis of 450 cancer patients over a period of twelve years by Lawrence LeShan of New York's Institute of Applied Biology. The findings revealed a commonality of life experience. Typically, the cancer patient has suffered a severe emotional trauma such as the loss of a parent early in life. For whatever reason, the tendency is to shy away from emotional relationships and instead put emotional energies into something else, such as a job or the role of a parent. Unfortunately, this emotional satisfaction is blocked by being fired from the job or by the fact that one is no longer needed as a parent. Their only emotional satisfaction is suddenly gone, their life energy, so to speak, is drained away, and the first symptoms of cancer appear as early as six months after the loss.

the heart diseases

The various illnesses collectively known as "heart disease" have been attributed to many factors in our society: cigarettes, high-cholesterol diets, and sedentary life. No doubt, all of these have some relationship to the incidence of heart disease.

But clinicians have long observed that persons suffering from the heart diseases seem to have common characteristics, and the picture we so often get is that of hard-driving, aggressive executives committed to completing a job, no matter what the pressure. They are committed (whether they want to admit it or not) to working long hours on a job with fewer and fewer vacations and with less and less recreational time and, in the end, without even the ability to relax off the job. Heart disease patients are the truly committed persons who put their hearts into their jobs until the pressure begins to kill them. Their calm exteriors belie the internal stress and pressure that they experience; yet they can continue to overwork and suppress their anger and anxiety until that moment when the internal stress "blows up" in the coronary artery. By then, the pressure is not so much a psychological difficulty as a medical emergency!

"Type A" Heart Disease Potential Victims

In 1974, a book entitled *Type A Behavior and Your Heart* was published by two researchers. They admitted that although some of the factors contributing toward heart disease in their patients could be linked to nonpsychological factors (diet, exercise, smoking), in at least half of the cases, these factors were absent. After more than thirty years of studying coronary disease in the hospital, laboratory, and consulting rooms, they concluded that a certain type of personality, which they labeled the "Type A" personality, had certain behavioral characteristics. These characteristics include an excessively high competitive drive, whether it be in business or on the golf links, a sense of continual pressure and not enough time to do everything they want to do so that they are always trying to do two or more things at once. They also are extremely aggressive, with a quiet rage that seems to seethe just below the surface. They generally have few hobbies or diversions outside their work and feel guilty when they relax. They also tend to abuse their bodies by eating too rich foods, drinking more than average, considering most recreations a waste of time, and putting their driving energies into work. They resemble what an early psychosomatic social scientist described as the typical heart patient, "They would rather die than fail."[17]

If you know someone who hates to wait in line, who strives to do too many things at once, who often seems to be in a hurry, who eats too much salt, who is a fast talker that jumps on somebody else's sentence when he or she speaks and cannot bear to dawdle or "just plain play," you may know a person racing to a heart attack.

the case for being "frightened to death"

As the mind-body interrelationship is being better understood, many people have suggested that we do not think of the mind *and* the body, or even of the mind-body but rather, of the *mindbody* or *bodymind*. That is exactly the meaning of the word psychosomatic. *Psyche* is the Greek work for mind or soul, and *soma* is the Latin word for body. It is becoming more and more obvious that a serious "psychological" trauma can have a profound effect on the body.

Voodoo Death

Psychologists began asking themselves whether or not the case for the *mindbody* relationship was strong enough to justify the stories of "voodoo death." We all have read about stories in which a native of some Caribbean island has died as the result of being cursed by a witch doctor or by some other psychological terror. Such cases have been described frequently by travelers, and one such case was described by an anthropologist who witnessed just such an event among the Australian aborigines. This poor victim was "boned to death" by his enemy.

The man who discovers that he is being boned by an enemy is, indeed, a pitiable sight. He stands aghast with his eyes staring at the treacherous pointer, and with his hands lifted to ward off the lethal medium, which he imagines is pouring into his body. His cheeks blanch, and his eyes become glassy, and the expression on his face becomes horribly distorted. He attempts to shriek but usually the sound chokes in his throat, and all that one might see is froth at his mouth. His body begins to tremble and his muscles twitch involuntarily. He sways backward and falls to the ground, and after a short time appears to be in a swoon. He finally composes himself, goes to his hut and there frets to death.[18]

Can such a thing be possible?

Laboratory Voodoo

In 1956 a trio of psychologists performed an experiment on rats which seemed to suggest that it is possible.

Insulin is the hormone that controls the metabolism of blood sugar. Most of us are familiar with the fact that if the body's pancreas malfunctions (so that no insulin is produced), the effect is the disease called diabetes. Fortunately, insulin can now be synthesized, and with daily injections of synthetic insulin, diabetic patients can live a fairly full and a longer life. Too much insulin injected into the blood stream, however, is also extremely dangerous and, in fact, can be lethal. This severe physiological reaction is called "insulin shock" and is accompanied by unconsciousness and even death. The psychologists (Sawry, Conger, and Turrell) injected rats with overdoses of insulin, and the result was unconsciousness and, in a few cases, death. At the same time that the rats were given these overdoses of insulin, the experimenters flooded the rats with a bright light. After the animals recovered from their insulin shock, the experimenters again gave the rats insulin injections and the bright light several more times. Each time the experimental animals fell into shock, and so on. Then the experimenters subjected the rats to a different experimental situation. Again under bright lights, they gave the animals an injection but this time the needle did not contain insulin but a harmless saline solution which produces no experimental effect at all. You can guess the results of this experiment. Even without the insulin, the rats fell into insulin shock which, for all intents and purposes, was indistinguishable from the reaction produced by the insulin. Evidently we can be conditioned or frightened to death.[19]

The Sufis tell an interesting story about human nature:
A certain Bedoin chieftain, while riding in the desert, met Pestilence. Reigning in his horse, the chieftain cried, "Pestilence, where are you going?"
Pestilence answered, "To Baghdad, where it is ordained that I am to take five-hundred souls."
The chieftain replied, "Well, see that you do not take one soul more; I am going there myself to raise an army." And both went on their way.
A few weeks later, the Bedoin chief met Pestilence, once more, riding in the desert and cried out to him.
"Pestilence, you lied. You promised you would take no more than five-hundred souls from Baghadad, but when I got there to look for brave young men for my army, they told me you had taken over 5,000."
"Nay, not so," said Pestilence, "I took only five hundred as I promised. Fear took all the rest."

Consignment to Death

One of the sad aspects of our society is our unwillingness to tolerate the old and the sick. We consign them to hospitals, to rest homes, or to homes for the aged. It has been observed time and again that many of the old people who are put into these situations do *not* get better but, in fact, very quickly go into a decline and death follows.

No matter what reasons are given to the aged parent for taking them to a nursing home (better care, round-the-clock service, other persons to relate to) the elderly person is not fooled by the reasons. One geriatric worker made the following observations:

Almost all older people view the move to a home for the aged or to a nursing home with fear and hostility . . . All old people — without exception — believe that the move to an institution is the prelude to death. . . . the move to an institution [is seen] as a decisive change in living arrangements, the last change he will experience before he dies . . . Finally, no matter what the extenuating circumstances, the older person who has children interprets the move to an institution as rejection by his children.[20]

applications and coping techniques

It must be obvious now that extreme stress results not only in psychological breakdown but also in physical breakdown. It is good to remember that life itself, even when we are going about our everyday humdrum routines, is *stressful*. Selye called attention, time and again, to the fact that we cannot avoid stress. It is a part of our everyday lives. Stress is part of the excitement of living, and we actually seek stimulation and challenging situations to avoid monotony. (Remember the monkeys who learned to do a task simply for the "pleasure" of getting a window opened in order to see the experimenters.) In fact, boredom itself is a stress situation.

Some of us actually seek extremely stressful situations. We challenge, for example, the records set by Olympic winners. We deliberately seek thrills by sky diving, or by climbing hitherto unscaled mountains. The deadly quiet between master chess players is only a surface calm, for underneath their apparent calm are intense emotions.

The remaining two chapters in this section will deal with specialized techniques and unusual therapies by which we can counteract some of the acute stress in our lives. There are many things we can do to remedy the more common stresses in our daily living, common sense activities that seem to help us minimize undue stress.

1. Remain Alert to the Stressors in Our Lives

As we go about securing better jobs for ourselves, making moves to further our professional career, and working hard at our work, it is wise to remember that all work and no play not only may make Jack a dull boy, but a sick one too. It is good to remember that *any kind of change* is stressful and to take on too many things at once may have a serious physical outcome. We do not suggest that you turn down an advancement in your job, but we urge you to remember that even this fortunate event may arouse anxiety, the anxiety to do well and the urge to "overdo" the work situation. A third or fourth child may be very welcome, but the problems of larger families do not multiply arithmetically but geometrically. Not only will there be that many more mouths to feed, but that many more children catch contagious diseases; that many more possibilities for expensive orthodontic work; eyeglasses; special shoes to be fitted (if one of them happens to have weak ankles or arches); that many more conferences with the school; and that many more involvements with PTA or Little League. If the parents are anxious to give their children "every advantage," there will be that many more music lessons, dancing lessons, and so on. We ask you to remember that when you "moonlight" a job to become more financially secure, that you may be overtaxing your body and spirit. Many of you who are now in school already are engaged in many kinds of activities including part- or full-time work, taking care of families, attempting to study outside your classes and doing, perhaps, many other things that are part of the educational scene.

2. Become Aware of the Small Signals in the Body which Tell Us that Our Physiological Defenses are Beginning to Crumble

The general adaptation syndrome suggests that we can build up defenses against profound stress and that we can thereby cope and function for a period of time. That level of adaptation, however, turns out to be a kind of supercharged bodily defense mechanism which cannot be maintained for very long. Running a machine at 100 percent power eventually results in the machine "burning up." Selye's research showed that much the same kind of thing happens with the human organism: if we demand that we function at peak levels for more than a short period of time, our defense system eventually collapses and the body then falls prey to disease. This effect is cumulative; as the numbers of stressors increase, the greater the likelihood is that one's body will "break down."

In chapter 3 we mentioned that all of us have our own symptoms of anxiety. Some of us may have a twitch that begins to act up (the kind that we think everyone can notice but when we ask them, they cannot see it). Others of us may have "butterflies in our stomachs" or begin to eat too much. We all also have our own physical symptoms that signal the "stage of alarm," that our body is beginning to show signs of stress. *This* person begins to get headaches; *that* person's sinuses are beginning to act up. One of the authors gets small swellings on the back of the head which indicates the lymphatic system (one of the body's lines of defense) is beginning to get infected. Another bodily symptom may be a joint that is beginning to flare up again with bursitis or arthritis, or one's "susceptibility" to hay fever or allergy may start to increase. These are the early warning signs that all is not well and that you ought to slow down.

Unfortunately, most of us tend to ignore these symptoms. Instead of calling in "sick" for a day or so, we "pop" a headache pill or an antihistamine, gird ourselves up and go to work or to school or that business party we do not really want to attend. Sure enough, later that day, we discover that our symptoms have gone away or are such that we can manage our responsibilities and the symptoms of stress, too. And we probably can. But if the pressure of work, studies, or family conflicts continue to pile up, our symptoms (which have gone away or which we have "blotted out" through aspirin and willpower) may suddenly erupt again in something more serious.

Some persons say, "Yes, but I've never been sick a day in my life. I've got a lot of physical stamina and I can do a lot of things." This is certainly more true of some people than of others. We caution you that your ability to drive yourselves, burn the candles at both ends, stay up late and get up early, and abuse your bodies, cannot last forever, and as all of us get older our ability to tolerate stress decreases. Sooner or later, we shall all "pay the piper."

3. Provide Yourself with an Occasional "Get Away"

It is surprising the number of professional and business people who never call in sick. Look at the attendance records of an organization, and you will notice that although many persons have used every possible sick leave, emergency leave, personal leave, there are others who have accumulated years of unused sick and other personal leave time. Despite the warning signals from their body that all is not well, these people are just unable to let go of their responsibilities. They worry that something might go wrong at the office if they are not there. They maintain their perfect record until, at length, they come down with something really serious like a heart attack, ulcers, or whatever. An occasional sick leave or "mental health day" will help prolong that eventuality, but only if you do not worry about what is going on if you are not there.

What you do with that day off is, of course, up to you. Some of you may just enjoy staying in bed with your favorite book. Others would feel better doing something constructive around the house, like fixing that leak in the plumbing or puttering in the garden. Just because you stay home does not mean you have to be really sick. You can just be sick and tired of the problems and the people in the office, and a day away will give you a new perspective on both the problems and the people.

There is another ironic note about what may go on in your absence at the office. Somebody else may take over the responsibility in your absence. One less thing for you to do! Or everyone may be so glad to see you back the next day, that the people giving you trouble may suddenly be more courteous and open to your suggestions. We cannot promise that this will happen, but it is certainly worth a try.

4. Learn to Understand the Language of the Body

Our body sends distress signals that bespeak more than just that something is wrong; it often indicates *what* is wrong (if we are willing to listen). If we have a headache or a backache, the questions to ask ourselves are "who or what is giving me the headache?" If it is a backache, who or what is on my back? Is it that party we dread going to? Is it a task we have taken on? Is it one of the kids or a relative whose behaviors are causing continual upheaval in the family? Take these clues as ideas only. Your body language and body signals will be singularly yours. Only you can interpret your body language. One person's headache may be quite different from another person's. Your cool, intelligent, objective self-analysis will provide you with the clue to the stressor (or stressors) in your life.

If we are coming down again with a "backache," who is "on our back," so to speak: the boss, the spouse, the kids? Here are some other clues to body language.

Lump in your throat? What situation would you like to cry about, or scream about, or is it something you just cannot "swallow"?

Knot in your stomach? What situation has you so tensed up you cannot relax? Or what piece of news can you not digest?

Abdominal cramps? Is there something going on in your life that is "cramping your style?" Do you feel squeezed by someone? Or are you in the middle of a situation or between two persons?

Cold or swelling of the mucous membranes (hay fever, sinus, etc.)? Has there been something in the last day or so that was particularly hurtful, something about which you did not cry—perhaps even denied that it made a difference to you but looking back now, you realize that it hurt you more than you had thought?

Sensitive areas in the shoulders? This is one of the authors' signals that we have taken on too much responsibility. We are beginning to feel "the weight of the world" on our shoulders.

Constipated? What are you holding on to "for dear life?" It could be that we are simply too busy to take time out for the calls of nature; on the other hand, we may be so tense and "tight" that we are unable to let the bowels function easily.

Diarrhea? We all have had attacks of diarrhea as the result of illness, but there is another kind that seems to come just before we take an exam or have to go for an important interview. Actors getting ready for a play frequently have to run to the bathroom just before curtain time.

5. Find Several Outlets for Your Creative Energy

Sometimes we get so involved in a project or a responsibility that we cannot separate ourselves from what we are doing. All our *emotional* energy is being put into *that* project or *that* responsibility. Our feelings of self-worth all are tied up in the *success* of *that* project or *that* responsibility. If something goes wrong, we have a sense of failure, not just in that project or that responsibility, but in *ourselves* as persons of value. For example, one of the most stressful situations in marriage is the conflict over how to raise children or what to do when they are acting up or having school problems. At these times, parents begin to feel a sense of self-doubt, that familiar, gnawing worry that "we didn't do something right." If we have invested our total concept of ourselves in "perfect, successful" children, we find our own self-worth going down the drain when they do not live up to our expectations. If we have devoted most of our time and energy into our career and suddenly find it boring or meaningless or more than we can handle, we may begin to wonder if life is worth living at all, and it is not surprising then that we begin to feel physically and emotionally low.

People who lead relatively *healthy*, rewarding lives have developed several areas of their lives. They may have a side hobby which challenges and gives them a sense of achievement. (We know a mathematics instructor who has developed two unrelated interest areas; Ham radio and playing a musical instrument in a community band. He also is gathering material for an eventual publication — *Teaching Math in High School*. These other interests help to sustain his general zest and enthusiasm for living which he takes into his classes. He can maintain his sense of humor even when the test grades in a certain class come in abysmally low.

During the middle period of his life, Winston Churchill experienced professional failure. All during the 1930s, he was considered a political pariah, even by his own party. He had to go into political retirement during those years, and very few people came to see him or to consult with him. He had many moments of depression and despair, but he kept himself busy, by painting, by writing *History of the English Speaking Peoples,* and by many other kinds of activities. He knew himself to be a person of worth, and he refused to let a temporary setback in his career change that attitude. Ultimately, as we all know, he was called back into Great Britain's highest office at the beginning of World War II, when Britain needed him most, and achieved his "finest hour."

6. Find Ways to Work Off Your Physical Tension

Some people do this automatically. They are particularly "physical" people, what Sheldon called the "mesomorphic type." These people will tell you, quite frankly, that they need physical activity to maintain a certain sense of ease, and they do it by playing tennis, swimming, or playing handball. After working up a good sweat, they feel physically and intellectually cleansed. A shower later also adds to their feelings of restoration. They have learned that emotional tension can be worked off by physical activity.

But many of us lead very sedentary lives. We sit at an office desk most of the day, behind a counter, or behind the wheel of our car if our business requires that kind of activity. Physicians advise persons with this kind of sedentary routine to get some kind of exercise. We do not suggest that if you have neglected your physical body to rush right out and join a tennis team — that kind of sudden exertion might just "do you in." But there are many appropriate kinds of activities for a person who has lead a sedentary existence. Recently there has been a rising interest in bowling and golf, two excellent sports for persons who do not otherwise work out. Golf, for example, has become known as the "executive sport," and many business organizations, recognizing the need for their executives to "get off their rear ends" to avoid a heart attack, encourage various types of athletic tournaments. Another type of activity that is becoming popular is yoga. The practice of yoga is a series of body "stretchings" that are done unhurriedly and calmly and which require as much sense of balance as physical activity. The books on yoga assert that not only does yoga increase the body's vigor, it also increases mental poise and peace of mind.

Finally, we make a case for the two most physically enervating activities: swimming and just plain old walking.

7. When Emotional Tension is Rising Dangerously High, Find Ways to Blow Off the Steam in Nonharmful Ways

Sometimes there are situations in which one would like to "tell somebody off" or "punch them in the jaw." But social consequences and psychological shame prevent us. What then to do with that anger and desire to lash out? We may be able to count to ten and cool down, but sometimes the anger is too deep, the sense of injustice too strong, and the suppression of the action is turned inward on ourselves, and we may feel irritable or depressed all day long. We snap at others, take it out on someone else, or we simply may seethe with indignation. We become aware that our blood pressure is rising. These emotions have their consequence: the acids of our stomach will increase, the increased adrenalin will keep our muscles tight, and we will have difficulty maintaining calm breathing. In these situations, we need to find a way to express our anger but in a place where it will not hurt anybody else.

Some Japanese business organizations have rooms where the workers can throw objects at pictures of the "bosses." How well it is working we cannot say, but many of us have our own, similar outlets. One psychologist we know has what he calls "aggression glasses." He buys inexpensive glasses at garage sales, and when he gets in one of his "furies," he takes out one or more of these glasses and smashes them against a stone wall. With every shattering glass noise, he finds his anger dropping away. He also finds a sense of penance for his anger in the job of sweeping up the glasss particles later so that no one will be hurt by them.

Sometimes we simply need to have a tantrum no matter how grown up or adult we think we are, but it helps if we can use the energy of our tantrum in a constructive way. A woman of our acquaintance takes her feelings of aggression out in scrubbing and cleaning. "I get so angry at my family, sometimes, I send them all out and then scrub the kitchen to within an inch of its life. The sheer exasperation I feel comes out in tremendous energy. I can scrub the oven in no time flat, mop up the kitchen floor in a few minutes, and even do some of the baseboards—all within an hour." She laughs at this point and says, "By that time, I am feeling so self-righteous that I tell my family to fend for themselves for a while, while I go out and indulge in some luxuries for myself, like getting my hair done or buying myself something I need. The family has learned to let me alone at these times. One can be conscientious and self-denying just so long, then I need to take care of ME!"

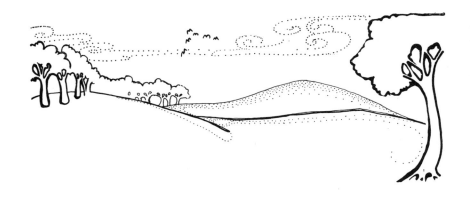

8. Finally, We Need Moments of Sheer Quiet and Relaxation

Related to the stress levels in health and disease is the paradoxical consideration that overstimulation and excitement can become a form of intoxication which, as Selye noted, feeds on itself. We can become addicted to being overstimulated or "high." For that reason people must learn to know themselves, what their essential needs for food, rest, and relaxation are, and even what variety they require in their relationships with the world (slowed down one day, bright and lively the next, etc.). Knowing our essential needs includes learning our own anxiety reactions — what they are, when they occur, and how we seem to adapt to their symptoms.

Finally, change — particularly a major change in one's life situation — is a stressor that cannot be safely ignored. Not only does traumatic (painful) change affect a person's balance and health, but even so-called happy or beneficial changes can be stressful, creating a crisis for the individual.

We live in a time of great sociological and technical change; we are being subjected continually to new inventions, new styles of dress, new modes of living, new forms of marriage and child rearing, and all of these experiments in relationships can become stressful, provoking emotional imbalances in one's everyday adaptation and thus enabling a disease process to attack the organism when they are prolonged. It behooves us, then, to learn new ways of meeting and dealing with our anxieties — recognizing and understanding them and ultimately finding ways to cope with and transcend them.

We need to find quiet moments for ourselves in which we do absolutely nothing. Many take up various types of meditation as a way to calm the body's overactive processes, of which we shall write more in chapter 5. All of us have our favorite ways to relax. Some of us find ourselves renewed by spending the day at the beach acquiring a tan. Still others like nothing better than leaning back in their favorite lawn chair on a cool summer's day and refreshing themselves with a cool drink and a book. Others find the quiet hours of fishing, under the sun and far from the shore, as fine a meditation as one could find.

Whatever our restful, quiet moments we need to have more of them in a time when so many persons and the public media take us away from ourselves and that center of quiet stillness within us.

conditioning and social learning: adaptation to sickness or to health

5

Much of our driving is the result of conditioned responses.

I. Learning: An Introduction to the Facts of Conditioning

    A. *Classical Conditioning*
        1. Conditioning and "unconscious" prejudice
        2. Stimulus generalization and "unreasonable fears"
        3. Phobias
    B. *Classical conditioning and our present state of being*
    C. *First impressions*
    D. *Experimental extinction and spontaneous recovery*
    E. *Operant conditioning*

II. Conditioning Makes Us Robotlike

    A. *The case of Sally*
    B. *The case of Michael*
    C. *The case of Thomas*

III. How We Unwittingly Reinforce Negative Behavior

    A. *The case of Marian*
    B. *The case of Patti and John*
    C. *Reinforcing children's illness*
    D. *Learning not to reinforce temper tantrums*

IV. Conditioning: The Potential

    A. *Shaping behavior*
    Shaping a shy child's behavior toward playing with other children

V. Deconditioning and Reconditioning as a Therapeutic Approach

    A. *Edmund Jacobson's progressive relaxation*
    B. *Tightening as a way of eliminating tension: Perls*
    C. *Wolpe and the conditioning therapies*

VI. Applications and Coping Techniques

learning: an introduction to the facts of conditioning

Learning is generally defined by psychologists as an *activity resulting in relatively permanent change in behavior.* That definition may come as a surprise to the reader who may have been taught to think of learning as something that happens in a classroom in which a teacher directs students' activities toward increasing their skills in reading, writing, and arithmetic.

In contrast to the formal learning which takes place in the classroom, we learn many things very quickly in the everyday world of living, working, and playing with other people. This kind of learning begins very early in life. We *learn* to speak, to walk, to smile (or not to smile), to cry and whine, and to have good manners — or to be aggressive and rude to others. We also learn to have a bad attitude toward some things that happen to us. For example, we adopt the opinions of others and consider them our own without awareness, often at a very early age, and sometimes even before the acquisition of words and language. As Freud pointed out, we learn many of our defense mechanisms and much of our life style before the age of six years — for example, to approach others with confidence and optimism, or to retreat from them so as to avoid problems. If as children we received real caring and support from adults, we may have learned in that way to trust adults and those in authority. On the other hand, if the adults in our early years engendered fear, we may have learned to fear and distrust adults and authority in general.

Freud maintained that people's characters are the result of their experiences with their parents and siblings and those fortunes or misfortunes of fate (death of a parent, early sickness, poverty, etc.) which any child may have to confront. However, it was not until Pavlov's classic experiments with a laboratory dog that psychologists found (began to develop) a rudimentary "scientific" method for studying how we learn these early skills and behaviors.

Classical Conditioning

The Russian scientist, Ivan Pavlov, is rightly considered the discoverer of one of the great psychological principles in learning. Oddly enough, Pavlov was not a psychologist but a physiologist, and his discovery of the laws of classical conditioning was a serendipitous event.[1]

Pavlov's main interest was in measuring the gastric secretions and other digestive processes in animals. In one experiment, he and his assistants had strapped down a large dog to measure the increase in the salivary reflex (amount of saliva secreted) when food was presented to the animal. A difficulty arose, however, when it appeared that the animal could not be made to begin salivating at a regular time.

The first few times the experiment was conducted, the animal

Much of what we call "learning" is the result of "conditioning," first discovered by the Russian physiologist, Ivan Pavlov.

began salivating when it *smelled the food* as it was being set down in front of it. After a few trials, however, the dog would begin to salivate when it *saw the laboratory assistant* approaching with the food. Then it began to salivate every time *the door to the laboratory opened.* Finally, the dog would begin to salivate when it *heard the approaching footsteps* of the assistant coming down the hall to the laboratory. These responses perplexed Pavlov; moreover, the intended experiment was being obstructed by the increasingly earlier onset of salivation. In other words, the assistants could not seem to get a consistent starting time for the onset of salivation, and it was thus impossible to measure accurately how much fluid the animal's salivary glands were secreting—the very purpose of the experiment!

It was Pavlov's genius to recognize that here in front of his eyes a phenomenon of learning was taking place, and he went on to study the processes at work. In time, he even began to understand some of the abiding laws of these processes. Pavlov realized at that time that he may have stumbled on a method of studying learning which could be generalized to those higher intellectual processes called "education," "habits," and "training." Pavlov's reasoning was approximately as follows: a dog does not have to learn to salivate at the sight and/or smell of food since it is born with this reflex—a type of reflex Pavlov called an *unconditioned response* (UR). Thus, anything which arouses an unconditioned response (UR) can be termed an *unconditioned stimulus* (US). What kinds of stimuli provoke the unconditioned response of salivation? For a dog, the presence of meat, milk, or water arouse the UR of salivation, so in this situation these particular stimuli were *unconditioned stimuli.* Ordinarily, if a bell is sounded in a dog's presence, the animal will perhaps prick up its ears and listen to it, but a dog will not ordinarily salivate simply at the sound of a bell. The bell, therefore, is not an unconditioned stimulus for the response of salivation—it is a *neutral stimulus* (NS). Then Pavlov rang a bell at the same time food was presented to the dog, a procedure called *pairing the neutral stimulus and the unconditioned stimulus,* and he observed a very interesting phenomenon: when the previously neutral stimulus of the bell was then sounded by itself (*without* the US of food), the dog began to salivate. The bell was no longer a neutral stimulus for salivation, since the dog had *learned* to salivate upon *hearing it* (without the accompanying food). Pavlov said that *the neutral stimulus (NS) had now become a conditioned stimulus (CS).* In psychological terms we might say that the dog had learned to associate the idea of food with bell ringing, although psychologists prefer to speak in terms of "conditioning," "stimulus," and "response."

CONDITIONING AND "UNCONSCIOUS" PREJUDICE.   Part of the importance of conditioning to our purposes is that many of our likes and dislikes, our fears, phobias, and anxieties, as well as many of our preferences for certain kinds of life situations, are conditioned (that is, acquired) at an early age.

For example, Pavlov's further experiments illustrated that if a dog were continually subjected to a shock (US) every time a bell (NS) was sounded, the dog very easily became conditioned to fear the *sound of the bell* by itself: When the bell was sounded, the dog demonstrated all the outward behavior of extreme stress and fear, as if it were being shocked!

In just such ways, say contemporary psychologists, we may have been conditioned to dislike blacks or whites. Consider, for example, a white child growing up in a prejudiced white family. If no one conditions the child, he may eventually begin to walk home from school with a black child with whom he has become friends. The mother in this hypothetical family sees the two walking home, and she is immediately horrified; she calls the child into the house and proceeds to deal with the child in an emotionally fearful way. Behavioral psychologists would say that the parent has given the child his first pairing of the stimulus *black person* (a previously neutral stimulus) with the stimulus *bad/horror/shame/negative/guilt*. As he continues to grow up, the child learns also that his father says "damn" everytime he uses the word "nigger" (in tones of contempt or hatred). Slowly, even without anyone telling him how to think or react to blacks, the child is being conditioned to dislike, distrust, and avoid associating with persons who have black skins.

A similar thing can, of course, happen in black families that carry forward hatred and resentment of whites. The children in those black families grow up similarly to fear and/or hate all whites as the result of conditioning in their early lives. Our prejudices against certain people or groups of people are early learned responses over which we have had, by and large, very little control. In childhood, we can be conditioned *directly* because we do not yet understand the subtlety of *nonverbal language*, that is, "*the sound of the bell which equals fear*," and so on. It is hard for any of us to trace where or how we learned prejudice—how to appreciate one set of values while deprecating particular races, groups, beliefs, or values.[2]

STIMULUS GENERALIZATION AND "UNREASONABLE FEARS". Further work in classical conditioning revealed another interesting phenomenon. Suppose an animal is conditioned to respond to a particular tone (say middle C) of a tuning fork. It can learn, for example, to salivate to the tone of middle C after some pairings of that tone with food. If another tone is sounded which is higher or lower than the original tone (say high C or low C), *the animal will most probably salivate to those tones also* (although not with the same intensity as in

Without attitudinal conditioning, children might grow up free from prejudice.

response to the original tone).[3] The animal will probably also salivate to other sounds which differ significantly from the original neutral stimulus: it may salivate to a buzzer, an alarm clock, or a doorbell. In other words, psychologists discovered that the conditioned stimulus can be *generalized* to other stimuli which are similar to it and without any more pairing with the unconditioned stimulus.

An American psychologist, John Watson, carried out an interesting experiment which illustrates this point very well in the now famous case of Albert.[4] Watson encountered Albert as a healthy, normal child of nine months. When various objects were placed in Albert's crib (such as a furry mask, a piece of cotton, a rabbit, and a dog), Albert showed no signs of fear. He did not even show fear when a white rat was put into the crib. On the contrary, he leaned forward to touch it. He did show fear, however, when a loud noise was made close to him.

In Watson's experiment, when Albert was almost one year old a white rat was placed in his crib and a loud noise was made nearby *as he leaned forward to touch it*. In fact, the loud noise was made every time Albert leaned forward to touch the rat on subsequent days. After this series of pairings, Albert began to cry when the rat was placed in his crib even when the loud sound was not made. The rat, which had previously been a neutral stimulus, had now become a conditioned stimulus capable of arousing the conditioned response of fear and crying in poor Albert!

Not only was Albert now afraid of the rat, but *he also was afraid of anything else that was white or furry* — as, for example, a white rabbit, white cotton, a dog, or a mask with a beard on it. None of those objects had evoked fear in their original presentation to Albert; rather, they had sparked his interest and delight. The fear stimulus (sound of a loud noise close by) that was associated to a specific object (white rat) had now become "generalized" (associated) with any object that was white and furry. This is what is meant by *stimulus generalization*. We do not know what happened to Albert when he grew up. He may have continued to evince intense fear when he saw a bearded man, without knowing why, or may have become phobic about rats, had a peculiar dislike for Santa Claus and everything connected with that jolly old man. And he may not even know why.

PHOBIAS.   A fear without a recognizable cause or "rational" explanation is called a *phobia*. Watson and his colleague, Rosalie Raynor, were fairly sure that direct conditioning and stimulus generalization probably caused some phobias, *particularly if the fears were engendered before the advent of language* – in other words, before we have enough words to make sense out of the thousands of events (stimuli) that affect us from birth to two or three years. Human beings, therefore, can suffer from many seemingly "unreasonable" phobias: fear of cats, fear of birds, fear of closed spaces, fear of heights, and the like. *It may be that one severely traumatic event* in one's life at an early age (or several less severe events) *can call forth a generalized fear to other kinds of similar objects or situations*, as in the case of little Albert. Far from being unreasonable, a phobia is simply a conditioned fear of great size, of some stimulus that happened in the remote and silent period of infancy. Sometimes this phobia produces allergies, and you may know persons who sneeze violently or break out in a rash in the presence of a cat or other furry animal.

Classical Conditioning and Our Present State of Being

In classical conditioning experiments, a first step in the precise measurement of what we call learning was made. Classical conditioning seemed, indeed, to account for some kinds of learning, particularly those learnings and behaviors that affect the so-called involuntary reflexes and functions: salivation, eyelid blinking, muscle tension, heart rate, and so on. It may also account for why we have pleasant reactions to certain objects while others have unpleasant reactions to the same objects. Because loud sirens have been associated with accidents, sickness, and death for so long, many of us still experience a rush of fear or find our hearts "skipping a beat" when we hear one in the distance. An acquaintance of the authors lived through the 1941 blitz in London as a young child, during the Battle of Britain. Even now, she reports, the sound of an airplane flying overhead fills her with dread, even though she has not experienced anything but pleasure in traveling by airplane herself since she was ten years old.

First Impressions

One of the principal goals of psychotherapists is to enable a person to achieve in the therapeutic situation the recognition that much of the behavior and emotional response to others is simply a generalized conditioned response to new but similar stimuli. Many men are unable to deal with women as individuals since they are, in fact, reacting to them as they once reacted to their own mothers, sisters, and daughters. If they liked their mother, their response toward other women will be generally favorable. If they disliked their mothers, they may be working out (or actually unleashing) their long stored-up anger, resentment, or guilt, not on their mother, but on the other women in their lives.

The same principle works in reverse. If a woman as a child had doted on her father, she may look for someone to dote on as a husband. If she disliked her father, she may seek revenge on men in ways she does not understand and of which she may not be aware.

Favorable and unfavorable first impressions of people also may be accounted for as *generalized responses to generalized stimuli*. Suppose your mother (of whom you were very fond) had a preference for blue and wore a certain pleasant perfume. Suppose you meet one day an attractive lady wearing a blue dress and enveloped in an aura of similar perfume. Would it not create in you a most delightful first impression? Of course, since she has created just such a delightful impression on you, you will convey this response to her in verbal and nonverbal ways as you communicate with each other. The fact that you find her so charming, no doubt, works a chemical magic in her, and she responds quite favorably to you . . . and so you fall in love.

Experimental Extinction and Spontaneous Recovery

Two other principles of conditioned behavior that Pavlov formulated are *experimental extinction* and *spontaneous recovery*. Going back to Pavlov's dog, the reader will remember that after the bell and the food had been paired (presented together) several times, the dog would salivate to the sound of the bell alone — that is, the dog was now conditioned to expect food at the sound of the bell. What would happen, Pavlov wondered, if over a long period of time only the bell were sounded—without food being given? You have probably guessed it: eventually, the dog stopped salivating to the sound of the bell—it "learned" that there was no food forthcoming and thus did not "expect" any. In psychological terminology, this phenomenon is called *experimental extinction;* that is, the conditioned response of salivating at the sound of a bell had been *extinguished.* We can say that although we can learn almost anything, it is possible to "unlearn" it as well.

There is a "catch." The catch is the phenomenon known as *spontaneous recovery.* Some time after the dog was no longer salivating to the bell (after experimental extinction had been achieved), the bell was accidently sounded one day and (much to the surprise of everyone involved) the dog salivated again! In psychological terms, after a response has been extinguished and a period of time has elapsed, the conditioned response may spontaneously recover—regain some of its strength without additional conditioning. The whys and wherefores of this phenomenon are speculative. Suffice it to say that knowledge of this phenomenon can aid in understanding why some of our fears, phobias, resentments, and jealousies may flare up long after the embers seem to have died out. If the person then learns not to "feed" (further condition) these negative emotions, eventually the response patterns will be extinguished completely.

Operant conditioning

The examples of the conditioning process that we have discussed so far all have one important feature: the simultaneous appearance of two stimuli in the environment which produces a conditioned (learned) response: that is, various environments condition us to behave in certain ways: to act, think, and feel, and to believe that given *this* event or person, *that* event will follow.

This model of learning seems to propose that we are nothing more than passive organisms reacting to the environment, a model more appropriate to the jellyfish carried along by the current until it comes up against another organism which it can eat (or which can eat it). Human persons and other higher animals, however, learn through their own conscious energic interactions with their environment.

The leading proponent of this second conditioning model, the American psychologist B. F. Skinner, calls this approach *operant conditioning* to account for the fact that animals learn also by *operating* on their environment as well as by responding to it.[5] In a typical operant conditioning experiment, a rat is put into a *Skinner box*—usually a cage equipped with certain mechanical devices. When first put into the cage, the rat will engage in *exploratory behavior;* it runs around the cage, sniffs, stretches, cleans itself, and runs around again and exhibits various other exploratory behaviors.

There is a bar in the cage which, when pressed, activates a mechanism that drops a food pellet down a chute to the rat. In the course of its exploratory behavior, sooner or later the rat is bound to accidently touch the bar, whereupon a food pellet is immediately released. The rat eats it and looks around for some more. When it does not find any more food, it may go to the opposite end of the cage, sniff, and wander around aimlessly. Eventually, however, it does manage to hit the bar again and is *reinforced* (rewarded) by another food pellet. This process is repeated over and over, and eventually the rat discovers that a certain action or behavior (pressing the bar) produces a reward—namely, food. The animal's behavior then becomes less random and more purposeful, and it quickly engages in pressing the bar and eating the released food pellets until it has had enough. This method of conditioning relies more on self-learning than does the classical conditioning approach.

Human babies, too, are not just passive organisms. As they grow up, they operate on their environment and experiment with a variety of behaviors. Some of these behaviors are reinforced, and others are punished by the environment. The "baby" of a large family indulges in "cute" behavior at the dinner table, and to its delight discovers that it is the focus of attention and laughter. The child now has been reinforced for acting in such a droll way, tries it again and again, and each time is thrilled with those familiar sensations of laughter and applause. When the child tries out these jokes at school, his or her classmates also enjoy the antics. The child has discovered a way of eliciting that longed-for applause from his or her audience, a pattern of reinforcement that could one day result in his or her becoming a stand-up comic.

conditioning makes us robotlike

From the foregoing discussion, it is easy to see how conditioning can predetermine our habits of eating, our habits of sleeping, our habits of talking and interacting and responding through the various thousands of conditioning experiences we have undergone, both reinforcing and painful. When we are completely unaware that many of our behavior patterns are indeed conditioned, we may then be considered *determined*—controlled ultimately by our past experiences and therefore "unfree." For example, when we are unaware of the choices available to us at a given moment and behave with old conditioned responses to a new situation, at that point and to that extent, we are more like automatons and machines — that is to say, *predictable* because we repeat old responses over and over like a machine.

English philosopher and novelist, Colin Wilson, described this conditioned aspect of the human personality as that part of oneself which is like a robot, nonhuman. Wilson pointed out how his own

According to the theory of conditioning, what we are is the sum total of all our conditioned responses.

robot (the conditioned part of himself) is very useful. For example, he does not have to *think* about walking, about driving a car, or about typing, since the response patterns for these behaviors are "programmed" into the nervous system, and his robot allows him to do these things more or less automatically. Extra energy thus is available which can be directed into his creative aspects — thinking, reasoning, deliberating.

But the robot in one's personality also imposes one enormous disadvantage (among others). To quote Wilson:

> If I discover a new symphony that moves me deeply, or a poem or a painting, this bloody robot promptly insists on getting in the act. And when I listen to the symphony for the third time, *he* begins to anticipate every note. He listens to it automatically, and I lose all the pleasure. He is most annoying when I am tired, because then he tends to take over most of my functions without even asking me. I have even caught him making love to my wife.[6]

Thus, we continue to do the same things, say the same things, use the same clichés, accede to the same demands from our environment — without question and without awareness. In Freud's terminology, this is the "unconscious" (unaware) aspect of ourselves. Whatever term we use to describe such behavior, it is astonishing how many of our responses are predetermined in ways of which we are unaware.

Our conditioning then can work against us when our own behaviors call forth rejection, ridicule, impatience, irritation, and anger from others. Let us look at some examples.

The Case of Sally

"Sally," a nine-year-old black child, had come to expect trouble (derision, hitting, name calling) from *all* white children because a *few* white children had treated her in this way. Accordingly, she distrusted the friendly advances of other whites. She had a negative, suspicious, hostile attitude toward all whites and kept otherwise friendly whites from trying to establish communication with her. In other words, she had not only developed a generalized response to *white* people, she even began to condition them to dislike her and stay away from her.

The Case of Michael

Michael is a youngster who received reinforcement from his environment in sports, so he has a certain amount of self-esteem and confidence on the athletic field. However, he has always been somewhat small in stature, and that continues to be a point of insecurity in his personality development. When he was in the lower elementary grades, Michael was hauled off the recess field several times because of fighting. As we investigated each incident, we discovered a common element in many of his fights: someone had called him a name which made him angry. These names generally referred to his small size: "shorty," "small-fry," "pipsqueak," "shortstop," "peanuts," and the like. Michael's reaction to these stimulus words was to prove to the name-caller that he may be short, but he also was tough and not someone to provoke too often. Consider, now, that Michael's behavior was so automatic that any casual reference to his size resulted in the inner command, "Fight!" As long as he had no other response but "Fight!" to the stimulus words, he was not in control of his own behavior. He was conditioned to respond in just one way. As long as anyone could arouse his anger and call forth the fight response in him through the stimulus

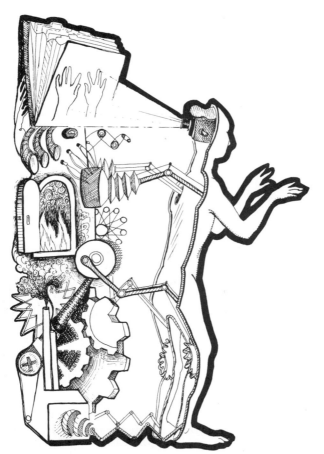

Social scientists ponder the questions: To what extent are we so controlled by our conditioning that we are merely robotized and nonhuman? To what extent, if any, do we exercise free will and choice?

words, that person was more in control of Michael's behavior than Michael himself was.

We have control of our behavior only when we have *at least two* (significantly different) *choices available.* Michael, seemingly (most of the time) had only one choice available, and that was the push-button reaction to fight when called one of these painful names, rather like the animals in Arzin's experiments (chapter 3). In his robotlike conditioned response (fight), Michael was as unfree as any other animal who attacks after a pain stimulus. That is what we wanted him to see and understand.

The Case of Thomas

Many of our values have been conditioned to our own disadvantage. "Thomas," a student, wants to be a better student. He probably has the capacity to get through college, but he lacks the motivation to study or even take his courses seriously. Thomas comes from a family which placed little value on education. His father used to take him on fishing and hunting trips and encouraged him to go out for the football team, and they had a most gratifying father-son relationship. His father never got past junior high school, however, and Thomas has frequently heard his father condescendingly refer to the university population as "eggheads." Thomas was conditioned early to value the "manly" things his father approved of, such as hunting and fishing, and he was conditioned also to look down on the pursuit of intellectual knowledge. Any stimulus associated with school, books, studying, or learning, simply "turns him off." *He has developed a conditioned response patterning against school.*

how we unwittingly reinforce negative behavior

We unwittingly reinforce negative behavior and illness in others. Many of the physical problems we have also are reinforced by our families. Let us take the case of Marian Kessle.

The Case of Marian

Marian's parents were neighbors of ours. Marian was the oldest of the four Kessle children, and her mother worried constantly about the fact that Marian was often sick, did not eat enough, seemed lethargic and was extremely underweight. To look at Marian, her mother's fears were justified. She was a "skinny" twelve-year old, who always seemed listless. Her mother had taken her on the usual rounds of physicians, to no avail.

Because we were psychologists, Marian's mother asked for our help. Although we were loathe to bring our work into the area of our friends and neighbors, Marian's mother was so insistent that she finally prevailed on us to come to dinner. What a revelation that dinner was! There were eight of us seated at the table: Marian, her three younger siblings, her parents, and ourselves. Although there were eight of us, most of the activity at the dinner table was centered on Marian. Just as Marian's mother had said, Marian picked away at her food and when most of us were eating dessert, Marian's plate was still piled high with food. Marian's mother kept up a constant barrage of statements directed to Marian urging her to eat, offering her something special that she had cooked and that she knew Marian liked, warning her of the dire consequences (like getting sick again) if she did not eat. It became readily apparent to us that Marian received more attention by *not* eating than if she had eaten like the rest of the children (all of whom were busily eating). With the constant visits to the doctor and her mother's continual verbal concern for her, Marian's mother was unaware that she was reinforcing Marian's non-eating behavior by her own constant attention to the child. Did we try to point this out to Marian's mother? We made some beginning statements about letting her eat whatever she wanted, and her appetite might improve. But we were met with such anxiety and hostility by Marian's mother, we knew better than to continue. There was obviously something deeper going on that only a professional relationship with Marian's parents could help. Psychologists learn to keep their professional and private lives separate. We did suggest that the community counseling center might be of service. Since we moved away soon after that, we have no idea how that situation turned out.

We *can* relate a situation in which we were able to use our professional services.

The Case of Patti and John

Husbands and wives can get trapped in similar vicious cycles of reinforcing behavior that inhibits interpersonal growth. John and Patti have been married for a number of years. During the early years of the marriage, Patti discovered that John on occasion awoke like a bear, a cross and irritable bear. To forestall that irritability, which she came to dread, Patti would prepare an an especially tempting breakfast on those days and an equally fine meal when John came home from work. In the beginning, this pattern of reinforcement seemed to work very well in placating the husband's crossness and irritability. Over the years of marriage, however, Patti noticed that her husband's morning irritability had become more frequent, even though he seemed to be pacified and made more mellow by the fine breakfast each morning. What she did not realize was how she was in fact reinforcing her husband's "negative" behavior in the morning: she did not realize that she served her *best* meals on the days John was at his *most* irritable and cranky.

Patti learned to serve both her own and John's best interest by preparing her delicious meals on the days when he was *not* irritable. In that way, at least, she reinforced his "good" moods, and his negative behavior gradually eased away from irritability and crossness.

Reinforcing Children's Illness

Parents can sometimes reinforce the syndrome of being sick. A couple of generations ago, when children became ill, they were put into a room by themselves, the blinds were drawn, the children were given evil-smelling, foul-tasting medicine, and other children were not allowed to visit them. In general, treatment of the illness was sometimes considerably more unpleasant than being sick. Getting well was its own reward.

Nowadays, parents are advised to treat a sick child differently—

Every time this young girl gets moody and/or sulky, her fiance "jollies" her up and gives her a lot of extra attention. What might be predicted about the frequency of her bad moods?

for example, to fix up special meals in pretty packages and to keep the child occupied and happy while convalescing. Many of our medicines today are made to taste like candy. A child may even get special little gifts from the family and friends, and if the illness is protracted, he or she may even receive letters from classmates at school.

Although we do question the severity of the older approach, it does seem wise nonetheless *not* to provide reinforcement for "sick" behavior. The limitation of the apparently more humane contemporary approach is that it may unwittingly reward sick behavior, thus providing reinforcement. A balance between these two approaches can be worked out by the thoughtful person, one that neither punishes nor rewards the child for his or her sickness.

Learning Not to Reinforce Temper Tantrums

What about a child who is having a temper tantrum? How can a mother deal with this behavior and not reinforce it? For example, she may give him or her a coloring book (if the child is still very young) or a special toy to play with provided he or she stops screaming. When the child begins to engage in the desired behavior, she can then further reinforce the behavior by remarking how well he or she is now behaving. Verbal compliments also are strong reinforcers.

Let us suppose that the child is not yet ready for this approach and still wants to have his or her way with the world despite the cost. For example, suppose he or she begins to scream again. The parent at that point had best simply ignore the child's behavior. But at the first moment he or she begins to play quietly, a compliment is then indicated.

Of course, the child can still express his or her frustration in not getting what is wanted by returning to the temper tantrum behavior. In that event, the mother can simply walk away from the uproar, or she can firmly remove the child to his or her room, saying quietly, "I understand that you are not feeling well. I want you to stay in your room until you begin to feel calmer and better. Then you can play [use your coloring book, etc.] again." Of course, at this point the child may throw the final tantrum. He or she can even go in for blackmail—for example, "holding his or her breath" as some children seem to do. But whatever the "defensive" behavior the child may choose to utilize in dealing with his or her current frustration, the primary consideration now for the parent is that the child *realize something is being expected of him or her*—and that the child can do it the "easy way" or the "hard way"!

conditioning: the potential

If we are conditioned in many subtle ways by other persons' responses to us and if we also, unwittingly, reinforce other persons' negative behaviors, is there some way that we can use the laws of conditioning for our benefit and those around us?

Shaping Behavior

B. F. Skinner, the psychologist who formulated the concept of operant conditioning, also formulated some fundamental ways to reinforce positive behaviors in others. He called it the "shaping of behavior." If one wants to train a pigeon to peck at a ping-pong ball, one begins by giving the pigeon a kernel of corn everytime the bird approaches the ball. Soon the pigeon is *walking toward* the ball, and again it is reinforced (given more food). The next step is to reinforce the pigeon with food only when the bird gets so close to the ball that it is *almost touching* the ball; now the pigeon will not move away from the ball. The final step in the reinforcement process is to reinforce the bird *only when it touches the ball*. Soon, the trainer has the pigeon pecking at the ball every time it wants something to eat.

Many animal acts are trained using just this kind of method of *shaping behavior*. In fact, two psychologists have made a business of training animals to perform at such places as Marineland, Florida, simply by shaping these animals' behaviors in the desired directions by a series of small learning steps.[7] We can shape animal behaviors very easily and very quickly. Is it possible to do that with human beings? In fact, we do just that when we tell children to say "please" and "thank you," and when they do so, reward them with a smile.

SHAPING A SHY CHILD'S BEHAVIOR TOWARD PLAYING WITH OTHER CHILDREN. In one nursery school, teachers devoted considerable time and attention to one apparently immature and withdrawn child who spent most of her time on the floor. When they failed to get the child to adapt to the school routine, they called in a consultant for advice and help. They discovered then that they had actually been reinforcing the child's withdrawn behavior by constantly giving her attention while she was on the floor and playing by herself. The consultant suggested that the first step toward enabling the child to interact with the other children (and to get the child up off the floor) was to stop paying attention to her (stop the reinforcement) when she was on the floor and *to give her reinforcement* (smile at the child, talk to her and pat her) *only when she got up to a standing position.* In a few days the child was standing for much of the time, and in two weeks she was behaving in a manner that was indistinguishable from the other children in the nursery. Furthermore, the teachers then proceeded to reverse the previous conditioning and reinforced the child only when she was down on the floor, playing by herself. In a few days, she was again withdrawn and staying on the floor for much of the time. As if that were not enough demonstration, the psychologists again reversed the reinforcement patterns (giving reinforcers again for *standing* behavior), and the child was standing on her feet, happily playing within a few hours.[8]

We have been asked by students and teachers to give more concepts and examples of shaping behaviors. Our own students have said that they were much enlightened by our discussion of how we unwittingly reinforce and shape negative behaviors in others; what can they do to stop what they have been doing and reinforce more positive and constructive behaviors? For a fuller appreciation of these behavioral techniques, let us begin by examining some of the basic principles and concepts of behavioral psychology.

1. *Behavioral psychologists do not necessarily seek causative factors;* they work on observable behavior. Freud believed that to help a person overcome a neurosis or "fixated behavior," it was necessary to discover the traumatic events and conflicts of the patient's early life. Hours of psychoanalysis were spent in therapy as the person endeavored to unearth from the unconscious, those repressed, narcissistic, and lustful desires, and their consequent punishment in the process of socialization. Much of our current counseling and psychotherapy utilizes intellectual insight into our past history and why we are the way we are. Behavioral psychologists may find the case history approach pertinent, but they are *more* concerned with *current* behaviors, how to extinguish undesirable behaviors and reinforce desirable ones. It matters little to them if Johnny's bad behavior in school comes from a child-parent conflict; they are interested now in how the teacher reinforces the behavior and how they can help the teacher to reinforce better behavior. They say that hours and hours could be spent in discussing the causative factors (if they can be discovered at all) but that all that discussion will not change the child's behavior. (Some behavioral psychologists believe that "neuroses" are simply "bad habits" of adaptation.) In fact, the therapy and counseling with children may only reinforce their attitude that there is something wrong or that the reasons for their problems are not *their* fault but their parents', teachers', or whomever. Interestingly enough, the results of a thirty-year, longitudinal study have just been released and are very disturbing to school counselors who believe in the "talking cure." Two groups of

delinquent youngsters were identified in the files of a northeastern counseling center. One group had received counseling and other kinds of remedial therapy; the other group had not. Now (thirty years later), a follow-up of these two groups revealed that the group that did *not* receive therapy or other treatment has not had as high a frequency of adult delinquency as the other group has had.[9] "Is it possible," some of our behavioral psychologists are asking, "that the attention received by the counseling *actually reinforced* the adolescent's delinquent behavior?" It is still too early to judge, but this report has shaken the foundations of social rehabilitation theory.

2. *Behavior is extinguished only when it is no longer followed by reinforcement.* If the laws of extinction hold, then a behavior is extinguished when it is not followed by a reinforcer. The key, then, is to discover what is currently reinforcing the child's behavior. It may be the very punishment, nagging and scolding the child, is getting because he or she has not discovered more socially rewarding ways to get attention (that is, to be reinforced). The teacher who screams at the class "cut-up" actually may be reinforcing the very behavior she does not want. After we identify the reinforcers, we need to find ways and means to *eliminate* those reinforcers. In the case of the teacher and child in the classroom, the teacher must stop directing her screaming and scolding to the child in question.

But, you may ask here, how can she put up with a child that is acting up? Anyone who knows the school situation is well aware that one child's behavior can be a continual disruption for the rest of the students. It can even be contagious, with the result that the whole class can become noisy. We suggest isolation until he asks to come back.

3. *Punishment should be used sparingly, since it is less effective than reward is.* For a while, behavioral psychologists argued that any kind of punishment was bad. They argued that even if punishment is severe enough to stop the behavior, it is only *suppressing the act,* not the *desire.* The behavior will simply go "underground," and the person will learn to become more sneaky or quiet about it. But most behavioral psychologists admit now that there are situations that must be quickly extinguished, which cannot be done through reinforcement. For example, we may need to punish a child for continually running into a traffic-filled street; in this situation, the child may need to be spanked to save his or her life.

Another aspect of punishment is that it does not teach new behaviors. The best punishment can do is to *stop* or suppress behavior until new behavior is learned. If we are going to punish a child, physically or verbally, we need to help that child learn new ways to behave — *behaviors for which he or she can be reinforced.* Other considerations for the use of punishment are listed in Box A.

Box A

If punishment be used, it is more effective when these principles are involved:

1. It is strong enough to be adequate. Weak punishment may simply give the child the idea that there is no real threat. Weak punishment is reinforcement.

2. Let the punishment fit the crime when possible. If a child has marked a floor with a crayon, let him or her spend the time and elbow grease necessary to clean it up.

3. Do not delay punishment. Experimental studies have shown that punishment, like reward, is most effective when it immediately follows the action. An overlong delay will tend to weaken the child's association with what he or she had done. Instead of saying, "you wait until your father comes home," you can tell the child to wait in his or her room until his or her father comes home. The restriction to the room is punishment itself and in that way you can get the father's help in the matter.

4. If you need to delay punishment, do it in such a way that the child does not have a pleasurable intervening activity so that he or she has "forgotten" what he or she has just done wrong.

5. Avoid rewards after punishment. Such a situation may simply reinforce a behavioral pattern of negative behavior-punishment-reward. There is a story about the little girl who hit her little brother and was slapped by her mother. The little girl began to cry, and her mother felt so remorseful that she gave the child a cookie. Later on that same day, the little girl again hit her brother in plain sight of her shocked mother and then held out her hand to be hit (and presumably to be followed by another cookie).

6. Whenever possible, let the punishment be constructive. If a child has broken a window, let him or her earn the money to replace the glass.

7. When the child gets old enough to reason logically, try to have him or her construct a method of making compensation. If he or she has come home late three nights in a row ask what he or she can do to make up for "worrying his or her parents unnecessarily." Involve the child whenever possible in the type of punishment.

4. *We need to identify and extinguish our own negative behaviors.* It is admittedly difficult to reinforce children for what they are doing "right"—especially when they have learned to elicit our screaming, yelling, and nagging. In fact, one might say they have, in turn, conditioned us to behave negatively. So another step in the process is to discover what *they* are doing that is arousing *our* negative behavior. Once we have done that, we need to find ourselves new ways to respond to *their* behaviors. Marian Kessle's mother, for example, would need to identify and extinguish her constant "nagging" at Marian at the dinner table.

5. *When possible, use nonrewarding extinguishers of behaviors.* The example of the child who whines for attention when guests are present or when one is making a long-distance call, must be very common, indeed, for we have had many requests on how to handle this. Frankly, this is a difficult one to overcome, but we have found two ways which seem to get results, judging by the feedback of parents who have tried them.

If the child, who is whining for a cookie in the middle of a long-distance phone call, is young, simply grab hold of him (gently but quite firmly). Children do not like to be restricted in that way. But be cautioned: he may suddenly start to whine louder to try to get away. Tell him you will let go when he quiets down. He may refuse to, so keep on holding him even tighter than before until he does so. Admittedly, this will make it difficult for you to talk on the telephone, but shaping behavior needs forceful measures. When he does stop his whimpering and whining, let him go. If he starts up again, repeat the process. He will get the message if you make sure that you are holding him forcefully, it must not be an embrace that is comforting, and you must not let him get away. The next time the phone rings and he is in the room, give him a *silent* (and that is very important) warning with your finger to your mouth to be quiet. If he does stay still, reward him with a cookie after the phone call. A few repetitions of these procedures will probably affect the behavior change you want. Of course, it would be better if you could completely nonreinforce him, by putting him into a room by himself, but that is not always possible when the child is small and you do not want to lock the door.

If the child is older, say ten or so, and he has begun to exhibit that behavior of asking for things in front of neighbors and guests, there is a very quiet, but very effective method of dealing with this behavior. Ask the child to *stop* asking now; it will be discussed after your guests have departed. Explain to him, quite openly *in front of your guests* that this is not the kind of thing to ask for when guests are present. If this behavior does not embarrass the child, ask him to leave. If he refuses, then apologize *to the guests,* quite openly in front of the child and in earshot of the child, for his behavior. The reason this method has been found so effective is that children, like all of us, do not like to be embarrassed.

6. *Help the child learn new ways to behave.* Teaching children new ways in which to behave is a more effective technique, behavioral psychologists tell us, than punishing them for undesirable behavior. If they are exhibiting negative behavior, we may be able to discuss this behavior with them and how they might behave more constructively. Sometimes children are simply unaware that they are doing anything wrong, irritating, or hurtful. We can "role-play" new ways of behaving. If they have been running into the house and inter-

rupting your conversation with a guest (to follow up our previous example), act out with them how they might behave. Have them practice coming in quietly and standing until you give them the nod to speak. Have them practice saying to the guest: "Hello, Mrs. Smith. Mom, can I speak to you about something?" Take part in the role-play situation yourself: become the guest or the child. Watch the children giggle merrily as you role-play immature and rude behaviors. If, the next time you have guests, they perform better (it does not have to be perfect), make sure you let them know you were aware of their improved behavior. Let them feel good about their efforts—that is the best reinforcer.

If you have two or more children, get all the children into the role-playing (all who are old enough to participate). The younger ones will learn much by just watching. Not only does it become a kind of fun game, the older siblings also will act as your reinforcing or punishing agents when the child forgets his newly learned behavior. They may admonish the child in front of you, guests and all, or they may volunteer at the table, "Johnny forgot his manners today when Mrs. Jones came over and you were on the telephone." Johnny may well sulk at that point but take no notice of his sulking: simply say, "Yes, I am aware of that. Johnny, can you remember your manners next time?" He may growl a "yes," he may even say "no"; again, take no notice. In all likelihood, he will not want to be the subject of his sibling's tattling again.

7. *Provide token rewards based on the child's age and interests.* We advise this particularly for the classroom teacher who has been yelling at a problem child to no avail and who now is desperate to find other methods to control his behavior. This will take some doing, and the case history method *will* be of advantage here. Talk to Johnny's parents and to his other former teachers, to find out what some of his interests are. And, of course, talk to Johnny himself. (We suggest talking to other adults who have known him, because Johnny may not be able to verbalize what he likes to do, or he may scoff at your attempts to "motivate" him.) When you have discovered something that he likes, follow it up in some way. For example, if he likes fooling around with model cars, bring in a model car, not a completely built one, but one that he must assemble. Tell him that for every three points he earns by good behavior (and make sure that you explain just what that good behavior is, like not talking for fifteen minutes or by raising his hand first when he wants to speak), he will earn a token. Behavioral psychologists call that *token economy*. When he has earned so many points (or actual tokens, like chips) he may spend, say, twenty minutes working on the model car.

A word of caution here. We are making this sound very simple—it may even sound rather simple-minded. In actuality, it will take much ingenious analysis on the part of the teacher to make it work. But work it will, for the authors have, in consulting with school teachers, seen it work. It becomes more effective if Johnny is not the only child in the class given token economies. Every child can become a part of this game. A young school psychologist, under our supervision, once, much to our astonishment, transformed a whole class of rowdy children in only a few weeks. What he did was make a list of all the children and, in class discussion with the teacher and students, listed desirable behaviors for every child in the class, even the "good ones" (who tended to dominate every class discussion). Every Friday afternoon he came into the class for about fifteen minutes and, again in consultation with the students and teacher, gave out small token rewards for the children who had improved in their given behavioral tasks. The token rewards were not expensive, they consisted of baseball playing cards, pencil erasers, free store calendars, and other inexpensive or free items. The teacher was very glad to see the young psychologist and his visits added to the Friday afternoon activities when it is sometimes difficult to keep students occupied with school work.

deconditioning and reconditioning as a therapeutic approach

In Chapter 4, we discussed how anxiety can make us tense and produce physical symptoms. In fact, physicians have estimated that upward of 50 percent of all the symptoms of persons who come to their office are the result of emotional problems rather than because of some dysfunction of the body itself. Some decades ago, an American physician, Edmund Jacobson, proposed a method of relaxation for his patients, which proved to be more effective than medicine was.

Edmund Jacobson's Progressive Relaxation

Jacobson hypothesized that since anxiety and stress increase muscular tensions, his patients could be relieved of many of their physical *conditioned tensions.*

He called his approach *progressive relaxation,* a series of exercises that his patients could use to relax their tensions and anxieties.[10]

Jacobson reported that correct application of his method, in which patients were taught to discover their tension patterns and then to exercise what he called self-operations control, produced the following results:

1. Patients began to recognize and understand who they were and, in particular, to recognize and find undue tensions in moments of stress.
2. They learned to relax in moments of stress.
3. They tended to become less worrisome, less hypochondriacal, and less dependent on others (such as physicians) for relief of stress.
4. Patients began not only to diminish their tendency to be hyperirritable and emotionally overexcited, they also replaced their overcharged life styles with calmer attitudes toward their problems.
5. They slept better, were able to avoid fatigue, were generally healthier in that they had better digestion, better elimination, better sleeping habits, and less hypertension (high blood pressure).
6. They became more objective about themselves and the stimulation from their environment, so they were not so greatly affected by stress and little irritations of daily life.

Jacobson's *progressive relaxation* method was a new approach in medicine and, like many new ideas and concepts, was not immediately accepted — particularly by his own profession. His popularity, then, is because of other workers in the field of human relations who began to investigate his approach, which relies not on medicine but on conscious physical relaxation of muscular controls. Since the method is relatively easy to learn, we summarize it here for those who want to try it out for themselves.

The instructions include procedures for gradually relaxing various parts of the body. When we are tense, we then tighten our muscles and thereby interfere with the natural operations of our muscular and nervous systems. Tense muscles increase not only one's sense of fatigue, but also the wear and tear on one's body (remember Selye's stress syndrome, discussed in chapter 4). Thus, tension decreases our efficiency and our capacity to handle the current stressful situation. (It very likely also hastens the aging process.) When we begin to relax muscles, the nerves which are embedded in the muscles also begin to relax, and eventually the entire nervous system and brain relaxes so that we can face the present conflict in a more relaxed manner. That is the basic thesis of Jacobson's theory.

The following is a brief description of Jacobson's method:

1. The person is instructed to sit or lie down on a couch — the prone position is preferable — in a private place with the understanding there is to be no interruption for at least one hour. Arms rest at the sides of the body and the legs are uncrossed. Eyes are open for the first three or four minutes, and then the person gradually closes his eyes. He does not open his eyes again even to look at the clock, for with closed eyes the person is better able to monitor his physical reactions.

2. After three or four minutes with eyes closed, the person bends his left arm at the wrist smoothly and steadily. If he feels a tightness in the forearm, this is a signal of tension, exactly what it feels like, so he can recognize all such signals in his daily life. The important strain to notice is *not* the one at the wrist. After he identifies the wrist strain, he is instructed to observe the much more delicate strain in his left forearm which is the *result* of his wrist action. This delicate strain in the left forearm Jacobson calls *control sensation*. It is these control sensations all over the body that Jacobson wants the person to recognize. Once the person gets in touch with the various control sensations in the various parts of his body, he learns how to relax each particular muscle.

3. *Going negative.* After the person has had a chance to identify the control sensation in his left forearm by raising and lowering his left wrist several times (which is called *going positive*), Jacobson instructs the person to *go negative* — that is, to let his wrist lie flat down and to relax his upper arm. But going negative is not just relaxing, it is an act of will to let go of the residual tension in the muscles of the left forearm.

This *going negative* may be a difficult thing for the person to learn because we tend to live so tensed up most of the time. Furthermore, there is residual tension in our muscles even when they are normally relaxed. Therefore, going negative is a much more concerted effort of relaxing than normal relaxing. Doing away with even small amounts of normal residual tension is the whole purpose of progressive relaxation, and, for this reason, it is a kind of relaxation most people have to *learn* to do.

From the authors' experiences with Jacobson's method, *going negative* (eliminating residual muscle tension) is a process of going so limp that all control over the physical universe is released and with it our cares and problems. There is even a feeling of floating which is quite unlike normal relaxation in which there is still some muscular tension present. Why do we not learn to relax so completely if it is simply the process of allowing our residual tensions to dissipate from our muscles? Here is Jacobson's reply:

To relax tension is the easiest thing in the world, for it requires just no work at all.
If so, why does not the nervous person do this easy thing? The answer is clear. The nervous person does things the hard way! He piles up his own nervous difficulties. The tense person has developed the habit of being tense. From habit, he fails to relax.
If you are a nervous person, it is time now for you to face the facts. It is easy to relax. You may be solving problems all day long and may be loath to give this up. Having realized this clearly (step 1), find the tensions (step 2) and go negative (step 3).
At this early stage of your training, you are nervous, anxious or disturbed, see what you are doing with your arms! Look for the tensions there! See what you are trying to do with your arms. Then proceed to go negative.[11]

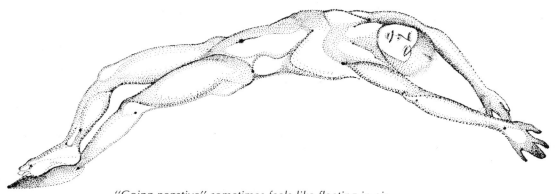

"Going negative" sometimes feels like floating in air.

4. Steps 1, 2, and 3 focus on tensions in the upper left arm. Step 4 is oriented toward finding the tension control sensations in the various parts of the body and eliminating them. Box B lists the remaining instructions in outline form.

By following carefully the directions in steps 1, 2, 3, and 4 and the chart in Box B, you will find yourself beginning to feel relaxed and more comfortable rather quickly—that is, if you practice the method every day and follow the instructions as they are given.

The relaxation program we have discussed so far is not the end of the method but, rather, the beginning of tension awareness. The next step is to take what you have learned from the couch sessions and to begin studying the tensions which build up as you go through your daily routines. Here is where the payoff is. For example, when you discover a tension beginning to build up somewhere in your body, give yourself the instruction, *"Go negative* for a few minutes!"* With practice, you will eventually be able to do just that—anywhere, anytime. You will then have learned to let go of the situation which is calling forth your bodily tension reaction and be more capable of dealing with what is happening to you in your present environment.

Tightening as a Way of Eliminating Tension: Perls

Frederick Perls, whom we discussed in a previous chapter, had his own variation of this relaxation method.[12] It differs somewhat from Jacobson's approach in that when a person felt tense, Perls advised him not to try to relax but to do just the opposite—*to tense the whole body.* He told the person to tighten every muscle: his facial muscles, his fists, his legs, his abdomen and buttocks—even to crouch, if need be, and get his whole body involved in the tightening-up process.

When the tension reached a peak—by then the person is sometimes shaking and trembling as he sustains the tension experience—he was instructed, "Now let go of your tension!" In Perls's approach, the person repeats this procedure several times until he is able to let go of his tensing. (If you practice this method for yourself, you will know for certain when the tension is dissolved—your breathing will begin to

Box B
Progressive Relaxation Procedure
  adapted from Edmund Jacobson, Progressive Relaxation,
  2nd ed. (Chicago: University of Chicago Press, 1938)

PART OF THE BODY	PROCEDURE TO IDENTIFY CONTROL SENSATIONS
Upper forearm	By raising and lowering the left wrist slowly several times
Upper front arm	By bending elbow several times about 35 degrees, which is felt in the biceps
Back of upper arm	By pressing arm down on two books
Front of lower leg	By bending foot up
Calf	By extending foot
Back of thigh	By bending knee back so that shoe is near but not touching the floor
Front thigh	By raising and lowering lef off and on couch
Abdomen toward the back and hip	By raising knee and bending at hip
Buttocks	By lying on two books and pressing lower thigh on them
Front part of abdomen	By pulling in stomach and diaphragm
Back, along spine	By arching back *up*
Chest	By deep breathing
Back, between shoulder blades	By bending shoulder back
Front chest	By lifting each arm one at a time forward and holding it over the chest
Top of shoulders and neck	By elevating the shoulders
Neck	By bending the head back, then down toward the chin, and to the left and right
Eyes	By raising the eyebrows, wrinkling the forehead, frowning, squeezing the eyes tightly shut, then looking in all directions
Speech region	By closing jaws firmly and then opening them, showing teeth as if in a smile and then pouting, protruding the tongue, pulling it back again interspersed with periods of relaxation (going negative)

operate consciously again, and you will know what it is to breathe with pleasure!) The *isometric exercises* which were popular a few years ago work on the same basis as Perls's method does. They are said also to supply lost muscle tone to the body and, in that way, to eliminate excess fat and flabbiness.

Wolpe and the Conditioning Therapies*

Joseph Wolpe is a physician who has been able to integrate the teachings of Pavlov, Jacobson, the learning theorists, and medical psychiatry into a modest but significant contribution to personality theory — modest in that Wolpe has chosen to study *one* phenomenon, namely, overt fears and phobias.[13]

To understand Wolpe's work, let us illustrate it with a case of extreme fear (or phobia). Let us take a cat first, rather than a person, and assume that we condition the cat to be afraid of a certain cage in a certain room. In other words, we turn a neutral stimulus into a negative stimulus (or learning) which says *FEAR* to the cat everytime the cat sees the cage. It is very easy to condition such a phobic response into a cat. All we need to do is put the cat in the cage a few times and shock it with electricity, and it will soon develop the pronounced stress response called *fear:* it fears the cage because this is where it experienced pain. If we place it in the cage again without shocking it the cat still will show the same symptoms of stress: it will "freeze" and exhibit "escape behavior" and do this many times before the symptoms begin to diminish. In fact, they may never diminish!

When a living organism (human or animal) is extremely fearful, it will ordinarily refrain from certain behaviors, such as eating. One has to be in some state of relaxation in order to eat. (Some humans seem to act in contradiction to this rule, but we cannot go into that curious behavior right now.) To return to the conditioned cat who has been shocked in the cage, Wolpe discovered that the cat would not eat, even when it was extremely hungry, if it even saw the cage. It would back away from the cage and arch its back, and its fur and tail would be standing on end. Wolpe decided from this piece of evidence that fear and eating are *antagonistic behaviors.*

If we take this conditioned cat and feed it in the same room, but

---

*Wolpe said that the experience of deep relaxation he has been able to engender with his approach is the experience of tingling, numbness, and warmth (personal communication, 1973). He said that these sensations arise when the person is relaxing that particular portion of the body he has so far kept under tension. This correlates with the sensory phenomena reported by persons in the beginning stages of what has been called *meditation*, or in the beginning state in yoga therapy.

first take away the cage, the cat will eventually begin to eat. When it is eating once again on a relatively fear-freeschedule, we can eventually and quietly bring the cage back into the room and place it in the far corner. The cat may then eat cautiously, periodically stopping to check out its environment ("to make sure it is safe"). From then on it is only a matter of time, patience, and sensitivity to the cat's level of fear for the experimenter to decondition the cat's fear of the cage, so that all of the original fear responses are eliminated. While the cat is eating, the cage is brought closer and closer to the cat until it can eat right next to the cage! That is the reconditioning process. We can say that it has been reconditioned *not to fear* the cage by encouraging behavior *antagonistic to the fear response* — that is, by encouraging it to eat. Wolpe put it this way *"If a response inhibitory of anxiety can be made to occur in the presence of the anxiety-evoking stimuli, it will weaken the bond between these stimuli and anxiety.* Because of that belief, Wolpe has the patient work on his anxiety *situations* and *symptoms,* rather than spending time talking about the *causes* of this anxiety as is the more usual approach in the classic "talking therapies."

Working on one anxiety situation and one symptom at a time, Wolpe's patients learn to identify *their specific symptoms of anxiety,* just as Jacobson enabled his patients to learn to identify their control sensations. Box C lists some of the many symptoms of anxiety. "Pure

Box C
Common symptoms of anxiety

Headache	Tenseness of body	Desire to run away
Excessive sneezing	muscle cramps	Tic in eye or elsewhere
Sighing (excessive)	Nervous cough	Muscle spasms
Overeating	Stuttering	Prolonged fatigue,
Not being able to eat	Mouth noises (like	weariness, listlessness
Chain smoking	tongue clucking)	Clammy hands
Insomnia	Talking too much	Biting lip
Nightmares	Unable to talk	Feeling cold frequently
Stomach cramps	Talking too fast	Hyperactivity
Diarrhea	Lump in the throat	Sleeping ten to twelve
Constipation	Dependence on drugs	hours a day
Nausea	Excessive perspiration	Vomiting or frequent
Butterflies in stomach	Blushing	queasy stomach,
Feeling faint	Fingernail biting	heartburn
Stroking beard or	Leg wagging	Heart palpitations
mustache	Rocking back and forth	Specific phobias
Hair twirling, pulling,	Gritting teeth	Clenched fists
or tossing		Feelings of choking or
		not being able to
		breathe

anxiety" is an unmistakable phenomenon: it clutches you in such a way that you unmistakably know something is happening that demands your total attention. But pure anxiety is such an exceedingly unpleasant experience for most of us that we begin to physically defend ourselves against it via defense mechanisms.

A person therefore needs to "get into" his or her feelings of anxiety and to acknowledge them. Once this first step is accomplished by the patient, Wolpe has a three-step method for deconditioning the person's fear *in a particular situation.* Suppose, for example, a man was once in a severe automobile accident in which he was badly shaken up, so much so that he now has a phobia about riding in a car — the kind of queasy feeling some people get when they contemplate flying from New York to Chicago in an airplane. The person may even be all right until he gets into a car and then becomes so full of fear he has to get out of the car immediately. That is what a car phobia, or a plane phobia, or any other kind of phobia is: a "gut reaction" so unpleasant that the afflicted person has to flee from the situation. Wolpe's *systematic desensitization method* attempts to deal with just these kinds of catastrophic fear reactions. In the case of the car phobia, this three-step method would be approximately as follows:

1. The therapist would first have the person identify all the situations associated with automobiles which call forth his anxiety-fear response — for example, the picture of an automobile, the smell of gasoline, and so on. Wolpe believed the person needs to identify at least twelve to fifteen such situations; these fear responses are then ranked in order, from the response that calls forth the highest level of anxiety to the one which is least fearsome.
2. The therapist now gives the person training in progressive relaxation without mentioning the car phobia, and the training continues until the person can relax readily and easily on command. That completes step 2.
3. The therapist now has the person examine the list of anxiety-evoking stimuli, and the actual desensitization method begins. Beginning with the least anxiety-provoking stimulus (for example, a picture of a parked car), the person is instructed to concentrate on visualizing that stimulus until he begins to feel his anxiety level for a few seconds. After a brief rest, the therapist now repeats the relaxation instructions and then reintroduces the same car stimulus. This procedure is repeated over and over until the person can visualize the parked car and still remain relaxed and anxiety free.

   Once the person can visualize the parked car and remain emotionally detached from the stimulus, the therapist now introduces the next, more anxiety-evoking stimulus from the list compiled in step 1. The same process of relaxation and concentration is used until this stimulus also becomes anxiety free. This continues up the scale of the person's fears until he can finally visualize his most anxiety-evoking fantasy (riding in the car in which he was hurt) and still remain calm, relaxed, and unattached to the stimulus. At that point, Wolpe said, he is free of his phobic symptom.

Obviously, all the fantasizing in the world would be of little use if there were not some payoff, tangible results which the person can use in his or her daily living. For example, can the car-phobic person who has gone through the visual desensitization procedure actually get into a car again and drive away anxiety-free—that is, without anxiety overwhelming him? Wolpe reported just such successful results with his therapy. In fact, Wolpe claimed some extraordinary cures. One of these is helping young persons with homosexual leanings to overcome their aversion to heterosexual coitus and to participate in intimate relations with persons of the opposite sex. Whether or not Wolpe's patient-clients actually achieved this, his approach has proved an effective approach in many extremely phobic areas.

Incidentally, it may come as a relief to some of our readers who are timid drivers, that one of the most prevalent problems Wolpe and his associates encounter in their clinic is a phobia about driving on the California freeways.

applications and coping techniques

We have emphasized how much of our present reality has been conditioned by forces beyond our control. These same facts of conditioning, however, can be used to our advantage if we have the wit to apply the laws of association in constructive ways. First, however, we need to discover how our conditioned responses have influenced our lives, so let us begin there.

1. Become Aware of Your Unquestioned Assumptions about Yourself.

It sometimes is startling to therapists to hear clients discuss themselves in broad generalizations. For example, we may hear them call themselves "dumb" or "subject to colds" or just being "naturally fat," as if it were irrevocably engraved in concrete, never to be changed. These beliefs about ourselves have become so much a part of us that we do not realize that we can be anything but how we always have perceived ourselves. These negative aspects of ourselves seem to us to be the "givens" of our existence. As long as we maintain these beliefs, they will emerge as self-fulfilling prophecies. It is as though we say to ourselves, "This is the way it has always been and so it must be for the rest of our lives," a conditioned, attitudinal "set." Thus we program our behaviors in the same rut year after year.

The first step in changing our self-programming is to become aware of our assumptions about ourselves. We need to discover what and how we limit our functioning, because we believe that we cannot change or that we have no alternative choices. We then need to decide what in ourselves we would like to change (either in ourselves or in our living conditions). The first step always is awareness.

2. Formulate an Effective Plan to Shape Your Behavior.

Wishful thinking does not get us where we want to go. We need now to formulate a precise goal of behavior. To draw from a real situation many of us have experienced, suppose you are having difficulty in math. There you are in class feeling rather stupid. Everyone around you seems to be understanding it, which only makes your feelings even worse. At this point, your years of feeling stupid will weigh heavily on you, to the point at which you may feel tempted to drop the course.

If these are your feelings and you are not past the drop-point in the course, dropping the course may be the "smartest" thing you can do. "He who fights and runs away, lives to fight another day." Besides, if you have taken chapter 4 seriously, you may be trying to eliminate the unnecessary stress in your life and at this point, your math course may be overstressful. There is no use attempting the impossible, or making your life needlessly difficult. But suppose that it is the beginning of the term, and your personal life is going easily. At this point, nothing is impossible. Say to yourself, "Well, I may never be a whizz in math, but I don't have to be a failure. After all, my feelings of failure stem from experiences when I was in third grade (or first grade or high school). But I'm older now, and I don't have to accept my feelings of insecurity about math in the same way as I did when I was a child. I can appreciate that I am fearful in this situation because of my years of conditioning, but if Wolpe could help phobias in people, I can help the phobia in myself." Think of your fear of math as a phobia, pure and simple.

Having decided you want to make a change in your math behavior, you now need to formulate a specific plan of action. For example, to continue with our math phobia, you may say to yourself "I'm not getting this by myself so I need help." There is nothing wrong with getting help. The mark of the successful executive is the ability to utilize all available resources. Have you ever noticed in your classrooms that it is generally the brighter students who ask the questions? The poorer students are those who keep their mouths closed and their questions to themselves because they are afraid of revealing what they do not know. So, start by being one of the smarter students and look around for someone who can answer your questions. It may be the teacher, it may be a student assistant, or there may be a special math lab in your college. If help is not available here, hire a math tutor!

This suggestion may nettle you since you believe yourself already to be overburdened financially. But you must consider what price failure might be. When you have a toothache, you find money for the dentist. When you are sick, somehow you find money for the physician. Your math functioning is sick, so go find a tutor.

Actually he or she is your behavior therapist. A person who is being paid to tutor you in math will be unbelievably patient. Whatever time you have with him or her is yours and yours alone. He or she is not trying to push you out of the office because of work to do. The math tutor is not trying to make you feel even more stupid but wants to help you. Furthermore, because he or she stays with you for every minute of that hour or half-hour, the tutor is watching you go through the processes and steps of the problem and will stop you as soon as you begin to make a mistake. In other words, he or she will be shaping your behavior in small, successful, successive steps. The tutor's immediate feedback and reinforcement of your successes will increase the probability of right answers in the future. You can relax with a tutor, and with a relaxed state of mind, you can begin to function better.

3. As You Build Your Desired Behavior Patterns, Eliminate Inappropriate Stimuli.

The math tutor is only one of the ways to change your phobic behavior about math. The next step is to plot out some specific time and place for your own studying and homework habits. Studying must become habitual like brushing your teeth. Self-discipline is simply built-up habits. Nothing interferes with those studying habits.

The first step in building up your studying habits is to set a specific time for them. Decide ahead of time *when* you are going to study. Make it so regular that when the appointed time comes to study you have a mental set that it is "time for studying," just as you automatically brush your teeth in the morning. Give yourself reinforcers for the study time: for example, devote one and a half hours to studying and then reward yourself for having done so by doing something you like to do, say, make a telephone call or watch your favorite TV program, or go back to your favorite "whodunit."

Before you get this far, you need to be very careful how you shape your studying behavior. Do not put yourself into situations for which you have learned other conditioned responses to the stimuli in your studying environment. For example, suppose you sit down at the kitchen table. Now the kitchen table has become a conditioned stimulus for the conditioned response of *eating*. No sooner will you sit there, then you may begin to think about *food*. So, although you finished eating only forty-five minutes before, you may find yourself standing in front of the refrigerator looking for that piece of pie left over from dinner.

Thirty minutes later, you decide to be more comfortable while studying (you are feeling a little groggy with so much food inside you) so you sit down in your favorite comfortable chair, from which you usually watch television. (In other words, that chair is the conditioned stimulus for the conditioned response, TV viewing.) You automatically reach for the television guide and without even being aware of it, you have been seduced into watching your favorite program.

It is now 11 o'clock. You are feeling a little sheepish about wasting the evening. Oh, well, you say to yourself, you can at least read the assigned chapter, even if you have to skip the math homework for tonight. So you resolutely remove yourself from the other people in the environment and seek the privacy of your own room. You prop up your pillows, flop down on the bed, open the text book and very soon . . .

You are asleep! The bed is a conditioned stimulus for sleeping, and you have been sleeping on it all your life. So much for studying.

The moral of the story is that you need to find a place to study that does not arouse inappropriate conditioned responses like eating, television viewing, or sleeping.

4. Create a Special Environment that Arouses the Conditioned Responses You Want.

Since conditioning can work to our advantage as well as to our disadvantage, you can use those same laws of conditioning to arouse a mental set to study. What you need, of course, is a place *where you do nothing but study*. After only a few days of this conditioning (that is, the pairing of the place to study with actual studying), you will have an automatic set toward the behavior desired. This study area need not be a separate room or study, although that is ideal. Most students just do not have that kind of space. A desk is fine, if it is not used for anything else, and a sign that tells others not to disturb you while you are sitting there and studying.

We can be quite dogmatic about this suggestion. It works! Many students actually have come back to tell us so. If you take it seriously, you are on your way to becoming a bona fide student.

5. Finally, Do Not Try to Change too Many Things in Your Life at Once: One Thing at a Time.

Trying to make too many changes in your life at once is a sure way to defeat yourself. If you set too high goals, you are bound to fail, which will result in discouragement and the desire to give up everything.

In all probability, you have many years to live. You need to define both long-terms and short-term goals. But trying to attempt to do them all or begin them all at the same time is wasting your energy. We have only so much energy. Beginning something new requires special effort. Give your best energy to one new project at a time. When you feel yourself well into one project and acquiring competency in it, then you can start a new project. There is a Chinese saying that *A journey of a thousand miles begins with a single step*. All you need to do is get a clear picture of where you are going and then to take the first step.

increasing our awareness of the physical self

6

A character neurosis acts like body armor in that it is a buffer against the pain of contact with the outer world. Physical activity may be helpful in breaking through the armor.

I. Introduction: On the Interface of Knowledge and Speculation

    A. Wilhelm Reich and character armor
        1. Segmental arrangement of the character armor
            a. The occular ring
            b. The ear, nose, and mouth ring
            c. The neck and throat ring
            d. The chest ring
            e. The diaphragmatic ring
            f. The intestinal ring
            g. The pelvic ring
        2. Is there any validity to Reich's armor theory?
        3. Unlocking the body armor
    B. The need for a sensory-aware body
    C. Learning to be sensorily aware

II. The Basic Bodily Needs

    A. The need for air
    B. The need for food
        Fasting
    C. The need for water
    D. The need for rest and sleep
    E. The need to stay in touch with pain signals
    F. The sexual needs
    G. Other kinds of needs

III. Psychobiological Awareness: Other Approaches

    A. Yoga
    B. Massage
    C. The relevance of any physical activity to body-mind integration
    D. Meditation
        Scientific investigation of meditation
    E. Biofeedback techniques

IV. Applications and Coping Techniques

introduction: on the interface of knowledge and speculation

In the last chapter we described the process of conditioning, how the forces of conditioning pervade our lives, and some of the effects of our conditioning. We concluded with some ways that conditioning, deconditioning, or reconditioning have been used to our advantage in handling anxiety. We also discussed conditioning as effecting change in ourselves. That chapter closely followed what are sometimes called the more rigorous aspects of psychological knowledge. Most of the material discussed has been fairly well substantiated by scientific demonstration, clinical observation, and clinical treatment.

In this chapter, we will go farther afield, into speculative psychology. We shall discuss theoretical matters that fascinate many of us, but we ask you to remember that many of these theories have yet to receive rigorous laboratory testing. We offer them because we believe it is as enlightening to consider the farther reaches of human thinking, as it is to accept the facts and laws of demonstrated experiments. Some of these ideas may seem, at first, to be radical, but remember that Freud's most accepted contributions to our current understanding of human personality also once seemed absurd even to his own medical profession. For years Carl Jung was ignored by American psychologists, and only now is he beginning to get the recognition he deserves.

If your interest is simply to advance your own growth, you may find something of value in the pages to follow — some methods or ideas which seem particularly suited to your present situation and life stage.

We will start this chapter with a discussion of Wilhelm Reich's work. Toward the end of his life, Reich had considerable political trouble, and there was some question also of his own emotional balance. For these reasons, perhaps, Reich's theories have not gained much attention except through his theoretical heirs, those who work in the area called *bioenergetics*.

Wilhelm Reich and Character Armor

Reich had practiced for many years the original Freudian methods of free-association therapy with considerable success. He noticed, however, that there are certain patterns of personality which do not profit from classical psychoanalysis, patterns of behavior which seemed to him designed to keep the person from becoming *aware of himself or herself, by deadening his or her bodily awareness.* Further investigation seemed to Reich to indicate that this deadening of physical awareness is accomplished by habitual *tensing of the muscles,* in much the same way people tense their muscles when they know they are going to get an injection—stiffening to ward off the pain!

Reich's theory is that certain persons have experienced so much psychological pain that they have become accustomed to walking, eating, breathing, and working with tensed-up muscles—as if to ward off pain (or any kind of stimuli from their environment). Certain parts of their body become stiff and hard from muscular tension, as if to provide some sort of psychic armor. A person with such "character armor" has a "character neurosis," which, said Reich, is much harder to treat than an "anxiety neurosis" is. Because anxiety neuroses are characterized by uncomfortable symptoms—headaches, butterflies in the stomach, flushes, depression, stuttering and the like—the person who has these symptoms is glad to get rid of them. The symptoms of a character neurosis, however, are *not painful* to the person—in fact, they *prevent* pain (or any sensation, for that matter) from entering into one's consciousness. Such persons do not want to give up the defending operation; it fits them too well, prevents pain, and wards off awareness. But in deadening themselves to the experience of anxiety, they also deaden and diminish their capacity for many other kinds of experience: awareness, free movement, free expression. In other words, their character not only protects them from imagined threat but also effectively prevents further growth.[1]

SEGMENTAL ARRANGEMENT OF THE CHARACTER ARMOR. Since we inhibit and suppress our emotions by tensing particular muscles, it is relatively easy for the discerning eye to see where a person's blocks are, according to Reich. Whereas the person who is fully integrated expresses himself or herself in coordinated, graceful, and flowing movements, a person with a character neurosis exhibits a certain lack of coordination in his or her movements, a stiffness where the body has become armored.

According to Reich, the body from the top of the skull to the base of the spine may be divided into seven segmental "rings." If one of these rings becomes armored, there results a characteristic stiffness, a certain "deadness" to feelings in that area and also (and most important) certain organic dysfunctions. These seven rings are distributed at various points of the torso, from the pelvis to the head as follows:

The Occular Ring.   The occular ring surrounds the head in the area of the eyes. If the occular ring has become armored, the person sometimes will seem to have a rigid face mask; the eyes, said Reich, will be "cold" and staring. The rest of the face may smile, but the eyes will remain stiff and unsmiling. Deadening in the occular ring also will result in a dysfunction of those areas. These persons may suffer eye strain, sties, and headaches centered on the eye area and on the sinuses.

The Ear, Nose, and Mouth Ring.   Persons who have deadened this part of the face may be very unsmiling. Their jaws will be tight, and they may grit their teeth. Hard lines may form around the mouth. If there is a deadening of this part of the body, these persons may suffer from infected sinuses, hay fever, and painful infections of the middle ear. They may have occasional toothaches and gum decay, and occasionally may be afflicted by cold sores on the lips or in the mouth.

The Neck and Throat Ring.   An armoring of this part of the body may produce sore throats or hoarseness. Other possibilities are vocal cord nodules or a *globus hystericus* (lump in the throat). Persons with this kind of armoring may look as if they have stiff necks, and they find it difficult to turn their heads easily from side to side.

The Chest Ring.   The chest ring covers the entire area from the neck to the diaphragm. Persons may have a caved-in chest, or, on the other hand, the chest may be pushed out, reminiscent of military bearing. At any rate, the chest is not flexible, and they may suffer from chest pains (real or imaginary), be vulnerable to pneumonia, tuberculosis, or emphysema. They may have asthmatic symptoms or general difficulty breathing.

The Diaphragmatic Ring.   The diaphragmatic ring covers the mid-torso. Persons who have armoring in this area may be subject to nausea or other stomach problems, including ulcers. They may have problems digesting food and need to vomit occassionally or suffer from "acid stomach."

The Intestinal Ring.   Persons with an intestinal ring may suffer from cramps, from any of the diseases connected with the vital organs in that area, including diseases of the kidneys, liver, and pancreas. Reich said that although this area was one of the most vulnerable to affliction, it also is one of the easiest to "unlock." Problems associated with this area are diarrhea, constipation, flatulence, and cramps.

The Pelvic Ring.   The pelvic ring is at the very bottom of the torso. People who have an armored pelvic ring will be vulnerable to the diseases of the sexual organs: menstrual cramps, problems with the uterus for women, and prostate gland cancer for men. Women may also be vulnerable to cancer of the uterus. Both men and women may also be afflicted with sexual problems, such as frigidity, impotence, or satyriasis.

IS THERE ANY VALIDITY TO REICH'S ARMOR THEORY?   As yet, we simply cannot give a definite yes or no to that question. We still are in the area of speculation. But we can consider some of the evidence that suggests this kind of armoring is possible. You will recall, from chapter 4, that hysterical conversion entails a deadening of a part of the body, "psychological" in origin since no known neurological dysfunction can account for the sensory numbness or muscular paralysis. You will recall also that hysteria blindness and hysterical deafness already are clinically documented. We know also that if we remain tense (so that our muscles are in a continual state of contraction), we will block off our feelings. For example, if a child knows it is about to get a spanking, the child automatically tenses up its buttocks to defend against pain. If a physician is about to plunge a hypodermic needle into our arm, even the bravest and best of us will tighten up to defend against the anticipated pain.

Both Reich and Jacobson (like so many other personality and social theorists) maintained that we live in very tense times and that we have developed defensive postures throughout our bodies. If that is so, then we have developed extremely armored bodies. Perhaps that is why we feel so relaxed and "alive" after a day of quiet fishing or after a day on the beach when we have loosened some of our armored tension. To help us minimize our bodily tension when we are not "on holiday," Jacobson devised a method to enable the person to relax deeply (or "let go," as he called it). Reich also had a method to enable the person to "unlock" the body armor. Reich's method, however is a much more physically active procedure.

UNLOCKING THE BODY ARMOR. To unlock the occular ring, Reich suggested that we use eye exercises: closing them tightly and opening them as wide as possible, frowning, looking around in all directions as physicians frequently advise to release tension, and finally "rolling the eyes." To unlock the lower half of the face, we can grimace and make faces (as children frequently do), stretch the mouth, stick out the tongue and curl it, and crinkle the nose. Unlocking the throat area involves more painful types of exercises, such as screaming, yelling, gagging, swallowing hard, stretching the neck, and turning the head from side to side. To unlock the chest, Reich suggested moving the shoulders around and up and down, as well as daily deep breathing. There are many exercises to aid the stomach and intestinal rings: forward and back bends, flipping the belly in and out (a yoga asana), and even belly dancing. Unlocking the pelvic area consists in imitating the bumps and grinds of the belly dancer.

The Need for a Sensory-Aware Body

Before we discuss other bodily approaches to personality integration, we would like to consider the body as a sensing organism and its relationship to our mental and emotional processes. We arrive at our emotional and intellectual understandings by two main avenues: from within as the result of our biological signals (glands, nerves, hormones, muscles, etc.) and from without as the result of what we receive through our senses—eyes, ears, smell, taste, touch, and pain. The more open we are to all these stimuli whether from within or without, the more alert we will be to our internal and external environments and the better we can understand what is going on inside and outside us. Some of us are sensitive to these internal signals and external stimuli, but others of us have closed ourselves off to an extraordinary degree, we have limited our sensory awareness. It has been suggested that neurosis may actually be the "closing off" of internal and external

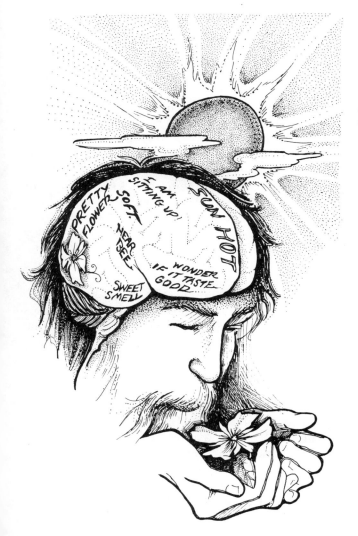

An integral part of personality integration is remaining open to, and aware of, internal and external experience: our feelings, our sensory data, our thoughts, and our motivations.

sensory awareness, and many of our therapies (like that of Reich) are designed to "bring us back to our senses!"[2] The person who has closed off bodily awareness and feelings seems to be saying, "I know that life may be kind of drab this way, but it is *safer*. I may not experience as much of the depths and heights that life can offer, but at least I can lay claim to less bother, less pain, less chaos, and unwelcome surprises!" This kind of emotional closing off has its physiological and intellectual correlates. The person who closes off bodily awareness is also closing off emotional and intellectual awareness. It is a two-way street. When we contrast the closed off person to the highly creative person, we discover that the highly creative person remains open to his or her bodily feelings and also to sensory experience. Abraham Maslow, who studied what he called "self-actualizing" persons noted that they allowed themselves full enjoyment of their physical senses: they ate well, slept well, were able to receive great satisfaction from loving sexual contact, and could appreciate the beauty of their world all their lives.[3] Such capacities require a body open to physical sensations and awareness.

A child is naturally spontaneous. It laughs, cries, is hungry, sleeps, or whatever from moment to moment. The young child lives in the here and now, and its world overflows with wonder. It is able to focus its attention on what is here and now. For that reason, its world is wonderful, full of wonder and excitement and aliveness. Is it in the nature of things that we must lose the excitement that we had as children?

Evidently not, for some persons never seem to lose the joyous appreciation of the moment. The artist and the poet somehow manage to hold on to the intensity of the *now* and the nearness of the *here*. Maslow and Rogers both found that their subjects had not lost their childlike ability to know joy in the present: to enjoy the scent of a flower, gain inspiration from music, see their wives and husbands as beautiful even after many years of marriage. Somehow their senses and perceptions do not become dulled to the moments of beauty that come and go so quickly.

Learning to be Sensorily Aware

What does it take to become more "alive" and more "sensing"? It means being aware of the body as a vibrating, pulsating, living, breathing, and perceiving organism. It means understanding some of our bodily needs for air and for food, understanding our "specialized" body hungers, and appreciating out need for sleep, rest, and recreation. It means recognizing the meaning of pain and other bodily symptoms that tell us all is not right. And it means developing our senses to their fullest capacity so that we can see, hear, taste, and experience all that life has to offer. It means taking care of our bodies and not abusing them with alcohol, cigarettes, drugs, and food, for all of these substances anesthetize our bodily feelings.

One of the great discoveries of psychobiology is that *emotions are bodily experiences*.[4] Fear, anxiety, anger, joy, and surprise all have their physiological correlates — changes in respiration, blood pressure, and salt, sugar, and hormonal levels.[5] All of these anesthetizers also have their consequent physiological correlates. When we abuse our bodies with toxic substances or when we neglect our bodies, we also are causing tissue and organ destruction.[6]

the basic bodily needs

It is good, then, to understand some of our basic bodily requirements so that we can keep ourselves in good working condition. People used to be fond of saying, "A sound mind in a sound body." We might add, "The sounder the body, the sounder the mind" and vice versa.

The Need for Air

Our most basic need as a living organism is for air (oxygen). This is a continuing need from conception to death. Without air, we die in short order. Without oxygen the cells of the body begin to die, even within a few minutes. If these cells are injured or die in the brain, there is a cerebral vascular attack (stroke), and there can be eventual paralysis and even sensory numbness to the body, coma, and death. Air is, therefore, a vital need of our well-being. Accidents leading to a lack of oxygen continue to kill miners, firefighters, caisson workers, and scuba divers. Babies can be asphyxiated at birth or suffer irreparable neural damage just from the lack of oxygen that can result from a prolonged and difficult labor. Our need for air is absolute, constant, and intense.

We probably are less aware of our need for air than for any of our other basic needs. It seems incredible that we scarcely pay attention to our breathing when we are living during what is surely one of the most "breath-taking" times in human evolution. Too many of us who live in a complex civilization breathe too often in a shallow way and too quickly: we do not give ourselves enough breathing room!

If this seems surprising, just compare for a moment your ability to sustain a single breath with someone who sings or acts — someone who

Pranayama, or breath control, is a yoga technique for psychological awareness.

has developed and trained his or her breathing apparatus. Our breathing, we soon find out, is much less well sustained, less deep, less even, and much more unbalanced.

How is it that civilized people in our times have developed this kind of shallow breathing? Psychoanalysts attribute this breathing behavior to our desire to avoid pain. Alexander Lowen, for example, noted that children seeking to avoid the pain of a spanking consciously hold their breath and tighten or "deaden" their bodies.[7] Has our civilization, then, become so painful for us that we have adopted this shallow breathing pattern in order to survive? Maybe so, but there are consequences. In tightening the diaphragm, one of the basic structures in the breathing apparatus, we begin a circular pattern of bodily desensitization to feelings and other bodily sensations, until we eventually live for much of the time on the edge of minor distress because of lack of oxygen. Lack of oxygen itself is one of the primary reasons for people's anxieties.

Frederick Perls, the first gestalt therapist, recognized our present inadequate breathing pattern as one of the several desensitization procedures on which modern people rely to avoid pain. Perls worked continually to help his patients and friends realize that they were not breathing adequately and that they held their breath in artificially, particularly in moments of anxiety. In other words, at precisely those times when they most needed an adequate supply of oxygen, they "forgot" to breathe. According to Perls, the experience of anxiety is related to the absence of an adequate oxygen supply in the body. The more stressful the moment is, the more people need to turn their attention to breathing. Indeed, in Perls's view, the so-called anxiety neurosis is an instance of chronic lack of breathing, and the first steps in resolving the neurosis are teaching people how to breathe well and fully again.[8]

It is never completely accidental when a particular emphasis or approach in psychology appears and becomes popular. Inadequate breathing patterns are to be found often in our contemporary society, and it follows that sooner or later someone is going to take note of that fact and to begin to prescribe for the difficulty. The gestalt therapy approach is one method of personality development which stresses the influence of breathing, and yoga is another. In the yoga view — and this is only one aspect of its comprehensive approach — calm, slow breathing itself deepens psychological awareness. This type of breathing is called *pranayama*, but the practice is never advised without a competent teacher. When we deal with breathing, we deal with life itself, and the consequences of tampering with this most basic bodily process could be extremely dangerous. Nevertheless, the practice of a few very simple, calm breaths daily does enable people to continue breathing adequately when anxiety threatens to overwhelm them.

The Need for Food

How do we know when we are hungry? Most of us would answer that question by saying "because of hunger pangs!" Research however has indicated that the sensation or "knowledge" of hunger does not depend solely on contractions of the stomach; other factors, such as blood, salt, and sugar levels, as well as emotional and physical factors, may also cause hunger. People may eat, not in response to hunger pangs, but just because they are tired, upset, or bored—or even when they are thirsty or cold instead. So the symptoms of experienced hunger are not limited to just hunger pangs. In one experiment demonstrating this phenomenon, animals without stomachs (their esophagus tubes were surgically connected to their intestines) still exhibited hunger behavior—in fact, just as strongly as control animals whose stomachs were left intact.

Obviously then, hunger stems from something besides contractions of the stomach. Yet many still hold to the myth that how we feel hunger is through hunger pangs. But given a list of other possible symptoms of hunger, people soon begin to identify (some for the first time in their lives) their own hunger-warning symptoms. Some persons, for example, get irritable and touchy, whereas others become more active (actually, hyperactive). Still others begin to feel drowsy and lightly sick; yet others begin to feel cool without realizing it. Of course, there are still those who never feel hunger at all—they know only that it is time to eat.

Changes in modern eating habits have had a lot to do with losing touch with hunger. For example, we consume *more* starch, *more* fat, and *more* protein than ever before. And we are getting fat on it all: fat from food intake and fat from our lack of exercise. Being overweight has become a nationwide problem in some industrialized societies, and in such cases dieting becomes a national pastime. Being overweight, we know now with some assurance, not only adds to the likelihood of heart problems but is also associated with diseases of the liver, kidneys, and other vital organs. Moreover, when we are overweight and have more bulk to carry around, we have less energy available to us for other pursuits and become tired more easily.

Stuffing ourselves with food makes us less responsive and less alert—anyone who has had the joy of a really full and delicious meal knows that! After a big meal, the processes of digestion divert so much blood away from other parts of the body (including the brain) that we are less capable of paying attention to the external world. We feel sluggish, apathetic, and unwilling to attend to anything other than digestion.

It is somewhat heartening to note that we are becoming conscious of the nonnutritive and toxic substances that we are taking into our bodies. We are beginning to realize how we have actually removed the most nourishing parts of grain kernels. We are beginning to examine how much refined sugar we are eating which has no nutritive value save calories, and which has harmful side effects. In one year

Obesity has become a national disease. A good dietary regime, together with physical exercise, can free us from this type of bodily armoring.

Americans ate less than a pound of sugar a century ago; we now consume over one hundred pounds of sugar for every man, woman, and child in the country. We are beginning to be aware of the toxic substances that some of us use to preserve and spice up our food. We are beginning to be concerned about the poisons we spray on crops, which we take into our systems along with the food. We finally are beginning to understand food as life energy, one which we must respect and appreciate if we are to be truly healthful people.[10]

FASTING.   Fasting (cutting down radically on the intake of fluids and solids) may well be a needed discipline for a person glutted with food and fat. Aside from a way of getting back in touch with the balance of bodily functions, fasting has been periodically recommended by religious communities as a means of searching for religious understanding and mystical communion. Fasting undoubtedly does sharpen the bodily senses, and it can trigger profound insights into the essence of oneself—that is, increase sensitivity to one's inner life and one's surroundings. One psychologist argues that fasting is a more natural avenue to an altered state of consciousness than drugs are.[11] This method of inducing altered states of consciousness has been practiced in many societies other than our own-including the Hindu, Zen, Judaic, Christian, and Islamic religions. The Indians of North and South America learned to fast as part of their traditional rites of passage, as did natives of other "primitive" societies. Since childhood, Americans have been fed the myth that a hearty breakfast is imperative for everyone. Actually, many people feel uncomfortable when they eat a large breakfast; they prefer to break their night fast later on in the day, after they have been up and around for a few hours. For others, eating is necessary in the morning just to be able to wake up. We do not recommend that anyone undertake a radical program of fasting except under the supervision of a qualified physician. The risks of tampering with one's accustomed dietary habits are great and may produce not a feeling of ease and growth but a profound physical crisis with equally serious psychological consequences.

The only myth here, of course, is that what is good for one is good for all. On the other hand, what we ask you to consider here is that we are *individually* different. Developing a more integrated personality in part requires that each of us discover how we differ in our physiology and psychology from others—in other words, find out what is best for ourselves and develop a therapeutic life style, provided, of course that life style harms no one else.

The Need for Water

In some respects, our need for water is more intense than our need for food. People can live for weeks, even months, without food, but a lack of water will cause them to lose consciousness within a few days and die soon after. Unlike hunger, whose symptoms tend to diminish after a time of fasting, thirst increases in intensity over time until the desire for water completely dominates a person's thinking, feeling, and perceptions: thirst eventually can drive a person literally "insane."

As with hunger, we know now that thirst depends on more than just the perception of dryness in the throat, mouth, and on the lips. Like hunger, thirst is triggered by an imbalance of chemical substances in the blood and by other hormonal-neuronal effectors. Our need for water is more easily appreciated when it is pointed out that more than 98 percent of our blood cells are composed of water. For example, our blood, lymph system, and the interior of our cell bodies all function in fluid balance. In addition, we give back water to the environment through sweat, tears, and urine. The intake of salt increases our need for water, as does warmth. In one sense, we may be land creatures, but we still need fluids to survive.

The Need for Rest and Sleep

Our need for periodic rest and sleep are other examples of the dynamic balance of the body. Although we still do not know too much about the physiological bases of fatigue or exactly why we need to spend approximately one-third of our life in sleep, we do know that the effects of sleeplessness can be devastating. For example, persons who go without sleep for long periods of time begin to exhibit a wide range of behaviors: lowered reaction time, poor judgment and confused thinking, hallucinations, and other symptoms that have been labeled "psychotic."[12]

It has been suggested that some of the symptoms of senility (disorganized thinking in elderly people) are due partly to their chronic insomnia. Worried (perhaps) by an awareness of approaching death, or kept awake because of physical aches and pains, elderly people often suffer from some form of sleep deprivation. When given sedatives that enable them to sleep, much of their pain and anxiety disappears, and there is marked improvement in their thinking and memory. Even adolescents and young adults who appear to be going through a similar form of "schizophrenic" episode may be acutally exhibiting the disorientation that occurs after weeks and weeks of intermittent sleeplessness caused by worry and anxiety.

Sleep disturbances seem to occur at certain life stages and in response to certain crises — failure in school, fear of being fired, illness of, or danger to, a loved one, financial pressure, disappointment and hurt in one's love life. We then may begin to suffer from insomnia because our daytime difficulties dominate our thoughts and, in truth, will not let us sleep. Or we may be afraid to go to sleep, to let go of our conscious controls and slip into unconsciousness. For some persons, sleep can be a frightening experience — when, for example, dreams keep getting more and more disturbing. Ironically, crisis periods in which we begin to lose sleep are the very times we need sleep even more than usual.[13]

The Need to Stay in Touch with Pain Signals

Pain (both psychological and physical) is a warning system: it informs us that all is not well within our internal universe. We have receptors for touch and pain, warmth and cold, proprioceptors, and the like throughout the whole body (inside and out) which can be compared to giant antennae bringing information that things are safe and well, or unsafe and not well. Lately, we have taken to anesthetizing this early warning system with drugs (aspirin, codeine, tranquilizers, psychedelic drugs, etc.). Such readiness to take drugs which are essentially painkillers and tension reducers results, however, not only in diminishing the experience of the pain itself but also in the more pertinent effect of taking our attention away from the causes of the pain. Pain is a signal not to be ignored, any more than the blinking red and yellow traffic lights which say "Stop!" "Slow Down!" "Proceed with caution!" "Yield!" Attention to all levels of our sensory awareness is one of the primary avenues to personality integration—which means that we need to learn to pay attention to our pain signals and to stay with those symptoms of our anxiety. This is a most difficult task, since the impulse to avoid pain is so instinctively fast that we hardly have time to focus on what is causing us pain before we run from it! Yet if we are able to focus in on this pain or that anxiety, the resulting awareness can tell us something about our current living.

The Sexual Needs

Sigmund Freud's initial psychological discoveries were made largely in the area of sexual repression. Freud was able to demonstrate, for example, that Viennese society for all its self-satisfaction, was largely a "sick" society—manifested, for example, by Victorian clothing, which was generally uncomfortably restrictive: a man's collar almost choked him, and a woman's corset was often so tightly laced that she "swooned." When Freud's Victorians went swimming, they did so in so many clothes that they seem now to us to have been fully dressed—

The Victorian era was sick insofar as bodily feelings were repressed, a tendency manifested by the fact that the body was kept hidden under strait-laced and voluminous clothing.

not only uncomfortable but dangerous! The Viennese Victorian era, Freud pointed out, was marked by suppression of sexual understanding and sensory awareness.

We know more today about the sexual nature of the human animal and therefore are freer in acknowledging the sexual side of our sensory reality. At least, we seem more enlightened than our Victorian predecessors were. Nevertheless, we are still incredibly naive about sex as an instinct, and sex as a socially learned attitude.

Part of that naïveté resides in the belief that our sexual responses are as instinctive as our other bodily needs are. This is not the case at all. Much of our sexuality is conditioned by our upbringing *and* by our cultural background *and* by our general state of health *and* by our personality type *and* by our emotional mood swings *and* by anything else that happens to be going on at the time — such as involvements with our job, upsets with family, and our professional endeavors.

Sexual maturation climaxes at puberty. At this time, the sexual glands begin to produce more actively the sexual hormones (estrogen and testosterone). Besides becoming increasingly interested in sexual matters, the young girl and boy go through many physiological changes labeled "secondary" sexual characteristics. In the male, these changes are an increase of muscular tonus, broadening of the chest; hair under the arms, on the face, in the pubic area, and elsewhere.

At the time of puberty, the vocal cords (which are not cords at all but membranes designed to prevent foreign particles from entering the lungs) double in length, thus providing the possibility of a lower speaking register. (Anyone with experience with stringed instruments will recognize the fact that the longer strings are those which produce the lower tones.) The vocal cords of girls also lengthen but not as much as boys' do. She undergoes some other physical changes. Her breasts develop, her hips round out, and her body adds additional adipose tissue to give her a generally more curved body form. She, too, develops pubic hair and hair elsewhere on her body.

The sexual urge of the young person becomes more pronounced, particularly in the young male. Indeed, he may have many erotic dreams, and nocturnal emissions are common among adolescents. The adolescent also may engage in masturbation, and it is fortunate that we are coming to understand that masturbation does not have terrible and dire consequences (as it was once believed). With the elimination of this superstition, masturbation is becoming more frequent among adolescent girls and women.[14] There seems, however, to be a difference in the sexual drives of men and women in terms of age. The male sexual drive is more intense than that of the female from adolescence to about twenty-five years of age, gradually diminishing thereafter; while a female's sexual drive starts more slowly and reaches a peak in the mid-thirties. This difference in age-related sexual drive may be a culturally determined factor, but it has been verified by much research. It would seem that, for real sexual compatibility, it would be better for older women to marry younger men than the other way around, as is the common practice in Western society.

Sexuality among humans is far more intricate, subtle and complex than it is among other life forms. Aldous Huxley called sexual behavior among lower life forms a "categorical imperative"[15] — there is very little choice in the mating and courtship of animals. If there is a receptive female animal, the male will copulate with her and that is that! Although there are fascinating stories of animals that mate for life, copulation among animals is a rather humdrum affair, and one observer of copulation between two baboons was rather surprised to note that the female baboon ate a banana during the whole affair.

The sexual act among humans varies according to the general aggressiveness or passivity of the female. Polynesian women tend to be much more active in their approach to men as compared to Western women. Western women, by and large, seem to require more courtship, affection, "romance," and sexual foreplay (preparation of the woman for coitus). Mangian women, on the other hand, are ready to engage in the sexual act without emotional or physical preparation and value a man who can achieve many orgasms in the sexual act. The Mangian man is not excited by the woman's breasts and buttocks as in Western society, but by the size, shape, and hair texture of her pubic mound.[16]

Western civilization has generally stereotyped the male and female sexual responses as predominantly aggressive, dominant, and assertive on the part of the male and more passive, responsive, and unassertive on the part of the female. But we are coming to understand this as a cultural role rather than as an instinctive role. There seems to be some indication that when women have played a generally secondary and passive role in the social-cultural-political world of a society, the woman has been passive in her sexual responses; when the woman has had a more equal social status, she also has been more sexually free and expressive. Our sexual behaviors generally are a reflection of our societal and cultural attitudes. Furthermore, when we observe animal behavior, we discover that it is generally the female that initiates the courtship and mating interchange, that she engages the attention of the male, and it is she that allows penetration when she is ready. There seems to be no such thing as rape in the animal world.[17]

Unlike other bodily needs, failure to satisfy one's sexual drives is not fatal. Celibacy does not necessarily lead to psychosis, neurosis, or other debilitating afflictions. If one is generally unable to endure frustrations of any sort, then that person may suffer most cruelly from periods of long abstinence. Let it be clearly understood, however, that sex is necessary for the survival of the species, but it is not necessary for the survival of the individual. Many rather sane and creative persons have been celibate for all or most of their lives without deleterious effects. We mention this because of a new myth that lack of sex will have dire consequences for the individual, a superstition that has no more truth to it than the superstition that masturbation will have dire consequences.

Another influence in the sexual drive is the person's psychological type. Introverted persons, who generally require more solitude and privacy than extraverted persons do, may also have less need for sexual interaction. Extraverted persons, who are more able to relate spontaneously to others, also may be more able to relate spontaneously on a sexual level. Persons who are endomorphic or who require a lot of physical activity, also may require more sexual activity than the average person does. We need not berate ourselves for the type that we are, or for whether we are getting all the sex we need, nor should we worry if we are closet satyrs. Americans tend to compare themselves needlessly with each other. As one wit said: "Ever since sex polls have been published, Americans think they must have sex twice a week—whether they want it or not!"

Our general state of health will influence our sexual drive, as well as our body's natural rhythms. When we are tired, emotionally or physically exhausted, or even if the weather is too hot, we are less inclined toward exertion in any area. The point to be remembered is that our sexual drives are a function of our personalities and a function also of the situational factors in our lives. Although the sexual drive is one of the basic physiological drives, it is mediated by our culture and our cortex.

Our understanding of homosexuality also has expanded as more and more sociologists and anthropologists report their research findings. The Kinsey report of sexual behavior in the United States revealed that although only 4 per cent of the population was exclusively homosexual, a much higher percentage of persons had engaged in both heterosexual and homosexual activity (37 percent of the men and 13 per cent of the women).[18] Although we in the West generally have been intolerant, some less developed societies have been much more tolerant of homosexual behavior. A survey of nearly two hundred societies reported that homosexuality was prevalent among seventy-six of them and, that of these seventy-six societies, forty-nine considered homosexuality an acceptable and normal sexual experience.[19]

Other Kinds of Needs

We have discussed only the most basic physiological needs. There are many more subtle and more individual needs. Some of these we share with other life forms; others are distinctly human. There is the need, for example, for contact, touching, and affection which is distinctly different from sexual and other emotional needs. Some people are "touchers"; they like to make contact with others through handclasps and handshakes, by putting an arm on another's shoulder, and by more intimate embraces; others prefer to maintain distance, have a "hands off" *territorial space* around them, and allow touching only after the relationship has won through their natural reserve. We do not have to decide which it is better to be, only to be aware that again there are vast individual differences among us and to respect those differences.

We differ also in the need for privacy and solitude, in the amount of physical activity we need. We differ in the amount of excitement, novelty, or challenge we need. Some persons prefer a quiet life of dignity and calm; others like a faster tempo, the excitement of competition, and problems to be solved. We differ significantly too in what gives us pleasure. For some, it is being outdoors. For others, it is creating beauty in whatever form their consciousness takes. In our everyday world of work and domestic affairs, we sometimes get so hassled that we neglect these higher human needs, but their fulfillment halps us to integrate our life process and stabilize our existence. What matters is that we understand and appreciate our individual needs and find the opportunities, whenever possible, to fulfill them.

psychobiological awareness:
other approaches

We already have discussed three therapeutic approaches to bodily awareness and psychobiological integration: Jacobson's progressive relaxation, Wolpe's deconditioning and reconditioning therapies, and Reich's armor unlocking. There are several other approaches. These have come to us from several sources: from a renewed interest in the psychology and philosophy of Eastern religions, from hospital and laboratory research in the general area of biofeedback and other states of altered consciousness, and from experimental growth centers such as Esalen, in Big Sur, California. All of these approaches have as one of their objectives: *the alleviation of stress and the reversal of wear and tear on bodily tissues.*

Yoga

There are many types of yoga. Some of them (as practiced by devotees in India, China, and even here in the United States) strive to attain a mystic union with the Godhead, a supreme level of consciousness. At this level, yoga is related to the mystic tradition of Christianity, Judaism, and Islam. Yoga itself means "union," the Sanskrit word from which the English word "yoke" comes. This meaning can be related to the Christian attitude of taking on "the yoke of Christ." Unlike Christian mysticism, a religious belief in God is not necessary to practice yoga. One can practice yoga regardless of one's religious viewpoints or lack thereof.[20]

The most common types of yoga include *karma yoga*, achieved through work and action (what the Christians call "salvation through works"); *jnana yoga*, achieved through study and knowledge (the intellectual and scholarly approach to human awareness); *bhakti yoga*,

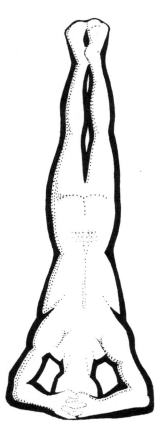

The up-side-down asanas, say the students of yoga, provide the brain and undersides of our organs with a nourishing blood bath of oxygen and nutrients.

achieved through devotion and selfless love; *mantra yoga*, a method of using sound and visualization to increase self-awareness; and *raja yoga*, the highest form and achieved only by experts. Raja yoga generally begins with another type of yoga called *hatha yoga*, the physical yoga we shall discuss below. The Hindus, even two thousand years ago, were well aware that psychological awareness is difficult to achieve in a weak or physically flabby body. They believed that to attain the highest states of consciousness, it was important to build the body's strength and endurance so that it could become a vehicle for the integration of body, mind, and spirit.[21]

Hatha yoga is a series of postures (we can call them stretching exercises) developed in India at a time when physical health and bodily ease were considered the first steps to personal growth and spiritual evolution.

We compared hatha yoga to the exercises of Western physical development, but there is a profound difference. The various positions in hatha yoga are not achieved as "violently" as in our Western forms of exercise but are done slowly, gently, rhythmically, and in a contemplative mood. The student of yoga first is taught to put the mind into a restful state of peace, and in that restful state of mind, the student moves from one yoga stretch to another. In actuality, yoga is simply a very practical and systematic method of toning the muscles of the body to achieve that kind of balance between control and abandon that a dancer feels or that a skier experiences when skiing "perfectly." Not only are the muscles of the body toned, but the postures (called *asanas*) also pull and stretch the whole skeletal system, including the spinal cord. Part of the aging process is the encrustation of calcium deposits within the cartilage and ligaments along with a general rigidification of the spinal system and a loss of elasticity in the joints.[22] The spinal-stretching postures of yoga seem to be effective in reducing these calcium deposits, thus counteracting arthritis, bursitis, and other afflictions, of the skeletal and muscular systems. Improvement has been reported by practitioners of yoga who have been afflicted with these conditions. There also have been reports of laboratory and medical studies which indicate a general improvement of physical and emotional health.[23] Books on aging generally agree that daily gentle exercising, even walking, can reverse some of the problems associated with years of stress and sedentary inactivity.

It is easy to comprehend the more conventional asanas, the ones which correspond to some of our Western exercises such as bending at the waist or touching our hands to the floor, but what can we make of some of the more bizarre yoga postures such as standing on one's head or twisting one's body into unusual positions? The practitioners of yoga explain it this way: our body is usually erect or lying down in a horizontal position. Our blood supply (which provides nutritive substances and oxygen to our bodily tissues and also drains away the wastes and poisons that have been built up) inevitably reaches certain parts of organs more easily than others. By reversing our center of gravity, we allow the blood to circulate more freely to our brains and to the undersides of our organs which normally do not get this kind of blood revitalization.

There has been little systematic scientific research on the effects of hatha yoga except those that were done rather informally by the survey method. One mass survey was carried out by *Mass-Observation* (the British equivalent of the American Gallup Poll).[24] One thousand students of yoga submitted reports of their yoga experiences. Only ten out of the one thousand respondents (or 1 per cent) reported no positive effects. The other 99 per cent considered their yoga instruction had done them considerable good, and many respondents were very enthusiastic. There were blanks for voluntary comments, and the following statements are typical of them:

"I have now a clear skin, calm temper, and a belief in the future."

"I have a more buoyant feeling and my friends are beginning to remark on the color in my face, which is natural—no make-up."

"I feel that my natural self has begun to exert itself. My mind and body are working in peace and close harmony."[25]

We can only hope that there will be more adequate research on yoga itself. There has, of course, been much research on the benefits of physical exercise of any sort in slowing the aging process. Some of the beneficial results include toning the muscles, increasing the circulation of the blood, trimming excess adipose tissue, and reducing the calcium deposits in the tendons and cartilaginous tissues.

Massage

One of the less active forms of awakening oneself to bodily consciousness is through massage, an age-old therapeutic method which decreases tension and engenders an experience of well-being and peacefulness. According to biblical tradition, the feet of a traveler were to be washed by the host or hostess, not only to cleanse his feet, but to encourage him to relax after his long and weary journey. In our own time, patients who are bedridden are given massages to increase circulation of the blood, to prevent bedsores and the other symptoms which follow from lack of movement. Persons who have had a debilitating "stroke" or who suffer muscle paralysis or loss of sensation in the limbs often are given special kinds of body massage and exercise.

All these techniques now have been gathered together to form a professional discipline called *physical therapy.* Athletes often are given massage to relax their bodies and to ease cramped muscles. We have long known that a skillful massage can ease tension headaches even more quickly than aspirin can.

Many books describe the various theories and approaches to massage. Noteworthy among them is *Sense Relaxation* by Bernard Gunther, who developed a series of exercises in which the person learns to touch, tap, slap, and stimulate his or her own or another's head, eyelids, facial muscles, chest, shoulders, limbs, and torso. Some of Gunther's exercises appear to be yoga postures simplified for the Westerner.[26]

The Relevance of Any Physical Activity to Body-Mind Integration

We have been discussing rather esoteric types of physical body-mind approaches to personality integration, although they are not nearly as mysterious when understood and utilized. We would like to make very clear, however, that one need not use any of these approaches to gain the benefits of physical enhancement. Those involved in any kind of athletic or bodily discipline will testify that using our bodies in any physical activity helps us to keep firm, fit, and young, whether it be playing tennis, swimming, dance and ballet, skiing, or whatever. Physicians extol the virtues of simply walking — if that walking be vigorous and full of zest. Time and again, we have been amazed at the extraordinary grace and youthfulness of the great prima ballerinas who have retained their physical splendor even into their fifties, and whose faces seem to us to be still firm with few wrinkles, saggings, pouches, and double chins. Surely, their physical fitness and attractiveness must reflect also a slowing of the aging process that comes from lethargy and from that lack of self-worth blamed on becoming "fat," hunched, and less mobile.

There are other advantages of physical exercise. Getting out and having a good game of handball or tennis, for example, does help to clean out the emotional upsets, just as the sweat from the body helps to cleanse the pores of the skin. In our daily interactions with others, we may find ourselves irritated, angered, or upset about a situation. These emotions may interfere with our work or leisure activities. In these situations, working up a "good sweat" in some kind of physical activity seems to cleanse these emotions, so we can operate more calmly and more rationally. It is certainly more constructive to run a couple of miles when angry than to follow the urge "to belt the s.o.b. in the nose."

There are many and varied physical activities that promote mindbody integration and creative potential.

Many of us live in a sedentary world and need to find ways and means for exercising our bodies as well as our minds. Many corporations, recognizing this, have begun to include athletic areas in their companies where their executives and white-collar workers can work out at the noon break or after working hours. Unfortunately, these areas tend to favor men, and we hope that in the future, these companies will make similar arrangements for women.

Meditation

Various forms of meditation have swept the country. Yet there is still abysmal ignorance of just what meditation is and is not. What it certainly is *not* is an esoteric and mysterious technique of transcendence known only by a few individuals known as "adepts." It is and has been a method of personality integration practiced by many of the major religions and even by many creative persons who were not particularly religious. The forms of meditation are as varied as the cultures from which they have arisen. Some types are derived from practices dating back some thousands of years; others have been developed in this century. Some types have achieved more prominence and popularity; others have been more scientifically investigated; and some have only reported in books. Each form of meditation has its own adherents and practices. Some types concentrate on sound, some on visualization; some incorporate movement, while others need stillness and quiet.

At its most profound level, meditation is a form of psychic experience, sometimes expressed as religious mysticism or as an "oceanic" oneness with the world. As a form of religious experience, it has been practiced by Catholic saints, Protestant mystics, Hassidic Jews, Islamic Sufis, Japanese Zen masters, Chinese Taoists and Buddhists, and Indian yogis, to mention but a few. At this level, it has been described as a method of experiencing the immediacy of the Godhead and to gain the meaning of life.[27] At its simpler levels, it is a method by which the person can calm the everlasting hum of the body's hopped-up energies and the mind's restlessness and anxieties, achieving at last peaceful harmony of the mind-body-spirit. It has been compared to an altered state of consciousness, to prayer, to communion with the eternal forces of nature, to inner reflection, to deep introspection, to visions and clairvoyance, to "inner listening" and to oneness with the universe.[28]

The media have emphasized the dramatic and mysterious types of meditation. In photographs, we are given a view of a transcendent being whose eyes are closed, sometimes in a trance. The person is sometimes seated in a "lotus position," with legs crossed and holding the fingers in a set position at the knees. Such photographs have frightened away many well intentioned people who know full well the difficulty of assuming such a position without months of practice.

All that is really needed to practice meditation is the willingness to commit fifteen to twenty minutes a day to it, in a private place free from noise and intrusion. All one really needs is a comfortable chair to begin the kind of "letting go" (described in chapter 5), devised by Edmund Jacobson to help his patient-students relax. There is nothing very mysterious about giving oneself a chance to withdraw for a small portion of the day and to rest one's weary *mind-body-spirit* away from the roar and tumult of the world.

Eventually, of course, each practitioner may want to investigate the various types of meditation. One person may feel most comfortable in a darkened room gazing at the light of a small candle. Another may prefer to use a *mantram*, a verbal or visual symbol to focus one's attention. Another may prefer to concentrate on an inspiring Bible verse. Still another may want to delve in the slightly more difficult "no-mind" of Zen Buddhism, the practice of ceasing all the thoughts of one's overactive mind and reaching a deeply contemplative mood with no words at all.

Laboratory observations of persons engaged in deep meditation confirm that the body does, indeed, seem to slow down and become more rhythmic. The muscular system becomes less tense; the breathing becomes deeper, calmer, and slower; the heartbeat slows; the blood pressure can be reduced; and, in general, the whole body seems to function more easily.[29] One may have many kinds of internal experiences. One may have a feeling of heaviness, of extreme lightness, or even of floating. One may suddenly see images as if projected on a screen. One certainly comes into direct contact with one's nonverbal inner dialogue with more heightened intensity. One may experience a strange sense of relief by not having to attend to all the usual daytime stimuli while in the waking state. One may have dreamlike experiences and not be asleep. One may receive subconscious material which may border on artistic creativity or experience some deeply anxiety-provoking, repressed material. It is certainly one way to get to know oneself.

People who begin to meditate will be surprised at the number of physical sensations that they may experience. Their nose may twitch or tingle, and they may get the same twitching and tingling in their hands and feet. We cannot as yet explain all these sensations, but they are certainly correlated with the change in muscle tones as one begins to relax more deeply than one ever has before. We generally keep ourselves so taut in the pace we usually follow, that our muscles, arteries, and skin feel vastly different when we are relaxed than in their usually contracted-constricted states.

SCIENTIFIC INVESTIGATION OF MEDITATION.   Until recently, the practice of meditation has been described only through field observations of yogis in trance states. Reports of these deep trances describe incredible feats, such as the actual slowing of the heart beat, reduction of oxygen intake, and the ability to blank out extremely painful situations. More recently, these adepts have been studied in the laboratory and reported in scientific journals. One team of investigators, with the willing permission of a yogi "adept," monitored his vital bodily processes during an extended stay in an air-tight box. The monitoring revealed that soon after his entrance into the box, the subject's heartbeat and breathing slowed, and within the first half-hour, dropped to one-fourth of its normal rate, far below the ordinary levels required for the maintenance of life itself. When the yogi was let out of his prison, he was discovered to be in excellent physical condition. This experiment has given more validity to the strange and extraordinary feats of the Indian yogis about which we have heard and read so much.[30]

Transcendental meditation is one of the best known and most widely publicized forms of meditation. We can be grateful to the practitioners of this meditation for their willingness and openness in being studied under laboratory conditions and for long-term, follow-up studies. There have been many articles which vouch for the long-lasting effects of TM (as it is called), and we recommend the footnotes at the end of the chapter for details. In general, physiological results obtained by transcendental meditation reveal the following among college students: increased blood flow and circulation, decreased oxygen consumption and a decrease in carbon dioxide production, increased skin resistance, an altered brain wave pattern, and a general "quiescence of the sympathetic nervous system."[31]

Biofeedback Techniques

The single area of the bodily approach to personality integration that has received the most rigorous experimental research is biofeedback. Under conditions of training, college students and patients from the general population have been observed to lower voluntarily their systolic blood pressure by using the biofeedback method. The biofeedback method is a technique by which people may become more in touch with their bodily reactions using feedback from an electronic monitoring device. The patient closes his or her eyes and concentrates on deep relaxation. When the brain-wave pattern goes into a less active state (Alpha, Theta, or Delta) than his or her usual active waking state (Beta), the monitoring device produces a tone which feeds back the information. Sometimes the subject reports a wonderful feeling of deep calm; sometimes the subject describes the experience as being close to God, or some other mystical description.

Another device for biofeedback is one that allows the subjects to observe their systolic blood pressure. By a learned technique, they can watch their own blood pressure go down and thus realize that they can control their bodily reactions, a great hope for the hypertensive patient! Observations of this group, as compared to a control group, reveal that the average subject was able to lower his or her blood pressure by about 12 percent. They also report that sufferers of tension and migraine headaches were able to relax sufficiently so that their headaches were diminished partly or completely by biofeedback techniques that allowed them to monitor their own bodily muscle contraction.

William Greene and his associates at the Menninger Foundation have helped sufferers from migraine and other tension headaches by what they call *autogenic training*. Autogenic training is an interesting procedure and seems to be something that a group of persons could try out on its own. The persons sit in a darkened room in comfortable chairs and with their eyes closed. The trainer repeats in a soothing, quiet tone (some participants have called it a hypnotic monotone) these kinds of instructions:

You are allowing yourself to relax . . . you feel yourself relaxing . . . you are allowing your head and neck to relax . . . you will allow the tiredness to drain from your body . . . soon you will be experiencing coolness in your head . . . you are allowing the warmth from your head to flow into your arms and hands . . . You feel the warmth leaving your head and neck . . . you feel the warmth flowing into your arms . . . (and so on).

The results of this training sometimes have been so surprisingly quick, report the trainers, that one girl got relief from a headache in only a few minutes.

applications and coping techniques

We have come to the end of Part 2, which has been devoted to the physical self. We have seen how mental and emotional stress can create physical breakdown and disease. We also have noted how the continual stress in our lives can age our bodies prematurely. We have discussed the increasing attention of psychologists to the bodily approach to personality integration. Finally, we have examined the need to remain sensorily aware of our internal and external physical environments.

It was not by chance that we placed this section toward the beginning of this book. We did so to emphasize that everything we do, feel, and experience, and the ways in which we behave all have an effect on our bodily functioning. We need a body that is "at ease" so that we are able to deal more calmly and easily with daily events. A body at ease promotes a mind at ease. Accordingly, we suggest that the person who is seriously interested in maintaining quality of life always be aware of the following points.

1. Devote Some Time Every Week to Physical Rejuvenation.

Our civilization allows us little time and opportunity to remain active. As children we ran and jumped, tumbled on the grass and rolled over, leaped into the air exuberantly and joyfully. We were natural "yogis," twisting, bending, and stretching our bodies. But as we grow older, more and more of our daily lives are spent behind desks, behind counters, behind the wheels of our automobiles. Sedentary activities take the place of active situations, with the result that our muscles, tendons, cartileges, vital organs, and glandular and nervous systems are slowly and insidiously aging prematurely. Our bodies are not getting the benefits of a healthy cardio-vascular system which provides oxygen and nutrition to the cells and tissues, and which disposes of the waste substances and toxic elements. By incorporating some form of physical activity into our everyday life, we slow down or actually reverse the effects of stress in our lives.

As well, physical activity helps drain the emotional tensions built up in the body, cleanses the mind of its emotional concerns, and paves the way for a fresh viewpoint toward living and its associated complexities. Physical activity, then, can be said to be one of the significant approaches to mind-body health.

Unfortunately, it is too easy to slide into a lazy attitude toward physical integration. We rationalize and make excuses to avoid the effort it takes to keep our bodies in good shape. We say to ourselves that we cannot take the time, that we have too many things to do, or that the pressures of home or office prevent us from doing what we know we should do. What is really happening is that we have not yet understood the significance of taking care of the physical self. When we get a toothache or earache that is screaming for attention, we get to the dentist or physician as soon as we can get ourselves an appointment. Aging and chronic diseases (like hypertension) are "silent killers" because they creep up on us unnoticed. We often are unaware of their toll—until it is too late. Physical integration needs to be an ever-present awareness in our consciousness. Time must be given for it just as time is given to the other functions of our lives.

2. Choose Physical Activities that Accord with Your Individual Differences and with Your Life Style.

When we discuss the need for physical activity with our students, we often hear the distressed response that they just cannot get out and jog every day, that they just are not the "racquetball" type, or that the idea of getting up each morning and doing the Canadian Royal Air Force exercises is not for them! To which we promptly agree.

Choose, therefore, physical activities that are in accord with your distinct preferences. For some that may be disco dancing or ballet. To others, swimming or golf may be more appropriate. It need not be an everyday event, but surely you deserve three or four times during the week to reenergize your body, for that is the real purpose of physical activity. Furthermore, a variety of activities will do you more good than the repetition of one type of exercise. Remember that what you are trying to do is to energize those parts of your body which are not usually used. Swimming develops the chest, arms, and legs, while disco or belly dancing invigorates the abdomen. You might very well have a weekly bowling date, go swimming on the weekend, and do yoga twice a week. A variety of activities exercises the different parts of the body and is a wholistic approach. The physical activity that you choose need not have the connotation of hard labor and exhaustion. Many professionals take time out on Wednesday afternoon or on Sunday for a game of golf. A good tour on the golf course is excellent, provided one does not use a golf cart but walks briskly from hole to hole.

3. Have Respect for Your Body.

It is sad that most of us take better care of our automobiles than we do of our bodies. None of us would think of driving our cars for 50,000 miles without a check-up or a tune-up. Yet, we forget to take care of bodily needs, go without sleep, live on junk foods, and visit our physicians only when we have severe difficulties. We called the chronic diseases silent killers, and so they are. Their progressions are slow but inexorable. We can abuse ourselves with drugs and alcohol and cigarettes for just so long until suddenly we feel the first chest pains, or a sudden blurring of our vision tells the physician that our blood pressure is approaching the danger level.

The body is the physical self in which we move and breathe. It is the structure through which we feel either joy or pain. It is by staying in touch with our physical selves that we remain rooted in reality. Emotions are bodily experiences, and by staying in touch with what is going on within us, we are more alert to what is going on around us; that is, we are more "intelligent." When we eat too much, drink too much, deny ourselves the sleep we need, or burn our candles at both ends for long periods of time, we actually anesthetize ourselves to bodily signals. We get used to heartburn or to acid indigestion and cover the minor aches and pains with aspirins and other analgesics. We become so used to chronic fatigue and discomfort that we do not realize that we can feel better. Ultimately, all the pill popping, chronic aching and fatigue blur our vision, deafen our hearing, and interfere with our accurate perception of what is going on "out there" in our personal lives and on the job. We have become "dull" human beings.

4. Respect Your Individual Bodily Needs.

We devoted one whole chapter to your individual needs. We hope that you have come to respect your individual differences. All of us differ significantly. For example, some of us have less need for the usual eight hours of sleep, but some of us may need more than the proverbial eight hours, particularly when the stress of our lives is greater than usual. Our nutritional needs vary. Some persons seem to need a hearty breakfast while others actually may feel slightly nauseated by the idea of eating immediately upon arising. While some persons feel physically invigorated by spending a day in the blazing sun and surf of the beach, there are some persons to whom this experience may actually be harmful. The latter may be those who have a vitamin A deficiency, in whom bright sunlight destroys the rhodopsin of their eyes; some persons are light sensitive and too much sunlight gives them eye strain; others have complexions that are injured by overexposure to sunlight.

Our reactions to climate differ significantly. Some feel exhilarated by cold weather and love nothing better than to ski, skate, or whatever, while others (who have poor circulation) may suffer during the coldest times of the year. Although most people enjoy a sunny day, some of us actually look forward to rainy days — our systems are made more buoyant by the increased negative ions of the atmosphere.

We have chosen only a few of the ways in which we differ in bodily needs. There are many physical differences among us. Harmony with the self is to become aware of those differences and to allow oneself to have those differences.

5. A Special Tip for Teachers at Elementary and High Schools.

Teaching school is especially trying. It is your job to keep thirty or more students interested in their schoolwork when most of them would rather be elsewhere. If you have been paying attention to this section, you know now how anxiety and stress can result in bodily and emotional fatigue. For many students, classroom work is *stressful* and *anxiety producing*. The symptoms of this stress and anxiety come out as class disturbance, acting up, or restlessness.

Physical activity will help reduce this emotional tension. You have seen it yourself after the children come back from recess. They may be a little overactive when they first come in, but in a few moments they settle down and seem to welcome a quiet period of desk work. Do not wait for recess to give them this emotional outlet. Every so often, give the whole class a chance to take a physical break. Get them up on their feet doing things, walking around, or (for small children) a chance to play "Simon Says." Give them a chance to use their voices (which is a type of motor activity) by singing or choral speaking. You may have encountered these suggestions in your educational methods courses, but now you can understand their special relevance to student well-being.

the emotional self: and the forces of society

THREE

our one and many selves: the search for integration

The group situation involves persons coming together to increase their personality integration and creativity.

I. Introduction: The Wide Range of Emotional Patterning

    A. *The Passive-Dependent Personality*
    B. *The Obsessive-Compulsive Personality*
    C. *Extreme Phobic Reactions*
    D. *The Severe Depressive Reaction*
    E. *Suicidal Depression*
    F. *The "Hysteric" Personality*
    G. *The Manic-Depressive Reaction*
    H. *The "Schizophrenic" Personality*
    I. *The "Schizoid" Personality*
    J. *Multiple Personality*
    K. *Psychopathic and Sociopathic Personalities*

II. The Development of the Dialogic Approach to Growth

    A. *A Very Brief History of Therapeutic Treatment*
    B. *The Use of Hypnosis*
    C. *The Development of Psychoanalysis*
    D. *Individual Psychotherapy and Counseling*
    E. *Sullivan's Interpersonal Approach*
    F. *Roger's Client-Centered Approach*
    G. *Group Therapy*
    H. *Growth Groups*

III. Two Insight Approaches to the Therapeutic Growth Situation

    A. *Transactional Analysis*
        1. *The Child-Ego State*
        2. *The Parent-Ego State*
        3. *The Adult-Ego State*
        4. *Aim of Therapy*
    B. *Gestalt Therapy*
        1. *The Figure-Ground Relationship*
        2. *A Gestalt Therapy Session*

IV. Three Therapies Directed Specifically to Behavioral Change

    A. *Implosive Therapy*
    B. *A Modified Implosive Approach*

C. *Rational-Emotive Therapy*
D. *Reality Therapy*

V. Other Therapies

VI. Applications and Coping Techniques

introduction: the wide range of emotional patterning

In the previous chapters, we looked at the commonalities and differences of fairly average human functioning. In this chapter, we shall consider some of the deviations of personality patterning. These extreme patternings occur if we have not had secure and constructive early experiences, or if the stress and change in our lives have become so severe that our usual functioning begins to break down. These breakdowns can happen to any of us from time to time, and we may find ourselves severely depressed, confused, disassociated, and even irrational. It may simply be that we have become so de-energized that we do not know how to integrate the events in our lives; it takes all we have to just keep going. In these situations, we may need dialogic therapies, either for a short time or for longer, until we can function better. We shall examine the different kinds of therapies and how they work.

The Passive-Dependent Personality

We already have discussed some of the fixations of personality patterning as described by Freud. One such personality patterning is the orally fixated person who gratifies his or her libidinal drive through the primary erotic zone in and around the mouth, which sometimes is manifested as excessive eating, drinking, smoking, and so on. Psychologically, this person remains passively dependent on the environment to take care of his or her needs. For example, you may know someone who is always asking your opinion about even the most minor decisions of living: what to wear today, what movie to go to see, or what kind of a present to buy for a friend or relative you do not even know. These persons may not even seem capable of taking care of their bodily needs. Although they are adults (in the physical sense), they have not yet learned to pick up after themselves; they leave their clothes about and their dishes in the sink; and they are constantly borrowing things from you because they have not bothered to replenish their own household store. All in all, they seem to expect the world to take care of them.

The Obsessive-Compulsive Personality

If the person remains fixated at the second level of psychosexual development, Freud said, he or she develops into an *anal* personality and exhibits obsessive-compulsive habits. He or she is excessively concerned about dirt, small details, and even the least bit of untidyness. As a result, he or she tends to be an overly tidy, excessively modest, compulsively exact person who "cannot see the forest for the trees." These persons may be obsessed with minor details and references to people you do not know, or they may go over the same subject time after time, driving you to boredom and confusion. Their offices are immaculate, their clothes creased and coordinated, and their work organized. All this is good, and sometimes these persons make excellent secretaries, treasurers, accountants, and computer operators in which exactness is desirable. But a hair out of place, a little dust on the furniture, a spot on their clothes, or papers slightly disarranged fills them with anxiety. Because they are concerned with the minutiae of daily living, they lack a larger perspective and often are passed over for positions of higher responsibility which require the ability to see the overall picture.

Still, these two personality patterns can and often do function fairly well in our society. We now come to those personalities which take a far more serious turn and which result either in the inability to cope adequately in our society or they become destructive to themselves or to the society in which they live.

Extreme Phobic Reactions

The obsessive-compulsive patterning (discussed above) can assume such an extreme form that it takes over the person's life. Whatever is disturbing the person becomes so obsessive that he or she cannot stop thinking the same thoughts over and over. In order to defend against these continual obsessive thoughts, the person develops counterphobic reactions and compulsive rituals to defend against them, over which he or she seems to have no control. A case history, reported by Davison and Neale, describes a woman whose anxiety about being attacked by germs was so overwhelming that she washed her hands no less than five hundred times a day. Not only did her hand washing occupy most of her waking existence, it also produced disfiguring and painful sores on her hands, wrists, and arms.[1] One is reminded of Lady Macbeth's compulsion to wash her hands as a way to rid herself of the guilt she felt for the murders committed by herself and her husband. While the others watch her strange ritual of hand washing, she is heard to murmur the fear of all such guilt-obsessed persons—the inability to cleanse themselves: "Here is the smell of blood still; all the perfumes of Arabia will not sweeten this little hand."[2]

The Severe Depressive Reaction

We all have experienced occasional bouts of depression, those times when everything seems bleak and hopeless and when we can see no way out of whatever desperate situation in which we find ourselves. Any attempt to cheer us up only sends us farther and farther into despair. We are not talking about these occasional situations that we all encounter at some time but, rather, of those people whose constitutional psychic functioning prevents them from being able to cope with the normal stress of living. Whether from an inherited predisposition or from severe deprivation in early childhood, they have learned a kind of generalized (conditioned) hopelessness and helplessness.

Sometimes we can suffer a depression so severe that we feel helpless and hopeless. At such times our physical and psychological energy can seem to drain out of us.

Whatever the cause of this severe depressive reaction, it has resulted in the abiding conviction that there is nothing they can do to change the events and sad course of their lives. One psychologist demonstrated a similar patterning in the laboratory. He conditioned dogs to shocks from which they could not escape. Later, he placed the experimental dogs and a control group (which had not been given this kind of training) in a shock situation in which there *was* an easily discerned escape. The control dogs discovered the escape and used it at the first possible moment. In contrast, the experimental dogs did not even try to escape. Instead, they remained passively tolerant of the shocks in a kind of dazed and helpless state. The psychologist reported also that the experimental dogs had a low level of norepinephrine, the hormone which helps to excite emergency arousal. He also noted that drugs which seem to mobilize the severely depressed person to overcome their lethargic state are the very ones which stimulate the production of the emergency hormone, norepinephrine.[3]

Suicidal Depression

Sometimes people have such severe depression that they choose the only escape from pain they can think of: suicide. One of the earliest studies of suicide was by Emile Durkheim. He first recognized the alienation factor in suicidal people's backgrounds and noted the frequency of the following situational factors: first, they were far from home and frequently had moved from a rural area to a large city with its more impersonal environment; second, they were out of contact with their families and old friends who had provided them with emotional support; and third, they were unable to establish new friends despite all the people around them.[4] Although some of Durkheim's statistics have been criticized, it still is true that suicides are more prevalent among those who have moved away from home and who have not succeeded in establishing new relationships. A recent follow-up study of attempted suicides among a group of adolescents confirmed many of Durkheim's conclusions. Of forty-five adolescents, twenty-three had lost one or both parents through death, divorce, or separation (many fairly recently), and two-thirds had lost or anticipated the loss of a parent, boyfriend, or girlfriend.[5]

But suicide is more than a situational occurrence. Many of us have had to confront the loneliness of living away from home and of feeling isolated and friendless. What, then, is the difference? Suicidal personalities often have suffered a crippling emotional deprivation in early childhood that prevents them from solving their situational problems. Anything may trigger the suicide attempt: academic problems in school, marital problems, and even conflict with parents. Paradoxically, suicidal students who blame their lack of academic achievement have done no more poorly than the average college students. Another study described "typical" suicidal students as older, lonely, friendless, and isolated psychologically from others.[6]

The "Hysteric" Personality

Another type of crippling reaction is called the "hysteric" personality. We already have discussed a few of the many manifestations of this disorder: physical symptoms by which the person converts free-flowing anxiety into disorders such as nonneurological paralysis or one disabling sickness after another. Psychologically, the "hysteric" exhibits a personality patterning in which the *feeling* function dominates almost to the exclusion of other traits. Hysterics literally are run by their emotions. They sometimes have been characterized as having a dramatic self-absorption, as if constantly "on stage." Their gestures are theatrical; their voices frequently have a considerably higher decibel level than the voices of those around them; and their conversation generally centers on themselves: *their* feelings, *their* emotions, *their* problems, *their* revelations, *their* families, and the injustices toward *them.* If we try to help these people, we soon enough discover that their difficulties are frequently of their own making and are exaggerated far out of proportion to reality. They are also ingenious at involving a vast number of persons in their emotional web: their families, their colleagues at work, their neighbors, their neighbors' children, even their minister, physician, attorney, and any person whose profession is to help such people.

They also are destructive to themselves. Psychologically, any small incident, any chance remark can set them off on their emotional rockets. They hamper themselves in their vocational careers since their fellow workers soon learn to avoid them, and their employers bypass them for positions that deal with the public and for positions of authority that need "cool heads" and rational decision making. At a physical level, they manage to incur organic problems which require surgery: removal of breasts, sexual organs, and other bodily tissues and structure because of cancer. One study which compared persons labeled "hysteric personality" with a group of "nonhysteric" personalities, found the hysteric group to have had three times the mass weight of organs removed—a gruesome but extremely interesting measure of personality disintegration.[7]

The Manic-Depressive Reaction

The manic-depressive reaction may actually be a type of hysteria in that these persons sometimes exhibit the type of functioning described as the "hysteric" pattern, with one important difference—in this personality complex, there are cyclic patterns. The first is the "high, euphoric" pattern in which these persons express great optimism about the present and the future, work out plans to improve their personal or professional life, talk and move with great energy, and concoct "fantastic" schemes to get rich, achieve fame, or gain power. They may undertake physical projects and actually accomplish them in record time. Their psychical energy is awesome. Then, suddenly, all the wind seems to go out of them, and they seem to go into reverse. They suddenly are "in the dumps," develop depression with its accompanying lethargy, and may even contemplate suicide.

The "Schizophrenic" Personality

In the so-called schizophrenic forms of deviancy, these persons seem to be out of contact with the normal, commonly shared experience of what it is to be human. Schizophrenia is not, as commonly believed, a "split personality." When we become schizophrenic, our behaviors and thought patterns seem strange and at times bizarre to other persons (sometimes also to ourselves). Sometimes, in fact, our emotional response pattern undergoes such a "sea change" that we seem to be "turned inside out." Schizophrenics may giggle inanely when confronted with a frightening situation and can just as easily (and as unpredictably) become morose and withdrawn—"dead people" who refuse to allow further stimulation from their environment to get through to them. These persons may even become *"catatonic"*—they may sit for hours without moving or may not eat or walk for long periods of time. They do not seem to be aware of things around them and may stand statuelike in an awkward position. Schizophrenics have other curious (to us) emotional responses: they can become morose when others seem happy—for example, at holiday celebrations—and can deviate in other directions thought "abnormal" by many in society.

The "Schizoid" Personality

"Schizoid" personalities appear to function as all the rest of us do. They work and support themselves and their families. They interact with others in the everyday world apparently without too much conflict and seem to carry on their daily round of activities with an apparent sense of direction.

The mark of schizoid personalities is that they seem to operate more effectively and completely than they really do. What distinguishes the schizoid life style is the "cool" and detached way of living with others. For example, they seldom seem to engage in spontaneous laughter, and many persons eventually come to see them as aloof, withdrawn, and emotionally disengaged. Such persons seem to prefer to work more with machines than with people and seldom have intimate relationships—the kind of relationships in which one is free to share one's inner thoughts and feelings. It is as if their trust in other persons is totally lacking. They do not seem to feel at ease or derive joy from human relationships as most of us do. Schizoid personalities therefore can appear to be withdrawn in company, for they say little and show few emotional responses. They may seem on the surface, nonetheless, to have everything in hand.

Though such personalities can be highly developed on the intellectual level and do well (even brilliantly) in their careers, they do not seem to enjoy or encourage the company of other persons. According to one personality theorist, their posture and facial expressions are characteristically stiff, mechanical, even robotlike, and their smiles seem masklike.[8]

Multiple Personality

Sometimes these persons are so fearful of the "dark" possibilities in their personalities that they attempt to repress all knowledge of their existence. These repressed emotions and feelings are still present even though they may be unaware of them consciously. When repression is complete and successful, these persons remain largely unaware of these dark impulses. But should these repressing defenses begin to fail, or even to break down, the dark impulses then can begin to emerge in an actual and distinct personality with a separate identity, not just as another aspect of personality.

There are many stories with the theme of multiple personality, such as Robert Louis Stevenson's novella *The Strange Case of Dr. Jekyll and Mr. Hyde* and Oscar Wilde's *Portrait of Dorian Gray*. But there have been actual cases of multiple personality recorded in medical history. One is discussed in a thoroughly absorbing book, *The Three Faces of Eve*, in which two psychiatrists describe their amazement and perplexity in discovering that a rather attractive but colorless housewife in her mid-twenties is harboring a repressed personality quite different from her public personality. The public personality

MULTIPLE PERSONALITY

Multiple personality in fact and fiction.

was completely unaware of her second personality, which emerged during periods of "headaches" and "blackouts." This second personality was cocky, brazen, aggressive, spontaneous, voluptuous—everything, in fact, that her public personality held to be unacceptable.[9]

Recently another, even more striking example of multiple personality was reported in the book *Sybil*. "Sybil" (a pseudonym) had been victimized by some of the most severe child abuse in the annals of child psychology. As a way of managing these childhood trauma, Sybil created for herself sixteen different personalities with distinctly different identities, interests, and even sexes. Although most of the sixteen identities were aware of the others and of Sybil, Sybil herself was unaware of their existence. The story of Sybil is at once the most fascinating and the most grisly of multiple-personality case histories.[10]

Psychopathic and Sociopathic Personalities

There is another kind of pattern which seems to be an *underdevelopment* of emotional behavior, called the *sociopathic* and *psychopathic* personality.

Psychopathics appear to value human life so little that they can snuff out another person's life much as we would slap down a mosquito—and with about as little sense of relationship with their victim! Interviews with psychopathic murderers seem to reveal just this curious lack of affect or feeling. They do not shoot or stab a victim in anger, rage, or fear. Nor do they kill him or her while under the influence of alcohol, drugs, or "voices"—as the psychotic personality often does. Psychopaths simply shoot their victims, stab them, run them down with an automobile, or push them out of a window—in cold blood. The psychopath is the extreme deviant.

There are "milder" forms of sociopathy. Sociopaths may not murder their next door neighbor, but they might "do him in" in other ways. They may sell him a car that is a "lemon" with full knowledge (and no remorse) that they have cheated the man. They may become an actual "carney" whose only object in life seems to be to fleece a "mark"—the general public. They may "borrow" money from a friend with no intention of paying it back, although they say they will. Or they may be professionals (physician, attorney, engineer, etc.) who are not living up to their codes of ethics.

We might call the sociopathic personality a "moral moron." There is much truth in this for sociopathic personalities, when confronted with their lies or how they have hurt others, show little real concern or embarrassment. They may declare that they are going to reform, but it is an acting job, pure and simple, in order to keep people bound to them or to get out of the mess they have made. A psychiatrist, Hervey Cleckley, who made a lifelong study of sociopathic personalities, considered it a form of insanity. But since sociopathic personalities hear no voices, have no obvious delusions, talk rationally, and are even rather charming, the psychiatric profession has not recognized the seeming rational exterior for what it is — simply *The Mask of Sanity.*[11]

Box A
Characteristics of the Sociopathic Personality

1. Superficial charm and "intelligence"

2. Delusions and other signs of irrational thinking

3. Absence of "nervousness" or psychoneurotic manifestations

4. Unreliability

5. Untruthfulness and insincerity

6. Lack of remorse or shame

7. Inadequately motivated, antisocial behavior

8. Poor judgment and failure to learn by experience

9. Pathologic egocentricity and incapacity for love

10. General poverty in major affective (emotional) reactions

11. Specific loss of insight

12. Unresponsiveness in general interpersonal relations

13. Fantastic and uninviting behavior with drink and also without

14. Suicide rarely carried out

15. Sex life impersonal, trivial, and poorly integrated

16. Failure to follow any life plan

(adapted from Hervey Cleckley, The Mask of Sanity, 4th ed. (St. Louis: C.V. Mosby Co., 1964).

the development of the dialogic approach to growth

We have named only a few of the devastating and destructive twists of personality patterning. What may be done for these personalities? What may be done for any of us, when we succumb to depression, near hysteria, a desire to run away from our problems, or any of the lesser forms of panic with which we are all familiar? To answer this, we shall study the development of another approach to personality integration — namely — dialogic therapy.

One of the best established ways to remedy problems today is therapy. *Therapy* and *therapeutic* come from the Greek meaning "to heal," and our *psychotherapy* today is (in that sense) the art and science of healing ills and suffering on the *psychological* plane. Much of that healing attention now focuses on enabling persons to cope with the pressures and tensions of our industrialized civilization.

For example, there can come a time for any of us when the difficulties in our lives have become so burdensome or when we find ourselves so prone to anxiety, that we feel emotionally crippled and unable to cope. At times like these we need some form of psychotherapy, no matter what we call it. The subheading names it as the "dialogic" approach, and that simply is therapeutic treatment through verbal interchange, as compared to the physical approaches already discussed in Part 2. Dialogic therapy may be private, between the person and a therapist or counselor, or it may be in a group of others who also are trying to break through limitations, conditionings, and stereotypic patternings.

A Very Brief History of Therapeutic Treatment

It must not be thought that what we call "madness," "insanity," "schizophrenia," or "bouts of depression" are modern phenomena. They have been described in literature since recorded history. Saul, King of Judah, is known to have suffered from severe depressions and to have become violent and even homicidal at times.[12] In some cultures — for example, among the American Indians — "mad" people were treated with respect, since they were thought to be touched by the gods. In Europe, in the Middle Ages, "insane" persons were thought to have lost their reason and sometimes even were thought to be possessed by demons. Since the devil was the personification of evil, "insane" persons were sometimes whipped, starved, or branded with hot irons in the belief that punishing the devil (who had taken over the personality) would persuade the evil spirit to leave.

Many of the mentally ill roamed the streets and byways in the latter years of the Middle Ages, and just starved to death or became victims of ridicule and cruel treatment. Some women were even burned as witches.

There was a small step forward in the treatment of severe personality problems when insane persons were placed in asylums. Un-

The word "bedlam" is a contraction of St. Mary-of-Bethlehem, an early mental asylum. The shrieking and howling of the inmates could be heard by the passers-by, and so the word "bedlam" has come to mean hubbub and confusion.

fortunately, these places were often not much better than prisons, and the inmates were frequently chained to the walls as other criminals were. The word *bedlam* — which has come to mean "a place of wild confusion and noise" — is actually a contraction of the name of a former insane asylum in Southwark, London: the Hospital of St. Mary of Bethlehem (Bedlam). The screaming of the patients could be heard clearly by passers-by, and the patients were sometimes exhibited like zoo animals (for a fee) to the curious and the thrill seekers.

Many kinds of treatments once used to heal the personality disintegration of persons now seem to us almost barbaric if not outright inhuman. In the snake-pit treatment, for example, the unfortunate patients were lowered by ropes into a pit full of snakes in the belief that the fright of the experience would shock them back into sensibility.

Treatment of insane personalities improved in France after the Revolution. A remarkable physician, Philippe Pinel, was put in

248

charge of La Bicetre, an insane asylum in Paris. To the astonishment of his colleagues and despite their ridicule, Pinel insisted on changing the environmental conditions of the inmates. He removed their chains, cleaned up the dung and filth, and let the sun shine into the dungeons where the inmates were housed. Pinel treated his disorganized personalities not as "witless" creatures, but with the same kindness and consideration he showed to other persons. His approach resulted in the improvement and release of many patients who otherwise might have remained in the asylum for the rest of their lives.

Pierre Charcot, another French physician, made another step forward when in the late nineteenth century he demonstrated that the apparently bizarre symptoms of stuttering, trembling, or the inability to walk and talk could be relieved under hypnosis. Charcot's discoveries in hypnosis and his treatment of the mentally ill constitute one of the really big breakthroughs in psychiatric treatment. He demonstrated, for example, that many of the *physical* symptoms and disabilities of the insane can have an underlying *psychological* cause and that if the cause is psychological, then the condition might be treated psychologically.[13]

The Use of Hypnosis

Among Charcot's students was a young Viennese physician named Sigmund Freud. Freud was already deeply interested in the problems of treating severe neurotic conditions and had come to Paris specifically to study under Charcot and learn his hypnotherapy. Upon his return to Vienna, Freud began to work with a colleague's patient, Anna O., a young woman suffering from "hysteria." This patient was a virtual cripple. Anna not only had trouble eating and sleeping, but she also had been suffering from frightening dreams at night and equally frightening delusions during the day. Using Charcot's hypnotic method, Freud enabled Anna to remember certain traumatic events in her earlier life, and as she began to remember those "lost" experiences in her life, her symptoms began to decrease in intensity.

The Development of Psychonalysis

One day, Freud was unable to put Anna into an hypnotic trance. To enable her to work out a dream she had had the previous night, Freud suggested that instead of being hypnotized she speak consciously of everything she was thinking and feeling about her dream. That was the beginning of Freud's method of free association.° What Freud had discovered was a "talking cure" for the neuroses of his day. We still are building and adding to Freud's original discoveries.

How does talking to a psychoanalyst seem to enable people to cope with the difficulties in living more efficiently? The answer depends on determining what interferes with their ability to grow in the first place. For Freud—who was then building a psychological theory of interpersonal relations—the basic interference with growth was *anxiety: how much* anxiety did the person experience? *With whom* was the anxiety experienced, and *how* did the person deal with it?

In his original theory of personality development, which he subsequently modified and extended, Freud said that children who experience too much anxiety or trauma (pain) have little choice other than to repress the conscious memory of these experiences—they try to forget them, in other words. These traumatic and painful interchanges with others are, however, not forgotten—they simply go underground—are buried or repressed in what Freud called the "unconscious mind." Repression demands much psychic energy. When too much of the psychic energy is directed toward repression, persons eventually can feel emotionally drained and mentally exhausted. They may even become so split off from themselves that they no longer are aware of their former thoughts, feelings, and experiences.

Those trapped in the vicious circle of repression may not realize exactly what the matter is. All they know consciously is that they feel tired and weak or that they seem to suffer from feelings of shame and guilt; they also can be obsessed with fears and phobias or may begin to experience similar kinds of nightmares and delusions as Anna O. did. On the other hand, they may need to go through a certain complicated ritual every night before they can go to sleep. They may find that they are unable to sleep more than a few hours a day—or that they need ten to twelve hours sleep. When one's life becomes frightening or painful, Freud said, look to the unconscious memory and to the anxiety which is bound up in that memory. That, in simple form, was Freud's original understanding of neurosis.

One reason our early childhood memories can be so frightening is that they represent a *child's* understanding of the world rather than the feelings and understanding of the adult state of awareness. What happens in the psychoanalytic relationship is that these previous memories—and the anxiety and suffering attached to them—are slowly and cautiously uncovered by the therapist and patient so they can

---

°In Freud's method of free association persons are supposed to be relaxed enough to speak of everything that comes into their "minds," their present awareness. This kind of honesty is bound to provoke change and growth, as Freud demonstrated in his treatment of many persons.

be worked through and assimilated into an understanding of the current self. Thus, they become not so frightening or shocking for the adult personality as they were for us as children. Suppose, for example, that a child, whose parents take care to protect their privacy, sees them engaged in sexual intercourse. That event may have seemed a violent struggle, and sexuality then may have been associated with anger and hostility and subsequently with anxiety and shame. If the child can recall that repressed childhood memory as an adult, however, he or she is better able to understand that what was seen was not physical violence but a part of the natural sexual order of things (which he or she is now ready to share).

In his work with emotionally handicapped persons, Freud developed the theory and approach of *psychoanalysis.* Our contemporary approaches to personality integration are modifications and variations of Freud's basic "talking cure." In the classical form of psychoanalytic treatment, developed by Freud, patients came to the therapist's office three to five times a week for an hour. Generally, they lay down on a couch so they could be comfortable and relaxed and better able to free associate, discuss dreams, and reconstruct daily problems. In that way patients were able to get in touch with those experiential aspects of their personalities from which they had cut themselves off. (The analyst, in Freud's method, sat behind the patient.) In working through these experiences ("finishing" them), the person in psychoanalysis became a more integrated personality. Freud (and later, his colleagues) demonstrated that his treatment approach worked — not for everyone, but for many.*

Individual Psychotherapy and Counseling

The kind of classical psychoanalysis that Freud and his students practiced has been somewhat modified over the past half-century. Psychoanalysis is still available today for those who can afford it and who need the continuous support of this approach while working through personality conflicts. Other types of individual psychotherapy also are available today.

Freud had been a neurologist and still considered himself a physician; in fact, he treated people so emotionally confused that they often were physically ill or crippled. Freud treated them as patients. He saw them regularly, sometimes for an hour daily. He gave them in-

---

*A person no longer has to lie on a couch to engage in psychoanalysis. Psychoanalysis is a much broader term and has a less precise meaning than it did in Freud's time. Today psychoanalysis denotes any therapy that systematically investigates a person's early memories and experiences and their effect on his or her present life style.

structions to lie down on the couch and to speak of everything, anything, that came into their minds. He interpreted their neurotic symptoms in much the same way any physician interprets symptoms today and gave them advice on what to do in much the same way a physician does today. It was essentially a doctor-patient relationship.

Sullivan's Interpersonal Approach

Psychoanalysis, transplanted to the United States in the twenties and thirties, was essentially more suited to the European aristocrat with plenty of time and money. Moreover, the American psychoanalyst, Harry Stack Sullivan, advanced the idea that a person who enters psychoanalytic psychotherapy is not necessarily ill or sick but is, more simply, experiencing difficulties in interpersonal relationships.[14]

With Sullivan, American psychoanalysis became analytic psychotherapy, or depth psychotherapy, and a more practical, weekly event in which two persons—the therapist (not "doctor") and the patient (or person)—sat together for an hour speaking to each other. The person no longer lay down on a couch and the therapist was in full view rather than, as in psychoanalysis, seated behind the patient. Since the person was not required to come to the therapy several times a week, this approach also placed the therapy within the financial reach of many who could not otherwise afford psychoanalysis.

Rogers' Client-Centered Approach

Carl Rogers took this idea even further and eliminated the word *patient* and replaced it with the word *client*. Both Sullivan and Rogers viewed themselves as consultants whose primary skill was in being able to be with other persons as they discussed the specific personal difficulties that had brought them into counseling or therapy.

Carl Rogers said that all persons have a "healthy" aspect that influences them to find their own directions and conclusions. The therapist's role, in Rogers's approach, is to act not as a "doctor" but as a sounding board, to reflect the clients' feelings, thoughts, and concerns so that they can see for themselves what they actually are saying, feeling, and doing. An advantage of Rogers's "client-centered" aproach to therapy has been that it encourages persons to grow toward self-direction: to find out for themselves what they want to do and be, rather than depending solely on the judgments of their therapist. Rogers believed that when people come to trust their *own* perceptions, *own* feelings, *own* thoughts, they come also to *value* themselves as a reli-

Box B
Characteristics of Persons Who Undergo Therapy

FROM	TOWARD
1. Talks about problems *or* cannot define problems; aware of symptoms but unable to see any connection between symptoms and headaches: "I don't know why I have headaches — they just happen."	1. Insight into how behavior creates problems: "My headaches occur when I have to go to my husband's social functions."
2. Highly self-critical; critical of environment and others: "I'm no good!" "They're impossible to work for."	2. More positive about self and others; accepts self "as is": "He has his problems like everyone else."
3. Fixated on past unhappiness and history: "I had an unhappy childhood."	3. More focused on present, the here and now: "I'm trying to work myself out of the knot I've got myself into."
4. Behavior is defensive and reactive to others' opinions and desires: "But my family wouldn't like it."	4. More willing to act on own feelings and desires. Acts more independently: "My decision may distress my family but I think they'll see the reasonableness of it."
5. Large perceived difference between "real" self and "ideal" self: "People see me as happy go lucky. I hide my true feelings."	5. Sees self as more integrated, less distance between what one really is and what one would like to be: "I am me and if what I am satisfies others, that's fine, if not, that's too bad."
6. More either-or, black-white thinking: "My mother is a bitch."	6. More differentiated perceptions, can see "greys": "Sometimes she is irritable."
7. Sees self and world as fixed, unalterable; problems are permanent: "There's no use even trying. The cards are stacked against me."	7. Sees self, world, others as more loose, fluid. The world does not lock one in; there are possibilities for change: "I'm beginning to see possibilities for future advancement."

(adapted from Carl Rogers, Client-Centered Therapy (Boston: Houghton-Mifflin Company, 1951).

able center of consciousness capable of deciding what to do with their lives.[15] (See Box B.)

It might be good to mention that it takes someone trained in listening to reflect another's thoughts and feelings and to keep one's own personal likes and dislikes out of the conversation. Can any one of us act as a "therapist" for another on that level of listening? Well, theoretically, we can—particularly if we know *how* to listen. Friendship requires that kind of sympathetic listening, and many of us have experienced that true sense of relief and release when we have been able finally to pour out our hearts to another human being who is listening—simply listening without interfering. But sympathetic listening is a great skill, and for most of us it is not easy since it demands impersonal attention free of judgments and the willingness to maintain an "unconditional positive regard."

Group Therapy

In group psychotherapy a therapist (or a number of therapists) meets with a number of persons once a week for one to several hours at a time. In group therapy, group members interact not only with the therapist but with each other; in fact, part of the therapist's function is to enable the group members to observe their own and others' behaviors and to encourage them to try out behaviors with each other that are more satisfactory to them personally. The group itself may vary from as few as five to as many as ten or twelve or even twenty persons. The group members develop close relationships, similar to those in a family. But unlike family relationships, the group members are not forced to live with each other day in and day out, so the conflicts within the therapy group have time to heal between sessions. A young man suffering from resentment of his parents is thus enabled to work on those resentments in the group as he interacts with his peers and older members of the group. Likewise, an older person is able to appreciate the young man's difficulties *without having to be the object of his resentment*. Through many kinds of interchanges (discussion, questioning, listening, nonverbal communication, even violent disagreement), the group members gradually develop insight into their own difficulties. They also come to appreciate the problems of other group members, and it often is a relief just to know that other persons have problems—that we are not alone! Members not only learn to share the group's attention with their peers but also can share vicariously in the work each group member does on his or her particular difficulties. For that reason a person may come to a group for many weeks, even months, sit quietly, and not seem to do any therapeutic work on his or her own difficulties, yet *still improve markedly.*

There finally is the matter of cost: an hour of group therapy costs about one-fourth the fee for an hour of individual therapy, which means that many persons can afford the group experience who would not be able to consider individual psychotherapy. When we add up all these advantages and then consider also the advances in the techniques of group interaction in the last twenty-five years, it is easy to see why group therapy is so popular and why the demand for it continues to grow.

Growth Groups

There are many approaches to group interaction. One is group psychotherapy, which we have just discussed, in which persons with moderate to severe interpersonal difficulties seek to alleviate psychological conflicts interfering with their capacity to grow. Another approach to group dynamics is the *growth group* method. One of the pioneer approaches in the growth-group movement is the communication laboratory developed by the National Training Laboratory (NTL) in Bethel, Maine. As it was originally planned, the NTL approach provided a

Psychotherapy is an attempt to get ourselves "all together."

place where business executives, office supervisors, plant managers, and similar occupational groups could study group dynamics (how people interact together) and so become more effective leaders. In the early years of the NTL, many who came to the training groups (called "T-groups") were sponsored by industrial corporations as a kind of in-service training program for leadership effectiveness in corporation management. Those who attended the NTL T-groups already were leading relatively effective and harmonious lives and wanted simply to further their skills in interpersonal relationships.

Many kinds of group combinations have developed in the past decade, which have been inspired by the growth group philosophy. Some of these groups specialize in working with business persons, church workers, married couples, professional persons in the social sciences, task-oriented groups for community, volunteer workers, and so on. There also are many names for these groups, including T-groups, encounter groups, sensitivity groups, human-potential seminars, and leadership-training labs. Although there can be sometimes subtle differences in emphasis among these various approaches to group process, most of the practitioners of growth group methods subscribe to what is now called "humanistic psychology."

A growth group seems definitely not the place for persons with acute or chronic interpersonal difficulties that will demand continuous attention from the group. (Such persons, we believe, belong in individual or group psychotherapy.) The growth group is suitable for persons who can function effectively in most areas of their living; it is oriented toward those persons who are willing and able to enhance the growth of the group and the persons in the group, without needing hours or days of the group's attention and time.

two insight approaches to the therapeutic growth situation

There has been a proliferation of growth group approach styles, differing in their purpose and methods. As we examine them, remember that not all of them will be to your taste. Some, to be sure, may sound very strange and bizarre; others will provoke your interest, but your own style may not warrant exploring this approach to any serious extent. But there may be one or two approaches that do apply to you and fit your personality structure or present needs. We add the same cautions here that we did in Part 2, in which we discussed some of the physical approaches to mind-body integration: let your head be your guide! You may well discover a growth approach that seems to you appropriate to your current level of development, life crisis, or life transition. Our aim in presenting these approaches is not as missionaries seeking to convert you but simply as an overview. Some of these approaches have been criticized by other workers in the field; some certainly are better for certain personality styles than for others; and some may be only for the courageous few.

Transactional Analysis

Transactional analysis was founded and formulated by a psychiatrist, Eric Berne,[16] and has been popularly translated by a psychologist named Thomas Harris.[17] Transactional analysis takes its name from its therapeutic approach, namely, to analyze any verbal or nonverbal transaction that occurs between two persons from moment to moment.

Within all of us, explained Berne, there is a complex of three psychic states: the *exteropsyche,* the *neopsyche,* and the *archaeopsyche,* which have been simplified to the *parent-ego* state, the *adult-ego* state, and the *child-ego* state. The three ego states develop separately and at different times. Moreover, they seem to operate distinctly within the human personality. (See Box C).

THE CHILD-EGO STATE.   The child-ego state is the most primary psychic state and, according to TA theorists, begins at the moment life begins — at conception. This state contains all the drives, needs, and impulses of the internal biological organism. At the psychological level, it is the *feeling* aspect of the personality. The child-ego state, then, is a complex of everything we have ever felt, wanted, tasted, smelled, and experienced as children, both the positive and negative aspects of our sensory and emotional awareness. We retain the child-ego state all our lives, no matter how mature and "adult" we may become.

The child in us has both its constructive and destructive elements. As a constructive element in our psychic make-up, the child-ego state represents our creative spontaneity (a child is spontaneous); our drive to venture out into the world (a child is adventurous); and our ability to laugh with joy, delight, and enthusiasm (for that is the essence of childhood). The child in us also has its negative aspects: our sulkiness (no one can be as sulky as a child); our temper tantrums (those "terrrible two" years); and our resentments and frustrations (the child's reaction to the "no's" of society). In other words, they include all those negative emotions and feelings that we also have as children.

THE PARENT-EGO STATE.   The parent-ego state begins to develop, said Berne, at the moment of birth and consists of all the "tapes" of the parents' verbal and nonverbal interactions with the child. In addi-

Box C
Our Three Ego States

CHILD-EGO STATE	PARENT-EGO STATE	ADULT-EGO STATE
PERMANENT DATA Internal events: Desires Bodily needs Curiosity Exploratory needs Feelings Discovery Experimental From birth (or prebirth) to five years	External events: Admonitions Do's and don'ts Rules and laws All verbal and nonverbal messages from adults from birth to five years Recorded as T R U T H S All the *How To's*	Evaluating Information gathering Thinking Open-ended judgments
WHEN OVERDOMINANT Always in the grip of *feelings* — anger, tears, sadness, irrational fears	Uncreative Inhibited Rigid Unquestioning Opinionated Narrow-minded	Too "studied" Lack of spontaneity
WHEN USED CONSTRUCTIVELY Motivation Excitement Creativity Growth	Productive habits Life saving Time saving	Is what I felt and thought as a child still applicable?

258

CHILD-EGO STATE	PARENT-EGO STATE	ADULT-EGO STATE
PHYSICAL CLUES	Furrowed brow	Listening attitude
Quivering lip	Pursed lips	Thoughtful
Tears	Pointing index finger	Interested in what person is saying
Temper	Foot tapping	Unperturbed
High-pitched voice	Hands on hips	
Shrugging shoulders	Arms folded across chest	
Rolling eyes	Wringing hands	
Downcast eyes	Tongue clucking	
Teasing	Sighing	
Delight	Clearing throat	
Raising hand for permission		
Nose thumbing		
Squirming		
Giggling		
VERBAL CLUES	"Always . . . ,"	"Let me see if I understand
I wish	"Never . . . ,"	this . . . ,"
I guess	"How many times . . . ,"	Who? What? Where?
I want	"You make me mad . . . ,"	When?
I don't know	"If it weren't for you . . . ,"	
I don't care		

Adapted from Thomas Harris, I'm O.K. — You're O.K. (New York: Harper & Row, Publishers, Inc., 1969).

tion, the child is constantly "recording" the interactions ("transactions") of all the significant adults with each other. Thus, the child is a kind of tape recorder of the external world around him/her for the first five years of life.

Specifically, the parent-ego state, as it develops in the person, consists of all those spoken rules and regulations of the parents (and older siblings), all the "shoulds" and "should nots," and all the non-verbal gestures, facial expressions, vocal murmurings, and postures peculiar to each of us. The parental role is largely to "socialize" the child, consisting of warnings, prohibitions, proverbs and maxims, injunctions to do something or not to do something, the imperatives "never" and "always", and the everlasting "Let me show you how to do it *right!*" Consequently, the parent-ego state within us is that part of us that says "no," "it can't be done," watch out," or "mark my words"—the fears, concerns, and guards we develop as we grow up.

THE ADULT-EGO STATE.   Berne believed that the adult-ego state begins at about ten months of age, for it is then that the child is becoming autonomous—learning to crawl and generally able to get around on its own. The ten-month old child is beginning to manipulate objects deliberately, to feed itself, to begin to point to things it wants, and so on. The adult-ego state is different from the parent-ego state in that the latter is "borrowed" from others and is introjected whole and without question. The adult-ego state is the "data-processing computer" which integrates the several sources of information coming to us: the *feelings* within that are the child-ego state: the *rules* and *regulations* proscribed and recorded by the parent-ego state; and the *understandings* we gain in our adult-ego state. If our adult-ego state is working well, then our distortions from childhood are "corrected" as we get older. Thus, if we are carrying a memory of resentment of our parents as the result of a disciplining, our adult-ego state allows us to form a new understanding of the events of that "terrible injustice," and we come to forgive our parents for the deed.

Still, all three ego states are present within us since all the recordings are permanent. We cannot erase them. Furthermore, if two people are talking together, six ego-states can be conversing with each other. To put it more simply, when two persons are having a verbal transaction, they may interact as if six different persons are talking with each other. As an over-simplified example, let us imagine a verbal interaction between a husband a wife:

HUSBAND: *(operating in adult state)* What happened to my cuff links?

    WIFE: *(operating defensively in child state)* How would I know where they are!

HUSBAND: *(operating reprovingly in parent state)* Because you borrowed them, and I knew you wouldn't put them back!

WIFE: *(operating in "bad news" parent state)* Just like all men, you always blame things on women!

HUSBAND: *(operating now in his child state)* Oh, so now you're on a women's lib kick!

WIFE: *(suddenly emerging in her adult state)* I'm being silly! I guess I meant to put them back and didn't. I must have put them in my jewelry box. I'll come upstairs and look.

HUSBAND: *(now returning to his adult state)* I guess I got my back up, too. Don't bother to come upstairs, I'm right here! Yeah, here they are.

Berne's group therapy attempts to enable each member of the group to recognize when he or she is being child or parent and to use them constructively. In that way, group members learn not to channel all their emotional conflicts through earlier fixated levels of responding and to be able to escape stereotyped behaviors. Thus, they have more clear choices available to them while interacting with others, who may be functioning at more primitive levels of responding.

AIM OF THERAPY.   The aim of therapy is to enable us to become aware of how we use ego states inappropriately and to learn how to use them to our benefit. Always remember that we can never (even if we wanted to) erase our child and parent "tapes"—they are permanent "recordings." Furthermore, each has its value in the natural order of things. The child in us is that spontaneous, alive, creative life force that gives us joy and delight and motivates adventure and relationships. The parent-ego state has its special function of self-preservation. (The child is naturally impulsive and headstrong, knows no fear and has no built-in safeguards for survival.) The parent-ego state is the accumulation of 5000 years of maxims and admonitions. If we eliminated these admonitions, we might very well never survive childhood. When used appropriately, the adult-ego state enables us to reason thoughtfully about our life problems, to reconsider the confusions and anxieties of childhood, and to escape from parental tapes so that we can become truly our "own" selves.

Berne said that the advantage of transactional analysis is that other approaches can take a long time to effect change, while TA is something the person is able to utilize immediately, by learning quickly to tolerate the anxieties of the past and to control the acting-out behaviors so characteristic of the child and which are self-destructive.

Gestalt Therapy

The essence of transactional analysis is freeing ourselves from our games and other ritualistic behaviors. Another therapy that seeks to do the same thing is gestalt therapy, formulated by Frederick (Fritz) Perls, a psychiatrist who trained many persons in this approach. It was Perls's contention that we do not operate as an integrated whole; that we have splits in our personality. We act out these splits in a constant struggle between our "top dog" and our "underdog." These two roles represent our parents who vied with each other for authority and dominance in the family unit, and which we have introjected within our personality. Do not be misled by the terms for these forces within ourselves for while the top dog frequently is the louder and more aggressive aspect of our personality, the underdog has powerful manipulative devices to get its own way—devices such as *martyrdom, weakness,* and *coyness* which topples the top dog fairly frequently.

Since we have these "splits" in our personalities, we tend to manipulate others into positions of top dog while we act as underdog (or vice versa). The aim of gestalt therapy is to enable the person to see the splits within the self and how they have been projected onto others. In that way, the person is able to become more "whole," which is precisely the meaning of *gestalt.*

THE FIGURE-GROUND RELATIONSHIP. According to gestalt psychology, we need to become aware of our sensory-experiencing as it changes from moment to moment, so that the meaning of the *figure* (what is occurring in the foreground of our conciousness) can be understood in relation to the *background* (all the possible stimuli in the environment to which we are not paying attention). When we can see both the *figure* and the *ground,* we have accomplished a complete *gestalt;* that is, we understand at that moment ourselves in relation to the world. The theory behind gestalt therapy is difficult to comprehend by reading about it (as you are now doing). Perhaps the theory will be easier to grasp by giving you a taste of gestalt therapy. The following is an actual therapy session with Dr. Perls himself, as it took place early in his professional career in the United States, and of which we were a part.

A GESTALT THERAPY SESSION. In this group was a pert and attractive young woman (let us call her Miss Y) who came into the group with a smile and a hello for each of the other members of the group, almost all of whom were men. The group had not "started" yet, for Perls frequently allowed the therapy to evolve out of the situational "happenings" (often much to the surprise and consternation of the group members, who felt "caught unawares"). Mr. X, one of the group members, made a seemingly joking remark to the young woman, Miss Y, that went something like: "I see you are being your usual flirtatious self." The attention of most of us was immediately riveted on Miss Y, but Perls turned his attention to Mr. X.

PERLS: What do you "see," Mr. X, when you look at Miss Y?

MR. X: (somewhat startled by Perls' attention) I was just making a joke!

PERLS: Let us examine your "joke." What do you "see" when you look at Miss Y?

MR. X: I really didn't mean anything by the remark—it was just a remark.

PERLS: Would you direct your attention to Miss Y now?

MR. X: Sure.

PERLS: What do you "see"?

MR. X: I see a pretty, kind of flirtatious girl, that's all.

PERLS: Would you direct your remarks to her? (Perls always asked the group members to talk *to* a person, not talk *about* the person— which he called "gossiping.")

MR. X: She heard me.

PERLS: We don't allow "gossip"; please direct your remark to Miss Y.

MR. X: All right, if you say so. Miss Y, I see you as being a very flirtatious person.

PERLS: What are you experiencing now, Mr. X?

MR. X: I'm looking at Miss Y, that's all.

PERLS: By experiencing, we mean what is going on in your body.

MR. X: You mean inside me?

PERLS: Ja!

MR. X: Well, my heart is pounding. You've made me nervous.

PERLS: (after some silence) Go on . . . what else do you experience?

MR. X: I'm feeling angry.

PERLS: Could you act out your anger?

MR. X: What?

PERLS: Could you act out your anger? Could you say what is making you angry at Miss Y?

MR. X: I don't know.

PERLS: Would you be willing to try?

MR. X: I don't know . . . maybe.

PERLS: Let us "see" your "maybe."

MR. X: Maybe I will; maybe I won't . . . Yeah, I guess I will. (to Miss Y) You make me mad!

PERLS: Could you tell her more how mad you are?

MR. X: I don't know. (To Miss Y) I get mad at women who flirt around with men.

PERLS: Could you tell Miss Y that you would like her to flirt with you?

MR. X: (suddenly very loud and obviously angry) Why should I! I resent her flirtatiousness. It's manipulative.

PERLS: Would you play Miss Y being manipulative?

MR. X: You mean act like Miss Y?

PERLS: (nods)

MR. X: I don't know if I can . . . All right, I will. (He then takes on a "female" voice and smiles to various persons in the room, saying "Good morning, dear" to each person. Although he does not do a very good job of imitating Miss Y, there is something authentic about his female impersonation.)

PERLS: Could you tell us who says "Good morning, dear?" like that?

MR. X: Why, Miss Y, whenever she comes in the room.

PERLS: You didn't hear me. Who says, "Good morning, dear?" to you like that? (It has become obvious to the rest of us that we have never heard Miss Y use that particular phrase when she greets us.)

MR. X: I don't know what you mean.

PERLS: Could you exaggerate "Good morning, dear."

MR. X: Good morning, dear. Good Morning, DEAR! GOOD MORNING, DEAR! (He is speaking very loudly now, almost screaming, and his face is red. He seems to all of us to be genuinely angry.) GOOD MORNING! GOOD MORNING! GOOD MORNING!
(The room is very quiet now after this—a few moments of intense silence.)

PERLS: What is going on now?

MR. X: (He is visibly shaken, and it takes a few moments for him to respond.) That was my mother talking. She always said that to us when she came into the room.

PERLS: Go on.

MR. X: I can just see her, the bitch! (There follows here a rather involved session in which Perls requests Mr. X to act out each member of the family on one of these occasions: his mother, his father, his brother, and himself. After almost twenty minutes of this "role-playing," Perls has Mr. X return his attention to Miss Y.

PERLS: Can you look at Miss Y now?

MR. X: Sure.

PERLS: What are you seeing?

MR. X: I see Miss Y (then after a few moments) I also still see my mother. It's like a double image.

PERLS: Ah! Can you put your mother into the corner of the room?

MR. X: You mean in my imagination? (Perls nods) . . . O. K., she's over there in the brown chair.

PERLS: Now regard, if you please, your mother in the brown chair. Can you see her clearly?

MR. X: Yeah.

PERLS: Now look at Miss Y, and see if you can see her clearly.

MR. X: Not very. She looks a little fuzzy.

PERLS: Ah. Now, try to shuttle between the brown chair to Miss Y and back again until you can see them both very clearly.

MR. X: O.K. (He spends a lot of time "shuttling" his gaze from the chair to Miss Y and back again).

MR. X: She's gone now.

PERLS: Who?

MR. X: My mother. She's faded out.

PERLS: Now look at Miss Y, please.

MR. X: Yeah, I can see her pretty good now. She's sitting there . . . (correcting himself) You're sitting there looking at me, Miss Y. (Miss Y nods).

PERLS: What is your experience?

MR. X: I'm not angry anymore, at least not at Miss Y. My heart's still pounding a little, but I feel calmer. (To Miss Y) I guess you're not as flirtatious as I thought.

This particular dialogue illustrates many Gestalt principles and techniques of which we can illustrate only a few. First, let us examine Mr. X's figure-ground relationship. The figure in this situation was Miss Y's appearance in the room and her greetings to the group members. The ground was Mr. X's background of his mother and his family interactions, of which he was unaware when he reacted to Miss Y's behavior as he did (his joking about her flirtatiousness, his acting out what he assumed to be her behavior, his first angry words to her). Because Mr. X was unaware of his ground, he also was unaware that his reactions to Miss Y were based on his own private history. He had *projected* on her his own unresolved difficulties with his mother, and the sibling rivalry with his brother. Whether or not Miss Y was actually flirting with the group members was inconsequential. What was important was Mr. X's "double image," how he "saw" Miss Y even in his very first statement, and how he was able to "see" her more neutrally afterwards.

The shuttling technique, demonstrated here, was one of the ways in which Perls enabled the person to "see" both the figure and the ground in proper perspective and to separate one from the other. Another principle of gestalt therapy is to stay with the *phenomenology* of the person: what he or she is experiencing "within"—bodily processes such as Mr. X's awareness of his heart pounding and also his faculty of sight, which in this instance became an important part of the therapy. (At one point, his vision actually became fuzzy.) Another aspect of the gestalt approach is the acting-out of intrapersonal conflict—in this situation, Mr. X's anger with his mother and sibling rivalry with his brother.

Finally, you will note that during the therapy session there is very little, if any, interpretation about what is going on. Perls declined to let Mr. X "intellectualize" his phenomenology; instead, he was encouraged to act it out, exaggerate it, and "be it." At the end of the therapeutic session, there was no discussion of his "problems" and no "interpretations." It was enough that Mr. X had become aware of his dualism; what he chose to do with that awareness was not Perls's concern.

Other transcripts of Perls's therapeutic sessions can be found in *Gestalt Therapy Verbatim,*[18] and there are several books by students of Perls's. Perls also wrote an unorthodox and fascinating autobiography, *In and out of the Garbage Pail.*[19] in which he reveals his own top dog and underdog in all their frank dimensions.

three therapies directed specifically to behavioral change

In the therapies we have discussed, the aim is *insight,* on the assumption that insight leads to change in behavior. The therapies we now will discuss have behavioral change *as a specific objective.* You already encountered one such therapeutic approach in Wolpe's deconditioning therapy in chapter 5. The objective of that method is to enable the person to face the feared situation (or phobia) under relaxed fantasy conditions and then to face the feared event in the "real-life situation."

Implosive Therapy

Implosive therapy is similar to Wolpe's desensitization therapy in that it forces the person to confront his or her phobic objects and dreaded fantasies. Implosive therapy differs from Wolpe's therapy fantasies in one noticeable way. In the beginning of Wolpe's treatment, the person is asked to relax until he or she can imagine the feared situation in its *least anxiety-provoking* aspect. Then gradually the person builds up his or her ability to face the next level of anxiety-provoking stimuli until finally the *most-feared* stimulus can be confronted. Not only is Wolpe's therapy a *deconditioning*, it also is a gradual *reconditioning* so that the person feels more and more confident of his or her ability to deal with the situation.

In contrast to the gradual process of Wolpe's approach, implosive therapy presents the anxiety-provoking stimulus right at the beginning *in its most intense form.* The therapist literally floods the person with anxiety-provoking stimuli. On first watching this kind of therapy, it may seem extremely cruel. The therapist bombards the person with a steady stream of talk about the terrible things the person fears most. The person may sob, cry, scream, and writhe in agony while the therapy is going on, which may take between thirty and forty-five minutes. Of course, if the person wants, he or she may choose to leave the room and never come back. But we must remember that the person has been informed of the therapeutic approach ahead of time so it has not been sprung unannounced. The proponents of implosive therapy add that if the person can endure the treatment, in spite of the terrible anxiety, there often is a sudden collapse of the whole feared phobia or anxiety syndrome.[20] Patients have frequently remarked that their whole defense system has suddenly collapsed, and along with it the fear or phobia. It is, of course, exhausting for both the therapist and the person and takes a particular kind of individual to utilize this approach.

What actually happens in this approach is open to interpretation. It may be simply that imagining the worst that can happen brings up all the repressed material from the unconscious, and this serves to eliminate the emotional trauma. This same phenomenon happens when a person interprets a haunting nightmare and discovers that the unknown is far more fearful than the known. Or it may be that the material which has been flooding the person over and over again during the treatment situation finally becomes so boring that the fear collapses out of tedium. The nurse who is afraid of blood at the beginning of nurse's training frequently loses that fear as soon as he or she has been in a situation a number of times in which the flow of blood is present.

We do not want to imply that one exposure to implosive therapy is adequate for the collapse of the feared situation or fantasy—although implosive therapists say it often is just that fast! Sometimes the person may need two or more exposures, even several, before the fear completely dissolves. The person often is told to do some "homework" by imagining the feared situation on his or her own through the week.

Wolpe has criticized this approach, and we certainly do not recommend it for the faint-hearted! Nevertheless, it seems to have worked for persons who have tried several other approaches to no avail.

A Modified Implosive Approach

Some therapists have adapted the implosive therapy approach, which prompted T. G. Stamfl, its founder, to decry the "watering down" of his method.[21] Despite this, we have developed a more moderate (even "watered down") adaptation of this approach to enable persons to overcome a particular problem, which we now describe.

Each of us has had certain "signal reactions" to something we have been called by others in our environment. These appelations may be racially and ethnically prejudicial, or they may be more personally insulting and call attention to a particular aspect of our physical being. Our family may have tried to prohibit or repress certain behaviors in us, and one of the methods that may have been used was to give us these "tyrannical" names,[22] and we were made to feel inadequate, ashamed, guilty, whatever. The object of them was to get us off balance, by calling us, "fatso," "stupid," "bossy," whatever.

It is just this "tyrannical" exploitation in which we find implosive therapy most helpful. When students in our classes or small groups indicate that they are under the influence of a tyrannical word, we ask them if they would like to drain that word of its power and poison. When their answer is affirmative, we use the following procedure, and so far it has proved 100 percent effective—one of the few therapeutic situations for which we can make this claim.

We ask these persons to sit in the center of the group and to tell us a little bit about how their particular tyrannical name affects them. They may describe their feelings of shame, guilt, embarrassment, confusion when the word is directed at them. Then we ask them to relax and to imagine that they are in an invisible, impregnable bubble. They can hear everything that is going on, but nothing can penetrate the bubble. Then we ask all the members of the group to call them by the feared stimulus word, whatever it may be. The group members each take turns in the name calling. When the persons indicate that the name calling is arousing negative feelings, we stop the procedure and say something like this:

In a few minutes, we are going to start the name calling again. But this time, we are going to ask you to visualize something quite obscene but which is going to take the power out of that word. What you need to do is to visualize, every time someone calls you (stimulus word), a giant turd coming out of that person's mouth. For that is all name calling is, somebody else's garbage—not yours. If you can remember to think of those words simply as giant turds, we are going to begin the name calling again! The louder the person shouts the word, the angrier he or she seems, the larger is the turd coming out of that person's mouth. Are you ready? All right, get back into your impregnable bubble again.

With that, we begin the procedure all over again, and in a very short time, the persons are smiling, giggling, and laughing. They have achieved a new gestalt, and the word has lost its power to tyrannize them.

Rational-Emotive Therapy

In a sense, we all use rational-emotive therapy when we are talking to people who are upset or discouraged about something. We try to explain the uselessness of being upset or "buck them up" when they insist there is no way out of their predicament. If they go on and on with their self-sabotage, we try show them how irrational that kind of thinking is. The difference between this informal level of therapy and what Albert Ellis does is largely a matter of refinement and expertise and the inclusion of a self-management program.[23]

Ellis explained that it is not the original situation that creates our feelings of hopelessness and despair but the nomological belief system that we attach to it which is the real cause of these feelings. Suppose, for example, that a person is a student having difficulty in his academic and social environment. He complains that he is stupid, that he cannot study, that he is a worthless person, and that he is a "born loser." At this point, Ellis explained, the person has himself all tied up in linguistic knots. Ellis educates his clients in general semantics and explains how their statements are irrational and therefore self-destructive. He has them practice turning their irrational statements into

One of the earliest attempts to integrate fragmented
personality was initiated by Sigmund Freud and other
psychoanalysts.

ones which objectify the problem. He tells them to stop generalizing by calling themselves names or categorizing themselves. (We have just discussed how *others* try to tyrannize us with words, what Ellis pointed out is how *we* tyrannize ourselves with labels.) He might ask our hypothetical student what he means by stupid and would it not be more rational to say simply that he has not yet learned how to study? What does he mean by worthless? Would it not be better to say that sometimes he feels discouraged, as we all do? In other words, he encourages the student to apply semantics to his self-reference system.

Ellis also starts the person on a program of self-management. If the student is failing math, Ellis may advise him to go out and find a tutor. He may give him some lessons on how to study and a study schedule which would start him studying thirty minutes a day with a gradual increase in the allotted time up to an hour or more a day. Ellis incorporates any technique into his method that will enable the client to manage his life more efficiently. The keynote in Ellis's rational-emotive therapy is DO IT. All the self-understanding and insight in the world will not get us to our goal without ACTION. People are instructed to go out and practice what they have discussed. Not only that, they must come back the following week and report on their activities!

If the first week's session has dealt with the student's tyrannical self-labeling as "stupid," the second week might be devoted to his calling himself a born loser. Ellis insists on asking, what does that mean? The student answers that he does not have any friends, that he does not know how to make friends, and nobody wants him for a friend. Ellis may glance sternly at the young man and ask him quite bluntly to describe how he has gone out and tried to make friends! Somewhat perplexed, the student may say that he does not go out much, in fact, he spends most of the time in his room watching television. "Well," demands Ellis, "How can you make friends when you spend your time watching television? You are not even trying!" Some RET therapists may order the person to take the television out of his room and to use the time he normally spends watching it in some kind of social activity. Ellis said that the therapist may have to act as a kind of mother hen, social counselor, teacher, anything to direct the person's energies toward the kind of competence the client is lacking. In this situation, Ellis might ask the student what he likes to do. Our hypothetical student responds that he used to like to bowl, and he likes to go to the movies. Who does he go with? questions Ellis. Actually, the student replies, he does not bowl anymore, and he generally goes to the movies alone.

Having this kind of information, Ellis and the student make a plan of social change and activity. The student will approach a person with whom he would like to make friends and suggest going to the movies. What if the person turns him down? asks the student. Go on to the next possible candidate for friendship. Also on the week's agenda: the student is to investigate bowling alleys and bowling tournaments and report back.

All of this may sound very pragmatic and like nothing that anyone of us could not do. To a certain degree, that is so but most of us offer advice and leave the person to his or her own devices for better or worse. The RET therapist is willing to use any action, technique, theoretical approach, or whatever to enable the person to effect change.

Reality Therapy

Reality therapy was formulated some thirty to forty years ago with the objective of enabling the person to overcome *failure*. Like RET, reality therapy stresses *doing*. The psychologist who developed reality therapy, William Glasser, did so to enable persons to overcome their feelings of failure.[24] As a psychiatric resident at a veterans hospital, he was struck by the number of people who were (in their own eyes and in the eyes of others) "losers" and "failures," such as the alcoholic, the mentally disturbed, the delinquent, and the chronically unemployed. Glasser noticed that one of the characteristics of "failures" is that they tend to bemoan their fate but to avoid the responsibility for it. Glasser's specific complaint was that although there was a lot of therapy, it was simply talk and not much action. Glasser is a man of action.

Before we paint an exaggerated picture of Glasser's frame of reference, we should state that Glasser does believe in dialogue, rapport, and other counseling techniques . . . to a point. Too much talking about a person's problems, Glasser believes, tends to overemphasize the person's problems and makes them the focal point of the patient's life style. What is needed, Glasser believes, is for the person to construct a plan of action and to formulate a *new* life style. Glasser does not want to reinforce the negative aspects of a person's thinking. Instead, he urges the therapist to talk about the normal things that good friends talk about, the good things that are going on in the patient's life as well as the not-so-good events. It is better, Glasser believes, to identify with the patient's strengths rather than with his or her shortcomings and limitations. Once an easy and open rapport has been established between the person and the therapist, Glasser proceeds to the next step in the therapeutic process: a program for effective change. Glasser admits that catharsizing emotions is beneficial but that the constant expression of misery, without some plan of action, will simply not help the person.

The questions directed to the person in therapy are as follows: *What are you doing about your problem?. What did you do last week? What do you plan to do today when you leave here? What do you think you could do before you come back to see me next week?* These kinds of questions are a constant refrain in reality therapy.

If the client in reality therapy insists that he or she has no choices the therapy then may be to suggest alternative paths of action. Glasser emphasizes that much reality therapy is done by planning responsible behavior. This planning must not be overly ambitious for that will simply invite more failure, which is just the pattern of behavior that needs to be avoided. If one plan does not work, another is tried.

Sometimes contracts are drawn up between the therapist and the person to motivate the person to work at his or her commitment. One of Glasser's convictions is that many problems are caused by people not living up to their contracts: thus, friendships are broken; employees are fired; parents and children find themselves at loggerheads — because people break their interpersonal contracts. A typical contract in reality therapy for an adolescent and parent might be something like this: if the adolescent cleans her room once a week, the parent will not nag about room cleaning for the rest of the week. Or it might

Encounter groups have developed many techniques to bring people closer together.

be: if the youngster agrees to go to school (not skip for one week), the parent will agree to give him one late night out on the weekend. It is an exchange of fair play.

No excuses are accepted for breaking the contract, but there also are no judgments or punishments. Rather, there is a redetermination of a plan of action, a new contract, and a new commitment. Glasser does not believe in punishment, since that is precisely what the delinquent, alcoholic, or "born loser" is seeking. If the adolescent does not live up to the contract, he has broken the contract so that the parent also does not have to allow him one night out late or use of the car. Thus, Glasser believes, the adolescent begins to realize that his behavior has consequences.

Reality therapy has been quite effective with delinquents, but Glasser is most concerned with the use of reality therapy as preventive education. He would like to see it incorporated in the school system from elementary school to high school and believes that when young people begin to understand that successful adult living is to set goals (first small goals and then larger ones), and then to accomplish those goals, they then may avoid failure altogether.

other therapies

There are other types of therapies. Some may raise eyebrows simply by mentioning their name, such as George Bach's "Fight Therapy."[25] There is a therapy called *est*, founded and headed by a man who calls himself Gerhard Werner. The training consists of a grueling four day marathon in which the participants go through a kind of endurance test. They are insulted, ordered about, verbally humiliated, and so forth, until their whole defensive gestalt system collapses, and they have nowhere else to go but up. The description of *est* sounds similar to implosive therapy except that it uses the group situation rather than the individual situation and the treatment is not personal but includes all the group members.

In addition to these more forceful therapies are the intradynamic therapies such as art therapy, Ira Progoff's diary-situation[26] and Assagioli's Psychosynthesis Approach.[27] Progoff developed some interesting ways for people to analyze their current situation by writing about their life history and their present process. It is essentially the novelist's process but no less valid because of it. Assagioli's approach is, admittedly, a desire to integrate the emotional-intellectual-spiritual point of view. Art therapy is another way to delve into one's psychic symbolism and is very close to dream therapy as a path toward self-understanding.[28]

applications and coping techniques

We have tried to be objective in our discussions of various therapeutic approaches. The reader, however, will want to know how to assess the therapies and how they can be used for his or her personal benefit and professional career. To answer these questions, we offer the following considerations.

1. For the Person Who Experiences Occasional Bouts of Anxiety, Depression, and the Like.

If you have experienced the kinds of feelings described in the earlier part of this chapter, you may be wondering if you are a "closet" manic-depressive or a catatonic personality. Many students do have these kinds of thoughts when they begin to study some of the emotional patternings we described early in the chapter. It is a kind of "intern's disease" (in which the young medical student believes that he or she has several of the esoteric diseases studied in pathology courses). Only this time, it refers to psychological symptomology.

In all probability, you are experiencing the usual everyday difficulties of coping with life. Being a student is not easy. You are doing your best to study, many of you are working, you all are concerned about your finances, and you are interacting with many persons at an intimate social level. Many of you also are trying to take care of a family. College is stressful. Besides coming out as physical symptoms, the stress will come out in bouts of alienation and depression. That does not mean you are seriously emotionally disturbed. It does mean that you may need to slack off a little, rethink what you are doing, and congratulate yourself on your accomplishments thus far, and to get some needed rest and relaxation.

The truth is that all of us, no matter how integrated we may believe ourselves to be, from time to time have days when life seems more than we can handle. We even may fall into despair and lie on our beds for hours rather than get up and face the day.

At these times, it is best to adopt the Taoist philosophy that all things always are changing—always in process. This problem will pass, so too will our lethargy and anxiety. All is ebb and flow. As we look back at our lives, we see that this is so; most of the things we worried about never happened and most of the problems we encountered were solved, and we were better persons for having gone through them. Just remember that we do not have to be adjusted all the time. We do not *always* have to cope successfully.

2. But Suppose That You Think It Is More Serious than an Occasional Inability to Cope!

Suppose you do think you have a long-standing problem, what can you do? Well, most cities usually have a counseling center where you can go, no matter what your finances are. Your own college and/or university probably has counselors who can help you sort out some of your difficulties.

Very frequently, it takes only a few sessions to "sort out your head" and for things to become more manageable. It is one of the blessings of these days, that no one thinks you "have to be crazy to see a shrink!" Those days are long past. It is better to process some of the unresolved problems that bother you than to suffer them needlessly. Just being able to talk about the things that are troubling you is helpful. The problems may still be there, but having someone with whom you can discuss them gives you the strength and support you need to see them from a more objective point of view.

3. Choosing Your First Group Therapy: Let Your Head Be Your Guide.

The reader may very well be feeling rather bewildered at the vast array of therapeutic approaches. How does one go about choosing an approach for oneself or to use in one's profession with patients or in educating adults and children? If you are looking for your first experience in the encounter groups, we can offer no better guide than Everett Shostrom's article entitled "Let the Buyer Beware."[29]

First, never respond to a newspaper advertisement. The encounter group leader should be a qualified professional who probably would not resort to newspaper advertising, which is not considered professional.

Second, do not participate in a group with fewer than six participants. Too small a group will not give a person "breathing room." The interpersonal dynamics can become so strong as to be almost overwhelming at times.

Third, do not enter an encounter group on impulse. Your decision should be made after thoughtful consideration.

Fourth, be cautious about participating in a group with close associates. You need all the privacy you can get, and strangers will not interfere with your privacy when you go home. Of course, there are exceptions to this rule. If you and a spouse are having marital problems and want to enroll in a Masters and Johnson sex therapy clinic, you go together. But in other situations it is a lot easier to discuss problems with a group of strangers just as some of us have had the experience on a long train or plane ride of a deep encounter with a perfect stranger.

Fifth, do not be fooled by attractive surroundings. The experience of the encounter group is an inner one.

Sixth, never stay with a group that has a particular ax to grind or an ideology that seeks converts. You want a broadly based experience so that you can choose your own path.

Seventh, never participate in a group that is not allied with some sort of professional group. Professional qualifications are the safest bet that you will receive expert leadership.

4. For Those Seeking Advanced Professional Training: Enlarge Your Professional Horizon.

There are many of you that will be going into highly interpersonal fields. Some may actually be thinking of clinical psychology or counseling; others may be going into a related field such as one of the health professions or education. Whatever your field, it is worth your while to add to your professional skills as you continue your education. Nurses and dental assistants may not think of themselves primarily as therapists, but they are involved in the therapeutic situation. Healing the body can be improved if we know how to help patients verbalize and deal with their anxieties. Furthermore, there are many so-called "apprehensive patients" in the dentist's chair. Knowledge and understanding of therapeutic techniques will benefit both the patient and the staff. Persons considering the rehabilitation areas may want to enroll in courses or workshops devoted to specialized approaches like reality therapy or rational-emotive therapy. If you will be working with nonverbal children or adults, you may want to investigate the therapeutic forms of art and music.

As you advance in your professional training, you may want to take advantage of training in gestalt therapy or transactional analysis. Professionals constantly seek to improve their professional qualifications and to enhance their techniques. Furthermore, your own integrity and creativity will expand.

5. Helping Another Person to Grow Requires Recognizing and Working with the Person's Strengths.

Carl Rogers emphasized the need of the therapist to *like* the person with whom he or she is working. He called it "unconditional positive regard." But what if we are working with an adolescent or sociopathic personality who is doing everything possible to annoy us or to dodge the real issues? It is difficult to maintain that positive regard when it seems the person is doing everything he or she can to obstruct our attempts to help. First of all, forgive yourself for giving way to momentary fits of irritation or discouragement. Then, try to discover at least one strength or attribute on which you can build. Glasser advises us to relate to the positive aspects of the person's character. If we get too caught up in people's miseries, complaints, or problems, we may simply reinforce their inadequacies, excuses, or limitations. It is better, says Glasser, to deal with them as we would anyone.

A psychiatrist we know is a consultant to a psychiatric ward. An old man of about sixty was brought in to the hospital because his depressions had become so severe he had hardly stirred forth from his small fishing shack and was on the verge of starvation. He was dirty, almost toothless, and he smelled! Our psychiatrist friend, on learning of the old man's occupation, brought in a large maritime map that included the man's own home territory, spread it out on the bed and asked him for advice on fishing spots in that area. The old man responded instantly, and the two spent several hours in the next two weeks discussing the best fishing areas, types of lures and bait to use, and things of interest to fishermen the world over. The old man responded more to that approach than he had to the medication and "professional" and conventional approaches that had been tried. He left in two weeks and went home considerably brighter in appearance and manner.

We do not want you to think that the old man was cured. He comes back every so often when the world seems a little confusing again. He and the psychiatrist talk about what seems to be bothering him, but both enjoy talking over fishing news as well. With a little medication and a visit every three or four months or so, the old man avoids being put in an institution and becoming a complete invalid.

6. Remember that You Cannot Become a Therapist to the Whole World.

As you gain more understanding of psychology and therapy and as you mature and become more compassionate, remember to safeguard your own emotional health. As a matter of fact, if you have chosen one of the interpersonal fields as your future career, the chances are that you are naturally warm and empathetic and that people gravitate to you for sympathy, understanding, counsel, and advice. As you learn professional techniques to enable others to grow, you may find that friends, neighbors, relatives, colleagues, and even people you do not know are knocking on your door for help.

You can only do so much. You cannot become therapist to the whole world. Although you may be personally gratified and even receive a certain amount of ego-satisfaction from the attention, the time will inevitably come when you will have to learn to safeguard your own well-being. How can you do this?

First, explain to people that, like all professionals, you have to be cautious about working with people that you know. Physicians are counseled not to treat or operate on family and friends. So it is with the helping professions, but what you can do is to *refer* them to agencies and/or specialists in the particular problem area. You might keep your own card file of agencies in your locale or elsewhere. Also keep articles from journals and a list of books that might be helpful. People seeking help will be grateful for even this much direction. You do not have to be the ultimate resource but just the first step in their own search for resources available. You may want to help them more directly, but referring them to the proper agency may be the most helpful thing you can do.

sex, love, and living together

Ultimately, love transcends everything we can say about it.

I. Introduction: The Quality of "Family Life"

    A. *And they all lived happily ever after: the end of the myth*
         The beginning of reality

    B. *Historical family and sexual arrangements: a brief survey*
       1. *Hebrew polygamy*
       2. *Greek bisexuality*
       3. *Roman infidelity and divorce*
       4. *Medieval courtly love*
       5. *Victorian sexual repression*

    C. *Sexual philosophy and mores*

    D. *Human sexuality as a function of individual differences*

    E. *Human sexuality as a creative act*

II. Human Loving

    A. *What the loving relationship is not*
       1. *Love is not jealousy*
       2. *Love is not possessiveness*
       3. *Love is not just sexual compatibility*
       4. *Love is not self-sacrifice and martyrdom*
       5. *Love is not the "all in all"*

    B. *Some realities of love and marriage*
       1. *Factors that influence choice of mate*
       2. *Predictability of future marital concerns*

    C. *What a loving relationship does include*
       1. *A loving relationship includes mutual support*
       2. *A loving relationship has many dimensions*
       3. *A loving relationship allows for individual differences*
       4. *A loving relationship includes emotional and spiritual renewal*
       5. *A loving relationship evolves*
       6. *A loving relationship stays in the here and now*
       7. *A loving relationship ultimately transcends everything we know about it*

III. The Wide Variation of Living Arrangements: Types of Marriages and Alternate Life Styles

    A. *Premarital sexuality*

    B. *Living together without legal contract*

    C. *Communal living arrangements*

    D. *Marriage styles: utilitarian versus intrinsic*

IV. Applications and Coping Techniques

introduction: the quality of "family life"

In no other time in history has there been such concern about how to form and keep close emotional ties; how to live together; how to work out the family difficulties; and how to help one another lovingly and creatively. Yet, the divorce rate is still rising. Men and women who do live together sometimes do so with anger, with resentment, or with just plain boredom. We see that parents and children often are bitter enemies, at least in the adolescent years; that children are abused and even mutilated by their parents; that adolescents frequently become delinquent; that rape and other sexual crimes are on the rise; and that many men and women live out the second half of their lives alone and lonely. The inability of humankind to live with each other in peace on an interpersonal level has been attributed by some to the "imperialism" of family life based, as it is, on authority rather than on love. David Cooper, in a book entitled *The Death of the Family,* asserted that we learn the basic inequalities, injustices, and alienations from our family interactions.[1]

And They All Lived Happily Ever After: The End of the Myth

As a consequence of the breakdown of our traditional behaviors and rituals, there now are new and experimental modes of being and living together: communal living, group marriage, multiple parenthood, "parents without partners," a new interest in open marriage, more liberal laws for homosexuality, adoption of children by single persons, and changing sexual roles with more equality for women. In addition, the last decades have brought new concepts of human sexuality: "swinging singles," homosexual "marriage," transexual operations, birth control, and marriage without children. It is no wonder that young men and women are bewildered about their future—a future which no longer seems to hold out a fairy-tale promise that "they all will live happily ever after."

This is not to say that the family is finished. Looking at the worst may be just the kind of beginning we need to make if we are to become fully conscious of living, loving, and being together. Marriage is a long-term investment of energy, so it demands the understanding that, of all the institutions of civilized life, the institution of the family has more difficulties, obstacles, and pain than any other.

THE BEGINNING OF REALITY.   It is time to begin to take seriously our involvement with each other on an interpersonal level. When the first blush of romance is gone from a relationship, when the stress and strains of everyday living begin to wrinkle a smooth relationship, when a family member begins to act in ways we have not expected (and which brings anxiety, shock, and grief to the rest), we need not crumble under it. Living together does not mean "sugar and sweetness" for the rest of our days. All relationships have moments of stress and pain as well as of delight. Love includes hurt as well as joy.

Despite the courses on marriage and the family, despite the counseling services to help family members understand and get along with each other, despite the attempt of our schools to provide sex education at an early age, and despite the books to help individuals in close relationships, we still are naive about the difficulties that arise when people live together, and we are terribly unprepared when they do arise.

If this chapter has a point of view, it is simply that living together and loving each other require constant attention and the desire to

We need to get rid of the fairy tale fallacy about love and marriage.

make a relationship work. It is a commitment to work together and grow together despite the stresses and strains of modern life. And we know also that all marriages cannot work.

Historical Family Structure and Sexual Arrangements: A Brief Survey

Family life today is difficult, sometimes almost impossible. In one sense, we *expect* more from the family, we *expect* more from love, and we *expect* more from our sexual relationships. Love, sex, and marriage have been idealized and connected in our fantasies as if they were the same. Such has not always been the case in either Western or Eastern history. Although Judeo-Christian tradition states that a husband and wife should "cleave together," forsaking all others and "be as one flesh," history has not always supported that point of view.

HEBREW POLYGAMY.   The Sixth Commandment in the Book of Genesis is "Thou Shalt Not Commit Adultery;" that is, not to engage in a sexual relationship with other than one's legal spouse. Before that, Hebrew patriarchs might have had one principal wife but were allowed to have concubines or even other wives (as did Abraham, Isaac, and Jacob).

The Sixth Commandment presumably was to reinforce the one-man-one-woman bonding, a return to Adam and Eve. (The word sex, incidently, comes from the Latin word, *sextus*, meaning sixth or sixth commandment.) Yet even after the Ten Commandments, Hebrew leaders continued to have more than one wife and many concubines, as in the stories of David (the shepherd king) and after him, Solomon, who seems to have engaged in the pre-Christian tradition of marrying princesses of other lands as a way of cementing relationships with foreign potentates. Furthermore, the Hebrews had a legal custom which, in Christian times, became a *taboo*: a dead man's next (in age) brother was expected to marry the widow of the deceased to perpetuate his "seed" and to provide security for her.[2] It was a kind of life insurance.

GREEK BISEXUALITY.   Athens may be said (at least at its highest cultural point) to have been a bisexual society. We admire that remarkable fifth-century Greek spirit (as it flowered in Athens), for its achievements in philosophy, architecture, sculpture, poetry, theater, mathematics, rhetoric, and for the concept of democracy, but when we take a closer look at the lives of famous Athenian men, we discover that their idea of a fully developed, loving relationship was not with women, but with other men. Generally, the most perfect relationship was between an older, wiser, more experienced man and a younger, more physically beautiful, and still growing one.[3] The relationship between these two was also that of mentor and student. Later, when the relationship dissolved and the younger man became more mature, he took, in turn, a younger male lover whom he instructed in the aesthetic and political aspects of living. This relationship was similar to the relationship we see today between an older man and a much younger woman. He delights in "molding" her character, taking a personal pride in her personality development; she, in turn, enjoys the husband-father-lover relationship that is a blend of her fairy-tale fantasies. This older man-younger woman liaison ends sometimes with an ironic twist: if the relationship does help her to grow she may, as the years go on, discover that, although she still admires this man, she has outgrown him, while he in turn has simply grown older. At that point she may look elsewhere for her emotional and sexual satisfaction. So it often was with the Greek older-younger male relationship, the difference being that they recognized the relationship was limited. Greece also had a tradition of female homosexuality. The word lesbian comes from the Greek Island of Lesbos, on which female homosexuality was supposed to be predominant. One citizen of Lesbos was the famous Greek poet, Sappho, whose poems suggest her own homosexual inclinations.

Why was Athens an essentially bisexual society? How did the Athenians continue their genetic line if it was a predominantly male-male bonding society? To begin, Athenian men were required to have at least one male heir before they were permitted to engage in such activities as going to war, so as to provide Athens with a second generation. If they did not have a legal heir, they were permitted to adopt one. But most Athenians did have wives and families, and many were not homosexually inclined at all but led totally heterosexual lives.

As for the homosexual element, we need to consider the status of women in Athenian society. By and large, women were illiterate and were kept at home taking care of house, servants, and children. They did not participate in political and philosophic life. Historians tell us that they must have been rather pathetic creatures, treated like chattel, not the kind of educated persons with whom the philosophers could converse on a high level. What could be more natural than for philosophers and others to turn for their "higher" emotional needs to others like themselves with whom they could share not only the pleasures of bed but the pleasures of philosophic and artistic discourse?

ROMAN INFIDELITY AND DIVORCE.   In Rome, aristocratic women had a high status, almost unparalleled in ancient civilizations. Although Roman women could not hold political office or vote, they could inherit land and wealth and were important behind the scenes of political life. Roman women were highly educated, and dinners and parties were not just orgies, but occasions to share influence and power, at which both sexes discussed philosophy, politics, esthetics, and the like. Early Roman society was based on the family, but in later years sexuality became part of the general political intrigue for which Rome became so famous. Although a woman could be divorced by her husband, he had to provide for her security, household maintenance, and even luxury, but divorce was far less prevalent than extramarital relations were. Love affairs between married men and women were far more frequent and sometimes not particularly discreet. Many famous Roman women are known to have taken and cast off lovers at will, provided they did not embarrass their husbands.[4]

MEDIEVAL COURTLY LOVE.   In the Middle Ages, there arose a rather interesting, romantic tradition. Since women had become politically valuable (they were assets to be married off to foreign royalty and nobility in order to establish and cement diplomatic relations), there was little chance for premarital romantic attachments between men and women. The young princess, duchess, or countess often was betrothed, even married, at an early age, anywhere from birth to adolescence, to the sons of foreign royalty and nobility. Most likely, she would not even see her husband until her wedding day. Or she might, on the other hand, be sent off to a foreign kingdom (with a small retinue of ladies-in-waiting and other servants) to live there and learn its language, customs, and duties. It must have been very difficult for them to leave their country at so early an age, cut off from family, friends, and everything familiar.

Although these alliances occasionally did produce warm attachments, the life of a royal female was never very joyful. Medieval castles were cold and damp and, frequently, filthy and smelly. They were dark, too, since windows with glass did not come until the early Renaissance. The "lady" of the house also had the burdensome responsibilities of maintaining order and providing food for her lord's retainers, army, servants, and for visiting lords with their retinues of serving men, sometimes even a small army. Although she might be addressed as "M'Lady," she was, all too frequently, not much more than an unpaid chatelaine or housekeeper. In addition to his wife, the master had his mistresses, some of whom he kept at court and elevated to a higher political position than his own wife, to her evident humiliation. The medieval lord of the fief was not a very glamorous person. Beneath his royal robes, he often was rather unsavory (bathing was not in vogue), frequently illiterate (Charlemagne, who established a school of learning in Paris, around A.D. 800, himself could barely write even his own name), and spent much of his time away hunting, fighting, or settling some minor territorial dispute. He spent little time at home, except between battles. In this bleak world, the lady of the castle led a lonely and isolated existence. She was expected to maintain sexual fidelity and medieval piety. Often she did. But sometimes, she had a romantic lengthy affair of the heart, which we now call *courtly love*.[5] The young man (who might be a member of her lord's retinue, a courtier, or a noble of a neighboring state) would put her on a high and romantic pedestal, pursuing her with poetry, music, and pleas of despair if she did not favor him with her heart, mind, and body. Much of his passion was sheer fantasy, just as movie and rock stars may be our fantasies today. She, in turn, was supposed to resist him at least for a time. If she finally gave way to his despair out of pity and love for his youth, it had to remain secret at all costs. If their affair was discovered (and it is exceedingly hard for us to imagine that it could long remain secret for castles were not very private places), then both were pronounced guilty and punished. The story of King Arthur, Queen Guinevere, and Sir Lancelot is an excellent example of courtly love. How much of this tradition was fact and how much was merely the myth of the medieval era is hard to say. In any event, courtly love did inspire some beautiful poetry.

VICTORIAN SEXUAL REPRESSION.   The Victorian era began in the early nineteenth century with the ascendance of Queen Victoria to the British throne. Women of that era were supposed to remain "innocent" and "pure" even in their married life. It was a scandalous admission for Benjamin Disraeli, the prime minister, to say publicly that his wife was an "angel in church" and a "courtesan in bed." There were "illicit" relationships, particularly between noble men and prostitutes, serving maids, or the governesses of their households. There was a tradition, also, of the governess or serving maid indoctrinating the adolescent sons in the mysteries of sexual pleasure. The governess who submitted (that is, was seduced) had to bear the shame of being a "fallen woman" while the young man was said simply to have sown his "wild oats."

Sexual Philosophy and Mores

Our history of sexual practices has been very brief. We could have mentioned, for example, the medieval attitude toward the "pleasures of the flesh." The Church elevated celibacy above the state of marriage, declaring virginity to be a superior way of life, a more likely one for the salvation of one's soul. This is still a tradition in Hinduism and Buddhism. Yogananda, the Indian mystic who came to this country, tells us in his autobiography that his parents engaged in sexual activity only once a year and then only for reproduction.[6] We also could have mentioned that homosexuality still prevails as an accepted fact in the predominantly Arabic nations.[7] We did not discuss the rather public sexual practices in certain primitive societies. Most Western persons would find it difficult to have sexual intercourse in the public conditions of these societies, as, for example, among the pygmies of Africa.[8]

Human Sexuality as a Function of Individual Differences

Social scientists have concluded that any form of sexuality between two *consenting* adults does not need society's sanction. Some social scientists have appealed to the general public for more tolerance of human sexuality in its many and diverse manifestations.[9]

Yet despite our more open approach to sexuality, it is remarkable how prevalent the fallacies of sexual behavior still are. For example, there still is, in this country, a phobic anxiety about homosexual rape and seduction of young boys. Although we may occasionally hear of a homosexual rapist or even of a homosexual murder, they are far less common than heterosexual rapists and murderers. We accept heterosexual rape and violence as an aberration of sexual behavior; homosexual violence also is an aberration of the homosexual life style. We need to remember that the homosexual perference has included some of the most remarkable and gifted persons of all times. Alexander of Greece, Julius Caesar, Richard the Lion-Hearted, Plato, Aristotle, Christopher Marlowe, Somerset Maugham, and Peter Tschaikovsky. Our sexual preferences are more diverse than are any of our other basic drives.

Generally, our sexual readiness and our sexual responses are closely tied to our upbringing, attitudes, goals, and socioeconomic background. For example, persons from lower socioeconomic strata tend to engage in much more frequent but much more *conventional* sexual practices. It is at the middle to upper levels of the socioeconomic strata that sexuality becomes more varied and less routine.[10] desire for sexual activity may originate at the reflex level but its potency, manifestations, and intricacies are influenced by our intellect. Even what arouses and holds our sexual interest varies from person to person and again is influenced by our sex, age, and so on. For example, research confirms that women are much more prone to fantasy, even violent fantasy, during sexual intercourse than men are. The woman may imagine that she is being made love to, not by her husband or lover, but by a total stranger—she may even imagine she is being raped by an unknown person.[11] We know, for example, that women need and value (at least in our culture) foreplay to be aroused to full sexual climax. Despite the Western tradition that the human male is the aggressor in sexual behavior, those who have studied sexuality in other organisms have observed that it is generally the female of the species that initiates and triggers the male sexual response.[12] In human sexuality, this triggering is done in highly sophisticated and subtle ways: in Victorian days it was the drop of a handkerchief and in medieval days, the delicate lowering of the eyes. In today's society, the sexual messages daily become more explicit.

Human Sexuality as a Creative Act

In every area of our lives, we can take a routine approach or we can vary it in order to make our lives more interesting and creative. When we sit down to a meal, it would be dull to eat the same thing day after day, week after week. We enjoy a variety of foods; sometimes we even go out of our way to eat something exotic. We do not wear the same clothes every day. We change our decor from room to room. We choose different books to read, according to our mood; sometimes we pick up a mystery because we want an escape, and read nonfiction when we want to be challenged.

We do not advocate license or sensation. But sex can become as monotonous as anything else can. Sexual sharing can be as varied and experimental as any other creative act. Two persons engaged in sexual intimacy for the first time need not feel driven to consummate the sexual act. Neither need they feel that all must go "perfectly" the first time, or even the second time. Impotency and lack of orgasmic climax is not a sign of deficiency. It may be the result of inexperience, anxiety, ill health, and a tendency to believe the fallacy of the "first-night ecstasy." Just as we learn to become more expert at dancing, golf, studying, carpentry, piano playing, or at any field of endeavor, so too we can we become more skilled in the actual practice of loving sexuality. Masters and Johnson proved, beyond a measure of a doubt, that couples who have difficulty with sexual intercourse, can unlearn their fear and learn sexual pleasure.[13] We could add that it is no psychological sin (that is, neurosis), to choose a celibate premarital existence and to enter marriage as a virgin. We stress this because of the many young persons who have to come to our office bewildered by the peer pressure they receive to lose their virginity as soon as possible. Their questions are: "Is it O.K. to follow their traditional desire to refrain from sex before they get married?" "Is something wrong with me when I resist?" "Am I really old fashioned?" To these questions, we can only answer, "You must do what is right for you and you only." It is far more unhealthy for you to engage in sexual activity only because you think you should or because you have been talked into it. One longitudinal study, comparing couples who had "tested" their sexual compatibility with couples who had had no premarital experience, showed no greater tendency to stay together.[14] Authenticity of personality comes from following one's own basic structure and orientation toward life and not the dictates and prejudices of others, in sexuality no less than in other areas of life. It is even "all right" to remain celibate for one's whole life if that is one's inclination.

How do two people learn to be more creative in the sexual act? There are, besides the Masters and Johnson type of clinics, many other centers for sexual education. Many publications and also films on sex education are available. But probably nothing counts so much as the relaxed communication and ease between two people as they increase their intimacy and caring.

human loving

It is far more difficult to discuss the loving relationship than the sexual relationship, simply because we do not know precisely what love is. Sexuality is concrete; love is an abstraction. Books on sexology can present diagrams of the female and male genitals. The sexual act can be illustrated by pictures or drawings of various positions of sexual intercourse, complete with text. There is much material on sexual practices in various cultures and societies. Researchers have correlated sexual intimacy, courtship, sexual activity with many other human variables. Discussing sex is relatively easy. But when psychologists broach the subject of love we tend to tread very softly. Love is not something we can see, touch or describe in a diagram, despite the number of personality theorists who have attempted to do just that. Frank Cox, in his book on human intimacy, said that the more we try to define love, the harder it becomes to analyze. He concluded that "love is what you make it."[15]

What the Loving Relationship Is Not

Before attempting to establish guidelines for the loving relationship, it is good to clear out the debris of mistaken notions. There are many fallacies in our society of how love displays itself. These fallacies are misleading and prevent our discovery and rediscovery of the loving relationship.

LOVE IS NOT JEALOUSY.   There is perhaps no more dangerous misconception than the one that jealousy is "the other face of love." A woman may enjoy her husband's jealousy, considering that to be a demonstration of her husband's love. But jealousy pertains more to the person who is exhibiting jealousy than to the subject of that jealousy. Jealousy implies a lack of trust in the partner as well as a lack of confidence in oneself in being able to retain the partner's attachment. A jealous person is not only jealous in love; that person will tend to be jealous of friends, relatives, and associates for many other kinds of attributes: their jobs, their salaries, their seeming good fortune, their good looks, everything in which he or she feels deficient by comparison. A jealous person is extremely hard to endure. The jealous person may not always express the jealousy directly; in that case, it will come out in devious and subtle ways: martyrdom, "game-playing" tactics involving revenge, irritability (such as slamming of cabinet doors), and sulking. The point to remember is that the jealousy (if the charges are unfounded) can never be stopped or satisfied by protestation, or even by proof, of innocence.

LOVE IS NOT POSSESSIVENESS.   One of the most destructive aspects of romance is the desire to possess the other's focus, interest, and energies all the time. In the first blush of attraction, it is natural for two persons to want to be together as much as possible, to learn about each other, and to share their interests and recreations. Eventually, however, as the two persons come to know each other well and have shared many mutual interests, there comes a time when both will have less need to be together, to do everything together, and to find complete satisfaction only in the other. A loving relationship, once it has been established, allows for individual preferences. But on occasion, one partner may not be able to loosen the hold over the other. This partner seems to need and demand constant attention and devotion from the other, which can be emotionally exhausting to say the least.

Unless we are very extraverted, most of us need some time to ourselves. For example, a man may like to go fishing alone or with friends, something which the wife may not enjoy, but she puts up a fuss every time he gets out his fishing gear. A woman may enjoy being politically active in the community, but her husband resents the time she spends away from home.

Sometimes this conflict of interests has a tragic outcome. The person may give up that pleasure, be it fishing or hunting, athletic or political endeavor. The person loses that joy or interest, and a part of the self atrophies. Sometimes giving up one's extracurricular enjoyment may be done with the best of intentions or with no seeming upset; yet, later in life, we find people admitting that they wished they had not done so. It comes as a relief for them to learn it is not too late, if they have the courage and conviction, to return to that pursuit that once meant so much to them.

LOVE IS NOT JUST SEXUAL COMPATIBILITY.   We have come

a long way in recognizing that sexual compatibility enhances the marital relationship. Yet, despite our more sexually liberated society, we may be overemphasizing the sexual component of a relationship. Sexuality is more than just sex. As one woman put it, "My husband can ignore me all day long, and then, at night, he wants me to slip into his arms for sex. I can't just turn on and off on a moment's notice. I try to tell him that but he acts like there is something wrong with me."

Women differ (as men do) in their approach to the sexual act. Some women are easily aroused and can have several orgasms. Other women have a slower (and deeper) rhythm and pace. Some people are able to enjoy sex for itself; for others, it is bound up with affection and general warmth, and for them, the sexual act needs a more personal quality, moments of shared quietness beforehand. Rollo May said that human beings are the only creatures who face each other in the sexual act; who can incorporate tenderness with hands, arms, body; and who can gaze into each other's eyes during the sexual act. Human love can manifest in emotional expressive acts of complex and extraordinary subtlety—the feeling of two becoming one, spiritually as well as physically.[16] Sexuality is not necessarily sexual prowess. Alan Watts pointed out that we could learn much from Eastern attitudes toward sex. In the West, he said, we have a compulsion toward the orgasmic climax—like our American attitude toward everything else, we feel that we must "get somewhere," must complete a project, accomplish something. We sometimes forget the *process* in our rush to the goal. We are in so much of a hurry to get to the office, we do not bother to look at the flowers so carefully planted at the entrance of our office building. Because we are preoccupied with bill paying, we overlook a child's demonstration of affection as he runs to meet us. So it is with the sexual experience. In fact, said Watts, we do not need to reach sexual climax at all—intimacy can be just as fulfilling, perhaps even more so, without orgasmic climax. This point of view may startle a few of our readers. We have become indoctrinated in the necessity of sexual climax. Watts added that there are pleasures to be had by the unfulfilled, nonclimactic approach which prolongs rather than satiates sexual ardor and attraction.[17]

James McCary stated, "Good sex means more than the number and quality of climaxes, frequency of coitus, positions assumed, or techniques used. The best sex is not merely a physical response but a mature affirmation of love."[18] Masters and Johnson added that unless the hearts and minds of the couple are also part of the act, the physical act of sex ultimately becomes boring.[19]

Surprising research on marital satisfaction has revealed that marital happiness does not necessarily depend on absolute sexual compatibility. Although a large percentage of men and women equated sexual compatibility with marital happiness, a number of long-term marital partners who had judged theirs as a "happy marriage," admitted that their sexual life was not as compatible as it is "supposed to be." In this instance, the couples attributed their marital happiness to other factors: tenderness on the part of the other along with thoughtfulness, a desire to please the other, and a "happy family life." These now classic studies revealed that "emotional support" and "doing things together" were two of the main ingredients of marital fulfillment.[20] One social scientist recommended affection rather than romantic love. Romantic love may grow from affection, he noted, while too often, romantic love is followed by disenchantment, even hostility when "the honeymoon is over."[21]

LOVE IS NOT SELF-SACRIFICE AND MARTYRDOM.   In their early eagerness to please the other, lovers occasionally become martyrs to the relationship. "I will be anything you want me to be; I will do anything you want if it will make you happy." In the beginning, the other person may delight in such devotion, but all too often, the readiness to subjugate one's individuality and interests has other unhappy consequences. The one for whom we are sacrificing ourselves begins to take us for granted, loses interest in such a submissive male or female, and may end by finding another partner who mystifies, excites, and provides constant challenge. If we invite such treatment, then, in all probability, we shall get it.

There is a continuing drama played out over and over again which many teachers and students will recognize. It goes like this: the young couple marry when the man is part way through college (or even just beginning) and the woman agrees, is even delighted, to put him through school. He is getting his M.D. or Ph.D., and she is getting her P.H.T. (Putting Husband Through school). Perhaps one, two, even three children come along. Now she frantically races to the nursery school or the babysitter to drop the children off before she goes to work and picks them up when she comes home. Sometimes her husband has a night class and cannot be home with her in the evening; sometimes she is typing part-time (to earn extra money); sometimes he shuts himself in the extra room so he can study. She understands completely, and though she is sometimes lonely and feels a little lost, she is proud to be able to contribute all her energies to him and to their future. She neglects herself physically, her clothing gets a little dowdy (she is saving money for next term's tuition or for doctors' bills), but she does not mind that. Sometimes she wishes she had a chance to go to the movies more often or go to a restaurant with her husband, but she "makes do" with her bag lunch at work. The end of the story? Many readers will have anticipated it. She manages the seemingly impossible; she gets him through school to get whatever degrees

Love is not self-sacrifice, nor the giving up of one's identity for the sake of others.

he needs. *She* feels a sense of pride and achievement. In the meantime, *he* discovers that he has "grown" but that she has not. While she is feeling noble and happy, he begins having small talks with her about his needs, their marriage, and so on, and the marriage ends in divorce. (Often there is another female in the background who steps into the role of the wife the minute the divorce is final.)

What can be done to prevent this gradual disinterest in an emotional relationship? Those who specialize in sex education have suggested many remedies. The woman can occasionally use seductive techniques, including clothing (or no clothing), "teasing," or "appearing suddenly in his den with two cocktails for them." The man may become a very aggressive, dominant lover (particularly if he tends to be passive in the relationship). Others warn against the "too much, too soon" approach which eventually ends in the satiation of one or both partners. Others have gone so far as to recommend aphrodisiacs, using mirrors, vibrators, and perusing sensuous literature and art. Still others advise "vacations from each other," extramarital affairs, and so on.

Frankly, much of this advice sounds rather mechanistic. Our approach would be to urge each partner to develop an internal sense of self-worth. By self-worth, we mean to continue to grow and to develop individual, self-rewarding interests and competencies. There is nothing so enticing as a vivacious person with interests. In that way, two people can bring to each other their outside interests and experiences and retain that original charm. But again, we urge that couples do what is most appropriate to them.

LOVE IS NOT THE "ALL IN ALL". "Falling in love" (whatever that may mean to you) is not the solution to all life's problems; it is not "the happy ending" of one's current existence; it certainly is not a magic pill that will bring eternal happiness for the rest of one's life. Falling in love (being romantically involved with a person whom we trust and admire) is certainly an exhilarating experience. Loving another human being is one of the richest and most rewarding emotions we can ever have. Life takes on a new dimension; we seem to move to another level of consciousness; and there is a special quality to everything we see, hear, or touch. We are transported from our everyday world to a place beyond anything we ever imagined. Time may seem to expand, and, paradoxically, one has a sense of timelessness. Love is so difficult to describe that even poets can only point to it with metaphors.

All that is true. But marriage counselors warn us that the rose colored glasses of lovers blind us to what the other person really is. We do not see the blemishes in the other person; he or she is perfect. And, of course, no one is perfect. Even the best of friends never get along perfectly. If you are getting along "perfectly," it simply may mean that one or the other is going along passively, giving up some aspect of the self for the other—a potentially destructive element already in the relationship. Relationship is give-and-take, understanding-misunderstanding, expectation-disappointment, and mutuality-conflict. Living, said Jung, is a matter of reconciling polarities—and so it is with love. After the rose-colored glasses are shattered, after we see that the other does have blemishes, after we understand that the other person is not perfect but has faults (as we all do), we will discover that all the problems we thought had disappeared magically are still there. Love does not remake the world. Love does not inherently change character (except perhaps temporarily). Love does not pay the bills. One of the most comic-tragic things we hear people say is "Oh, I know he/she is stubborn/irritable/jealous/lazy/(whatever) but I'll change all that after we get married." No one is ever radically changed by love or by marriage.

Some Realities of Love and Marriage

FACTORS THAT INFLUENCE CHOICE OF MATE. We hope that no one still believes that marriages are "made in heaven." The persons we are attracted to, come to love, and eventually marry are not those far away from us in geography, personality, or status. The very reverse is more often true. We tend to become attached to a person with whom we have frequent contact. Social science calls this the *propinquity* factor. We are really more apt to marry the boy or girl "next door" than some stranger from far away. What is more, we tend to be attracted to persons like ourselves, who come from the same general social class, age, race, ethnic group, and religion. We even seem to marry those of similar intelligence.[22]

Opposites may attract, but we will get along better with people who have similar attitudes, interests, background, and values. There is one exception to this general principle: Men are more willing to marry women who are less educated, who come from a lower stratum of society, who are younger, or who are less intelligent. Women, evidently, prefer to marry a man who is generally "above" her in all these factors.

PREDICTABILITY OF FUTURE MARITAL CONCERNS. It may be "speaking to deaf ears" to suggest that when two people are considering marriage (or to produce children in a "free love" situation), to consider all aspects of genetic tendencies. If you knew that there was a genetic tendency in the family of your loved one to inherit blindness or deafness, or to develop a dreaded disease, would you seriously discuss the advisability of having children? If you knew that in twenty years, your loved one may be bald (his father is bald) or fat (her mother is fat), would you still be attracted physically to him or her? Someone has said (and we wish we knew who) that if you want to know what your lover will look like in twenty years, take a good look at his or her parents and grandparents. Eventually, beauty fades; we begin to get that middle-age spread; our faults become more pronounced; and we are heir to physical ills. We become more and more (not less and less) like our parents as we grow older.

Do you agree about how to raise children? If not, there may be problems if one comes from a permissive home, and the other comes from a more disciplined home. Two of the most common causes of marital arguments are money and children. Have you discussed the management of both? The present society is a changing society. Women are going out into the world of work; men are sharing more and more of the domestic responsibilities and burdens. Have you talked this out? Or have you assumed that all of these aspects of living together will fall into place naturally? If so, you may be in for some

very unpleasant surprises. Have you put on a "good face" to the other—what Jung called the *persona?* Or have you both shared enough
time together, and worked and played at enough tasks to allow some of
that mask to drop off and to see each other at your worst? Our intention
is not to throw wet blankets on the budding of love and romance but
simply to have you consider some aspects of loving and living together on a long-term basis.

What a Loving Relationship Does Include

In turning now to the qualities inherent in the loving relationship, we
walk on very soft ground, for although many persons have tried to
define what love is, the essence of love often seems to elude us. Although Freud was very courageous in revealing the sexual taboos of
his society, he did not say much about love. It is easier to discuss the
biological aspects of sex with children. It is becoming amazingly simple to teach couples how to be sexually intimate with each other
(thanks to Masters and Johnson) but it is still very difficult to grasp the
essence of the truly loving relationship.

A LOVING RELATIONSHIP INCLUDES MUTUAL SUPPORT. Most
of us have known persons who seem incapable of being truly loving.
They still are egocentrically concerned about *their* feelings, *their*
unhappiness, and *their* problems. With these people, the relationship
often seems to be a one-way street. No matter what we do to try to
please them, it is like a bottomless well. They seem always to find
something else to fret about, to complain about—the need for constant
demonstrations of love seems endless. When we try to discuss *our*
feelings, *our* concerns, *our* problems, they seem unable to get beyond
their egocentric phenomenology. They are children still, emotionally
and morally, unable to comprehend and appreciate another's needs.
This kind of a relationship can be exhausting since it is always *we* who
solve problems, comfort, and nourish the other.

"He does all the talking. He never listens to me."
"I can't get her interest when I talk of the things I'm interested in."
"There is nothing at home for me but her endless upset. If I'm upset,
she just gets more upset, so I've learned to keep my mouth shut."
"I'm never supposed to be anything but happy and nurturing. I nurture
him, I nurture the kids, I even nurture his parents. Who nurtures me
when I need it!"

A loving relationship needs thoughtfulness on both sides, the
willingness to give and take, and the understanding that both require
attention and compassion. When there is a long-overdue need in a

person, someone will step in and fill that need. Suddenly, the man finds a woman at the office who seems genuinely interested in *him* again, and not just what he can provide. She finds a lover who allows her to talk about herself occasionally.

A LOVING RELATIONSHIP HAS MANY DIMENSIONS. We do not always have to "love" the other. Sometimes we can get bound up in guilt or remorse, because we get angry at the other, irritable, or downright nasty. When we are young, we either "love" our parents or "hate them": *either-or*. That is the child's one-dimensional world.[23] If we are not fixated at this child's level, we come to understand that our love for a person has many dimensions: pain as well as joy, and conflict as well as agreement. Carl Rogers noted that sometimes when persons come for counseling they are confused about their feelings toward another. During counseling the person may discover he or she is truly angry at the spouse, and that it is all right to be angry.[24] Sometimes the person feels many emotions: impatience, upset—even, at times, indifference. These experiences do not mean that "love has gone out the window," it means, rather, that there is a crinkle in the relationship that needs attention. The first step in ironing out that crinkle is recognizing that, at that moment, we do not feel "loving," that we do feel impatient, upset, angry—even indifferent. We stop the "tragedy" and step out of the "personal" aspect—we become more "impersonal," less defensive, and more open to what is going on with ourselves and with the other person. It is a little like saying, "Oh, I see that we have come to an impasse for the moment. Let's see if I can understand what is happening from my side and from your side. He/she thinks/believes/wants this, and I think/believe/want that. It doesn't mean we don't love each other; it simply means we have hit one of those chuckholes or bumps that occur in any relationship." The thing we have to do is to see if we can talk it out, not at the top of our lungs, not by hurling accusations at the other, not with defensiveness, but with a willingness to share our point of view and to grasp that of our partner. We do not always have to be together; we do not always have to agree; and we do not even always have to resolve the situation *right now!* We can, at least, agree that we need to back off from each other for a while and resolve our differences when we both are calmer and less defensive.

One therapist, George Bach, boldly asserted that we need to learn to fight with each other and named his approach "fight therapy."[25] That may work for the aggressive person. What we may really need to do is to learn to fight fairly. Learning to fight fairly requires several ground rules and the cooperation of both persons. For example, fighting fairly means not accusing the other of crimes but pointing out what disturbs us. Fighting fairly means discussing current situations, not all the problems from "day one" of the relationship. Fighting fairly means allowing the other person to express his or her feelings, to get them all out and not to jump in with, "Oh, I see, sure, I'll do that," or "Oh, I'm sorry, I won't do that again." Fighting fairly means making sure both end feeling that they have arrived at a reasonable solution.

A LOVING RELATIONSHIP ALLOWS FOR INDIVIDUAL DIFFER-ENCES.   Although we may marry persons similar to ourselves, we are, at the same time, always different. A loving relationship recognizes those differences and allows for them. We know a man and woman who have been married many years. Each of them was married before and each brought into their relationship two children. The man is in business, highly successful, very extraverted, gracious, and with a generosity that has contributed to his success. The woman has a different kind of personality, multifaceted, artistic, and participates in many community art projects with others. She also is involved in community affairs which is a little more difficult for her husband since his job necessitates many trips away from home. Despite their differences, they have maintained a good relationship. The husband says: "I get a kind of reflected glory out of my wife's artistry and activities and enjoy getting in on that part of life to which I am, by nature, unaccustomed. I think she feels rather the same way about my business and other pursuits." They seem to recognize their two worlds and allow each other full freedom to pursue them; yet, at the same time, they enjoy those opportunities when they can share the overlapping moments. It has not always been easy for them; they have had to go through many soul-searching encounters with each other, since they have experienced some of the value shifts Levinson has discussed in *The Seasons of a Man's Life* (chapter 1).

One of the aspects of the parent-child relationship, particularly in the adolescent years, is the "generation gap" that both experience. The father may want the son to "follow in his footsteps," and he is disappointed when the son's inclinations and interests seem to point in other directions. A mother may feel confused because her daughter does not value the same things she does. An example: a young lady we know has a mother who is a socialite in her community, a socialite in the very best sense of the word. She involves herself in charitable pursuits, is a fund raiser, and gives banquets or dinners for liberal causes. The mother dresses very well and is a vibrant and outgoing person. By contrast, the daughter is introverted and does not value the gracious life. While she has a distinct type of beauty, she prefers jeans and other casual clothes, shuns make-up, and is, of all things, a farrier; that is, she shoes horses. Learning to be a farrier required almost a year of training. Although she was the only woman in the class, she was deemed an outstanding student. She is now trying to get into the college of veterinary medicine—to the dismay and bewilderment of her mother, who was taught that a lady does not do those kinds of things.

Allowing the other person his or her individual differences allows that person to grow. Allowing yourself to "own" your individual differences allows you to grow. Each person in a dyadic relationship needs space for those differences—this is ultimate freedom.

A LOVING RELATIONSHIP INCLUDES EMOTIONAL AND SPIRITUAL RENEWAL. The commitment to allow each other to express individual differences, also necessitates the commitment to plan moments *together* and not just through the children. Although the American ideal is to have a wonderful family vacation together with the children, children can interfere with the relaxed, private intimacy of two people. Part of the attraction of a premarital or extramarital affair is the fact that the two persons are sharing something together free from the constraints of a small tot pounding on the bedroom door at those precious few moments of intimacy; free from the nagging routine of dishes, mowing the lawn, gathering dirty clothes for the laundry, or fixing the plumbing leak. How can two persons have a loving relationship when one or both are too exhausted to do anything at the end of a weary day but collapse in bed? The two persons are just living in the same house as contrasted with being together in a private place with time to relax, talk, and have a drink or watch the sun set, walk, or whatever. Studies of sexual frequency in marriage reveal that as each child comes along, the frequency of sexual intimacy decreases.[26] Parents owe it to themselves to leave the children occasionally at home with relatives or babysitters and plan an escape from the endless routine of diapers. Children can be a source of joy, but they also are demanding. Unfortunately, the most critical time for this escape comes at the very time when money usually is the most scarce. When babies come along, the wife has had to quit working, income is reduced, and the bills pile up. Yet, this is the time when both need to find ways to be with each other. If the couple have no relative with whom to leave the children, they still might find other couples in the same economic situation who would be willing to "pool" the children. You take theirs for a time so they can get away, and they take yours so you can get away.

There is more to being together than simply time and privacy. There needs to be a sharing of mutual interests. Some of the most happily married couples (in this marriage-disillusioned society) are those who work together: both practice medicine, do research, teach, or are in business together. The work binds them: they can share ideas and projects or simply discuss their individual interests. If a couple does not have this specific work interest, they certainly must have had

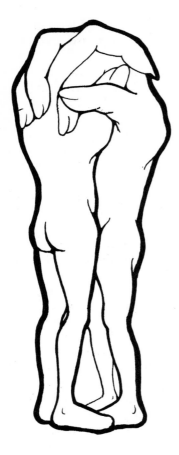

*Love is a coming
together of the body,
mind, and spirit.*

something in common when they first knew each other. If they met on
the golf course or tennis courts, have they continued this interest or
have they abandoned even this special enjoyment? Did they once
enjoy gardening? Do they still? Did they used to go to the theater or
football games, but recently is it just too much trouble to secure tickets
in advance and arrange a "football" or "theater" party with friends?

A LOVING RELATIONSHIP EVOLVES.   There is a natural evolution
in the loving relationship, just as there is a natural evolution in the
process of our lives. Our needs change from one developmental cycle
to the next, as Erikson put it. Our values are different from one era to
the next, said Levinson. In the early days of knowing each other, the
romance of the relationship dominates. There seems to be an ever-
present need to be together, to talk, to touch, to caress, and to share
physical intimacy. But given enough time and privacy, this terrible
urgency begins to recede, and other needs begin to take over: the

need to put down roots, establish a life structure, pursue career goals, begin a family, and generally establish one's position in the community. The loving relationship requires an understanding of these elements, and some of its libidinal drive is diverted into other experiences. In that sense, the passionate desire to be together evolves into the excitement of sharing the activities of communal living and of looking forward to and planning for the future. As the life cycle continues, and if the relationship has been constructive for both persons, there is another dimension: having shared years of emotional experience. Having lived so long together and becoming familiar with the other's moods and subtle nuances, you can begin to talk a kind of "shorthand." Meanings do not have to be "spelled out." A situation may suddenly be the occasion for a humorous or nostalgic reminiscence. Having weathered emotional storms and temporary setbacks, each has a wealth of knowledge of the other, and when one of the partners has had a hard day or receives bad news, the other knows instinctively what to do to help.

A LOVING RELATIONSHIP STAYS IN THE HERE AND NOW. One of the problems in any relationship (friendship, parent-child, husband-wife, lovers) is the tendency to assume that people and relationships will remain the same. People's conceptions of us remain what they were when they last saw us. This probably happens in one way or another to every college student when he or she goes home after being away at school. The college student will feel different and is different, to some degree. But family and friends will still consider the college student as he or she was before. So it is with the persons in the loving relationship. Presumably, over the years, we both have grown; presumably, we have been pursuing our own creative and individual needs; presumably, we have been evolving from one life-cycle to another. Our own needs will change; so will the other's needs.

We need to remember not to assume that what was right for one or both partners remains right year after year. It may come as a surprise to us when we hear our partner begin to express hopes and dreams never before expressed, perhaps not even experienced. This is not the time to say "But you said you never wanted . . ." or "If I had known that you would suddenly want to do this, I never would have married you in the first place."

We may suddenly discover that our partner (who has seemed happy and satisfied with life in general) is expressing ideas and needs completely alien (seemingly) to his or her past life style. The person may be at the Age 30 or Age 40 Transitions, to use Levinson's formulations, or may be at the point of life that Jung called the "search for one's soul."

A LOVING RELATIONSHIP ULTIMATELY TRANSCENDS EVERY-
THING WE KNOW ABOUT IT. No matter how much advice you may
receive from us or any other authority, the loving relationship transcends everything we know. We may be able to list some of the factors
contributing to long-term marriages; we may be able to provide some
insight into what can destroy a relationship. But, ultimately, no one
can provide you or any two human beings with a prescription for happiness, successful marriage, or love.

Nor can we really describe the loving relationship. It is more than
sexual compatibility; it is more than the satisfaction of personal needs
or the search for the "neglected function"; it is more than just having
someone conveniently in the background. Love has less to do with the
pelvis than with the heart. It is less what we can *receive* from it than
what we can *give* to it. It is less *expectation* than *commitment*. Johnson and Masters, those masters of sexual intimacy, end their book, *The
Pleasure Bond,* with a chapter on "Commitment." All the sexual techniques in the world do not replace the truly caring affection and regard two people have for each other. Masters and Johnson:

This is the foundation on which all future affectionate relationships will
be constructed. The search for (sexual) pleasure—and pleasure is an
infinitely deeper and more complex emotional matter than simply sen-
sual gratification—continues throughout life. The quality of marriage is
determined by whether the pleasure derived exceeds the inevitable
portion of displeasure that human beings must experience in all their
associations. Where there is more displeasure than pleasure in a marriage, a husband and wife are more aware of the obligations of marriage,
than they are of its rewards. It may clarify the subject if their bond is
characterized as a *commitment* of obligation.
In contrast, there is the commitment of concern, a bond in which a man
and a woman mutually meet their obligations not because they feel
impelled to do so. They do so in response to impulses, desires and convictions that are deeply rooted within themselves, not all of which do
they fully understand. When they act in each other's best interest, even
though this may at the time be in conflict with their own immediate
wishes, they are saying to each other, in effect: "I care very much about
your feelings—because your feelings affect mine. Your happiness adds
to mine, your unhappiness takes away from my happiness, and I want to
be happy.[27]

Furthermore, the essence of the loving relationship will always
be more than any authority can ever know about it. Any two persons
bring to their loving relationship their individuality, backgrounds,
interests, and creativity. The loving relationship between two persons
is not, cannot, be the same as that of any other couple. All of our "do's
and don'ts" are merely suggestions for interpersonal harmony. They
may not work out in practice. There are no absolute prescriptions for a

loving relationship any more than there are absolute prescriptions for mental health, success, or even life.

Psychologists and psychiatrists are not magicians. We are people very much like yourselves trying to comprehend what living is all about. We observe people, we try to make our observations objective, and we draw conclusions. But we are well aware (most of us, anyway) that there are no magic love potions. Each couple must work out their problems, their despairs, and their barriers no matter what kind of advice and suggestions we may give. In the next chapter, we will discuss some verbal and nonverbal techniques for relating to each other, and these techniques should be helpful in communicating, one of the very important ingredients of emotional relationships.

Finally, none of us knows what two people can experience together in a loving relationship. It is an unpredictable, continuing process.

the wide variation of living arrangements: types of marriages and alternate life styles

Americans have inherited the Judeo-Christian-Puritan-Victorian tradition of love, marriage, sex (in that order) as if they were one concept: lovemarriagesex. This is called *monogamous marriage* and implies virginity before marriage, fidelity within marriage, and remaining together until death. We noted that monogamous marriage is a concept, perhaps an ideal, which has not been generally sustained in either current society or in the past. This ideal, however, has merits in providing mutual physical and emotional support, dividing labor, and nurturing the new generation. In our time, the ideal of monogamous marriage has been somewhat modified by societal sanction of *successive* marriage; that is, lovemarriagesex first with one person and then with another. But living arrangements vary far more widely than even this. Although some of these alternate life styles are admitted by only a small percentage, the actual percentage who do practice these bonding styles may be much larger than we know. At any rate, let us take a look at some of these other bonding arrangements.

Premarital Sexuality

One of the significant findings of the Kinsey report, one of the first sociological studies on the sexual behavior of Americans, was the double standard of American morality at that time (just after World War II).[28]

Although both men and women openly subscribed to the belief that sex was unacceptable before marriage (but more so for women than for men), personal interviews with thousands of Americans revealed that this verbal attitude, sanctioned by the churches and by our prevailing societal ethic, was not upheld by research data. Although men espoused the view that women should enter marriage as virgins, they also believed it was better for the man to have some experience before marriage. Premarital sex for men was deemed to improve the chances for marital satisfaction, but it was thought that premarital sex somehow "sullied" the woman. Indeed, even after marriage, men were more apt to condone their own infidelity but not the infidelity of their marriage partner. The actual frequency of premarital sex among both men and women was considerably higher than was expected by the sanctioned mores of our society. At the time of Kinsey's report, some 85 per cent of American males had had sexual intercourse before marriage, and about 50 percent of American women had had sexual intercourse before marriage.

Subsequent studies of premarital sexual frequency indicated that it has risen considerably and is still increasing. The most ambitious survey since the Kinsey report, one which interviewed over two thousand persons, revealed that by the early seventies premarital sex had become even more widespread. The *Playboy* survey, as it is called now, revealed that about 75 percent of unmarried women under the age of twenty-five admitted to having had premarital sex.[29] The Playboy survey has been more or less confirmed by many other surveys.[30]

Not only has the frequency increased, there also has been a change in attitude toward premarital sex. By the early seventies, Morton Hunt reported that both men and women had adopted more liberal attitudes toward premarital sex. Eighty-four percent of the men thought premarital sex was acceptable for males and almost as many (81 percent) considered it acceptable for women (under certain conditions such as degree of "real" emotion and affection).[31] Even the Gallup polls announced that a far smaller number of persons considered premarital sex as wrong. In 1969, 68 percent in a Gallup poll were still against premarital sex, but four years later only 48 percent still believed that; a significant change in attitude in so short a time. Attitudes, as any psychologist can tell you, are extremely hard to change. Yet our attitudes on sexuality are changing at an astonishing rate, faster even than our prejudicial attitudes toward ethnic groups.

Among college students, the question has become not so much whether or not premarital sex is permitted, but what kind of premarital sex it should be: casual, with one's fiancé(e), or a trial marriage.

The double standard of morality is beginning to dissolve and whatever scruples persons may feel about the "collapse of sexual morality," we cannot help but applaud the collapse of the hypocritical double standard.

Living Together Without Legal Contract

Some writers call it "living together without marriage," but we are reticent to use this because of the prevalence of common law marriage, which always has been a quasi-legal arrangement. Common law marriages are recognized by certain states, to the extent that if a person can prove a common law relationship with a deceased person, he or she can claim some or even all of the inheritance of the deceased. It should be noted that these situations may be very difficult to prove, and although two persons have been living openly together in a community and known to other persons as having a common law marriage, the matter of claiming these kinds of benefits is difficult, to say the least.

We do not have exact figures of the number of persons who are living together at the present time. We know that, as a practice, it is fairly widespread among college students. In Florida where there is a high percentage of elderly people on retirement pensions and social security, the number of old persons "cohabiting" is quite high.[32] Why do they not marry? Their social security benefits will be lowered if they do. They may be old, but they are not demented. They prefer to live together for companionship and for sex (yes, even for sex — despite the prejudice of the young), but they remain single so that their combined income is not reduced.

In nonlegal living arrangements, there are many pros and cons. Certainly, one comes to know another person better, his or her *real* self (the shadow as well as the persona) than in the kind of romantic dating in which each sees the other dressed up and "at his or her best." Some wit once said, "If love is blind, then marriage is an eye-opener." Many high-school friendships have broken up as the result of rooming together in a college dormitory or apartment.

It is in living together that we really become aware of our differences. It is then that we discover that the other person's habits of messiness and leaving clothes around may interfere with our standards and life style of orderliness. Or perhaps one person has an "alpha" rhythm: that is, he or she enjoys getting up at dawn, is cheerful and full of energy. We may be, on the other hand, a "beta" type who likes to sleep late, wakes up in a fog, hates talking before our second cup of coffee, and only really gets going sometime before noon. At night, we are ready for excitement and will be up till one or two in the morning while the other has collapsed at nine or ten. Or we may find that our tastes differ radically in terms of entertainment, friends, the ability to listen to loud music, eating habits, and the like.

In that respect, at least, living together before marriage certainly tests the "romantic illusion." If, after a period of time, each knows the other's limitations and strengths and would rather live with that person than another, then both may feel better about entering a legal status marriage.

On the other hand, living together in our society is fraught with problems; difficulty with parents, for example, who are of another generation and who do not know how to handle visits and have little experience with persons living together openly. We have, as yet, no terms for persons who live together. We cannot ask, for example, "how is your husband?"

Another problem is the breakup of the two persons living together if and when that should happen. With a legal *marriage*, one can get a legal *divorce*. A contract is made legally; it also is legally broken. It is a kind of information processing to other persons in the community, that what was is no longer: a modern rite of passage. No such formal ceremony exists for breaking up a living-together arrangement. Although the breakup may be easier in one sense (it is not costly and does not require lawyers), there is another sense in which legal divorce has advantages: A legal divorce is a signal that the person is no longer married and is thus available for other kinds of sexual alliances, though many divorced persons frankly state that their reintegration into the general community is difficult.

There is another aspect to living together that has come to our attention and which has seemed to us to be almost tragic in its consequences. This relationship sometimes becomes not a commitment of both persons to each other, but the manipulation of one partner by the other—rather like reaping all the rewards of living with another without sharing the burdens and responsibilities.

One example is of a young man who began living with a woman for whom he cared deeply. They had two children. After the birth of the first, and, even more so, after the birth of the second, the young woman proceeded to change her life style. She left more and more of the care of the two children to the man and began to exhibit what society calls "promiscuous behavior." The young man was extremely hurt but, as he said, he got used to that and eventually found other people for his own emotional satisfaction. What binds him to the relationship with this woman (even yet) is his love for the two children. When he suggests that they separate and that he take the children to live with him (for she has demonstrated no great love for them) she says that legally they are hers, and if they separate, she will simply take the children with her.

He could take the issue to court, since the birth certificate lists him as the father. Our legal system, however, generally adheres to the principle that children are better off with their mother. He is investigating the possibility of proving her "unfitness" as a mother, but this is very complicated. Her parents want the children; they are quite well to do and can afford to pursue the matter in the courts. If the suit fails, the young woman may cut the relationship off so completely that the young man may never see his children again.

Admittedly, this is an extreme situation; most persons would not treat each other that way. But we would like to tell you now about a situation which *is* fairly frequent. There are many variations of this story, but it generally goes something like this. The young college woman discovers that she and a young man have a lot in common, and are very attracted to each other. They have sexual intercourse. In the beginning, he goes home to his own apartment or room, but eventually (sometimes quite soon) he begins to stay overnight and to leave for school the next morning. After a while, he may spend the weekend there, sometimes several days. He leaves some of his clothes there for a "quick change." Later, they both agree that it is silly for them to have two apartments when they can save money by sharing expenses with one. So he begins to live at her place . . . and this is where the story gets complicated. What happens now is not clear, but the girl ends up no longer going to school, at least not full-time. *She*, somehow, has become the wage earner since the young man is *not* working. She now is in the position of the married woman earning her PHT (Putting Husband Through), and the girl senses that he has begun "to live off" her and does not know how to claim her rights. She still is emotionally involved with him but their relationship begins to smack of paying him to live with her. He grows careless about his habits, reaches into her pocketbook for extra cash, and if she is good to him, he is willing to sleep with her. One variation of this story was told to us by a young lady who "woke up" when she went home unexpectedly early one day and found him in their bed with another woman.

Communal Living Arrangements

Another form of emotional and physical "bonding" is when several or many persons live together communally. Historically, this arrangement has taken many forms. The medieval church and certain Eastern religions and philosophies worked out communal style habitation for the express purpose of salvation, economic survival, and cooperative efforts for "good works." Traditionally, these monastaries and convents ordained celibacy as one of its tenets on the grounds that freedom from the pleasures of the flesh allows the spirit to transcend earthly attachments. In fact, these situations sometimes deteriorated into nonlegal sexual bonding. Lest there be any misunderstanding, do not believe that celibacy always leads to this kind of *sub rosa* sexuality. We hasten to add that, for many centuries, the religious life was able to maintain denial of the flesh fairly well. Nor should we perpetuate the fallacy that celibacy, any more than masturbation, leads to emotional ill health.

In the United States, communal living has been tried in several different situations. Members of the Mormon church attempted to live polygamously until they were hounded out of state after state and finally even outlawed in their final home, Utah. In the nineteenth century, a Protestant sect, in upstate New York, which came to be known as the Oneida community, practiced a kind of group marriage in which every member of the group was considered married to every other member.[33] Although they had sexual intercourse, they managed to forestall pregnancy evidently by means of a practice known as *coitus reservatus* or *coitus interruptus*,* or by engaging in sexual relations only after the woman had completed menopause. This group remained active for over thirty-five years before it disintegrated through internal and external pressure.

Modern Israel established settings for communal living in its *kibbutzim* (singular, *kibbutz*). The kibbutz style of living is mainly monogamous, but the care of the children is communal and so is the shared work of food preparation, garbage disposal, crop raising, and other household activities. Meals are eaten together. In Israel, even the women are drafted into the army or other branch of military service. There have been some interesting studies done on the personalities of kibbutzim children. One striking characteristic of persons raised together in communes is that they do not tend to become sexually attached to each other. They describe their feelings for each other rather like those for brothers and sisters.

More modern living arrangements have sprung up since the so called "sexual revolution" of the early sixties, but most attempts at long-term, stable, communal existence have not been very successful. Communes are highly individualistic. Some are a kind of informal group marriage with several men and women living together and shar-

---

Coitus reservatus and *coitus interruptus* is the practice in which the man withdraws from the woman before ejaculation or orgasm.

ing the job of parenthood. Others are essentially monogamous, but the members of the commune still share property and the responsibility for child rearing. Communal living, whether it be on a religious basis or a political basis (as in Israel), is an attempt to relate to a group of persons for the mutual benefit of all. Many of these groups still tend to leave the household and child-raising duties to women, while the men take over the physical labor involved in maintaining the economy.[34]

Marriage Styles: Utilitarian versus Intrinsic

Just as there are many types of life styles, so also are there various types of marriage styles. Two investigators, John Cuber and Peggy Harroff, studied "fairly happily married," prominent couples: They were considered happily married both by themselves and by others who knew them.[35] The researchers were surprised that happily married couples did not necessarily resemble each other. In fact, they concluded from their study that there were at least five basic marriage styles. By marriage style, they meant how the couples lived together, raised their children, interacted with others in their social milieus, and related to each other sexually. These five styles could be grouped under two general headings: the utilitarian marriage and the intrinsic marriage.

The intrinsic marriage is what is thought of as a romantic relationship, with each partner finding the other "indispensible" to fulfilling emotional needs. They share as many activities as they can, and each values and needs the physical and psychological proximity of the other. The fulfillment of emotional needs is a source of strength for both partners as well as a source of creative energy. Within intrinsic marriage are two subcategories, the *vital* intrinsic marriage and the *total* intrinsic marriage. The difference is a matter of degree rather than of kind: the *total* couple attempts to interact with each other as much as they can, while the *vital* couple shares fewer activities and less time together. Nevertheless, both types of couples just "click" with each other; their loving is profound, and conflicts, while they may be heated, can be resolved.

The utilitarian marriage is less personal, and the couple spends much less time with each other and at home. They may sleep in separate bedrooms, spend considerably more time in outside activities and with others and may have casual extramarital affairs which may be known and accepted by the other spouse. Yet the couples have a fondness for one another and have worked out a fairly viable relationship. Within utilitarian marriages are three subcategories: the *passive-con-*

genial, the *devitalized,* and the *conflict-habituated.* The passive-congenial style of marriage is frequently found in middle-aged couples who have never experienced any real depth of emotion for each other but who entered marriage in a cool, nonromantic way: They shared interests and each had a "commonsense" attitude toward raising children, and managing careers, home, finances, and so forth. The devitalized utilitarian marriage probably began with a vital interest in each other (and originally may have been an intrinsic marriage), but common interests and activities ceased to be shared emotionally. There is little overt tension or conflict but their emotional and sexual interaction has become devitalized and infrequent.

The third kind of utilitarian marriage is the conflict-habituated marriage and, in fact, this conflict tension becomes the mode of relating.

One may think that the only satisfactory marriage is the intrinsic marriage, for it obviously is what most of us hope for when we are young. Unfortunately, there is a "catch-22" in the intrinsic marriage: it is much more vulnerable to swift change and deterioration. Because the persons put so much emphasis on each other to supply their emotional needs, sexual gratification, and so on, the intrinsic marriage does not seem to be able to sustain the demands on it for too long and ultimately may end in divorce, mutual conflict, or the more benign state of utilitarianism. The passive-congenial marriage which was utilitarian from the start has much less strain and tension, and the couple seldom experiences the same disillusionment and subtle resentment that a vital or total intrinsic couple may feel when the romance has faded.

applications and coping techniques

We have taken some of the "romance" out of marriage, and that is as it should be, for it is the romantic part of marriage that dies. Romance is the flower, the bloom of the blant, that fades. Love is more than romance. The flower fades, but the plant, if tended and cultivated, and cared for, will survive the droughts and torrents. Love is the putting down of stable roots, the shooting forth of many branches, and the eventual blooming again. But like all growing things, enduring relationships need cultivation.

Every marriage counselor will have his or her favorite techniques for long-lasting relationships. You eventually will have your own techniques. No list can include them all, but we offer the following basic ones.

1. Maintain Direct and Sane Communication with Each Other.

Without communication, there is no relationship. Sometimes the first sign of a breakdown in a relationship is a breakdown in communication. Both persons begin to retreat behind a wall of silence, punctuated only by hostile and terse questions and answers. Although silence may be less immediately painful than screaming battles, silence ultimately can become the *modus operandus* of the marriage. The end has already come.

Raging battles, on the other hand, may clear the air, but the wounds suffered may permanently injure one or the other so that the marriage itself becomes disabled.

The issue then, revolves around how to confront the issues at hand—even those painful to discuss—without causing permanent wounds and without retreating into hostile silence. (See Chapter 9.)

2. Allow Your Relationship to Grow, to Change, and to Process.

Life is process. So, too, is every relationship in process. Erik Erikson formulated life as a series of crises to be worked through, tasks to be accomplished, and competencies to be mastered. We may have mastered trust, autonomy, initiative, industry, and identity as individuals, but Erikson warned us that these tasks are never completely achieved once and for all, that it is a matter of a "favorable ratio." *We need now to relearn these tasks in the marriage relationship.* We need to develop *trust* in each other but also *trust* in ourselves. We need to develop a cooperative style of living together but also to establish *autonomy.* We need to find ways to interrelate but also to maintain our own independence and *initiative.* We need the *intimacy* of love but also to maintain our individual identities, and so on.

These tasks will not come all at once. Trust and intimacy will be more important earlier in the marriage, while self-identity and autonomy will become more important later. When the children begin to leave the nest, the relationship may experience once again the need for a new kind of intimacy, and so on. The enduring marriage is one of discovery and rediscovery.

3. Make Room for Each Other as Part of Your Basic Commitment.

Many things interfere with marriage. Children come, financial burdens increase, and job demands take precedence. Sometimes we sacrifice ourselves for "the sake of the children," or we bury ourselves in our work, or we mediate our relationship through other persons. Little by little, we are like two persons simply living under the same roof. It was not anything we did to hurt each other; it just happened — by errors of omission.

We may begin to talk to each other through the children. When he asks her about the news of the day, she replies that Johnnie had to stay home from school because of a cold. Their talk revolves around others: invalided mother, so-and-so at work today, the neighbors.

We need time to be together, to renew ourselves with each other. We need privacy away from intrusions, even the children, so that we can become acquainted with each other once again and rediscover each others' concerns, feelings, hopes, aspirations, and even the changes that have come about since our last encounter.

4. Encourage Each Other to Pursue Emerging Interests, Ambitions, and Individualities.

Marriage is not possession, nor is it ownership. It is a matter of two persons who come together for mutual sharing. Each person has unique interests and abilities which need to be encouraged.

Give each other space and room to grow. Give each other some privacy and time alone. You are separate entities with distinct and individual personalities. Your likes and dislikes do not have to coincide precisely. Marriage is a coming together, but there is an ebb and flow to relationships, and sometimes there must be a pulling apart before we can come together again in true remeeting.

Furthermore, as you grow and mature, you may discover that you now would like to venture into activities and pursuits that did not interest you earlier. Allow your partner to do the same. Love allows the other to grow. Love has respect for the other person's individuality. Both of you will become more exciting persons as the result and therefore more exciting to each other.

5. Surprises are Fun, but It Is Planning Together that Makes a Relationship Enduring.

A man we know became somewhat more affluent. He wanted to do something for his wife for their anniversary, so he bought her a new car and surprised his wife with the keys to it on the morning of their anniversary. Her reaction was hurt. His reaction was anger at her hurt. It was an event that cropped up many times in arguments over the next few years. He was angry that she did not appreciate his gift; she was hurt that she was left out of the decision.

Although we generally are more neutral, we have to agree this time with the wife. Such "surprises" can do irreparable damage, though he may have had good intentions.

All major decisions and many minor ones need to be made together. Marriage and living together is a partnership, and a marriage of minds does not happen when there is a silent partner. Working out the details of a project or the various aspects of problems as they come along brings people closer together.

6. Remember that It Is Sometimes the Little Things that You Do Not Do that Erode Your Marriage.

Most persons in a marriage are aware of the big problems. These are the things that you quarrel about or are the bones of contention. If the two of you are at all serious about making a marriage last, you continually work at these problems. In the background, however, are the many small omissions that may be causing serious (and silent) erosion, things that may seem too small and petty to be mentioned but which foster resentment, hurt, and feelings of neglect. For example, one partner may forget that the two of you agreed to go out to dinner and works late at the office. Or one partner forgot to mention an after-dinner meeting, no big thing, since neither of you had special plans for the evening. Nevertheless, it just "slipped the mind," and the other partner begins to feel that he or she is just not important enough to be kept informed.

There is a way out of this and an easy one. Keep a common calendar of events. List all dates, meetings and invitations. Review it daily and weekly. Check in with each other before making other dates or commitments. In the morning, before one or the other of you leave, review what is supposed to be happening during the day and evening. We do this with our office colleagues, surely we can do it for each other.

7. Finally, Remember that No Two Marriages Are Alike and None is Perfect.

Live for yourselves and not for those around you. Work out the details of your life in a way that is viable for both of you, regardless of how others are living their married arrangements. There are, ultimately, no do's and don'ts except those that the two of you contract together.

language: our spears into plowshares

Open communication between two persons can be a profoundly therapeutic experience.

I. Introduction: The Power of Language

II. General Semantics

Barriers to communication: poor listening habits
1. *The person who jumps to conclusions*
2. *The person who closes his or her mind*
3. *The person who listens only to words*

III. Improving Our Communication: The Art and Science of Listening

A. *Learning to listen*
B. *Listening as the basic form of communication*
C. *Factors affecting our listening*
D. *Listening is more than hearing: it is also attention*
E. *We can learn to listen*
   1. *Good listening is focused attention*
   2. *Good listening requires an objective attitude*
   3. *Good listening is encouraging the other to speak*
   4. *Good listening requires empathy, not sympathy, and not projection*

IV. Learning to Understand the Speaker's Phenomenological World

A. *In the beginning, keep silent externally*
B. *Keep silent internally (do not jump to conclusions)*
C. *As you listen, develop hypotheses only*
D. *Test your hypotheses with the other person*
E. *Becoming aware of our prejudicial listening*

V. Learning to Speak Effectively

A. *Learning not to accuse and blame*
B. *Instead of accusation and blaming: "self-revealment"*
C. *Make requests, not demands*
D. *Self-assertiveness: stating clearly what you would like, or need, or want*

I. Nonverbal Communication

    A. Cultural determinants of nonverbal language

    B. The speaker's paralanguage

    C. Body posture

    D. Incongruent body-speech language

    E. Territorial space

    F. Personal distance

    G. Touching

    H. Clothing

    I. The use of silence

VII. Applications and Coping Techniques

introduction: the power of language

Humankind is gregarious. We tend to congregate together, to live together, to divide our labors for the benefit of all, to share in the education of the young, to come together for thanksgiving and rejoicing, and to seek the company of others when we are at low ebb. We are tribal beings. No other species has developed a way to communicate with each other as we have done through the miracle we call language. With language, humankind became capable of producing civilization. Through the *spoken* word, we can make known our wants and needs to others in our environment; through the *written* word, we have been able to leave a recorded history so that what we have learned does not die with us but is transmitted to the next generations. Through *sound put to music* we can come together for folk song and opera. Through language, we are capable of scientific thought by which we can analyze problems and hypothesize solutions. Language helps each person define his and her individuality; that is, we have the means by which we can proclaim to others in the world: *This is who I am.* And through language, we can ask that other most important question: *Who are you?*

Language, then, is a powerful and magnificent tool. Used effectively and creatively, it is an instrument whereby we can invent a better and more humane world. In that respect, language is what we use to build friendship. Language is what we use to work out differences between management and labor. Language is what we use to work out treaties for trade and disarmament between nations.

But language is a double-edged sword. The same language that can be used to promote good will and understanding can also be used to cause hurt, anger, suffering, and ill-will. We can use language to build bridges, but often we use it to build walls and barriers. We can praise and bless with language, but we also can curse with it. Language can be used to make peace treaties, but also declarations of war.

The study and scientific use of language has become a specialized science called linguistics. We shall turn our attention now to one area of linguistics, called general semantics. General semantics attempts to improve our communication so that language may be used not as a weapon but as a force for saner and more rational ways of interpersonal living.

general semantics

Alfred Korzybski, the founder of general semantics, went so far as to say that the way we use our language can make us scientific or irrational, sane or insane.[1] Consider, for example, the following: a man we know complains continually about his job: his supervisors are unreasonable; his colleagues are uncooperative; and his students are "dumb" and "trying to get away with things." Now all of these may have some measure of reality, and we do not want to imply otherwise. This man, however, never lets up on his pet topic. His working conditions are his constant subject matter to his friends, to his family, and to any of us who will listen to him. We suggested to him once that he discuss his contentions (in a rational and calm way) with his colleagues and supervisors. His retort silenced us for good: "No use trying to do that. Nobody will listen to me!" There is some truth to this, for many of us have become weary of his same old record, and we begin to edge away when he starts up. The point is that this man is "gossiping" continually. He may not call it gossip—he thinks that gossip is what women do with each other. He may call what he does griping or letting off the steam, or even voicing legitimate complaints. But the fact is that much of his creative energy is going into self-sabotage. He is giving himself a "mind set" that his working life is hell and that he is the target of his students and the scapegoat of his supervisors and colleagues. He is not trying to work out his personal upsets with others; he is actually promoting more and more disharmony within himself and with others. In short, he may be driving himself insane, and paranoia may be just around the corner.

Barriers to Communication: Poor Listening Habits

Irving J. Lee, one of the best known linguists of his day, was not only a very effective communicator himself, he was expert in enabling others to improve their linguistic skills.[2] He was employed by many types of organizations (military, business, educational institutions) to train persons to understand why communication breaks down and what to do about it. One of the first things he did was to talk about how people build barriers to effective understanding. In particular, he called our attention to three kinds of persons who contribute to communication breakdown. All three persons demonstrate poor *listening* habits, and *listening* is the basic process of communication. There is the person who jumps to conclusions; the person who closes his or her mind; and the person who limits his or her listening by listening only to words.

322

THE PERSON WHO JUMPS TO CONCLUSIONS.   Persons who jump to conclusions assume that they know the answer to whatever is going on with one or more persons. Should someone miss an appointment, we may say, "I knew he wouldn't take this seriously." If a teenager is late coming back with the family car, we may comment, "I knew he wouldn't act responsibly." Now that may be so. On the other hand, the person who missed the appointment may have had an accident, gone to the wrong office building, or have been given inadequate instructions to get there. The teenager who is late with the car may have noticed on the way home that the tank was low on gas and is spending some time hunting down a gas station so that there is gas in the car when we want to use it the next morning. When we jump to conclusions, we are in the trap of believing that we know everything there is to know about the situation. And, of course, that is *never* possible.

Assuming that we know *everything* there is to know about a situation is, as psycholinguists point out, an *unscientific* approach to human affairs. Social scientists, who are in the business of making their observations more scientific are aware that no matter how carefully they design research, they may come up with misleading or inconclusive results because of something they did not account for, something they call an "intervening variable." What we *observe* is one thing and what we *conclude* from that observation is another.*

Let us give an example from our own experience. We college teachers are not so impervious to student reactions as one may think. Despite our occasionally cynical remarks and professional competence, we are, at heart, very susceptible to the attitudes of our students. We like to know that we are being understood, that our lectures are interesting, and once in a while perhaps even inspiring. Although we may not admit it, a student who looks bored may threaten our ego; our feelings may even get ruffled if a student yawns in class.

Now if this does happen we have made an assumption. We have jumped to a conclusion which may or may not be true. That person may indeed be bored. But there are many other possibilities for the student's yawning, he or she may be on a night shift and the yawn reflects extreme fatigue; the student may be ill and the yawn is part of the general symptoms of sickness, or the classroom may be stuffy and the yawn is the student's physical reaction to lack of oxygen, and so on.

A colleague of ours has a very effective way of emphasizing what happens when he jumps to conclusions or makes assumptions about other people's behavior. He writes the following phrase on the board:

*Law courts attempt to separate observations and inferences by allowing witnesses to report only what they saw and heard and not what they conclude about what they saw and heard.

I ASSUME

When he has written that, he then draws some diagonal lines between a few of these letters, like this:

I ASS/ U /ME

and adds:
"When I make an assumption, I make an ass out of you and me."

THE PERSON WHO CLOSES HIS OR HER MIND.   Some of the most discouraging behaviors are those exhibited by persons who close their minds. These persons not only set up barriers to further communication with others, they also prevent any further growth in their own mental processes. Persons who close their minds tend to make the following types of statements:

"That's it! I've said it! There is nothing more I wish to add."
"I've listened to his arguments over and over again and I don't care to hear them again."
"No matter what else they bring up, I've made up my mind."
"Don't tell me . . . (whatever). I don't want to hear it."
"You can't convince me!"

Teachers sometimes experience this attitude with students, and students may even make these kinds of statements. But sometimes they communicate this attitude with all kinds of nonverbal postures, gestures, or expressions. These students are the ones who sprawl in front of us with arms folded and an expression that says, "Go ahead, talk. I dare you to teach me something." Most of our readers are probably familiar with these students. No matter what the instructor is trying to say, they have an argument—not a legitimate argument to elicit any further information or enlightment, or to bring out another point of view—but a barrage of statements that sabotage the teacher's attempts to make a meaningful lecture.

Persons who close their minds to what others have to say or to opposing arguments both verbal and written, prefer to believe that they know the answer and the whole answer. They hold their own opinions on the subject; they consider only those facts that they consider pertinent; and they reject any new information that does not fit their conclusions. General semanticists urge us to remember to keep ourselves open to new facts, to listen to others' opinions, and to be willing to change our minds or at least to modify our present positions. Otherwise, we continue to harbor superstitions, to hold onto prejudicial and stereotypic thinking, and to close ourselves off from further growth.

Communication means not closing ourselves off to what another person is trying to say to us.

General sematicists have devised a way for us to remember to keep our minds open and to remember that, although we are trying to make precise statements, we can never say everything. They ask us to add the abbreviation "etc." to our statements. Etc. stands for the Latin word *et cetera* which means "and so forth." We cannot very well go around always adding etc. to our writing or to our speaking, or we would sound very pedantic. But we can remember that when we make conclusive statements, we are thinking inaccurately, closing our minds, and preventing ourselves from intellectual growth. Here are some examples:

"My wife is ALWAYS on my back."
"He NEVER understands what I'm trying to say."
"Women are too emotional."
"Don't ever expect a man to understand things like that."

What these statements are doing is generalizing from one or a few persons to all persons, or from a few instances with one person to all behavior. We all tend to make these kinds of statements which blind us to the exceptions. We see or hear only what we want to see or hear. We have closed our minds to anything which might be different from our expectations.

325

THE PERSON WHO LISTENS ONLY TO WORDS.   Words are very inadequate to convey all the information and emotion that we intend. When we hear a person make a statement, we need to know what the person means by certain words. The words people use to convey information, then, can actually lead us to very wrong interpretations. Let us cite an example. Suppose, for instance, a foreman says, "From now on there will be no more personal phone calls," and this actually happened in a company with which we once were associated. Suddenly, company morale dropped to zero. Workers began to mutter to each other. A few employees actually left because they were incensed at the idea that if there were an emergency in their homes, their spouses would have no way of reaching them. When the matter was brought to the attention of the company management, they realized that the foreman's statement was misunderstood, miscommunicated, or misinterpreted. The foreman was simply carrying out management policy, so he was not mistaken. A policy had been established in which employees would no longer be able to make or receive personal phone calls, that is, the kind of phone calls people can make just as easily at lunch or on a coffee break. Of course, if there were an emergency, they would be allowed to receive and to make phone calls. *That is not what they had meant.* But the employees had heard only the words. No one had elaborated on what was *intended.*

Very few of us are gifted orators, writers, or poets who use language competently. We say things carelessly and abruptly. Such statements are open to misinterpretation and can hurt others even when no such hurt is intended. We need, therefore, to understand that how a person says something may be very different from what he or she really means. We need to discover, if we can, exactly what the person was trying to say.

Children (and adults who are still children emotionally) have a tendency to listen only to words. We frequently hear children say about a teacher, a parent, or another child, "But he said . . ." or "She said . . ." adamantly refusing to listen to reason and hanging the other person on his or her words. People in great emotional or mental anguish may not have the coolness of mind to try to explain what they mean. Out come the words, and they come out so badly that we take offense. Even when we are cool, there are frequent breakdowns in communication. Most misunderstandings between people at work occur because of a breakdown in communication. This is such a cliché that we are apt to overlook it.

Language, then, is *more than words.* The actual words we use can lead us astray, sever lines of communication, arouse negative reactions, or prevent constructive action. We need to remember that *what people say is not necessarily exactly what they mean,* or it may not be *all* that they meant to say.

improving our communication: the art and science of listening

We have discussed only a few of the factors that bar effective communication. We could have listed many others. The area of psycholinguistics (how people use language and the effects of language on behavior) is fascinating, and some of you may want to delve into this area a little further. We will now turn our attention to how we can improve communication. The first step is learning how to listen.

Learning to Listen

Ever since we were babies we have been listening: listening to our parents, listening to our teachers, listening to the radio or to television. We listen to our friends and to political speech makers. We listen to our employers or our colleagues. We spend innummerable hours listening to everybody else at various meetings. Why, then, do we have to learn to listen? Sometimes we may feel that it would be nice to wear ear muffs to prevent ear pollution.

Listening as the Basic Form of Communication

We do not listen well. Perhaps we do not listen well just because listening has been so much a part of our lives. Yet listening is undeniably the first step to effective communication. We spent considerable time in the preceeding section discussing the person who listens only to words. Now we need to understand how to listen for meaning. Listening, real listening, is more than a skill; it is an art.

Some years ago, two psycholinguists, Ralph G. Nichols and Leonard A. Stevens, wrote a book on the research on listening, entitled, *Are You Listening?*[3] It has become a classic in psycholinguistics, for it summarized much of the research done on how much we listen, how accurately we listen, and to whom we listen.

Quoting a number of studies, they concluded that we listen far more than we talk. Dieticians were once asked to keep a log on how much time they spent on each of the four communication skills associated with their jobs: reading, writing, speaking and listening. There were 110 dieticians in 48 states and the District of Columbia who responded to the request. Here are the results:

Reading	4%
Writing	11%
Speaking	22%
Listening	63%

Dieticians in supervisory positions spent *three times* the amount of time in listening than in speaking. Other surveys have generally confirmed this.[4] *Listening is our most fundamental communication level.* Yet Nichols and Stevens noted that very few colleges and universities teach listening skills. There are courses in *speed reading, speech making, interpersonal communication,* business, and creative writing— but no courses in listening..

Factors Affecting Our Listening

Studies of listening reveal that we tend to hear what we want to hear and listen to what we want to listen to. We tend to "turn off" when we do not like what is being said, if we are bored, or if there is something about the person we do not like. Have you ever heard a student say, "I can't learn anything from him." If we listen further, we may hear the student say something like this: "I just don't like him. I don't like his personality." He or she has stopped listening. It is not so much that they cannot learn as they will not learn. One of the characteristics of successful students is their ability to learn from anyone, even those with irritating personalities, who are boring, or whatever. They have learned to get around their own resistance to listening; they are more interested in what the instructor is intending to convey than in how he or she says it.

Besides our attitude toward the speaker or the subject matter, there are many factors which influence our ability to listen: people's rate of speech (how fast or slow), accent (they may be immigrants or have a very distinctive regional accent), volume (voice level), the atmosphere of the room (whether it is visually distracting, for example), the temperature of the room, air, acoustics, and competing noise.[5]

But most important of all is our *attitude.* Whether we *want* to listen and to understand will determine how attentive and open we are to what the speaker is saying. No other single factor is of such importance in how well we listen.

Listening Is More Than Hearing: It Is Also Attention

The human mind is amazing in its ability to see or not to see, to hear or not to hear, and to perceive or not to perceive. Most of us are aware that although blind persons do not hear any better than sighted persons do, their ability to use their hearing has been so much more developed that they can find their way about their physical space by paying attention to the echoes in the room.

A clinical psychologist we know spends much of his professional time counseling students and other persons in his academic environment. As a therapist, he is considered outstanding. Yet his wife complained to us she could not get her husband to listen to her, and at home he often seemed "deaf." We asked the psychologist if he would be willing to take a series of audiometric tests. He was willing and did so. There are two kinds of hearing tests. One is for *pure sound*, which indicates whether there is actual hearing loss or whether the person has an adequately functioning auditory apparatus. The second hearing test indicates how well people are *using* their hearing or what attention they are giving to the spoken word; that is, a test for *speech reception*. The two hearing tests revealed a very interesting fact. Organically, the psychologist had very adequate hearing for a man of his age. But when we gave him a speech perception test, the results were dramatic. The profile leaned toward the kind of loss people exhibit when they do not want to listen. The psychologist was as amazed as we were by the results of the tests. While discussing the results (which seemed at odds with his reputation as a skillful counselor), we wondered if time of day were an "intervening variable" in his hearing. We had tested him at 4:30 in the afternoon on a normal working day. By that time, he had spent several hours in counseling and in a two-hour staff meeting. We asked him to come the next morning at 8:30 before he began his day. He again was willing and appeared early the next morning. Again the results were dramatic. The selective hearing loss he exhibited the afternoon before now was gone. He was hearing well and paying attention to speech. Again we discussed the results. It was he, himself, who drew the following conclusion: after many hours of listening to people's problems in counseling and to people complaining in committee meetings, he simply withdraws from listening when he leaves the office. He has had enough, so to speak. He turns off. Whether these results aided the man's marriage, we do not know. We only know that it was a lesson for us.

We Can Learn to Listen

If poor listening is a matter of bad habits, listening can be improved by developing good habits. It is not easy to learn how to listen, but it can be done. We know this because if there is one thing that psychologists, counselors, social workers, psychiatrists, and so on are good at, it is listening. But it is not automatic. It is something we spend months and years developing in our professional training.

GOOD LISTENING IS FOCUSED ATTENTION.   Call this *concentration* if you like. Doing anything well requires concentration, whether it be hitting that golf ball with a balanced swing, typing accurately, painting, or laying bricks. We focus as much of our consciousness as we can on the person; not only on the *words* of the speaker but what the speaker is *not* saying and the difficulty and ease with which the communication is forthcoming. We watch for nonverbal as well as verbal clues. We try to stop the thoughts in our heads (our projections, assumptions, opinions) as much as we can so that we can attend to the speaker. The speaker has our undivided attention or as much as we are able to give. We do not hurry to respond. We give the speaker as much space and time as possible to express the content.

This kind of focused attention is very difficult. The average rate of speech for most Americans is 125 words per minute (give or take some words to account for regional differences: New Yorkers talk much more quickly and Georgians talk much more slowly). But we think much faster than we talk. A study was done in which persons were required to respond to information given at various rates of speed. It was found that college subjects could comprehend spoken material at 300 words per minute. Furthermore, some outstandingly fast readers could scan reading material at better than 1,200 words per minute.[6] If we can comprehend speech and read at these levels, we must certainly be able to think at these levels or better. That means that while someone is speaking, we can be thinking about something other than the speaker's words. Real listening demands the elimination of internal speech, as much as possible.

GOOD LISTENING REQUIRES AN OBJECTIVE ATTITUDE. Acquiring an objective attitude is the single hardest thing to do in real listening. Making judgments of what people are saying or doing or how they dress or where they come from is natural. We make assumptions about what lies behind the words and actions of others: we want to know what really "makes them tick." We have learned over a time that people do not always reveal themselves when they talk; they sometimes camouflage their real feelings or motivations.

Nevertheless, no matter how much we know about the deviousness of human nature, real listening is accepting the person's words without making judgments. Carl Rogers, in teaching his students to be good therapists, advised them to adopt an attitude that has become a classic phrase of therapy. This attitude is *unconditional positive regard* — the ability to accept without negative judgment everything the person is saying and also what the person is trying to say.[7]

Under conditions of complete acceptance, we help create a safe climate for the person to express his or her inner condition. The speaker can begin to drop his or her defenses. Almost all of us have one or two friends or relatives with whom we can be frank. We know that this person is on our side, so to speak, and we can confess our frailties, mistakes, and pettinesses, because they do not judge us — they love us.

GOOD LISTENING IS ENCOURAGING THE OTHER TO SPEAK. In daily life, we can not create that special climate of safety that is the mark of true therapy. Life is too busy and too fast. But we can make an attempt to try to understand the person. We can try to understand the speaker's frame of reference, even if it is not our own. We can listen to what the speaker has to say and to encourage the speaker to express what is difficult to express. We do this by listening and nodding and asking pertinent questions and not by jumping in and giving our own opinions. We listen, despite how the person is speaking (angrily or sorrowfully or boringly).

Consider, for example, what happens when our spouse suddenly erupts with an all-or-none statement: "You never listen to me!" Of course, we all fail to listen sometimes, but that is not what our spouse really means. That statement has been blurted out under the stress of extreme emotion. We can get defensive and holler back some retort like "Well, if you would stop bitching, I would listen," or "Of course I listen; you're being irrational." That kind of retort simply exacerbates the desperation the other person is feeling. What our spouse may really mean is "There is something of extreme importance I want to tell you or share, and I need you to listen and understand." But few of us are given that kind of coolness at the moment of stress. If we can understand that, then we can provide the person with the time in which to express the emotion or thought that lies behind that sort of statement. An attitude of positive regard or at least of alert attention to the moment will enable us to say something like this: "Look, I know I don't seem to listen at times, but I've had a lot on my mind. I'll try to listen now if you'll speak a little more calmly." Or if events are pressing on us, we can say, "I haven't got the time now, but how about later this evening after I have finished what I have to do?" If our spouse wants to remain unreasonable, this kind of comment is not going to help. But if our spouse is at all reasonable, these types of comments will bring a certain amount of relief, and he or she will be able to relax and speak more calmly.

As supervisors on the job, an employee coming in late for the third, fourth, or fifth time may really anger us. But if we challenge him or her while we are angry or irritable, we are only going to make that person more defensive than he or she already is, and that will only create further disharmony between us and the employee. As an employer or supervisor, we need to understand the difficulty the person has in getting to work on time. Perhaps that person has no car or a car that is more often *in* the repair shop than *out* of it. If this is the case, then we might be able to help the person find a solution. If the employee is one of those who has difficulty getting up in the morning (and there are many of us like that), perhaps the person would be willing to work a later shift. There are many solutions to a problem — but first we need to discover what the problem is. Discovering the real problem needs a receptive attitude on our part, a willingness to *listen* without boredom, anger, or irritation.

GOOD LISTENING REQUIRES EMPATHY, NOT SYMPATHY, AND NOT PROJECTION.   One of the qualities of good listening is the ability to be able to to empathize with the person. Empathy is an interesting word. It implies a quality of sympathetic understanding, but it is not sympathy. What is the difference between empathy and sympathy? Sympathy can have either or both of two characteristics. One of these characteristics is "I feel so sorry for you, you poor thing." In other words, *pity*. Pity has a certain superiority to it. It is a kind of condescension at the plight or unhappiness of the speaker. That kind of attitude does not help; in fact, sometimes pity aggravates the situation. That is the second characteristic of pity.

All of us have probably had the experience of seeing a child fall down while riding on a tricycle on the street. We may see him get up and look around to see if anyone has seen him. If no one is present (because we are looking out of the window), he may very well brush himself off and get back on. But if we suddenly run out and sympathize with him by our words and concern, off he goes howling, convinced that something very terrible has happened to him. That is one of the effects of sympathy. It creates an atmosphere of distress which seves only to confuse, distort, and enlarge the problem.

We can see that sympathy is a *judgmental* type of listening, which is not helpful to the speaker. Another judgmental characteristic of listening is *projection*. You will remember from chapter 3 that projection is a defense mechanism. It is the one in which we attribute our own feelings and ideas to others. As a defense mechanism, it is a denial of our own feelings and thoughts.

For example, a rather jealous individual tends to assume that everyone experiences jealousy. A person who experiences jealousy frequently has difficulty believing that there are other persons in the world who do *not* become jealous. Those persons may have other problems, but jealousy is not one of them. A jealous person will attribute his or her characteristic jealousy to others. That is projection.

There is another kind of projection which novelists and playwrights utilize. They project feelings and thoughts into the characters they write. This is one of their creative talents and not to be confused with the defensive projection we have been discussing. But most of us are not authors. We need to remember that we can never really know other persons. No two of us experience exactly the same feelings and thoughts. They may be similar, but they cannot be the same. All we can do is to establish some common understanding.

We do that with *empathy*. Empathy, in the psychological sense, is a combination of understanding and compassion. We attempt to understand what the person is feeling and how the person is analyzing the situation. But we do not pity the person. We listen with the awareness that all of us have problems and we try to understand the speaker's particular problem. We do not presume a righteous attitude; we do not project what *we* would think, feel, or do onto the person. Rather, we try to understand what the person is thinking, feeling, and wanting to do. But we do not get so caught up in the person's plight, that we *suffer the person's symptoms*. That does not help the speaker at all because then there would be two unhappy persons instead of one. This tendency to suffer the other person's symptoms is what professionals in mental health fields learn to avoid, which is essential. After all, we go into one of these professions (psychology, psychiatry, social work, nursing, whatever), wanting to help others in distress. But we learn quickly that if we identify too strongly with the other person, we go home after a day in the office with depression, guilt, and aches and pains. It is sad that the suicide rate among psychiatrists and psychologists is very high. One of the reasons may be that they have taken on the despair and alienation of the persons with whom they have been working, and the emotional overload has become too great.

learning to understand the speaker's phenomenological world

How can we begin to understand and appreciate the other person? The first step is good listening, and we have discussed several attributes of good listening. The next step is to try to come as close as we can to the person's *phenomenology*. We do that by always being aware that no matter how close we do come to understanding how another person feels, we can *never* completely know the other person's world. We can come close, but our phenomenological worlds can never coincide completely. One of the fundamental mistakes that very good friends or enthralled lovers make is to assume that they are completely united in thinking and feeling. Sometimes we hear a person say, "Oh, we are just alike; just like twins (or brothers or sisters)." It comes as a shock when they have a serious disagreement. As we attempt to understand one another, we must remember that all we can do is get an approximate picture of what is going on with the speaker.

In the Beginning, Keep Silent Externally

How then do we go about getting as accurate a picture as possible of the other person's world and that person's plight? First of all, we *keep silent*. We keep silent externally and do not jump in with sentences like "Oh, I know exactly what you mean!" or "How awful!" or "You poor thing." We may respond with a nod, perhaps, or by a gesture that says "Go on, I'm still listening," or with an indication that although you may not be saying anything, you *are* listening, you *are* interested, and you *do* want to hear more, or as much as the speaker is willing to tell you.

Keep Silent Internally (Do not Jump to Conclusions)

Do not jump to conclusions in your thinking. Do not assume that just because you may have had a similar problem you understand what is going on inside the speaker. You may be quite astonished to find, that although the two of you have shared a similar kind of problem, the speaker's reactions are quite different from yours. For example, the speaker may be discussing the agony of a recent divorce. You also may have had a divorce. But, whereas your reaction was relief in getting out of a bad situation, the speaker may be feeling lost and insecure.

As You Listen, Develop Hypotheses Only

When you begin to think you may have an idea, a picture, or an understanding of what the person is trying to say, view it only as an *hypothesis*. This is what scientists try to do. No matter how sure the results or how conclusive the data, scientists know that someday their research may be replaced by a better explanation. A good listener has this scientific caution. Even when we begin to gain an intuitive grasp of the other person's feelings, we are cautious in coming to a firm conclusion. We remember that when a person is trying to discuss something that is emotionally loaded, it is difficult to get it out logically and calmly. This is particularly true when two persons are having a serious argument or disagreement.

One of the strange things about human nature is that when we are upset at another person, we cannot always say what is really bothering us right away. We may say something like, "You never think my opinion is worth anything!" when we would really like to say, "I don't feel very adequate with you. I feel stupid and don't know what to say when you talk to me." It is easier to accuse somebody of a sweeping generality than it is to confess our own feelings of inadequacy and unworthiness. We must understand that a person's first words may be very far from the real difficulty, and that these first words sometimes are only the first stab at trying to express feelings of hurt and rejection. One of the lessons that psychologists and counselors learn is this: that the most important thing a person says often comes in the last five or ten minutes of their hour together. It has taken all that time beforehand to get to the point of being able to express their most worrisome feeling or idea.

This is not to say that we have to wait a whole hour just listening. But we can allow the person to talk before we have to jump in with "Oh, I understand now. Well, that's silly." When you are beginning to think you know what is bothering the person, make that only a hypothesis, one which can be modified in the course of the discussion.

Test Your Hypothesis with the Other Person

Testing your beginning hypothesis with the speaker is one of the most helpful things you can do to establish communication with the other person. This is generally good advice whether it be an argument with a friend or spouse, a committee meeting at which someone is trying to express an opinion or an objection, or even sitting in a classroom trying to understand what the instructor is saying. Instead of making assumptions about what the person is saying, we need to learn to ask questions that help us confirm or correct our understanding.

We need to learn to ask questions like, "Is this what you are saying?" "Is it like . . .?" or "Is what I think I hear you say accurate . . .?" and put our tentative hypothesis into words, indicating that we are still open to further clarification of what the speaker is saying.

At this point, the speaker may say something like, "Well, almost, only it's not quite like that," or "Yes, that's what it is!" Now we and the other person are coming closer to sharing our phenomenological worlds. We know when we have arrived at it because we each feel a common bond. Psychologists call this process "feedback," and it moves communication along over the sometimes difficult terrain of interpersonal conflict to a sense of openness and honesty with one another.

Becoming Aware of Our Prejudicial Listening

As indicated earlier in this chapter, listening comprises the majority of the time spent in communication, but it is difficult to listen well. We grow up with certain attitudes of "right" and "wrong," "good" and "bad," and with other prejudicial attitudes. We are not speaking of the prejudice of one ethnic race or religion toward another. We are speaking of those subtle prejudices which are so much a part of our existence that we are scarcely aware of them. For example, we may pride ourselves on being careful with money, so when we are listening to a person who reveals his or her extravagance and is consequently in a shaky financial position, we must be careful not to color our whole attitude with a feeling that "since he or she has made this financial mess for himself or herself, he or she deserves it." And so we stop listening. Or if, in a meeting, a fat person is talking, we must be careful not to let our prejudice against obesity arouse a dislike for what that person is saying. If someone is expressing himself or herself badly in a committee meeting and is upset and arrogant, we must try to listen to what that person is saying, *despite* how he or she is saying it. The speaker may seem to be foolish but what he or she is trying to say may have some degree of validity, worthy of attention.

Prejudice means prejudgment. As we get older, most of us become less prejudiced and more tolerant. It is one of the benefits of increasing age.

learning to speak effectively

Now we shall go on to the other side of the communication process, the one in which we have major responsibility for speaking. As we have implied, the speaking-listening situation is a two-way street, and the desire and ability to express oneself can be hampered or hindered by the listener's attitude. Still, there are many things we can do as speakers to encourage the listener to listen to us, just as there are many things the listener can do to encourage the speaker to speak.

Learning Not to Accuse and Blame

One of the foibles of human nature is to blame our problems and plights on to others and when we are overwrought, this tendency increases. This tendency has many names, such as *projection, scapegoating,* or *rationalization.* Unfortunately, some persons adopt this attitude as part of their life style. As long as they blame others for their misfortune, they will never achieve the kind of self-understanding that leads to more harmonious, rewarding, and creative living. It is a kind of psychological trap.

Whatever situation we find ourselves in must to some extent be partly of our own making. *Conflicts with other persons,* crisis situations at work or at home, *involve us as well as other people*. We need to start then, as we attempt to iron out wrinkles in our relationships with others, to be aware and wary of accusing or blaming others for our unhappiness.

Furthermore, accusing others of this and that puts others immediately into a defensive position. They may have no alternative at that point but to deny or to retaliate. What may have started out to be an attempt at peace suddenly becomes another battle in the interpersonal war. Eric Berne calls this "courtroom" with one spouse playing plaintiff and prosecuting attorney and the other spouse playing victim and defense attorney.[8] Sometimes another person or persons may be called in to act as corroborative witnesses, judge, or jury. As with most deadly games, nothing is achieved in the end but confusion. As we read newspaper accounts of labor-management disputes or summit meetings between opposing forces, we sometimes mutter to ourselves that civilized people really ought to be able to learn to get together. We forget that we ourselves have difficulty even in a one-to-one situation with another person who we feel has wronged us. As long as we have the attitude of being the injured party, our attempts to iron out difficulties are merely motions which mask our wish for revenge.

Sometimes getting something off our chest is very cathartic, but some prefer to go around with hurt or angered feelings. They wear an air of martyrdom or aloofness. When we ask them what is wrong, they snap, "Nothing!" At least the person who is talking angrily is getting it out.

But while we are "getting it off our chest" and feeling better, we may be making the other person so miserable and alienated that the last thing he or she wants to do at that point is hear another word. We may have so alienated that person that we have closed off any further communication, for a while anyway.

Instead of Accusation and Blaming: Self-Revealment

There is an alternative to starting out with accusations and blaming the other person, and that is, self-revelation or "self-revealment."

Carl Jung called the outer personality the *Persona*, or mask, we wear to hide out real selves. This mask is our public personality.[9] Later Carl Rogers noted that people who have been engaged in therapy for some time, begin to drop this mask and allow themselves to be what they really are, or as many of Rogers' clients put it: the "real me." What these persons discovered was that the *real me* who comes out of hiding is not unlikeable at all. Since the *real me* is so often more authentic than the mask we ordinarily wear, other people seem to like us more and be more willing to listen and get to know us. Revealing the *real me* encourages others to be themselves as well, so they in turn are willing to take off their masks.

Self-revealment takes courage. It is difficult to reveal that one is feeling inadequate, stupid, confused, or fearful. We are afraid others will think less of us, and sometimes this may be so. But more often than not, others can relate to us very easily when we are brave enough to come out with honest statements about ourselves. When others witness our willingness to admit to our human limitations, they too are more willing to admit to their limitations and mistakes. An apology from another elicits admiration from us.

In the beginning, genuine self-revealment is difficult. But when practiced over a period of time, it becomes easier, and we discover its rewards. Finally, self-revealment is so much lighter than the burden of pretense and ego-defensive posturing that we wonder why we ever preferred the mask.

We adopt the mask, the Persona, early in life. Young boys are taught not to cry; young girls are taught there are certain ways they can behave and cannot behave. It starts within the family group and continues through school. The culmination of masking probably comes as the result of interaction with our peers in high school. Adolescents strive desperately to be accepted by their peers. Individuality is not appreciated at this age as much as conformity to the ideal personality of the prevailing group. The adolescent who is not part of the inner circle feels somehow unacceptable. It is an unusual adolescent who can dare to be different and that brave young woman or man pays the price.

Thus, the mask is cemented at the high school level. One of the delightful aspects of college is that one is now in an environment in which one can relate to others more candidly.

How does self-revealment work? When we begin to iron out a difficulty with another, we do not start out saying to another, "Look, I've been a big fool and please forgive me." That is a very remarkable way to begin and is frequently just the kind of frankness that can shatter the walls of Jericho. But that is to take a very cold plunge into the process of self-revealment and may be more than we can manage, at least, in the beginning. If we are used to self-revealment, we can make a statement like that and not be fearful of the consequences. We have learned to be frank and if the other person rejects it, (or us), or tries to take advantage of it, we simply shrug our shoulders and walk away. Our ego has not been damaged. We have done what we thought we should do and if the other does not choose to respond, there is nothing more we can do now. *Our ego is no longer invested in what the other person thinks of us, but in what we think of ourselves.* We have done what we could. Now it is their move. (In time, the person may be able to reflect on our peace offering and reopen communication with us.) This kind of self-support does not come all at once. It is something toward which we grow. Like all other aspects of living, it is a process of maturation and experience.

If self-revealment is new to the reader, we suggest that he or she begin gradually.

One might begin with a statement such as:

It isn't easy for me to say this, so I would appreciate it if you would just let me get this out before I lose my courage.

Look, I'd like to straighten out this difficulty between us, and I don't know exactly how to go about it.

I know we are having some conflict here, but we are both reasonable people. I'd like to see if we could arrange a time to do it when we are both relaxed and with no one else around.

I'm feeling very upset about this, and I'm sure you must be too. I would like to explore our feelings with each other if you would like to as well.

These kinds of statements "test the water." If the other person responds at all positively, one can go on to the next level of self-revealment such as:

"Part of the difficulty is that I feel very inadequate about this situation. I got defensive and said some things that weren't as accurate as they could have been."

"I'd like you to know that I have a tendency to get steamed up about things. You know, 'I fly off the handle.' I'm always sorry about it later. Of course that doesn't help the situation now. But I'm calmer and I think I am in a better position to work it out with you."

These are a few of the beginnings one can make. You will be able to say things in a way no one else can that is relevant to your situation, yourself, and the other person. You never need to be a doormat and invite being walked on. If the other chooses "to take advantage" of your willingness to be open, leave it at that and go about your business. If the other person makes concessions on his or her part, despite the awkwardness he or she may feel, take it in stages. Remember that the other person is probably feeling just as nervous as you are. But from this encounter may come an openness and a friendliness that you could not have imagined.

Make Requests, Not Demands

Suppose, for example, you live with someone who is not as tidy as you are, be it a spouse, a child, or a roommate. You come home to clothes strewn all over, dishes in the sink, and ashtrays full of ashes. Instead of screaming, "Damn it, clean up your mess," you can state your needs much more directly: "Look, I get nervous when there is too much untidyness. I would like to come home to a neat place. Would you put your clothes away, do your dishes, and empty your ashtrays?" You have stated your needs clearly. You have put it as a request instead of a demand. And you have been polite. Unfortunately, a really untidy person cannot change overnight. But if the person has simply gotten careless lately but appreciates tidyness, too, this small request may be just the thing he or she needed to respond.

At this point, the other person may say, "Sure, but I'd like you to do something for me. I have a 'thing' about stockings in the bathroom. Will you dry them in your room instead of hanging them on the shower rod?" or "O.K., but do me a favor, too. Please turn the stereo down after eleven o'clock at night. I'm not a night owl and I need my sleep."

Self-Assertiveness: Stating Clearly What You Would Like, or Need, or Want

We have urged you not to accuse or blame. We have suggested that you reveal yourself. Now we encourage you to state as clearly as possible what you want or need. We tend to assume, in this life, that other people are just like us. We want them to read our minds, as if we all are psychic. When a despairing spouse says to an aggravated partner, "Well, what do you want?"—the partner may respond, "If you don't know, I won't tell you." Now what good does that do? We may be fearful of coming out and saying what we want. We may have learned that it is not right to be assertive. Yet, effective communication needs clear communication.

Learning to be assertive is learning to enunciate your needs clearly. It is being frank about yourself rather than being aggressive toward the other person. When waiting with three or four others at a counter, and the salesperson turns to the customer who came in after you, you can assert yourself calmly and politely instead of aggressively and accusingly. An accusing statement goes like this, "Wait a minute, this isn't fair. I was here first." How is this accusing? You are implying that either the salesperson or the customer was unfair to you. An assertive statement makes reference to yourself, not another. "Pardon me, but I believe I'm next," is *assertive*, not hostile or aggressive. You will notice most people will give way to this kind of assertive but nonaccusative statement. It takes time to develop an assertive but nonhostile attitude. Learn to analyze your statements and the statements of others. Speaking is an art that can be learned. Speaking well gets you to where you want to go. Not speaking out or speaking with hostility gets you nowhere or gets you into a place you do not want to be.

nonverbal communication

Besides the words we use, there is another dimension to language, one which does not rely on words at all but on body movements and sounds. It is called nonverbal communication and includes all those sounds, postures, gestures, expressions, and movements that accompany the speaker's words or the listener's attitude. We tend to think that the verbal aspects of communication carry most of the message being communicated and relegate the nonverbal accompaniment to the background. Yet one estimate of the amount of actual face-to-face message being sent and received between two persons amounted to no more than 35 percent of the verbal communication; the rest was sent and delivered by nonverbal means.[10] The listener's willingness to listen and to indicate interest has an encouraging effect on the speaker. The speaker, whether or not he or she is aware of it, is constantly checking with the listener to see if the message is not only received but welcomed.

Cultural Determinants of Nonverbal Language

We are not surprised when two persons from two different language backgrounds have difficulty understanding each other. Trying to talk to a native French or Spanish person with our high school or college French or Spanish is never as easy as we hoped it might be. That is because there are so many dialects in each major language and much slang in every dialect. It may come as a surprise to learn that nonverbal communication also is distinguished by country or area. People who grow up in the same vicinity develop common nonverbal language habits and have far less trouble communicating with each other than those who grow up farther away. This is true even in our own country. Southerners find Northerners cold and aggressive; Northerners are apt to be put off by the friendliness of Californians. The British with their reserve draw back from our general American willingness to relate to almost anybody anywhere on our own terms. We seem to them brash and perhaps a little rude.

All of these underlying cultural determinants of our communication with each other has been called "the silent language" by psychologist E. T. Hall.[11] But that may be a misnomer, for part of our nonverbal language is the intermittent sounds we make as we speak or listen to another person, such as *hmmm, uh-huh*, or even that sound, *unh*, which we sometimes stick into our speech and which indicates to the listener that we are struggling or groping to find the right words.

The Speaker's Paralanguage

One of the barriers to effective communication often is not *what* the person says but *how* the person says it. Without realizing it, the speaker may say something which arouses resentment, hostility, and downright anger in the listener. A gentle reminder may sound like an outright rebuke, with the result that the listener may suffer indignation or humiliation. One often hears a person say, "It wasn't *what* he said that made me upset/angry/disgusted/insulted, it was *the way* he said it. By and large, if a supervisor or a foreman or a business manager speaks softly and slowly, the employee will be more willing and able to listen without getting defensive. If the speaker's message comes out loudly, quickly, and with a note of irritation in it, the listener is more apt to listen to the emotional quality than to the words being spoken.

As an experiment, say the following statement as if you were talking to an employee in two different ways: first, as if you were understanding and sympathetic to the employee's plight, and then as if you

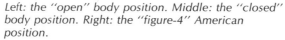

Left: the "open" body position. Middle: the "closed" body position. Right: the "figure-4" American position.

were very impatient with the employee's "stupidity." To make the experiment even more dramatic, ask several of your friends to do the experiment with you. Divide these willing subjects into two groups and deliver the messages one way to one group and the other way to the other group. Ask each volunteer to tell you what you were saying, thinking, and feeling. The statements are:

Will you please suspend all phone calls for a few minutes?
Miss Jones, step into my office for a minute. I would like to talk to you.
Mr. Jones, just what do you think is the cause of this particular production breakdown?

If you have carried out this experiment with any zest, you will discover that when you give the message "kindly," the subjects will have a totally different comprehension of the statement than when it was delivered "angrily," "loudly," or "impatiently." *How* we communicate actually may be at odds with what we are trying to convey. "A soft answer turneth away wrath" the saying goes and so it does, most of the time. Our tone of voice, the pitch and volume of our speech register, and the rate and intensity of our communication, all influence the listener's comprehension.

Body Posture

The ways people sit, hold their arms, cross their legs, and watch or do not watch the speaker influence us. Even such subtle clues as the flickering of an eyelid, a raised eyebrow, a certain tenseness and alertness of the body indicate how the listener is receiving the message whether he or she agrees or disagrees, is interested or bored, and so on. The speaker, aware of it or not, picks up these clues and will shift the line of argument, hesitate, speed up, or slow down the communication and make more or less of an effort to clarify what he or she is saying.[12]

For example, psychologists are particularly observant of the person's general body posture. The person may be exhibiting an openness in bodily expression: relaxed, leaning back easily and receptively, or even sitting with a forward thrust as if wanting to catch every word. Or the person may be exhibiting a closed system; that is, the person sits back, not forward, appears tight and tense, arms and legs crossed, brows furrowed, mouth pursed, and perhaps with the face turned slightly away so that the person is not looking straight at us, but out of the corner of the eyes.[13]

Some Common Nonverbal Language Signals

	HEAD AND FACE	HANDS AND ARMS	LEGS AND FEET
Open, interested attitude	Open, smiling, eye contact May tilt head, nod	Uncrossed, unclasped, hands relaxed, fingers loose, open-handed	Uncrossed, on floor
Defensive, closed attitude	Head may be tilted but away, a frown or "tight" mouth, looks out of corner of eyes	Arms crossed or hands clasped together, tight fists, may hug upper arms.	Crossed
Unconcerned or indifferent attitude	May seem open, even a little smile, but does not have "intense" quality of interest	Hands behind head or over back of chair	May be *very* open, even have one foot over arm of chair or *"figure-4"* crossed legs
Procrastination or stalling for time	Does not look directly at person, will seem fairly open to give that impression	Tends to keep arms and hands busy, lights pipe, takes notes, changes position	*"figure-4"* position of legs
Bored	Looks at ceiling, legs, papers, watch, stifles yawns, looks at others	Drums fingers, kicks crossed leg, may doodle.	May shift to several positions of legs and feet
Evaluating, thinking, skeptical	Scratches head, purses lips, strokes beard, squints eyes, introspects for a few moments	"Steeples" fingers, rests chin on cupped hands	
Suspicious, secretive	Looks out of corner of eye, covers mouth while talking	May use left hand or arm to gesture, keeps hands in pocket, may "steeple" fingers	Keeps legs crossed at ankles
Nervous	Shifts glance from people to ceiling to wall	May have hands clasped or moving in and out of pocket	Legs may be pressed together, or will rock while standing

(Caution: These are not absolute; observer must evaluate person's individuality and look for *clusters of gestures*)

...NERAL POSTURE	CLOTHES	DISTANCE	SOUNDS	MISCELLANEOUS
...ert, may ...n slightly ...ward	Jacket may be unbuttoned, or takes coat off.	Draws nearer	Murmurs agreement, asks questions	
...dy leaning back ...slightly away	Buttoned	Tends to put more distance between self and other	Mainly silent, or asks negative questions	
...bably leaning ...ck in relaxed ...overly re- ...ed position	Unbuttoned, casual clothes	Keeps distance or pulls farther away	Slight murmur or quiet	*"Figure-4"* position, one leg crosses the other at ankle
...ems relaxed ...cause he or ...e wants to ...pear un- ...ncerned	Seems casual, may keep coat unbuttoned	Tends to *keep distance* or moves slightly away	May ask broad theoretial questions	May smoke
...ifts body ...d moving ...pers, etc. or ...ts head in ...nds	May fidget with clothes, removes real or imaginary lint	Tends to keep distance	Sounds of movement, paper rustling Sighs or gives noncommital "mm-mm"	
...ay lean ...ck with a ...it and see ...itude	May roll up sleeves, unbutton coat, loosen tie		Makes small grunts, murmurs, asks pertinent questions, may be very silent while thinking	
...rned slightly ...away, ...nds and arms ...se to body	May have collar up, keeps gloves on, stays buttoned up	Keeps distance from other, with back to wall, or (for quick exit) close to door	Remains quiet, listening	
...ifts a ..., makes many ...gestures	Fidgets with clothes	Hugs wall and keeps distance	Clears throat or coughs	

Incongruent Body-Speech Language

Sometimes what a person says belies what his or her body is saying. For example, a person may be saying, "I see," "go on," or "that's very interesting," when his or her body posture is conveying the very opposite message. While the speaker is mouthing interest, comprehension, and agreement, the speaker's body language may be saying something else. The speaker's face may be slightly turned away, arms may be crossed, and he or she may be in state of tight muscular tension; in other words, exhibits a "closed system."[14] Which should one trust? If it has to be one or the other, we would sooner trust body language than words. We learn to dissemble early in life, that is, to be kind rather than brutally truthful, to be cautious about what we say rather than being open, and to be diplomatic rather than precise. Thus, our words frequently *camouflage* our real feelings and thoughts instead of expressing them. If we must choose between verbal language and body language, we choose the latter. Our bodies do not lie. If we are tired, it shows in our slumped shoulders; if we are angry, it appears in a certain set of the mouth, a flash of the eye, or a flare of the nostril.

In fact, many therapists take body language into account when dealing with their clients or patients. We become very sensitive to small bodily movements, sudden tensing of the muscles, or tapping of the fingers. Some psychologists believe that in our society, at least, there are certain physical signs that suggest that if the person is not downright lying, he or she is at least not telling everything. According to these psychologists, these gestures include nose touching, nose rubbing, pursing the lips, and so on.[15] We suggest that these not be taken at face value, however. Each person develops, in the course of a lifetime, certain idiosyncratic movements and to read a person requires either knowing that person very well or years of experience in the art and psychology of interpersonal communication.

Territorial Space

Scientists who have studied animal behavior have described what they call "territorial space." In animals that tend to herd or breed together (such as penguins) the breeding animals demarcate their nesting areas. Should another penguin stray into that magic circle, the nesting penguins scream, flap their wings, and exhibit altogether aggressive movements until the invading penguin retreats. Those of you who have owned dogs will have noticed similar kinds of behavior. One's pet dog establishes a certain territory, and if a neighboring dog enters that space, your dog becomes heroically aggressive until the neighboring dog slinks off. The farther your own dog goes beyond its territorial space, however, the less courageous it becomes. Suddenly the two dogs are on the neighboring dog's territory, and now our aggressive watch dog suddenly becomes timorous and is chased back. The same has been noticed in sticklefish; in fact, it is a common animal behavior.[16]

Humans, too, establish territorial space. We tend to have certain "favorite spots," an armchair or a special place on the couch. When that space is taken by another person in the family, we feel a little outraged. Children frequently fight over "I was there first;" that is, "That is now my territorial space." Children delight in establishing territorial space.[17] Given a room to share, two children will divide the room very carefully into "mine" and "yours." This is part of creating a personal universe for oneself.

It is not remarkable that this kind of behavior appears in the work and social situation. Committee members at weekly meetings tend to return to the chairs that they first sat in.[18] If committee members come late and find someone in their chairs, they appear a little confounded as if the other person has taken something from them. We speak of our home as "our castle" and we would be offended if we found someone in our house without our knowledge. People "own" their offices in the same way, or their particular bench in the workshop. We speak of a person being "insensitive," "naive," "unsophisticated," or even "young" if that person is unaware of our territorial space and "invades" our domain without permission. Part of becoming experienced in the ways of the world is learning to be sensitive to another's space. We learn to approach a lunch table and ask others if it is "taken." This question is a "testing of the atmosphere." If the persons at the lunch table do not want strangers, they will indicate that they are having a private conversation, and we know to move on. If they laugh and pull a chair out, we know we are not invading a territorial place this time and that they are open to newcomers. Even when we enter a library, there are certain unwritten rules about sitting at a library table. If the library is occupied by only a few persons, we tend to sit at a table not already occupied. If the library is rather crowded, then we know we can sit at a table where there is another person, without undue invasion of territorial space.

Personal Distance

Even if we are not within our own home territorial space, we tend to carry around with us a zone of space that is ours, and we do not welcome people intruding on that space unless we have given them a signal that they may do so. E.T. Hall even established a correlation between the actual space in terms of inches. A close space of three to twenty inches between two persons indicates intimacy, a distance of two to five feet impersonal distance, and over six feet is public distance.[19] Woe to the young student who walks up to the stuffy college administrator as if he were approaching his best friend! One may observe a certain discomfort in the administrator's bearing; indeed, the administration may well be offended.

In our culture, close space between persons seems to be allied to sexual intimacy, in contrast to what it is in Arab cultures. Strangers in the Mid-East will approach each other very closely while bartering. We Americans do not like a total stranger walking right up to us, within our "personal" zone. Certain persons are so threatened by this invasion of their personal space that they may even get angry and resentful. Persons who have difficulty in ego-strength or in self-control (such as schizophrenic patients and those with histories of violence) are much less able to tolerate invasion of their personal space and tend to lash out if their personal space is violated.[20]

Becoming sensitive to communication with others, then, is also becoming sensitive to their need for space, privacy, and becoming aware of the signals that go back and forth indicating that the distance can be changed. When persons are at odds, they need a larger space between them; as they come to agreement, the space can be narrowed and often is. It has been noted that in meetings we tend to look at those who agree with us and eventually end up sitting closer to our allies.[21] After a series of meetings, committee members will begin to "polarize;" that is, the conservative members will tend to congregate on one side of the table, and the radical or liberal members will tend to congregate on the other side. In order to offset this polarization, committee chairpersons sometimes will ask the members to take different seats. Even this mechanical tampering with the geography of a committee room may affect the psychology of its members.

Touching

We vary also in how we seek to touch each other. In one sense, touching another person is related to the amount of *affect* in our own personality patterning. If we were raised in a family in which there were many open demonstrations of affection, then we would be likely to touch other people when we engage in close personal communication. If, however, we were raised in a family in which people were reserved and undemonstrative, we would tend not to embrace others or want them to touch us. Cultural factors also are important. Few Englishmen would be able to embrace another Englishman closely, and to be kissed by another Englishman would be offensive to him. Yet French and Russian and Italian men embrace each other warmly and openly. A professional colleague of ours came back from an anthropological tour of the Fiji Islands somewhat dazed by a custom among the natives of that particular region. If the natives welcome you into their society, he told us, they embrace your genitals — that is their equivalent of a handshake! He had been welcomed several times!

We need to be sensitive to the cultural determinants of touching, not only in our working relationships with others but also in our social relationships. If we touch another person who is uncomfortable with this aspect of paralanguage, we may not realize that we have deeply offended him or her. In our culture, women have more "private zones" than men, so that to invade her personal distance and to touch her too soon on early acquaintance may, indeed, shock her sensibilities.

Another intriguing aspect of touching is the interplay between married persons when one has come from a warm and "demonstrative" family, and the other has come from a reserved and undemonstrative family. If, for example, the husband has been used to touching and embracing in everyday communication, he may feel quite bewildered when his wife withdraws from him. This withdrawal may appear to him to be a rejection of his affection, which may have consequences in the sexual relationship. She may interpret the touching and embracing as a sexual signal, when for him it is simply a part of his everyday communication. She will be confused when the husband does not follow his casual touching with active sexual advances.

Still another aspect of our tendency to touch or not to touch is our psychological type. Extraverted persons will be more apt to touch other persons by offering handshakes or putting an arm around another person's shoulders during discussion. Introverted persons will not be any more willing to engage in close physical contact than they are to engage in close psychological contact.

Clothing

Our first communication about ourselves to others probably is our dress. Clothes and hair style certainly convey how we wish others to see us and also how we see ourselves. It is part of our Persona or public face. We inform the world that we are "strictly business" in our business suit, dark colors, and attaché case. Or we announce ourselves as "strictly casual" if we appear in jeans, sneakers, and loose-flowing hair.

Historically, clothing has reflected the climate of the times. In

English history, we can trace the political-social milieu by the variations of costume. The flowering of Elizabethan literature and drama was reflected by a flowering also of Elizabethan costume. Both men and women wore brilliant, sometimes gaudy (to our minds) colors with jewels and medallions woven into the fabric. When the Cromwellian forces took over around 1640, dress became the familiar black, buttoned-up garb of the Puritans. Women were no longer permitted to wear plunging necklines. With the Restoration, there appeared again very low necklines for women, and lace collars and cuffs for men. The Victorian era, with its repressed sexuality, was reflected in the many layers of clothing that both men and women wore. After World War I, the sexual freedom of the "flapper" era was expressed through short dresses, bare arms, and lower necklines for women, and more casual clothing for men. Some writers have suggested that the current tendency of women to wear jeans and pantsuits reflects an androgeny between the sexes, that is, more equality in their roles. That may very well be so, but we have not become so androgynous that a man may walk around in a dress or skirt.

The Use of Silence

Silence also is communication. It may mean, on the one hand, thoughtful listening, self-examination, and introspection; on the other, it may mean resentment, anger, or disagreement: it depends on the other nonverbal messages being sent.

Some persons are so uncomfortable with silence that they jump in to stave off the embarrassment that may be generating. A group of people who have been talking excitedly together becomes anxious when the conversation dies down and there seems nothing else to say. When there is silence in a work situation, one can simply leave, since the need for communication has apparently ended, but in a social situation, when one does not feel free to leave, silence is very difficult. Each member of the group gropes lamely for a new subject to provoke the interest of the group. Probably one of the real "acid" tests of easy and profound friendship is when two persons can allow silence to fall and be comfortable and easy in that silence. It is in silence that we walk together on a country lane watching the fall leaves; it is in silence that small murmurings become the most intimate of communications; it is in silence that we know that we have achieved a depth and profundity in our being with each other.

It seems appropriate that we started this chapter on language with the need to listen and that we end with the silence that comes between two lovers or two friends in intimate and deep communication.

When discussing a difficult situation, it is facilitating to involve other activity such as a long walk.

applications and coping techniques

1. Remember that Communication Is a Process that Extends Over Time.

When we try to straighten out an interpersonal difficulty, we sometimes make the mistake of thinking that we can iron out the wrinkles of a situation in one grand, open discussion. That may happen, particularly in a misunderstanding of one specific difficulty. More often than not, however, most communication difficulties are of more long standing. A let's-settle-this-problem-once-and-for-all approach may lead to disappointment and discouragement. A more realistic approach is to realize that the communication process takes time. One session is not enough; one discussion is not enough; one solution may not be enough. In fact, one discussion may indicate the need for many others, since any interpersonal difficulty has many ramifications. Furthermore, seeing what needs to be done is not the same as doing what needs to be done. It is easier to talk about something than it is to put it into practice.

Two of the most frequent arguments between married people is the use and distribution of money, and expectations and discipline of children. Each partner has grown up in a family which has different ideas about spending and saving money, and differing ideas about what children should and should not be allowed to do. Let us discuss one of these, the distribution of financial resources. Generally what happens is that one partner is more apt to spend freely, while the other is more cautious and self-sacrificing in order to pay the bills and save a little. Getting at the root of this problem is not going to happen in one session. It will require several sessions just to discover what the budgetary needs of both are, an analysis of where the money is actually going, and subsequent discussions on how the money slipped between the cracks while no one was looking. It may require discussions of long-range financial goals and also of short-term emergency situations. Finally, it will require ad hoc meetings when one or the other of you thinks your partner has broken the general guidelines you both established. Those of us who work in any type of organization or institution know very well the endless number of hours in weekly meetings that it takes to discuss the many ramifications of any problem. Allow this type of discourse to occur in your relationship with someone else. State flatly before the discussion starts that you know this is only the first of many meetings and that you will need to have follow-up discussions.

2. Approach the Communication Process as Calmly as You Can.

When we are upset, hurt, disappointed, or angered by something someone else has done, it is very easy to let these feelings out in accusations, name calling, and other offensive tactics. Although it may do us a lot of good to get these feelings out, we may so hurt or alienate the other person that the damage done is irreparable. But, you may ask, what do you do with your angry or hurt feelings? You can do a lot of things. You can write your anger out in a blistering letter or memo (this has a wonderfully cathartic effect) but never mail or send it. It is useful only as a way to let *you* know what is ailing *you*. Or you may decide to vent your feelings with someone other than the person with whom you are upset. That is useful, too, since that person may be able to see the other person's side and help you get a more objective viewpoint. (Make sure, however, that the person you confide in is not a gossip, or you may rue the day you discussed the matter with him or her.) Or you may decide to have a fantasy conversation with the person in which you get all those things off your chest. However you do it, get the steam out before you sit down with the person. The intent of the communication is more valid when it is not the desire to rake up old problems but to seek solutions to current ones.

3. Allow Each Person to Interpret His or Her Motivations, Feelings, and Desires.

We want to avoid accusations and blame and to increase self-reveal-ment and self-assertion. We accomplish this only when we refrain from interpreting the other person and interpret ourselves instead.

For example, we may start the discussion of the money situation by saying, "I feel as if I don't get a chance to buy the things I need" rather than "You spend so much money, there isn't any left over for me, so I have to scrimp." The other person may then say, "Well, I didn't know there was something you needed. Why didn't you say so?" At that point you might reveal a deeper concern, "Well, I'm a more saving type than you are, too—it's just part of my character, but I really have been wanting such-and-such," instead of saying. "Well, you nev-er ask me if there is something I would like to have."

The two of you might then come to an agreement that a list of priorities can be drawn up. You may then decide on both a mutual budget and an individual budget.

4. Avoid Discussion, If at all Possible, When One or the Other of You Is Tired or Under Pressure.

Even if both persons are fairly calm and rational people, environmental stress may be such that one or both of you will tend to snap or become irritated unnecessarily. Be open and frank about it. If one of you starts to discuss a sensitive area, tell the other that right now would not be a good time for you to get into it since you feel harried and pressured, and you want to approach the problem as objectively as you can. There are few things so terribly urgent that a few more days of delay will hurt.

5. Be Aware of Your Paralanguage.

Particularly watch your tone of voice. If you raise it unnaturally loud or hear yourself speaking stridently, you are putting the other person on the defensive, and your discussion may end up as another verbal battle. In fact, you can even say, "I feel myself getting an angry tone of voice which I don't want to do, so I think I'd like to just have a few moments to collect myself, and try again a little more calmly." The other person will take that kind of a cue with admiration and will attempt to emulate it.

If the other person's paralanguage seems to indicate that the discussion is becoming more than he or she can handle (by moving away or by retreating into hostile silence or by beginning to shout), you might want to verbalize it in a very gentle way, "Are you getting irritated now, because I don't want to cause that. Perhaps we should postpone any further discussion. But if it is true that you are upset, I'd like to hear just what exactly it is that is bothering you."

6. Give Both Yourselves Enough Space and Distance to Move Around In and Breathe Freely.

When handling a sensitive situation with another person, do not get into a small cramped room in which your intrapersonal-interpersonal dynamics are going to bounce off the walls. In chapter 7, we cited Everett Shostrom's advice to avoid a cramped room in an encounter. You need room to breathe. So it is in any discussion situation. A person who is agitated can drain some of the emotional tension by getting up and moving about.

A walk is a fine way of discussing something emotional since it allows both persons to talk or not talk, to stop and talk and then to walk on, perhaps silently for a while, each thinking out what has just been said. Or perhaps you are working together on a joint task, painting a house or raking the lawn. There may be no finer time to discuss the ins and outs of a situation since both of you are involved in a task together. You can speak intermittently and return to the task. There is a lot of breathing room here, and the dynamics are much less pent-up than when both of you are in a face-to-face, claustrophobic situation.

7. Test Each Other Frequently to Make Sure You Are Really Hearing Each Other and Getting a True Understanding.

In the beginning, this technique may seem a little mechanical, but it also is one of the most effective techniques for interpersonal communication. It tells the other person that you really are listening, that you really want to understand, and that you are interpreting the speaker accurately. It also enables that person to recognize if he or she is or is not communicating clearly. In psychology, this technique is called "feedback" and is one of the most helpful tools in communication and education.

8. Keep the Discussion Between the Two of You and About the Two of You.

If you can manage it, keep other parties out of the communication. Third persons put one or the other party at a disadvantage. Furthermore, the third person is not privy to all the facts, and even if you think you can relate all the facts, you cannot. The third party will believe whoever sounds "right," and of course, "right" and "wrong" is not relevant.

In your discussions also keep the reference between yourselves. To bring in something Aunt Mary or Dr. Jones said is tactical, but tactics are more related to war than to honest self-revealment. What is happening is related to both of you, and the moment you go beyond both of you, the discussion has deteriorated. Stay with the topic at hand, and handle one thing at a time. This is not war or manipulation but a desire to work something out.

9. Adopt a No-Fault Attitude.

Discussions of this sort are not a matter of somebody being right and somebody being wrong. Do not keep a score card to tally points made by who was right. Go beyond judgment, adopt a no-fault attitude, and get on with the business of clearing out the underbrush and cutting a clear swath through the forest of miscommunication. There is no need to apologize for yourself, and do not insist on apologies from the other person. Apologies set up a "right-wrong" dimension, and that is a polarity you wish to avoid. Remember that what is needed is for both to see where the communication has broken down and to find ways to make needs and desires more explicit in the future.

10. For Parents: A Tip in Teaching Children How to Communicate.

Children learn much more from example than from instruction. They will adopt their communication style from you. In families in which parents have learned to communicate well with each other and to work out individual differences, children will be more able to do that later on in life. As you and your spouse become more comfortable with and adept in working out interpersonal problems let your children in on your process. We tend to think that we should never argue or confront each other in front of our children. That is certainly true if we cannot manage our hostile or angry feelings. But if you have worked out ways to "process" your misunderstandings and situational conflicts, your children will gain much from being able to observe how you do it. Later, in their adolescent years, you and they will have a much easier time managing conflicts and crises.

the unconscious self: our symbolic language

FOUR

CHUANG TZU

LAST NIGHT I DREAMED I WAS A BUTTERFLY;
NOW I DO NOT KNOW IF I AM CHUANG TZU
WHO DREAMED I WAS A BUTTERFLY, OR A BUTTERFLY
WHO DREAMED IT WAS CHUANG TZU.

dreams and dreaming: royal road to the inner kingdom

10

I. Introduction: Sigmund Freud and The Interpretation of Dreams

    A. *The physicalist explanation of dreams*

    B. *A brief history of dream interpretation*

    C. *Freud's clinical subjects: his patients, his family, and himself*

    D. *Basic elements of Freud's theory of dreams*

        1. *Latent versus manifest dream content*

        2. *The dream work*

        3. *Condensation*

        4. *Displacement*

        5. *Visual representation of abstract ideas*

        6. *The universality of dream symbols*

        7. *Sexual symbols*

II. Jung and the Discovery of the Symbolic Self in Dreams

    A. *Freud and Jung*

    B. *The constant polarities: our dual natures*

    C. *The personal versus the collective unconscious*

    D. *The archetypes of human personality*

        1. *Our sexual duality: Anima and Animus*

        2. *The Persona and the Shadow*

    E. *The mandala symbol and the integration of personality*

III. Two Examples of Dream Therapy

    A. *Ginny's dream: the child bride*

    B. *Brooke's dream: a Jungian dream*

IV. Applications and Coping Techniques

introduction: sigmund freud and the interpretation of dreams

It is relevant, we believe, to note the date of the original publication of Sigmund Freud's *Interpretation of Dreams*. The first manuscript is dated 1899, but that is an error. The book actually made its first appearance in 1900, and it seems to us now that it was the first indication that the twentieth century would explore the realms of inner existence. After twenty-five hundred years, humankind would begin to heed the ancient Greek dictum: know thyself. Until then, a huge area of human awareness lay unexplored, which we call the *unconscious*, and in which, Freud asserted, are the origins of most of our motivations and personality.

The unconscious aspect of human personality has become so much a part of our current understanding of ourselves that it is hard for us to realize the furor created by Freud's theoretical formulations. We take for granted now the "stream of consciousness" approach of modern novelists, by which they allow the readers to see into the inner, uncensored flow of their characters' random thoughts, but this approach is one of the direct results of Freud's work in psychoanalysis. We no longer are surprised or confused when the main plot of a televised or movie story is suddenly interrupted by flashbacks or other cinematic techniques that reveal a person's unconscious motivation. As a result of the psychodynamic movement, twentieth-century art was able to free itself from the restrictions of conventional representation and realism, and to experiment with nonrealistic methods of expression such as symbolism, surrealism, and abstract art. In fact, looking at it now, we recognize that the significance of Freud's work was better understood by novelists, poets, playwrights, and painters than by Freud's medical and scientific colleagues, a fact which astonished and hurt him. Freud expected some reaction from the Church, but he never expected the extent to which he would be ridiculed, condemned, and ostracized by his own medical and scientific colleagues. It was ten years before the six hundred copies of the first edition all were sold. Freud allowed some of his disappointment to show in the preface to the second edition, published in 1909.

If within ten years of the publication of this book . . . a second edition is called for, this is not due to the interest taken in it by the professional circles to whom my original preface was addressed. My psychiatric colleagues seem to have taken no trouble to overcome the initial bewilderment created by my new approach to dreams. The professional philosophers have become accustomed to polishing off the problems of dreamlife (which they treat as a mere appendix to conscious states) in a few sentences—and usually in the same ones; and they have evidently failed to notice that we have something here from which a number of inferences can be drawn that are bound to transform psychological theories. The attitude adopted by reviewers in the scientific periodicals could only lead one to suppose that my work was doomed to be sunk into complete silence.[1]

Eventually, of course, *The Interpretation of Dreams* went through eight editions during Freud's lifetime and was translated into every major language. The original manuscript netted Freud only a few hundred dollars and gained him the opprobium of Victorian society, for what Freud was saying to that society was not pleasant—he was saying that the dreams of the men and the women who were his patients showed clearly that their society (which prided itself on its conduct, ethics, and belief in progress through science and technology) was producing *neurosis*—that is, not healthy persons but sick people. Freud's rationale for this assertion came through his explorations into dreams and dreaming.

The Physicalist Explanation of Dreams

The nineteenth century had relegated the strange events and experiences occurring during sleep to a neat and tidy explanation. Dreams were simply a reaction to physical distress. For example, if people dreamed of being guillotined, it was the result of something which had fallen on their head as they slept or because of the bedclothes that were choking them. If they dreamed that they were in a boat and the boat were in danger of sinking, they needed to urinate. Scrooge, in Charles Dickens's novel *A Christmas Carol*, probably summed up the physicalist theory of dreaming when he reacted to his "night visitor" as nothing more than "a bit of undigested food."[2]

This approach to dreaming came as a relief to the educated people of the nineteenth century. Since the beginning of time, dreams had been haunting people with their sexual content and other confusing elements that disturbed peace of mind. Frightening dreams were, in fact, called "nightmares" in Old English because they were believed to be caused by monsters *(mares)*. During the medieval witch-hunts, erotic dreams were seen as the work of devils *(incubi* and *suc-*

cubi) which invaded the souls of innocent men and women. There is probably not one of us who cannot sympathize with Job's desperate cry, "You frighten me with dreams and terrify me with visions."[3]

It was comforting, then, for people in the nineteenth century to be able to rid themselves at last of the disturbing belief that there was something real or important going on in their dreams. After all (they could say), these events and experiences happened during the "sleep of reason"! Clearly there could be little correspondence between these strange aspects and happenings of the dream self and those everyday experiences of the sensible, mature, and virtuous person in the waking state! The explanations of rational science provided just enough impetus for them to dismiss their dreams as essentially unimportant. Then there appeared *The Interpretation of Dreams*.

Freud asserted a preposterous, even scandalous, idea, that dreams were not meaningless and unimportant at all but were indicative of a very deep and essential part of our personality, one that lay hidden beneath our conscious mind. He maintained always that dreams were the "royal road" to this unconscious and that we would do well to treat them seriously and to learn to understand them.

He said also that dreams reveal the savage, infantile, uncivilized aspects of the self which each dreamer would prefer to ignore. He said, as well, that the lusty, exhibitionistic, and aggressive dream-self is just as valid a self as the one each person attempts to construct in the waking state. He said, finally, that the denial of the existence of this lusty and aggressive self in Victorian society was one cause of the psychological conflicts in that society.

A Brief History of Dream Interpretation

Freud's contributions to the theory of dreams, as original and monumental as they certainly were, nevertheless did not burst full grown and independently from Freud's intellect. Ever since people differentiated between their waking and dreaming states, they have been fascinated by dreams. There was a considerable amount of literature on dreams by Freud's time, much of which Freud knew and which he quoted extensively in his book. We summarize that history briefly now to set the stage for Freud's original insights.

First, the Old Testament is not only a source of accounts of dreams but is one of the first handbooks on dream interpretation. For example, Joseph's position as a dream interpreter was good enough not only to secure his release from prison but also to gain him the chancellorship of Pharaoh's court. Joseph's dreams may also have prompted his being sold into slavery, for he dared to interpret two early dreams as a prediction that one day he would be a mighty lord before whom all his brothers would bow down.[4]

Solomon at the beginning of his reign, illustrates very clearly that the Hebrews believed that God could use the medium of dreams to appear to men.

You may remember that Solomon had not always been the heir apparent, for he was not the oldest son of King David. It must have come as a surprise to him, then, when he became successor to the throne. At any rate, God appears "in a dream" to Solomon and says: "Ask what you would like me to give you." Solomon's dream-self displays an astonishing humility in his reply:

My God, you have made your servant king in succession to David, my father. But I am a very young man, unskilled in leadership. Your servant

The Old and New Testaments indicate that the Hebrews and early Christians relied on their dreams for divine guidance.

finds himself in the midst of this people of yours that you have chosen, a people so many that its number cannot be counted or reckoned. Give your servant a heart to understand how to discern between good and evil, for who could govern this people of yours that is so great?

The Bible notes that God was pleased by this response and answered:

Since you have asked for this and not asked for long life for yourself or riches or the lives of your enemies, but have asked for a discerning judgment for yourself here and now I do what you ask: I give you a heart wise and shrewd as none before you has had and none will have after you.

But God rewarded Solomon even further:

What you have not asked I shall give you too: such riches and glory as no other king ever had. And I will give you a long life, if you follow my laws and commandments as your father David followed them.

And then to remind us, the writer repeats again the setting of this dialogue: "Then Solomon awoke; it was a dream."[5]

The New Testament also provides many instances of divine revelation and guidance through the medium of dreams. For example, in the book of Matthew, when Joseph discovered that his bride-to-be, Mary, was pregnant, he was sorely distressed; but being a man of honor he did not want to expose her publicly, so he decided to divorce her quietly. The Lord's angel, however, Matthew went on to say, appeared to him in a dream and told him not to be afraid to take Mary for his wife for her conception was "by the Holy Spirit."[6]

Later, the Magi, after their visit to the child Jesus, failed to inform Herod of the child's whereabouts – as he had instructed them to do – for they had been "warned in a dream not to go back to Herod" and thus returned to their own country by another route.[7] The Angel of the Lord appeared twice more to Joseph in dreams: first to tell him to take his family and flee into Egypt,[8] and then again to tell him that it was safe to return to Israel.[9]

In the last hours of Jesus' trial, there also is that well-known moment when Pilate, ready to pass sentence on a man he realized was not a criminal, received a plea for mercy from his wife:

Now as he was seated in the chair of judgment, his wife sent him a message, "Have nothing to do with that man; I have been upset all day by a dream I had about him."[10]

Most religions we know of have recorded dreams and interpretations of dreams. In fact, the earliest extant book on dream interpreta-

According to the Talmud, "A dream uninterpreted is like a letter that is not read."

tion, the so-called Chester Beatty Papyrus, dates back to 2000 B.C., from Thebes (in the ancient kingdom of Upper Egypt).

The stone inscription on the Sphinx at Giza records that Thutmose IV obeyed instructions which came to him in a dream. His instructions were to clear the statue of sand, and the inscription records that Thutmose did, indeed, carry out the commandment.[11]

The Talmud records that a certain Rabbi Hisda regarded dream interpretation as essential to personal guidance. Said he, "An uninterpreted dream is like an unread letter,"[12] a point of view which the psychoanalytic school of Freud later was to reiterate.

Mohammed, the prophet of Islam, made a practice of relating his dreams each morning to his disciples and having them relate their own dreams. The art of dream interpretation was dignified as a science by Mohammed and his followers, who considered it one of the higher orders of natural philosophy.[13]

During the Middle Ages dreams became associated with devils and demons, an outlook on dreams which was to continue until the

366

eighteenth and nineteenth centuries. Yet even in those years, as Freud points out in his book, philosophers had intimations of the real meaning of dreams.

It will perhaps be clear to the reader by now that Freud did not begin empty handed when he undertook his master work on dreams. But it was Freud's particular genius to pull together the many diverse insights and intuitions of these other ages and to integrate their intuitions and discoveries systematically into his own clinical work as a psychiatrist.

Freud's Clinical Subjects: His Patients, His Family, and Himself

All great philosophers, scientists, and artists draw upon themselves as they struggle with new ideas and new directions of expression, and so it was with Freud. As part of his investigations into the unconscious, Freud reported and interpreted twenty-eight of his own dreams for his readers. From them, Freud formulated his theory of the psychology of dreaming and validated his investigations by gathering hundreds of other dreams from patients, colleagues, and even relatives.

It was not an easy task for Freud, for such self-revelation necessi-

Freud analyzed many of his own dreams. This dream is an example of condensation.

tated considerable risk to himself as a person and as a professional. It entailed speaking of subject matter taboo in his society, namely sexuality. We also need to remember that Freud himself was a Victorian gentleman, a scholar who by nature and training would have been naturally loathe to reveal himself so candidly. He actually confessed this several times in the eighth edition of *The Interpretation of Dreams*.

Although we are aware now that Freud's theory of dreaming was incomplete and that other investigations would extend his theory and develop still other approaches to dream theory, Freud still stands out as the father of contemporary dream theory, the benchmark against which any dream theory must be measured, examined, and understood in our time.

Basic Elements of Freud's Theory of Dreams

In this section we will discuss Freud's scientific terminology for investigating dreams.

LATENT VERSUS MANIFEST DREAM CONTENT.   Basic to the psychoanalytic theory of dreams is Freud's assertion that every dream has two levels. The first is the *manifest* or surface dream, the actual pictorial-auditory dream we remember upon awakening. The second level of the dream Freud called the *latent* content, to emphasize his belief that there is a truth hidden (latent) behind the manifest content. In other words, we disguise the real meanings of our dreams.

Why do we disguise the real meaning of our dreams? Freud's answer: our dreams are repositories for our hidden wishes, particularly sexual wishes and aggressive impulses. Indeed, said Freud, when such thoughts, feelings, or wishes invade our conscious awareness we tend to forget them very quickly. (That is where psychoanalysis comes in; it enables people to remember forgotten material — or more explicitly, to unearth material that is not so much forgotten as *repressed*.) For Freud had discovered that "forgotten" material is simply driven below conscious awareness and "down" into what Freud called our unconscious mind. This process of forgetting he called *repression*. Repressing an idea, feeling, or wish requires a lot of effort, Freud added, for our repressed urges are constantly striving to come "up" to our conscious mind again. Repressing requires considerable psychic energy, therefore, to keep impulses below conscious awareness.

The wish to kill one's father, for example, may be repressed consciously and transformed in a dream of seeing one's father melt away like a snowman. The wish to expose oneself may appear in a dream as having one's clothing blown off by the wind. The wish to have inter-

*Freud noticed the correspondence of house symbols
and a woman's body.*

course with one's mother may be expressed as making love to a woman who has no face and is therefore unrecognizable. If such desires were expressed literally in one's dreams, however, the censor would become immediately operative, the dreamer would then wake up.

THE DREAM WORK.   Dream work is fitting meaning into the unreal quality of many dreams. Strange or half-familiar persons float through our dreams, and events occur which seem either trivial or bizzarre. But Freud had a gift for expecting objections to his ideas. Just because one's dreams seem to be filled with irrelevant details, one must not suppose them to be insignificant! Everything that appears in our dreams is significant, even if they are the usual things of everyday life such as walking along the street, picking flowers, or throwing a snowball. But what if the dream seems to be just a rerun, so to speak, of the events of the day? Freud had an explanation for that, too. Dreams, he said, use the "left-over refuse" of the day as symbols for what the unconscious wishes to express. For that reason, it is essential to pay attention to every single element in a dream, no matter how insignificant that element seems to be.

CONDENSATION.   According to Freud, a dream is always economical in expression, even laconic in its manner of conveying its message. A dream expresses ideas and feelings always in the briefest way possible. For that reason, one dream symbol can stand for many things simultaneously. For example, a giant may stand for all the authority figures we have ever known: one's father, a policeman, or a schoolteacher. Or a soldier may stand for an army, or a book may represent knowledge in general. These are called *collective objects* or *collective persons.*

When words are part of the dream process, they tend to be *verbal condensations.* Freud gave many examples of verbal condensation in his book, but since they are puns on the German and/or Yiddish language, they lose much of their force in their translation into English.

One of the dreams Freud reported is an example of just such a process of condensation. A medical colleague once sent a journal article he had just written to Freud. Freud thought it overwritten, as well as overrated by the author for its scientific value. That night, Freud had a one-sentence dream: "It's written in a positively *norekdal* style." Analysis of the word *norekdal* revealed to Freud two different condensations: first, the word *norekdal* is a play on two German words for "colossal" and "pyramidal;" and second, the word is also a combination of two characters in Henrik Ibsen's plays: Nora in *A Doll's House* and Ekdal in *The Wild Duck.* Freud then remembered that his colleague (the author of the paper) had also written a newspaper article about Ibsen some time earlier which Freud also had read. Newspaper articles have a peculiar style which is actually called pyramidal, and journalistic adjectives tend toward exaggeration. Freud chose not to make further inferences at this point—at least not in print. It is not too difficult for us to infer that the author, in Freud's opinion, had written his scientific paper in much the same exaggerated style as his previous newspaper article had been. (Notice, incidentally, how much space it has taken to translate Freud's one-sentence dream—a good example of dream condensation.)

A good way to know whether a semifamiliar figure or object is a product of condensation is to analyze the various elements. It may "look like A perhaps but may be dressed like B, may do something we remember C doing, and at the same time we may know that it is really D."[14]

DISPLACEMENT. Sometimes we dream a seemingly senseless dream, very neutral in tone, one which seems to have no emotional quality or purpose. Freud was particularly specific about such a dream. These kinds of "neutral" dreams, he said, very often disguise extremely violent, narcissistic, or primitive impulses and desires. Freud called this type of symbolism *displacement*. For example, a man dreams that he was throwing a wheel to his father. The latent interpretation of this dream revealed a deep-seated hatred by the man for his father whom he considers tyrannical; in fact, he wishes the old man were dead and out of his life. He might have dreamed that he had shot the man with a "revolver," but instead the manifest dream leads away from that taboo wish and instead disguises the wish by having the man throw something to his father which "revolves." In fact, the dream continues with the revolving instrument being thrown back and forth between the father and the man, further displacing the taboo wish by turning it into something as innocuous as a game of "catch."

VISUAL REPRESENTATION OF ABSTRACT IDEAS. A third explanation for the use of dream symbols, said Freud, is that often dreams attempt to describe abstract ideas that are difficult to express. The unconscious part of ourselves is concrete, rooted to things which can be expressed visually. For example, Freud noted two dreams which translated abstract ideas into concrete visual representations. The first was of a man who dreamed he was planing a piece of wood. At the time of the dream, the man was in the process of revising and refining an essay he was writing, and the dream translated the idea as smoothing out and refining a piece of wood. A second dream, also by the same man, involved the visual image of a printed page falling away. In this instance, Freud said, the man was concerned about losing his train of thought as he was revising the article.[15]

THE UNIVERSALITY OF DREAM SYMBOLS. Freud went to great length to disparage the superstitious dream omen type of book (still

When we are in the dream state, we are freed from the laws of space and time. Dreaming is an altered state of consciousness.

popular today) that supposedly reveal the future in much the same way as a palm-reader claims to prophesy future events. He had, over and over, insisted that dreams revealed not the future but the past. But toward the end of his life, he was able to admit with some degree of humor that some dream symbols seemed to be so universal in content that one might well produce a new kind of "dream symbol book," with the understanding that the symbols pertain more to a person's childhood conflicts than to prophecy. (Freud was adamant about superstition or mysticism of any kind!) In fact, he had come to understand that symbols are very much the same wherever they surface—in folklore, myths, legends, dreams, parables, or even jokes. The dream interpreter thus must not only know the dreamer's personal associations to his or her dream symbols but also study the symbols of literature, mythology, religion, art, and the like. He or she needs to be, in other words, an educated man or woman who understands the whole panorama of human existence.

SEXUAL SYMBOLS.　Freud's society was one of the most repressive eras in history, particularly in regard to human sexuality. Many of the dream symbols that appeared in Victorian dreams represented the sexual aspects of life. If Freud tended to oversexualize dream symbols, we can forgive him now since he was battling the hypocritical double standards of those days. He viewed elongated objects such as neckties, knives, sticks, spears, and even bananas as symbolizing the penis, and boxes, chests, cupboards, and even ovens as representing the vagina. Rooms, in dreams, also could represent women, and so could boats, cars, and other kinds of "boxes" which carry people around. A train going through a tunnel would be an excellent symbol for intercourse, as would also such physical activities as rocking in a chair, climbing, and swimming.

In a dream, a child is often symbolic of the genitals; so playing with one's child could be symbolic of masturbation, according to Freud. He noted that the male penis is sometimes called by a male name. In English, for example, the words *dick* and *peter* are used to denote the penis. Similarly, fear of castration may be represented in a dream by having a finger or a leg cut off or even by a tooth falling out. The snake is then obviously a representation of the penis, particularly if the dreamer is a woman who is afraid of sexual intercourse.

Freud did not confine his investigations to symbols of the human body. He saw that the animal world was a rich source of symbols and symbolic representation. For example, the dislike children have for their brothers and sisters can be symbolized by small, obnoxious animals and vermin. On the other hand, a woman who dreamt that she

Common symbols for psychological transitions.

was plagued with vermin Freud viewed as symbolic of pregnancy and as an indication of the woman's loathing of the event.

A dream concerning direction can have several meanings. *Right* and *left* are used commonly in our language in symbolic ways — for example, the *righteous* way or the *right* way — whereas the *left (sinister* in the Latin) denotes illegitimacy, even homosexuality. The directions *up* and *down* can represent success and failure, as they also can represent the sexual parts of the body, with breasts represented by "upstairs," and "downstairs" referring to the genitalia.

These few fragmentary illustrations can only begin to convey the panorama and depth of Freud's thought, how thought provoking the objects and symbols in dreams can be for self-knowledge and personality integration. We hope that we have given the reader a taste of Freud, just enough incentive to encourage further reading. Freud is highly readable and even when, to our eyes, he is clearly wrong or when his vision is unclear or myopic, we cannot deny him his rightful place in the history of ideas.

Freud was one of the giants of the twentieth century, who reshaped our understanding of the nature of people. Perhaps no one said it better than Carl Jung, one of Freud's most brilliant students:

> Freud's greatest achievement probably consisted in taking neurotic patients seriously and entering into their peculiar individual psychology. He had the courage to let the case material speak for itself. . . . He saw with the patients' eyes. . . . He was free of bias, courageous, and succeeded in overcoming a host of prejudices. . . . By evaluating dreams as the most important source of information concerning the unconscious processes, he gave back to mankind a tool that had seemed irretrievably lost.[16]

jung and the discovery of the symbolic self in dreams

By the time Freud published the second edition of his *The Interpretation of Dreams,* a devoted group of psychoanalysts had gathered around him in Vienna. Many of these analysts were eventually to make original contributions to psychoanalytic theory and to achieve public renown in their own right; for example, Wilhelm Reich, Alfred Adler, Otto Rank, Karen Horney, Ernest Jones, Wilhelm Steckel, and Carl Gustav Jung — to mention a few. We have chosen to speak of Jung and his theories because Jung's works, in particular his work on dreams, led psychology to a wider understanding of dream symbols.

Freud and Jung

It was common knowledge among the original psychoanalytic group that Freud considered Jung the "crown prince" who might one day take over the leadership and direction of Freud's psychoanalytic congress. Although that was a flattering possibility, it was also a considerable burden for Jung, for he was twenty years Freud's junior and one of the youngest members of the psychoanalytic movement. Freud, however, considered Jung brilliant, and his feeling for Jung came close to that of a father for a favorite son. This period was a time of great importance to Jung's personal and professional life. He had been a relatively unknown Swiss psychiatrist who was just beginning to feel the stirrings of genius within himself when he met, in Freud, the kind of seminal teacher he needed.

Nonetheless, by 1914, Jung knew he could not unequivocally accept Freud's approach to personality. He was a more solitary individual than Freud was, and he felt himself constitutionally unable to assume the function of a "crown prince." (See Chapter 2, Box C.)

The turning point in their relationship came when Jung acknowledged that he could no longer accept Freud's "exclusive sexualistic conception of dream symbols."[17] To be sure, Jung believed that dreams could convey powerful biological messages from the unconscious (as Freud taught), but Jung also believed that sexual content in the dream itself could be symbolic.

Suppose, for example, a man dreams that he is pregnant and is going to have a child. A Freudian analyst might interpret this dream at the sexual level of content and then might say that the dream represents a wish-fulfillment of the person and possibly also homosexual overtones in the man's personality. A Jungian analyst might suggest a different interpretation of the dream. Knowing the man to be a writer or a scientist, for example, he might suggest that the dream is a symbolic representation of the person's intuition that he is on the verge of "giving birth" to a literary work or to a scientific discovery.

For Freud dreams were mainly *retrospective*—that is, concerned with past unresolved, infantile conflicts and instinctual needs. For Jung, however, dreams not only represent the *present*, they could even portend *future* plans, imaginings, hopes, and desires.

The radical differences in temperament and outlook between Freud and Jung resulted in the eventual withdrawal of Jung from the Viennese school led by Freud. It was an event that was painful for both men, for both were geniuses, and genius is sometimes blind to its own "shortsightedness." Neither Freud nor Jung found areas for reconciliation after their break, though Jung was to acknowledge Freud's contribution to his own theory later on in his autobiography.

Jung returned to his beloved Swiss mountains and lakes and, except for journeys to the United States, England, and Africa, he remained at his home to work in comparative isolation for the remainder of his life. As he said himself, he became accustomed to being misinterpreted and merely tolerated by the psychological world.[18] There is little doubt that, until the last decades of his life, his psychological approach to personality was considered too mystical for American scientists to take seriously, though his writings and theories had been respected in Europe for some time.

The Constant Polarities: Our Dual Natures

Throughout the ages, philosophers, writers, theologians, and scientists have been concerned with the apparent duality of human nature: our possibilities for good and evil, our sublime achievements and our equally murderous atrocities, our capacity for transcendental awareness and our biological limitations.

Freud opened up discussion of the existence of *polarity* in the human personality in his theory of human *bisexuality* (that is, that each person has both *male* and *female* components), and in his conception of the mind being separated into *conscious* and *unconscious* functions. This principle of opposition, or polarity, became pivotal in Jung's own psychological theory. Jung wrote, for example:

The sad truth is that man's real life consists of a complex of inexorable opposites—day and night, birth and death, happiness and misery, good and evil. We are not even sure that one will prevail against the other. Life is a battleground. It has always been and always will be; and if it were not so, existence would come to an end.[19]

But if human nature is divided into oppositional tendencies, how, then, may we deal with these polarities? More important, *is it possible for us to reconcile our divided nature and become whole,* at peace with ourselves and our world?

Jung concluded in one of his final essays that it is not—that there always will be a constant opposition of these forces in our personality, and that the best we can do is allow ourselves to recognize, accept, and harmonize these forces. In that respect, Jung emphasized the process of human development. He may have been influenced by the concepts of the *Tao,* the mystic philosophy of China developed some two thousand years ago. Tao philosophy stresses the eternal ebb and flow of consciousness. In Taoism, this ebb-and-flow is called *yin-yang* and represents the dualities of existence: the dark and the light, the feminine and the masculine, the receptive and the creative, the intuitive and the rational, the dominant and the yielding, and the external and the internal. Whole people, those that Jung called *individuated* persons, are better able to integrate these aspects of existence and of themselves beneficially and creatively. He set as a goal the reconciliation of these opposites in personality development and in daily living.

We already discussed several of these polarities, including Jung's concept of extraversion-introversion, in chapter 2, but Jung called attention to several other polarities which we shall discuss in this chapter. First, however, we need to understand Jung's concept of *racial* or *collective* memory, a concept which was to alarm even Freud, who begged Jung not to get "mired down in mysticism." If this concept seemed strange to even the radical Freud, you can well imagine the opposition Jung encountered from more conventional scientists. It has only been in the last few years that psychology textbook writers have been willing to include a discussion of the collective or racial memory.

The Personal versus the Collective Unconscious

Like Freud, Jung accepted the conscious and unconscious levels of personality. But whereas Freud had posited only a personal unconscious, Jung posited two types of human unconscious. Besides the personal consciousness which marks the beginning of our individual existence from birth on, Jung asserted that we are heir to another aspect of memory, which he called the collective or racial unconscious and which we share with all other humans. Taking the human fetus as an analogy, Jung pointed out that in the mother's womb, the developing embryo-fetus undergoes the phylogenetic history of the human race; that is, it goes through the stages of evolution leading up to a human, progressing from a one-celled organism, through a "fish" stage (complete with gill-like structures), until eventually the fetus becomes recognizable as a higher-order primate and finally resembles a human infant. Just as our *bodies* have evolved over millions of years so, too, according to Jung, our human personality has evolved psychologically—and we carry this psychological evolution in our collective unconscious. This archaic heritage, said Jung, explains some of the primitive, more savage sides of human personality, that aspect that emerges in violent interpersonal and international conflict. But within this racial unconscious, said Jung, there also is both the intuitional and rational dawn of human consciousness, as it emerged and developed through countless centuries and eons. If we are able to recognize these primordial forces within our nature, we not only will be able to harness our destructive urges, we also will be able to tap the deepest and most creative wellsprings of inherited wisdom, by getting in touch with the polarities within our nature and with something that Jung called the *archetypes* of human personality.

The Archetypes of Human Personality

Jung's definition of the archetype is a bit too elusive for many rational scientists, and there have been many interpretations of what Jung meant by archetype. The word itself has the same root as archeology and archaic, indicating something very old and deeply rooted in the development of humankind. More specifically, archetypes are prototypes of the first emotional-intellectual understandings and experiences of early humankind. Our earliest forebears were not rational (as we know it) in their thought processes: they explained natural occurrences with emotional interpretations. Let us give one of Jung's examples. Early humankind was, no doubt, awed by the daily return of the sun as it rose each day in the east to lighten the night. Since they were unable to understand this intellectually, they personified the rise of the sun in the myth of a sun god who not only lightens the darkness of the night but who also enlightens human consciousness. Said Jung, "The archetype is a kind of readiness to produce over and over again the same or similar mythical ideas. Hence it seems as though what is impressed upon the unconscious were exclusively the subjective fantasy-ideas aroused by the physical process."[20]

What is important for us to understand is that Jung believed that humankind still has the tendency to process our emotional experiences in much the same way as our earliest forebears did. These emotional "predispositions" or "potentialities" still shape and influence our perceptions, no matter how modern, rational, scientific, or liberated we may believe ourselves to be.[21] In order to clarify what Jung meant, let us look briefly at two of the archetype polarities which Jungians believe to be the strongest forces in our personalities and which still emerge in our mythologies, our personal fantasies, and, particularly, in our dream symbols.

OUR SEXUAL DUALITY: ANIMA AND ANIMUS. Freud shocked many of his readers when he wrote that we all are biologically and psychologically double-sexed. Even though children are generally born masculine or feminine (with either male or female sexual organs), we retain much of the biology of the opposite sex, which he believed accounted for homosexuality. In fact, Freud believed that most of us have a certain latent homosexuality, even if we are predominantly and satisfactorily heterosexual in our adjustment. Such a statement no longer is so shocking to our more open sexual society and with our more liberal views toward homosexuality. We more or less accept that we do have both elements within our nature, even if we are predominantly one sex or the other.

Jung extended this thesis even farther. In cultures which insist that certain behaviors are "masculine" and certain behaviors are "feminine," there develops a deeply significant polarity in our personalities, which he called the *Anima* and the *Animus*. If a young boy is taught to feel ashamed of his crying, told to be a "man," frowned on when he exhibits his softness and tenderness, and is made to think that such emotions are "feminine," he will come to resent or repress this side of himself and become lopsidedly "masculine." The modern slang for this type of personality is "macho" or the "machismo" personality style. He will emphasize his physically aggressive aspects or his intellectual self, and repress his emotional and intuitional aspects. But we can only repress this side of ourselves; we cannot destroy it. Those denied, repressed aspects of the male will coalesce (to use Jung's word) in his unconscious and influence his behaviors in ways of which he is unaware. Sometimes, even, Anima breaks through and takes over his personality, and he finds himself bewildered by his own actions. Let us consider two examples.

Suppose a man prides himself on being a "real man," as being "tough" or unemotional, capable of handling himself cooly in every situation, and suppose that this is generally true of most of his behaviors. Let us then suppose that he suddenly has an experience which makes a tremendous emotional impact on him. This experience may be so moving to him that its impact cuts through his "tough skin," and he finds himself out of control, crying perhaps, or at least overwhelmed by passions he has never even dreamed were possible. His own emotions may so confuse him that he finds himself not only bewildered but wondering if he is "losing his mind," so strange does he seem to himself. In one sense he has "lost his mind," at least that part of his mind with which he is most familiar, but he is in touch, perhaps for the first time in his life, with a deeper aspect of himself, a "mind" that he has long denied. He probably is not going crazy; he may be, in fact, more in touch with himself than he ever has been before; he is in touch with his Anima.

Jung's second example is on the other side of the emotional spectrum. The intellectual man, who has prided himself on his calm, unemotional, rational life style, may suddenly find himself exhibiting a strange negative streak that comes out as irritability, hurt feelings, jealousy, all of those things he has ascribed to women.

Probably we all have witnessed this "change of character" in some man that we know, perhaps our father, an uncle, or husband, and we have wondered what has come over them. What has come over them is simply the other side of themselves—their *Anima*.

Some men are more in touch with their Anima than others are and are in less conflict with their softer selves. Usually, these men are those we call artists, romantics, or idealists. Shakespeare said that "the poet, the lover, and the madman" are alike, and it may be because they allow their Anima more dominance over their personalities. The poets speak of their muse, the lovely goddess of inspiration; the lover speaks unceasingly of his beloved; and the madman flees from his demons, who, more often than not, are pictured as hags, witches, or she-devils. All of these are aspects of the soul—for that is what *Anima* means. Jung explained that the muse who inspires the poet, the beloved who seems to the lover the embodiment of all beauty and goodness, and the hag or witch who frightens the madman all are really the man's search and discovery of the denied feminine aspects of himself.

The Anima may be a frequent visitor of a man's dreams. It is that part of himself trying to break through the constraints of his unconscious mind so that he can take the next step in his psychological evolution. Jung said that the Anima could appear also in daydreams and fantasies, but that this experience may be so overwhelming that the mind could feel "shattered" by the experience. In a man's dreams, the Anima is less overwhelming, except when she appears as a hag or a witch and awakens him as in a nightmare. More often, she is gentler and appears as a strangely beautiful or exotic creature, a divine goddess, or as a vague presence of soft femininity who cannot be seen or heard but of whom one is aware. How can a man know when a woman in his dreams is the embodiment of his own Anima and not a "real" woman? He instinctively knows that he has experienced something he has never experienced before. There is something magical, "numinous," unearthly (if you will) about her. He awakens with a sense of awe, filled emotionally and spiritually (Jung was never afraid to use the word "spiritual"). Perhaps the men who are reading this will have a dim or even a vivid recollection of such a dream. If so, perhaps they will realize that such a dream came at a particular time of their life, a time when they were on the verge of something "new" within themselves, or when they were filled with more energy and creative spirit. Do not be misled because the dream was erotic. Such biological symbolism simply means that there is a true blending of both sides of one's personality and infusion, even for a moment, of the dual aspects of one's nature.

The Animus is the denied "masculine" aspects of the female personality. The Animus, like its counterpart, the Anima, is the coalesced and opposite-sexed component of the female. In cultures in which the woman has been taught to repress her intellectual and assertive self,

Three aspects of the
Anima: the Virgin, the
Mother, and the Hag.

in which intelligence and aggressiveness is considered to be a threat
to a man's status or disliked and rejected by both sexes as "unfemi-
nine," these aspects of her personality will go underground and remain hidden or latent in her personality.

If a woman does not accept this so-called "masculine" aspect of
herself, said Jung, she can evolve into that rather pathetic creature:
the colorless, uninteresting mother/housewife with no identity as a
person in her own right. Her conversation centers on her children, her
house, her husband, her surgeries — there is nothing else of herself she
can put forward. When her children are grown up and gone, her husband deeply involved in his work, she feels incomplete for the rest of
her life since so much of her identity went with her departed children,
and her husband no longer has the same kinds of need for her that he
once had.

On the other hand, said Jung, she may take another route: instead
of subjugating herself to the men of her family, she can become an
opponent, combating men and trying to conquer them. This opposition may be forthright and open, or it may assume more subtle forms of
manipulation such as acting helpless, or by mothering her husband,
or fawning on him until he feels trapped by his relationship to her.

Every so often, however, even the most self-negated female may
assert herself as a personality and astonish her family. She may begin

by becoming dimly aware that something is wrong somewhere. She feels lost, perhaps, or incomplete. She may realize she is buried, or dying, or at least stagnating. The feelings may mount until she strikes out desperately in some direction searching for something unknown. Or she may suddenly wake up one morning and take stock of herself quite rationally and, with a certain brutality, decide on a new life style.

At these times, her Animus may come to her in dreams. He is an opposite-sexed figure who is not known by her in her waking existence but who somehow seems strangely familiar. Her masculine self may frighten her, and she may awake "in fear and trembling." If she has been a "dumb blond" or been raised to be a sweet and soft "Miss America," this part of herself breaking through may be experienced as shocking or border on the forbidden. She even may fear she is becoming lesbian. But that is only her emotional reaction, for her assertive and intelligent side has been seen as "masculine." In her dream, she may picture herself wearing pants or in men's clothes. She even may find herself turning into a man.

Fortunately, the past decade has seen an unfolding of assertive strength in Western women and it will be interesting to watch the directions this process will take in the years to come. From our point of view, we wonder what Jung would have had to say about this emergence of the Animus from "the closet" and into the open.

It is fairly easy for us now to accept our masculine-feminine dualism. Physiology has provided us with much information about the presence of both masculine and feminine hormones in every human being. We know, for example, that a rise in the level of testosterone (the male hormone) in the female will produce what we consider secondary masculine characteristics, such as more facial hair, hardening of the muscular structure, and so forth. It also is true that an increase of estrogen (the female sexual hormone) in the male will produce some secondary feminine characteristics. We know that the masculine-feminine balance in any human being is very fragile at best.

THE PERSONA AND THE SHADOW.   The Persona is the more recognizable of this pair of archetypes. In a way, it can be correlated with the word *personality*. The Persona is that part of ourselves of which we are conscious and that which we see when we look into a mirror, but it is only the outer husk of what also lies within. The word Persona means *mask*, the kind of mask that the ancient Greek and Roman actors used on stage. Most people cannot see beneath the masks we wear, and sometimes we ourselves are not aware that our public personalities are just that: the masks that disguise other aspects of ourselves. The poet, T. S. Eliot expressed it well when he spoke of putting on "the face to meet the faces that we meet."[22] The Persona can also be thought of as the role we take on, the stereotypical image we adopt as we become lawyers, physicians, or even psychologists, wise and omniscient. It also can be thought of as the way we portray ourselves as "sexy," "pure," "noble," or whatever.

There is something behind our Persona or mask, said Jung, and that is our Shadow. If the Persona is everything we like about ourselves, then the Shadow is everything we dislike about ourselves, the darker side that we deny and shun. But we can never turn away from it, for our psychic Shadow, like our real shadow, clings to us even when we turn our backs on it. Then, of course, there is a large part of ourselves that we do not know. We project our Shadows, to become our scapegoats.

In the history of humankind, we have tended to externalize the conflicts within us, said Jung. What is "evil" in ourselves we project onto others. Thus, we find scapegoats upon which to unleash our fury, our fear, our rejection, and so on. Some of the classic scapegoats have

The Shadow is that aspect of ourselves that we deny, but that we cannot get away from.

been the "Jew," the "nigger," the "Indian," the "gypsy"—anyone who seems different from ourselves. In our dreams, the Shadow is that fearsome person or thing that can frighten us. For a man, it may be an evil magician, the devil, or even a gorilla who is chasing him. For a female, it may be a witch or another same-sexed female monster or animal.

An interesting aspect of the Shadow is that it may not be necessarily evil to others—in fact, the Shadow often can represent some aspect of us about which we are simply embarrassed, even though others may admire that characteristic. For example, a businessman who prides himself on being penny-wise and not given to spontaneous acts of charity, may dream of a foolish man giving money to a beggar—his own dislike of impulsive acts of spontaneous generosity. A woman who thinks of herself as sexy may dream of a puritanical woman who is punishing her, that is, her inner woman who is ashamed of her flirtatiousness or promiscuity.

How may we recognize our Shadow-self in our dreams? The most obvious answer is that the Shadow-self is, in contrast to the Anima or Animus, the same sex as ourselves. The second way we can recognize the Shadow is that there is something quite familiar about the person, but again, it is not like anyone we know in our waking life. Generally, if we keep analyzing the dream, we begin to recognize that there is something about the Shadow that is similar to some part of ourselves, some part we dislike or some aspect of ourselves that bewilders us. For example, one man's Shadow turned out to be the fun-loving, spontaneous, maybe even irresponsible side of himself. The dreamer, himself, was a cautious person, very responsible, perhaps even over-responsible and conscientious. The Shadow person of himself was the side that wanted to break through his tendency to take on so much responsibility and to have a little fun. He saw his Shadow as irresponsible but that may have been simply his own overcautious self. He was probably not the type who would ever do anything foolish, even if he did loosen up quite a bit.

There is another clue to who the Shadow might be. Frequently in a dream we often start off with another person by our side who seems to be doing everything we are. That other person may be a little indistinct and may even suddenly drop out of the dream and reappear later. Sometimes that person even seems to be a shadowy twin self. Then we should ask ourselves, "If I were to divide myself into two different persons, how would I characterize my two selves?" The dreamer above said that he was highly responsible but that there was a self that resented how much work he took on, and he called it his "irresponsible self."

The Mandala Symbol and the Integration of Personality

A mandala is generally circular though it also can be a square or even a "squared circle." Mandala drawings and paintings have appeared in many cultures in Western and Eastern societies and have been used for meditation in Eastern religions for many centuries. A mandala may appear as a wheel, something akin to Ezekiel's wheel in the sky as in the Bible story, or it can be a four-sided cross or square, as in the medieval tradition with the Christ figure at the center and the four evangelists at the cardinal points.

Jung became interested in mandala symbolism very early in his professional life as a psychotherapist, and he noticed that at certain psychological crisis points some of his patients began to have dreams and sometimes fantasies in which mandalas appeared. These dreams not only had great significance for these persons, but in many instances there also followed a resolution of the person's particular psychological conflict — and a notable step forward in his or her growth and understanding — once he or she worked through the dream in which the mandala appeared.

In Jung's theory of personality the mandala came to symbolize the integrative forces at work in personality. Indeed, he believed, when

Two examples of mandalas: Left: derived from the Hebrew-Christian-Judaic tradition; Right: a Tibetan mandala.

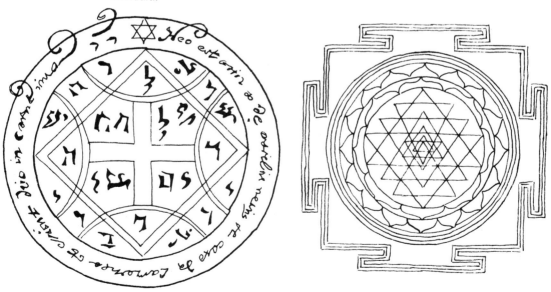

these figures begin to appear in dreams, they point toward an oncoming wholeness, unity, and harmony in the personality and the personal life. For that reason, Jung encouraged his patients to work on these symbols during the therapeutic session and also to draw and paint the dream symbols in detail. For in making the dream symbol objective on the canvas, there will be a necessary distance or impersonality which enables the person to understand more fully what he or she currently is experiencing. Jung himself painted many mandalas over his lifetime, and he appears to have used such paintings both as a creative discipline (to "externalize" the psychological forces stirring within his personality) and to understand objectively what he was experiencing in his own development.

two examples of dream therapy

Learning to interpret one's dreams is not as difficult as one may think. In fact, our experience has been that, with only a little encouragement, most persons are able to get in touch with their dream symbols very quickly. Our method of dream interpretation is somewhat eclectic, since it draws from Freud, Jung, Perls, and many others. Mainly we ask persons to relate their dreams in the present tense and then with gentle questioning encourage them to make their own associations from the dream symbols. Sometimes we may get a flash of intuition about a certain dream symbol, and then we ask them if our flash fits. The dreamers always are encouraged to correct our impression or to validate it. *The key is to stay with their actual words.*

Many of our students have become very accomplished in recognizing their dream symbols. The following are two dream sessions. The first dreamer was a very young girl; it was her first time in a college dream group, and the dream took quite a long time to unravel. The second dream session was with a woman who had had many experiences. Because of her rich background, the dream session took only about five minutes to tell and another five minutes to interpret. The two dream sessions reflect very clearly the differences in the dreamers' backgrounds, education, and experiences.

Ginny's Dream: The Child Bride

GINNY: In my dream, I am in my car and I am going to my boyfriend's house. Only I can't see anything around me like houses and trees because it is all gray and dark. But anyway, I keep driving along this road, and then I come to my boyfriend's house—only it's a garage. And I pull up in my car, and he puts gas in it. Then suddenly I am not there at all, but sitting in a room in a house and it seems as if he has kidnapped me, which I can't understand because my boyfriend is very nice and wouldn't do such a thing.

O'CONNELL: Go on.

GINNY: Well, anyway, there I am in this room, and I have my head down on my arms, and I'm crying and crying. And *here's* another strange thing! My father and my brother are also in the room with my boyfriend and me. And the three of them, all of them, are sitting there and laughing at me. And, of course, I keep thinking, "They are laughing at me." And I don't understand why they don't help me or something. And then I wake up.

O'CONNELL: Besides the fact that you have a feeling your boyfriend has "kidnapped" you, is there anything else that seems very strange in your dream?

GINNY: Well, there's the fact that my father and my brother and my boyfriend are all sitting there, just laughing at me. Because I have a good relationship with all three. You see, I'm kind of the baby of the family, so my father and brother kind of pamper me. And my boyfriend is nice, too. Only in this dream, they seem to be laughing at me.

O'CONNELL: All right, let's walk the dream through again. Start from the beginning and try to remember every detail you can and stay in the present tense as you did before.

GINNY: Let's see, I'm in my car and I'm driving on this country road, I think, and it's very dark out so I can't see the cars or houses or anything.

O'CONNELL: OK, let's find out what the car means to you.

GINNY: I don't know.

O'CONNELL: You're the only one who knows. Play-act the car. Talk as if you are the car. Begin: "I am Ginny's car."

GINNY: I am Ginny's car. I am driving her along a country road, and I'm running out of gas.

O'CONNELL: Ah, that's interesting. What does "running out of gas" mean to you?

GINNY: I don't know . . . well, maybe getting tired. Yeah, I guess that's it. Getting tired.

O'CONNELL: Do you get tired often?

GINNY: Oh, I see what you mean. Yeah, that's true, I guess I'm going along the road of life. Can that be right, and I'm getting tired . . . ?

O'CONNELL: All right, now what about the grayness. Can you transform yourself into the grayness?

GINNY: You mean play-act the grayness? It was just gray.

O'CONNELL: But we want to find out how you put the grayness in your dream rather than sky or sun.

GINNY: OK. But I don't think it'll do any good. It doesn't mean anything, it was just gray.

O'CONNELL: Nothing is ever "just" in a dream, Ginny.

GINNY: Well, I'm the grayness in my . . . in Ginny's dream. I'm kind of like fog, and I cover everything up. make it hard to see. . . . Hey, does it mean I feel like I'm driving along and don't—can't—see where I'm going? I'm kind of like confused?

O'CONNELL: Sound right to you?

GINNY: Yeah. Can I go on?

O'CONNELL: *(Nods affirmatively.)*

GINNY: So I get to my boyfriend's house, only when I get there he's in a garage, you know, like a filling station. And he comes over and pumps gas in my car. I guess that means something sexual. I guess it means I want to sleep with him.

O'CONNELL: I don't know. Let's find out what it means to you. What's your boyfriend's name?

GINNY: Tim.

O'CONNELL: All right, become Tim in your dreams and let's see what he's doing there.

GINNY: I'm Tim. I'm Ginny's boyfriend. We're going to get married . . . *(stops)*. I don't know what else to say.

O'CONNELL: I'm putting gas in Ginny's car.

GINNY: Oh yeah, I'm putting gas in Ginny's car. . . . *(Smiles.)* That's really funny. That's what he does to me. Everytime I begin to feel kind of low and moody, he kind of fills me up . . . you know, charges me up. He's always so enthusiastic about everything. And I'm never really sure about anything, it seems. So I begin to have doubts about something and he comes along and he kind of just straightens out all my problems. And he's always cheerful and good-humored, I forget all my moodiness.

O'CONNELL: Very good. You're really getting "in touch" now. Go on with your dream.

GINNY: Well, suddenly I'm not at the garage anymore but at my boyfriend's house. I don't know how I get there, I'm just there. And I'm at this table with my head down on my arms and I'm crying. And the strange thing is my boyfriend is just sitting there and laughing at me and so is my father and brother. And it seems like I've been taken there against my will. And so I just cry more and when I wake up, I'm just sad that nobody cared how I was feeling. There I was crying my heart out, and they all just sat there and laughed at me!

O'CONNELL: It seems strange to you that your father is laughing, too.

GINNY: I know it. He was always very nice to me. I have always been kind of the baby of the family. So it sure hurts me in the dream that he just laughed at me.

O'CONNELL: All right, let's find out what that means. Play your father laughing at Ginny.

GINNY: OK, but I don't see what that's going to do.

O'CONNELL: Well, go ahead and try.

GINNY: I'm Ginny's father and I'm laughing at Ginny. And there's Ginny sitting at the table crying because I'm laughing at her. . . . Wait a minute . . . that's not right. I'm not laughing *at* her. Ginny thinks I am, but I'm only laughing *with* her. Only Ginny's not laughing, she's crying. That's strange. I guess I'm not taking her crying seriously.

O'CONNELL: So in some way, your father is not taking you seriously about something. Or your brother and boyfriend either?

GINNY: That's right. (*Silent a moment.*)

O'CONNELL: What is it that you're worried or scared about that your father and brother and boyfriend won't take seriously? In real life. Is there something?

GINNY: Yeah, that's funny. There really is. They think I get worried about foolish things.

O'CONNELL: And what foolish things are you worried about?

GINNY: Well, whether I should get married or not. I keep trying to tell them that maybe I'm too young to get married, but they all just tell me I'm being silly or something. I really feel as if I haven't lived yet!

O'CONNELL: How old are you Ginny?

GINNY: Eighteen.

O'CONNELL: Do you have a feeling that maybe you're going to be a child bride?

GINNY: Yeah!

O'CONNELL: In your dream, you are taken to your boyfriend's house against your will.

GINNY: Yeah.

O'CONNELL: In real life, Ginny, do you feel a bit as if you're being "kidnapped" into marriage?

GINNY: Wow! That's just how I feel! Oh, wow!

After some time elapsed, we asked Ginny to translate her dream symbols into everyday language.

GINNY: I guess I feel lost and confused about getting married and I don't know if I should or not. I am pretty young, I guess. Anyway, everytime I tell my boyfriend I don't know if we should get married—in real life—he just tells me not to worry about it and talks about all the things we're going to do and everything. So I get convinced it's the right thing to do because he makes it sound so exciting. But I guess I'm not really sure it's the right thing to do because I haven't really lived yet, and I feel a little as if I'm being kidnapped.

Brooke's Dream: A Jungian Dream

The second dream was related by a much older, beautiful woman who has had many tragic experiences, including the suicide of her husband seven years before. She has had to raise her children by herself and to continue to manage a 170-acre farm, virtually alone, which took all her available energy and spirit. The dream she related was as follows:

In my dream, I am in a plowed field which seems to be very fertile, but nothing is growing on it. As I am looking at the plowed fields, I am suddenly aware that I am leaving the ground, am looking around and rising into the air. I see the blue sky around me like a dome and as I look down, the furrowed fields are no longer earth but water, ocean, only with the same texture and quality of the plowed fields.

When she finished relating her dream, she added that she thought that she understood most of the dream.

O'CONNELL: Relate what you understand.

BROOKE: Well, I'm like the furrowed fields. I have a lot of richness in me, fertile like the land, but I haven't produced anything for a long time . . . since my husband died.

O'CONNELL: Go on.

BROOKE: The rising in the air seems to mean that I am beginning to leave off being so rooted to the earth and allowing myself to expand like the air.

O'CONNELL: New ideas, new goals. What about the water?

BROOKE: The water represents the nourishment of the earth so things can grow. The only thing is that the water-land is still brown — nothing is growing yet. But the potential is there. I am at a place where I want to do something for myself.

O'CONNELL: (After a pause) Brooke, do you notice that your dream contains three of the four universal elements? Do you recognize them?

BROOKE: Earth, air, and water.

O'CONNELL: What's missing?

BROOKE: Fire!

O'CONNELL: What does fire represent?

BROOKE: I have to put a fire under myself!

O'CONNELL: The fire of creation.

BROOKE: Yes. That fits very well. I better get "fired up."

All we can say at this point is that a person who is as introspective as Brooke proved herself to be in her first dream session needs very little guidance from dream guides such as ourselves. There is a postscript to this dream session. After another term at the college, Brooke decided to go into a paraprofessional program in counseling. Her aim was to acquire enough skills to help her work with other men and women who, like herself, had experienced the tragedy, the suffering, the guilt, and the despair that accompanies suicide and, at the time of this writing, she is pursuing that objective.

There are many good books for those who wish to pursue their personal study of dreams, and we encourage you to peruse them, remembering always that a particular symbol interpretation may be relevant to one dream but not to another. You always are the final arbiter of your dream symbols — let no one tell you otherwise.

applications and coping techniques: how to remember and interpret your dreams

In the years since Freud and Jung and other pioneer psychoanalysts made their studies of the dreaming experience, there have been significant breakthroughs in sleep and dream research. For example, we now know that all of us dream, even those who do not remember dreams. So "I don't dream," would now be more accurately "I don't remember my dreams."

Second, sleep and dream research have shown that, depending on what we consider to be a dream, we dream more or less almost all night long![23]

Third, the fact that one is dreaming can be observed by others, for dreaming is accompanied by observable physiological changes in the body. Just as emotional reactions in the waking state can be measured

Some dream symbols are very easy to understand. Ask yourself what they might mean in real life.

with scientific instruments, so also can dreaming, with such accuracy, in fact, that the research scientist can specify when a person is in the "deep dream state."

Dream and sleep research now tell us that we dream many times during the night when asleep and that dreaming may account for as much as 85 percent of sleep. Dreaming, therefore, accounts for almost a third of our lives (since we spend approximately a third of our lives asleep).[24]

Some persons seem to remember their dreams better than others do. If you are a nonrememberer, there is hope for you, too—if you want to put the time and energy into that project.

The guidelines which follow have been used for several years with all kinds of persons in teaching them how to remember dreams. Although they may seem rather obvious, these pointers have proved useful to many persons, and we hope they will be useful to you as well.

1. Tell Yourself Before You Go to Sleep that You Want to Remember Your Dreams.

This is a crucial first step for people who have difficulty remembering their dreams. It is a kind of autosuggestion technique that seems to work. Some persons report instant success, but if you are a "nondreamer" (that is, a nonrememberer), it may take many suggestions before this technique pays off. Remember that you have spent most of your life not remembering so do not be discouraged if it takes several weeks to overcome many years of resistance. Remembering dreams is not easy for most of us; it takes practice.

2. Try to Wake Up Quickly!

Dreams are forgotten very quickly, so quickly in fact, that within a few seconds of waking up, we can have forgotten them. If you wonder why this is so, let us give an analogy that you may understand. Once in a while when we are discussing something during the day, we lose the thread of what we were trying to say. If that is true even in our waking existence, it is that much more true of our nighttime thoughts. As soon as we begin waking up, our daytime thoughts push our previous ones (our dreams) away. We now know that the dream we remember is the last one we had before waking up. Also, if we are the type that wakes up slowly, we will have difficulty remembering what we have just been dreaming. So it is important to try to wake up quickly. One of the reasons that nightmares are so well remembered is that we wake up very quickly, and we have no interfering thoughts that allow us to forget them.

3. Wake Up Earlier than Usual.

If you are one of those persons who wakes up slowly, find an alarm clock that will startle you awake. Set the alarm for a little earlier than usual so that you can "catch" yourself in the middle of a dream. As the time approaches for us to wake up, report the sleep researchers, our sleep stages gradually become lighter, and our dreams begin to merge with our early morning thoughts. So the technique of waking earlier than your normal time sometimes produces results.

4. Keep a Notebook by Your Bed and Write Down Everything You Can Remember.

People frequently insist they can remember their dreams, but the truth is that even if we have a very vivid dream, we may very well forget it by the end of the day. Our waking life is filled with so many of the urgencies of living that we simply forget what seemed so vivid on first waking up. Psychoanalysts, writers, and other introspective persons keep a special notebook by their bedside so they can record their dreams or whatever they can remember about them. Please accept that everything we dream is significant. Freud insisted on it, and so did Jung, and so has everyone who has made a serious study of dreams. We may not always understand the significance immediately, but pursuit of our dream symbols will eventually reveal it.

5. Do Not Run Away from Nightmares.

When we have a bad dream, our tendency is to try to put it out of our minds as quickly as possible. It may come as a great surprise that most of our nightmares, once interpreted, usually turn out to be amazingly benign.

For example, a student of the authors' once had the following dream. She was in her kitchen preparing a meal when she saw a horde of Chinese soldiers marching down toward her house and about to descend on her. She awoke trembling with the feeling that if she had not waked up, the soldiers would have marched over her house, her, and all her existence. Her only initial clue as to the meaning of the dream was the color of the uniforms of the soldiers: red and green. When asked what red and green symbolized, she answered rather puzzled, "Christmas . . . but I don't see what . . ." and then she stopped and a look of astonishment came over her face. She then told us that she knew exactly what the dream meant. Every Christmas, her husband's family, two adults and four children, came for a visit. The six of them together with her own family of five (her husband, three children, and herself) made eleven people she had to take care of, entertain, feed, clean up after, and so on. Although she enjoyed their visit, she also was overwhelmed by what seemed to her, at times, to be an army of people to take care of: everyone had a grand time at Christmas but her. We can certainly sympathize with her anxiety and irritation, but her dream was certainly not as frightening as it was when she did not understand it.

Likewise, death dreams do not need to be interpreted literally as signs of impending physical death — at least not in the authors' experience. For a very elderly person or someone clearly on a self-destructive course, a death dream may have some such related significance. But in general, if you dream that a friend is dying, it is more likely that he or she is "dying to you," that your relationship has become "dead," that what you once had together is now over. A dream of one's own death (again, in the authors' experience) generally refers to the end of some aspect of one's personality, the loss of innocence, perhaps, or the end of one's tendency to be impatient, or the destruction of some part of the ego.

If your dream deals with death, figure out what part of your personality is "dying" or what person is "dying to you."

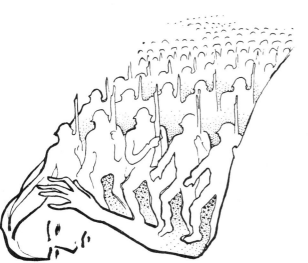

Nightmares are never as terrifying when they have been understood.

A young woman dreamed that her brother was in a coffin and stirring around. She understood finally that her brother was, in her eyes, "asleep, even dead" to the world around him, but that maybe he was beginning to show signs of waking up to who he was and what he was doing with his life.

A word of advice: do not ever be frightened of taking a death dream literally; there is only a million-to-one chance that death in a dream means literal, physical death! Most of the time what is dying, or ceasing to exist for us, is a *relationship* with another person, or some *aspect of our behavior* we no longer need. Such dreams sometimes enable us to see that a relationship with another person is no longer possible, and if we look closely enough, the dream may even tell us why this is so.

In the event of dreaming of your own death, it is usually some aspect of yourself dying—usually a part you no longer need, such as your hopes or your immaturity. A woman we know has had death dreams regularly all her life, and she is still going strong! "When I have a death dream," she says, "I know I am in for another personality change or stage of growth. Sometimes," she adds wearily, "I wish I wouldn't grow so much."

Look then for another dream soon in which there is a baby or small child. This is that new part of yourself that is being born or some undeveloped aspect beginning to grow.

6. Review Your Dream Notebook Every so Often.

Calvin Hall, who has studied the relationship of dreams has noticed that dreams may have a continuous thread.[25] One of our students had a series of four dreams over a period of time which she was able to relate to her own development as a person.

In the first, she was studying for a test. In the next dream, she awoke in horror because she had been found cheating on a test. In a later dream, some four weeks later, she dreamed she was being tried and convicted for a crime. Some months later she dreamed of caging a tiger. She interpreted these dreams as her struggle to control her own fierce temper.

The dreams were reflecting something I have been trying to learn for a long time (studying for a test), which is not to lose my temper. The next dream reflected a moment in which I backslid (cheated). Then I really determined to do something about my bad temper (the trial). I think locking up the tiger means I am successfully controlling my temper.

7. Trust Only Yourself and a Trained Dream Interpreter to Interpret Your Dreams.

Your dreams are your private, inner world. Only you have the key to your dream symbols, no matter how apparent they may seem to others, your friends and peers who are only too glad to interpret them for you. These well meaning "armchair psychologists" may well put you off the track with their interpretations or frighten you to death, generally with something which is not accurate at all. How do you know what is an accurate interpretation? Simply this: the correct meaning will just seem to "fit"—it will make sense—and it is probably not frightening. The experience is something like suddenly remembering something which has been on your mind but which you have not been able to think of, like remembering the name of an old friend or acquaintance.

8. Consider Your Dreams as Potential Sources of Wisdom, Solutions to Problems, Inspirations, and So On.

There are many anecdotes about scientists, artists, and writers who, in their dreams, received creative inspiration and discovered solutions to complex problems or received guidance on what path to take regarding a life situation. A well-known example is August Kekule's suggestion of the structural formula for benzene in 1858. Kekule had been working to discover the arrangements of the atoms in the benzene molecule for some time, and then, in a dream, he saw the atoms fitted together in a certain pattern which proved subsequently to be correct. This led to the development of the many compounds containing carbon.

Research on highly creative individuals by human behavior scientists has confirmed that truly gifted individuals, whether they be scientists or artists, are very much in touch with their creative unconscious. We shall discuss this further in chapter 13. Suffice it to say here that dreams are a truly creative expression of every person. In actuality, you are the writer, the director, the scene designer, and the actors of your own dream plays. In fact, we know a humanities and art professor who encourages his students to paint their dreams as a form of creative expression. Using his idea, we encourage our readers to draw, color, or paint their dreams. Sometimes, this becomes the simplest route to one's own dream symbols and interpretation. Jung frequently painted his own dreams, and you might want to look at his paintings.

9. When Searching for the Meaning of Your Dream Symbols, Be Open to Symbolic Art and Literature Wherever You may Find It.

When asked how to know what kind of studies are necessary to be a psychoanalyst, Freud replied: a study of the humanities—literature, mythology, religion, art, archeology, and anthropology. We advise the same for understanding dream symbols. As Jung pointed out, symbols tend to be universal to all cultures. Writers and painters use symbols consciously and from the depths of their creative unconscious. One of the interesting facets of dream symbolism is that it seems to agree with symbolism in art, literature, religion, mythology, and the like. Freud pointed this out and so did Jung. Blue has always been the color of love and devotion in religious art: in medieval art the madonna is usually dressed in a white robe (standing for purity) but cloaked with a blue mantle (for her love of humanity). Blue also often represents love, lovingness, compassion, tenderness, and/or devotion in dreams, depending on the shade and hue. In fact, love is often red (passion) as in Valentine cards, tenderness and affection sometimes appear as pink; deep blue is a deep and devoted love. But we repeat that these are general symbols; you, yourself, may have a different association with it, and only you can make that judgment. For example, blue may have a different meaning for you; it may mean "having the blues," being depressed, or, as in the case of one young Britisher, it may represent loyalty: "true blue."

Numbers are often significant—particularly since we are a very number-conscious culture. We identify ourselves by our age, our birthdate, and our social security number. We live in terms of number of minutes, hours, days, months, and years. We celebrate brithdays, holidays, and anniversaries. We deal in money, and even how much mileage we get to a gallon of gasoline. We need not go on. The essential thing is to get in touch with the significant numbers in your dream and discover the meanings to them. Three rabbits in one lady's dream stood for her three little helpless, sweet, and very un-toilet-trained children. One man dreamed of three doors, representing three possible alternative courses of action among which he was then trying to choose.

Those familiar with the symbolism of numbers may recognize their significance in dreams. Of particular interest, we think, is the number forty. We often say that "life begins at forty." Jung said that at forty, a person begins to take an interest in his or her transcendent-spiritual life. Students of the Bible will recognize the significance of the number forty, so often does it appear in both the Old and New Testaments. When Noah escaped the flooding of the earth, the rain continued for forty days and forty nights. When Moses led his people into the wilderness, it was for forty years. Catholics traditionally practice a forty-hour vigil during Lent in commemoration of Jesus' *withdrawal from*

A significant key to understanding your own dream symbols is to "own" every part of the dream.

the world before his crucifixion. Putting all these together, what may we discern about the number forty? Let us suggest that forty denotes the radical transformation of a person or a people. God transformed the world of Noah through forty days of rain. Moses kept his people for forty years in the wilderness to weed out those who had grown soft and weak in Egypt and to produce a new generation of strong, desert people. The "forty-hours' vigil" represents the internal preparation of Jesus in Gethsemane for his final journey into Jerusalem and his ultimate illumination. Jung said that it is true that a new understanding of life is possible around forty, and thus we begin again. Can such symbolism be accidental? The longer we study this, the more we think not.

10. When You Run into Difficulty Interpreting Dreams Symbols, Act Out the Symbol.

The psychologist Frederick Perls had the dreamer play out every aspect of the dream — whether it be a person, an animal or an inanimate object. Perls's thesis was that every detail of the dream was some part of us or our projection of the world. Whereas Freud called dream interpretation a "royal road" to the unconscious, Perls called dreams the "royal road" to personality integration. Perls's contention was that it is not necessary to have a cognitive understanding of our dream symbols, only to be willing to admit to every aspect of our dreams. By "playing" each dream symbol, the person is able to "process" the dream material without cognitive understanding.

the search for authenticity: discovering our fairy tales, games, scripts, and myths

Our unconscious motivations and aspirations emerge not only in our personal lives, but also in our myths, folklore, fairytales, literature, art, architecture, music, and social mores.

I. Introduction: Myths, Folklore, and Fairy Tales

    A. *Sigmund Freud: totem and taboo*

    B. *Folklore and fairy tale*

    C. *Erich Fromm: the inner wisdom of fairy tales*

    D. *Bruno Bettelheim and the uses of enchantment*

    E. *The significance of fairy tales to our own lives*

II. The Child's World-View: Animistic, Inconsistent, and Inconstant

    A. *Jean Piaget: the intellectual development of the child*
        1. *Sensori-motor stage*
        2. *Concrete operations stage*
        3. *Formal operations stage*

    B. *Piaget's stages of moral development*

    C. *Lawrence Kohlberg's stages of moral development*
        1. *Stage 1: Hedonistic and self-evident moral reasoning*
        2. *Stage 2: Moral judgment based on approval by others or on stereotypic thinking*
        3. *Stage 3: Empathic orientation*
        4. *Stage 4: Strongly internalized stage*

    D. *Primitive thought processes versus rational thought processes*

    E. *The fairy tales people believe and the games people play: Eric Berne*

III. Therapeutic Approaches For Our Games and Life-Scripts

    A. *Jacob Moreno and psychodrama*

    B. *Assertiveness training*

    C. *Fritz Perls: owning one's projections*

IV. Mythic Forces and Themes: Carl Jung

    A. *The wisdom of the wise ones*
        1. *The Wise Old Man*
        2. *The Wise Old Woman*
        3. *The Wise Child*
        4. *The child as "Trickster"*

    B. *A therapeutic approach for expanding consciousness: "mind games" and creative fantasy*

    C. *Mythic themes and human motivations*

V. Applications and Coping Techniques

402

introduction: myths, folklore, and fairy tales

In the chapter on dreams, we studied how our unconscious motivations and conflicts, wishes and fantasies, hopes and aspirations emerge in highly symbolic ways in our dreaming state. In this chapter, we shall examine how these factors dominate our waking existence in the way we interact with each other from day to day. They also form the great underlying themes which contribute to what Alfred Adler called our life style (chapter 2).

Many of the great personality theorists (Freud, Jung, Adler, Fromm, Horney, etc.) agreed that these unconscious forces make their appearance not only in our personal lives, but also in legendary literature of all kinds throughout the ages and across cultures. We shall investigate the relevance of these themes to our own lives. If some of this material seems to you to border on the fantastic do not be alarmed. Accept only what you can and shelve the rest as interesting but not yet convincing. But remember that when Freud first published his *Interpretation of Dreams* his ideas were rejected even by his own profession. All new ideas need time to take root and bear fruit. The same has been true of all those who have ventured beyond the known: of Darwin, of Galileo, of Einstein.

Sigmund Freud: Totem and Taboo[1]

In his formulation of the male child's psychosexual development, Freud relied heavily on the story of Oedipus. Freud postulated that myths and fairy tales are more than mere stories, that they contain the fundamental truths of psychological functioning.

Freud believed that our myths and fairy tales represent our strongest taboos (partricide, matricide, fratricide, incest, cannibalism, etc.) or the deepest and most repressed aspects of psychological evolution. The reason that they are so forbidden is because they pertain to our deepest instinctual, narcissistic desires, not only affecting the development of the child but the development of the human race itself. He believed that taboos were established to prevent the destruction of society. Freud postulated that humankind once revolved around a strong, primordial totem-father who claimed for himself all the females of the herd and prevented the young males from claiming any of the sexually mature females. In those early times there was no prohibition against incest, just as there is no such natural repulsion among lower forms of animal life (gorilla, chimpanzees, horses, dogs, etc.). Then the young males of the tribe would band together in rebellion and overthrow the patriarchal domination of females (much as stallions fight over the mares of the herd). In order to prevent this kind of anarchy and to preserve the tribe, each small tribe or society eventually evolved the laws prohibiting incest, patricide, fratricide, infanticide—all the acts considered taboo! Thus arose the prohibitions and mandates against marrying close female relatives, which we call incest.

Freud's theory of totem-father and taboo received considerable criticism by some social scientists, but others give it credence. Most personality theorists seriously consider the idea that myths and fairy tales contain some of the primitive wishes, fears, and conflicts of child development. Freud, himself, considered mythology and folklore as a necessary ingredient of a rational society. Since we can never root out the savage and primitive instincts of our *id* but can only repress them, they still form the basis of our deepest motivations, no matter how hidden they are. Furthermore, said Freud, the more they are repressed and denied, the stronger their drive is to be expressed. Dammed up or not worked through, they can emerge in horrifying ways.

We may not do such monstrous things, said Freud, because we catharsize them through reading, hearing, or watching them in legend and literature. Freud believed that fairy tales perform the same function for children as the Greek myths and plays did for the fifth century Greek. In plays, the Greeks watched their gods and goddesses play their games of love and war and revenge on each other, using (all the while) innocent human men and women as their unknowing and tragic pawns. If we are to believe Homer, the Trojan War was fought because a jealous goddess was seeking revenge for having been slighted.

Folklore and Fairy Tale

Eventually however, the human race ceased to believe in deities that performed acts of murder and incest and genocide. Eventually, humankind began to accept a new concept of Deity, that of a Father-God, so unlike anything that had been previously conceived, that no graven image could be made to show His Unimaginable Being. The

The pagan gods and goddesses were dethroned but not destroyed. They reemerged as the elves, goblins, leprechauns, trolls, and witches of folklore and fairy tale.

next step in religious evolution was a Son-God, so loving and compassionate that He would give his life for mortal beings, no longer the pawns of whimsical or cruel gods but now recognizing themselves as the "children of God." Mortals now could transcend their original sinful natures. Such a profound reversal of theological meaning and symbol was a radical transformation of human psychology, a transformation of spirit that only the most elevated of men and women could understand. Despite the spread of Christianity throughout the pagan world, most human beings retained deep in their unconscious, a belief in malevolent or mischievous entities who still needed to be feared and placated. Although the pagan gods were dethroned by the early Christian missionaries, they were not annihilated. The ancient gods and goddesses may have been stripped of their powers, but they were not dead by any means. They went into the unconscious to emerge as the fairies, witches, elves, and goblins of folklore and fairy tales. But even in this demoted status, they continued to embody the irrational and primitive hopes, fears, and wishes of humankind. Even now, to children, they are very real entities.

Those who have studied folklore and fairy tales tell us that fairy tales differ from myths and sagas, in that fairy tales are not connected with any specific country or locale; nor are they identified with a specific person. Fairy tales happen in an indefinable past ("Once upon a time . . .") and usually do not involve gods and goddesses. To be sure, the main characters of fairy tales have names, but these names always point to some specific but impersonal characteristic or rank, like the King, the Queen, the Wicked Stepmother, the Prince, the Fairy Godmother, or the Wicked Witch. Sometimes, a character may have a symbolic name, such as Snow White (a person of goodness and beauty) or Sleeping Beauty (indicating both her beauty and the spell she is under), or Prince Charming (referring to both his rank and personality).

The essence of the fairy tale, then, is *plot*, which often is simple, and ends usually, with a happy ending. Do not be misled by the innocent beginning: "Once upon a time far away . . ." and the ending ". . . and they all lived happily ever after." For between these two innocuous phrases, the fairy tale deals with the fears and taboos of humankind. Some persons think that fairy tales are so barbaric that many of the fairy tales of the brothers Grimm have been eliminated from children's fairy tale anthologies and those which are included have been "cleaned up" considerably. Fairy tales are very unlike the gentler messages of Christianity with its gospels of love and compassion, and are filled with murder, revenge, mutilated bodies, and witches who poison others and cast spells on the innocent. No turning the other cheek or forgiving the enemy as in the Christian message;

the evil doers must be punished, their powers destroyed, and they must be made to suffer for their crimes.

Why, then, have fairy tales held such fascination for children? Because, say those who have studied them, fairy tales, like the great myths of the world, retell the eternal themes of existence: good versus evil, poor versus rich, weak and helpless versus strong and mighty, and ultimately crime and punishment. They deal also with the existential problems of fear, death, injustice, and despair.

There is another reason for their continuing fascination: they hold out the promise of love, hope, justice, and deliverance, and they teach a kind of morality, primitive as it may be. Evil is eventually punished, the good are eventually rewarded, the poor become rich, the weak and helpless are elevated, the ugly duckling becomes beautiful, the heart's secret longing is fulfilled, and all who deserve it, live "happily ever after."

Finally, say the personality theorists, the fairy tale embodies our familial conflicts, wishes for revenge, adolescent rebellions, and hopes and struggles for self-identity. In fairy tales, said Freud, our parents appear as the kindly king and queen while the child identifies with the prince or princess of the stories. As children, our parents seem to us to be wonderful, majestic beings who can do no wrong, the benign rulers of the child's realm. Then comes that shock of awakening when the father and mother no longer appear so benevolent—they punish us or treat us sternly. This is the beginning of our ambivalent feelings toward our parents. The mother is then no longer the "good queen" nor is the father the "good king." In the child's eyes they have been transformed into the "wicked king" and the "wicked queen" or "wicked stepmother." But children are told to love their parents; to hate them is wrong. Thus, as children we resolve this conflict by identifying two mothers: a good mother who is "nice" and does what we want, and a wicked stepmother who is "mean." In the fairy tale, this resolution appears as a "good queen who died in childbirth" and the "wicked stepmother" whom the good king married in his bereavement. Children are able to hate the wicked stepmother because she is not really related to them. After all, their real mother would never do mean things to them.

It is in just such ways that fairy tales enable children to catharsize their angry feelings toward their parents and other confusing problems of existence. Take, for example, the problems of the youngest child in a family who generally feels shoved around by his or her older siblings and can be actually heard to complain that he or she has nobody to push around. These kinds of resentments and desires are wonderfully manifested in those fairy tales in which the youngest child is the hero or heroine. Generally, these fairy tales begin, "There once was a miller who had three sons . . ." and it is the youngest son (whom no one had ever considered very smart or competent) that succeeds in the world, outwits the giant, destroys the wicked witch, releases the princess from her spell, and gains her hand in marriage from the grateful king and queen of the land. On hearing the happy ending of the fairy tale, the youngest child in the family (who almost never beats anyone at anything) is given the renewed hope that someday, he or she too will do something a little bit better, or smarter, or bigger, or braver than his or her siblings.

Erich Fromm: The Inner Wisdom of Fairy Tales

These symbolic themes have been pointed out, time and again, by many of the great personality theorists of our times. They draw our attention to the fact that although a child may not understand these symbolic meanings in any conscious way, they are important to shaping the child's *faith* and *hope* in the future, and the *will* and *determination* to overcome the obstacles and problems of life. Erich Fromm called folklore and fairy tales the "forgotten language"[2] of childhood but forgotten only consciously, for the folk wisdom of the fairy tale remains rooted deeply in the child's unconscious.

Fromm made another significant statement about the value of fairy tales and folklore: they explicate the mores of society in ways understandable to the child, although the child may not understand them fully until later. Fromm cited the classic tale of Little Red Riding Hood. Why does this story, asked Fromm, remain so popular decade after decade? The tale begins with a mother's advice to her daughter: one must be kind to older people, and so Little Red Riding Hood is sent off to visit her grandmother. But, warns her Mother, do not stray into the woods because terrible things may happen; there are wolves in the forest. So Little Red Riding Hood is instructed to stay on the straight and narrow path to her grandmother's house.

But even beyond the logical explanation for the popularity of this fairy tale, Fromm went on to explain, is another symbolic element. No matter where the story is found, one element never changes: the child's red cloak which is so much a part of the story that it is included in the title. That is not by chance, said Fromm. On the contrary, the red riding hood represents the color of emerging womanhood: the color of the menstrual blood which marks her passage into another significant state of existence. Once that symbol is understood, explained Fromm, the rest of the symbolic meanings fall into place. The thirteen-year old girl may no longer read fairy tales, but she may remember what can happen when she innocently takes up with a wolf. What is the denouement of the story? It takes place in grandmother's house where the wolf is lying in bed urging the child to come nearer and nearer. Is there any way now to deny that this is one of the most cleverly disguised seduction scenes of all literature? Of course, in the knick of time, the young woodsman comes and saves Little Red Riding Hood from the clutches of the seducer. Usually, the woodsman turns out to be a suitable young man who not only saves the heroine from the clutches of the villain but will ask for her hand in honorable marriage.

Bruno Bettelheim and the Uses of Enchantment[3]

Bruno Bettelheim won world-wide recognition for his work with children, particularly with psychologically damaged and emotionally disturbed children. He urged parents, educators, and anyone who works with children to restore fairy tales as part of children's education. The unique art form of fairy tales, he said, has been largely replaced with meaningless primers, preprimers, and "realistic" children's literature which are mainly to teach reading skills and to offer information. There is nothing wrong with these educational objectives, said Bettelheim, but they lack the richness and meanings of folklore and fairy tales.

Bettelheim stressed that the problems presented in fairy tales are existential situations that all of us must one day face: the death of a parent, the emergence from childhood into adulthood, the problem of good and evil, the search for another with whom to share one's bed and board, and the hope that we may eventually establish a worthwhile life. These themes are not presented in an adult way, of course, but are presented so that a child can understand them. A child's understanding of the world is magical: a realm of enchantment not unlike their thought processes.

Of particular significance, we believe, is Bettleheim's analogy of fairy tales to dreams. In dreams, said Freud, adults enact their worries, guilts, and wish fulfillments in a safe and symbolic way. Fairy tales provide the same kind of cathartic relief for children. Jack, the famous giant killer, represents the child's desire to outwit the giant adults in his or her environment. Hansel and Gretel destroy the "bad mother" (now safely disguised as the "Wicked Witch") in the same way she was going to destroy them. But since it is not the real mother in the story that is destroyed, but only her evil replacement as a witch, the child does not have to suffer guilt and remorse for that fantasy.

Furthermore, the evil forces that fairy tales embody are the "evil" impulses within the child's own psyche, which are subdued in the end by the child's own desire to be "good." Said Bettelheim:

Those who outlawed traditional folk fairy tales decided that if there were monsters in a story told to children, these must all be friendly — but they missed the monster a child knows best and is most concerned with: the monster he feels or fears himself to be, and which also sometimes persecutes him. By keeping this monster with the child unspoken of, hidden in his unconscious, adults prevent the child from spinning fantasies around it in the image of the fairy tales he knows. Without such fantasies, the child fails to get to know his monster better, nor is he given suggestions as to how he may gain mastery over it. As a result, the child remains helpless with his worst anxieties — much more so than if he had been told fairy tales which give these anxieties form and body and also shown ways to overcome these monsters. If our fear of being devoured takes the tangible form of a witch, it can be gotten rid of by burning her in the oven!

He went on to say that modern parents wish to deny that their children have murderous wishes and want to destroy the people that they also love. These parents assume that by having the children read only stories about good and rational persons, their children will identify with goodness and reason. Nothing could be further from the truth, Bettleheim warned, for by denying the child access to stories in which savage and monstrous acts are committed, the child is never able to catharsize his or her own frightening impulses. By hearing of these deeds in fairy tales, the child is relieved to discover that he or she is not the only one who imagines such things. The monsters and the taboo acts of fairy tales enable the child to feel part of humanity despite the evil wishes of his or her fantasies. Moreover, punishing the monsters, witches, demons, and dragons helps the child allay consequent guilt and remorse and assure that the evil impulses in his or her own being have been eliminated.

The Significance of Fairy Tales to Our Own Lives

If we have been fortunate enough to have had fairy tales as part of our childhood education, we may recognize the significance of one or more of them to our own existential maturity.

Remembering the fairy tale or childhood story that once meant much to us is one way of getting in touch with the developmental stages in our lives. When the authors asked their students to remember what childhood story was significant to them and to determine what meaning it had, one young woman wrote:

I think the story of Snow White and Rose Red meant a lot to me. Although [my sister and I] were very close, I always felt like Rose Red. For some reason, Snow White is the main person in the story, and she gets the prince, and Rose Red only gets to marry the prince's friend. My sister was fair and I was dark, just like Snow White and Rose Red, and I always thought she was much prettier than me and had more boyfriends somehow.

A shy young woman wrote:

The story of the *Three Billy Goats Gruff* was a very important story to me. I guess because the three goats gruff all were aspects of me. I am usually very shy and quiet and can usually only make a little noise like the littlest goat gruff, and I am kind of defenseless. The middle-size goat gruff is like me when I have enough courage to assert myself a little more. And the large billy goat gruff is me when I'm angry and really make a loud noise. But I can't do that very often.

The girl went into counseling and worked very hard on a "big billy goat gruff" voice so she could make herself heard when need be.

A young man admitted that the reinterpretation of "Jack and the Beanstalk" hit close to home:

As a matter of fact, he wrote, I was the youngest of four children and I was a comparatively late child. My family consisted of my parents who were much older and three sisters grown up by the time I was three or four. So here I was just a little tot, surrounded by all these grown-ups (and a lot of them were female, to boot), and I was always being told I could not do this and could not do that. I was fascinated by "Jack and the Beanstalk," and I used to get a large charge out of the fact that he outwitted the giant and brought him down. I can see that I identified with Jack, and the giant was all the grown-ups in my family. And I also have a sneaking suspicion that I get a charge still out of outwitting my boss, or my father, or anyone in authority. I'll have to look into this.

Writer Michael Hornyansky adds, "Beauty and the Beast should be read by every pretty girl who places too high a value on masculine good looks and by every unfortunate boy who knows he's a prince down deep."[4]

the child's world-view: animistic, inconsistent, and inconstant

The demons, monsters, witches, goblins, and all those eerie inhabitants of folklore, myths, and fairy tales may seem much more bizarre to adults than to children. As we become adult we begin to realize certain truths: that the universe is lawful and orderly; that our behavior has consequences; and that if we come to understand cause and effect, we can begin to control our own lives and master our own destinies. We are not at the mercy of demons, witches, and gods. The world is safer when we understand that what happens to us is, to a large extent, of our own doing. We are not the targets for malevolent spirits. This kind of adult world view was a distinct advance in human psychology and took many eons to evolve. Human thinking first was a world of *animism*. Primitive humankind did not understand the natural phenomena of the world. When the skies thundered ominously and lightning struck down people, children, cattle, and trees, primitive humankind imagined that their animistic gods were angry. When sickness and plague decimated a society, the priests and shamans of the tribe met to discover what taboo had been broken, who had broken it, and how this terrible wrong was to be righted. If the locusts swept over the village fields or a child was eaten by an alligator, people assumed that the demons had taken revenge for some unwitting insult.

To placate the gods, sacrifices were offered: human sacrifices and, eventually, animal sacrifice in place of humans. In the Book of Genesis, Abraham was prepared to sacrifice his beloved only son, Isaac, to Yahweh until Yahweh stayed his hand. Until only comparatively recently, the Hawaiians (whom we consider a peaceful, gentle people untarnished by the evils of civilization until the invasion of the white missionaries) sacrificed a virgin to the goddess Pele every time her mountainous volcano erupted. Until only recently in the west of Ireland, platters of milk were put outside cottage doors to keep leprechauns from playing their spiteful pranks.

The world was a fearful and confusing place to the primitive mind. Sad and tragic events were comprehended as the will of the gods, and a suffering humanity lived in fear and dread of them.

Children live in just such animistic worlds. The events of their lives seem to be ruled by forces that they do not understand. There is no better example of this than Lewis Carroll's story of Alice as she wanders in those curious realms of Wonderland and Through the Looking Glass. Consider Alice's various adventures. Upon eating and drinking magic substances, she grows so large that she finds herself a giant or so small she cannot reach the table. That is precisely the predicament of children. No matter how old they are, they are "too big" to do some things but "too small" to do other things. Alice often encounters a rabbit who is always running off somewhere, muttering that he is late and forever consulting his large gold watch: a child's view of the adult male in our society. Alice discovers someone holding a baby, but when she gets close enough to have a good look at it, it turns out to be a little pig. If not made ashamed of their feelings, children will not hesitate to voice their rather negative opinions of babies others fawn over. Alice finds it very difficult to make sense out of this confusing world in which a cat smiles mysteriously (although, as far as Alice can see there is nothing at which to smile), or in which some strange adults sit around at tea parties or suddenly scream "off with their heads" for no reason at all. To children, adults do seem to smile for no reason. Sometimes adults do seem to be as silly as the Mad Hatter's tea party visitors. And adults do seem to explode over nothing (at least to a child's point of view) and shout out dire threats of punishment. What better explanation of the tale of the Jabberwocky than that it is the child's comprehension of adult conversation.

Does this animistic theory of primitive thought processes have any basis in fact? To answer this question, we turn our attention to the work of two psychologists who have devoted their professional lives to children's intellectual and moral development: Jean Piaget and Lawrence Kohlberg.

Jean Piaget: The Intellectual Development of the Child[5]

Jean Piaget is a Swiss psychologist who early in his life was extremely interested in *epistemology,* or the study of *how we know what we know.* As a young psychologist he helped develop the Binet-Simon Test of Intelligence. This test was eventually brought to this country and standardized for American norms and is now known as the Stanford-Binet Test of Intelligence. Piaget always was interested in those children's responses that differed significantly from adult thinking. As a result of many years of study of his own three children and of others, Piaget concluded that children's thought processes have definite stages of development, which are related to age rather than to intelligence. His theoretical formulations are complex, and we can do little more than describe his stages of the development of thought processes: the *sensori-motor* stage, the *concrete operations* stage, and the *formal operations* stage.

SENSORI-MOTOR STAGE.   In the first two years, children primarily respond to sensory stimuli and make connections between those sensations and their own motor responses. It is a great achievement when children finally make the connection that some pleasureable sensations are not internal but come from external objects separate from themselves, such as mother's breast. For much of this infantile existence, before this neural connection is made, children's thought processes are disconnected sensations and experiences. It takes many experiences, for example, for infants to connect kicking off the covers and the sensation of coldness.

The child's phenomenological world is such that things appear and disappear by themselves. If we were to put a ball in front of a child at this stage, the child sees it and may even want to play with it. If we remove the ball and hide it behind our back, the child cannot understand that the ball is still present but hidden; to the infant, the ball is gone, as if by magic. It is a discontinuous world in which events happen of their own accord; adults come and go mysteriously, and objects appear and reappear without connection.

CONCRETE OPERATIONS STAGE.   Eventually, as the child grows up the world begins *to connect*. As adults we develop certain neural perceptions that psychologists call "constancies." If one shows an adult a ball at close range, the ball appears big. If one shows that ball to an adult from far away, the ball seems very small. As adults, we understand that the ball has not shrunk in size, (nor has the person holding it, for that matter), we understand that the "small" ball is now at a great distance from us and only appears to have shrunk, and the differences in the size of both the ball and the person is the result of depth perception and perspective. In psychology this is called "size constancy."

Little by little, the child learns that objects have permanency and that they do not disappear simply because they are not visible. Nor are they smaller just because they are far away. The world itself is becoming full of objects, whereas before it was full of disconnected sensations and movements. The infant associated *sucking* with the bottle; now the child begins to distinguish his or her own sensori-motor responses from the object itself. There is a *bottle. Sometimes he or she sucks on the bottle.* These two events now are distinguishable. The child perceives the world, and perceives himself or herself, as manipulating it through concrete operations. The stage of concrete operations lasts from infancy (somewhere between one or two years of age to about eleven or twelve years of age).

A significant part of this stage comes around seven or eight years of age when the child is able to learn the principle of *conservation*. Before this time, the child has mastered one-dimensional thought processes but is unable to consider more than one of them at a time. For example, if we were to take some colored water and put it into two different types of glass beakers, one that is short and fat and one that is long and thin, and ask the child which contains the most water, the five- or six-year-old would point to the taller beaker. But suppose we demonstrate to the child that we can pour all the liquid from the taller beaker into the shorter beaker and then ask which beaker holds the most water, will the child change his or her mind? Actually, he or she cannot. The child still points to the tall beaker. In his or her mind, something which is taller is bigger. The child cannot integrate the second principle that although something may look shorter, it can be fatter and therefore can contain the same volume of liquid. The fact that we can make the bigger and shorter beaker look as if it contains the same amount as the tall thin one seems like magic to the child. At seven and eight years, he or she can begin to accept two variables in his or her thinking process; that is, the child can think in terms of "but" and "if."

FORMAL OPERATIONS STAGE.   The final maturation in the thought process, said Piaget, comes around eleven or twelve years of age, and he called it the stage of *formal operations*. It is at this stage that the child can achieve the same kinds of rational understandings and complex abstractions that the adult has. It is only at this time, Piaget believed, that the child is capable of what we consider scientific thought—the ability to make an hypothesis but also to consider alternate hypotheses at the same time. In other words, it is at this time that the child can project what seems to be the case but at the same time be able to imagine what is not apparent and yet may be possible.

If Piaget's views are correct, they suggest that the educational drive to teach certain mathematical and scientific methodologies at earlier and earlier ages may be wrong. If we attempt to teach sophisticated inductive and deductive reasoning skills before eleven or twelve, most children will simply be confused. What is important here is that until a child reaches the age of eleven or twelve, he or she does not operate with the same kinds of thought processes that the mature and capable adult does. The world of children is a disconnected series of events over which they often seem to have no control.

This same disconnection also operates in children's moral development. Piaget's views of children's moral development, like his views of children's intellectual development, emphasize gradual evolvement.

Piaget's Stages of Moral Development[6]

Piaget concluded that before the age of seven or eight, children are incapable of any real moral reasoning. Children's psychology is *egocentric*; they are unable to appreciate the effects their actions have on others. (Freud might say that the child is still being ruled by the *pleasure principle*.) What is clear to children is that some things are wrong or forbidden and that other things are allowed. Children are guided by *rules* but are *incapable of understanding that there are reasons for these rules* and that the reasons apply to violating the rights of others. Piaget called this the stage of moral realism.

Piaget's second stage of moral development begins at about the same time as the stage of concrete operation (at about seven or eight years of age). Now children begin to perceive that certain acts are *good* and *bad*, not just that they are allowed or forbidden. They have been interacting with their peers and can see that others do bad things (although it seldom applies to themselves). Their sense of justice is being awakened and a grim justice it is! Not only is good behavior to be rewarded, bad behavior should be punished and punished severely. One might call it the stage of *crime and punishment*.

The third and most mature stage coincides with the stage of formal operations (at around eleven or twelve years of age). Children now can begin to understand the *relativity of moral decision making*. Two persons may commit the same kind of bad behavior for entirely different reasons. If a rich child and a poor child both steal, children of eleven and twelve can begin to appreciate the extenuating circumstances that might be applied to the case of the poor child and be much more understanding and forgiving. This stage can be called *autonomous morality, moral relativisim*, or *morality of cooperation*. Children's sense of justice is beginning to be influenced by thoughtfulness, and blind obedience to authority is beginning to give way.

Lawrence Kohlberg's Stages of Moral Development[7]

Kohlberg's work was based on a series of interviews with boys from ten to sixteen and thus represents a somewhat later age range than Piaget's subjects do. Kohlberg's subjects were given problems of moral dilemma similar to the rich child-poor child problem above. Each problem given to these boys involved "right" and "wrong," and the boys had to consider complex moral issues which involved extenuating circumstances. Kohlberg suggested four sequential stages of moral development, ranging from middle childhood through adolescence and adulthood. He concluded that the highest moral reasoning is reached by a very small proportion of mature adults!

STAGE 1: HEDONISTIC AND SELF-EVIDENT MORAL REASONING. This kind of reasoning predominates in middle-school children (although a few fourth- to sixth-grade students exhibit higher moral reasoning). It is essentially a hedonistic, pragmatic orientation in which children are concerned about their own rights and become incensed if they are violated, whereupon they call in an authority to straighten things out. When children do consider the needs of others, it is based mostly on personal gain. Occasionally, the middle-school child does think of others in a less egocentric way but only when it is very visibly demonstrated.

STAGE 2: MORAL JUDGMENT BASED ON APPROVAL BY OTHERS OR ON STEREOTYPIC THINKING.   Another level of moral judgment is achieved at about the ages of eleven, twelve, or thirteen. At this time, children are more willing to consider the rights of others or to be generous. These considerations and acts are not so much internal as reached through external factors, "because he is a good guy," "because my friends will like me better," or "because if I help him now, he'll help me later." The real motivation here tends to be stereotypic and arbitrary judgment ("He's O.K. so let's help him") enlightened by self-interest or by some vague notion of "good and bad" behaviors.

STAGE 3: EMPATHIC ORIENTATION.   It is not until high school that most boys are able to extend themselves to others on the basis of sympathetic responding, role taking, and concern for the other. At this time, the boy will defend his response to moral issues by stating "I know how he feels," "I care about people," or "I'd feel bad if I didn't help." At this stage, he is putting himself in the other's shoes. As boys get older, they begin to have a less egocentric point of view and can begin to understand another person's point of view and feelings.

STAGE 4: STRONGLY INTERNALIZED STAGE.   The final stage of moral development is one not achieved by everyone. It shares with stage 3 the qualities of empathy and concern for others, but it has a more abstract quality. It is based on the person's own internalized standards of behavior and moral principles. At stage 3, we can sympathize with one person because of that person's dilemma; those who reach stage 4 can consider the plight of a group of people or even of all humankind. The person expresses the need to live with himself or herself, "I couldn't live with myself if I didn't help." Their comprehension of the world and the relatedness of all humankind is gradual and is related to age and experience.

Primitive Thought Processes Versus Rational Thought Processes

Little by little, as children begin to understand the cause-and-effect consequences of their own behavior, they give up their magical and fairy-tale thinking. Just what is fairy-tale thinking? It is the belief that things happen to us without logic, without cause, and without reason. If things go wrong, it is because the evil forces in the world (like demons, witches, and malevolent spirits) have cast a spell upon us; if things go well, we are the fortunate recipients of a fairy godmother. It is a world in which good and bad are absolutes. People who oppose our wishes seem to the primitive consciousness to be the forces of evil; those who advance our aims and fulfill our desires are viewed as the forces of good. It is the simplistic thinking and one-dimensional world of early childhood. It is the kind of thinking that puts the control of our lives (as well as the responsibility for our actions) outside ourselves.

Suppose children are asked why they did something. They cannot answer. They do not know themselves. Something "made" them do it, or somebody told them to; after all, they could not have done it of their own free will! They do not know how it happened. As a matter of fact, some children will deny that they did it. Having said that, it becomes the truth! It happened "of its own accord"—as in the fairy-tale world in which anything can appear or disappear, inanimate objects talk, and people put spells on you!

Some infants may never even go beyond the stage of sensory-motor development; they live in a world of "disconnect," as with autistic children. Or, if the ego development has not been well developed, under moments of stress, the adult can revert (as in the case of extreme emotional breakdown) to primitive levels of consciousness. We say that they are having hallucinations because things seem to happen without apparent cause or connection. Or they may be unable, as in the case of sociopathic personalities, to understand that the tangled webs in which they are caught are of their own making. Sociopathic personalities have one common characteristic: they blame others for their plights, unable evidently to connect their behaviors to their difficulties—like the evil spells in fairy tales.

The Fairy Tales People Believe and the Games People Play: Eric Berne[8]

Eric Berne, author of *Games People Play*, has written about adults who also harbor unconstructive fairy tales and fantasy. A common one, Berne said, is the Santa Claus fable—the belief that if one plays one's cards right or if one is especially good or dutiful, then "Santa Claus" will some day reward that person. But, as Berne told his patients, there is no Santa Claus! Using his transactional method of psychotherapy, Berne was a "debunker," a slayer of dragons and other mythical beasts who prey on the energy and vitality of human personality. If you want something, Berne asserted, you better get off your duff and begin to work, and stop complaining! Berne's method aims at what Maslow called actualizing oneself. Berne's approach may seem iconoclastic, but people seem to understand it and make good use of it. In *Games People Play*, Berne showed how many of us act out neurotic scripts/fairy tales/plays/games over and over again. The first thing to remember about these neurotic scripts (conditioned behavior patterns), is that they are repetitious—we keep repeating them and therefore fail to learn anything. Second, since they are circular, they are highly predictable. The "neurotic" person is much more predictable than is the highly integrated, creative person. Take, for example, the game a wife sometimes acts out called "If it weren't for . . . ." The game she is playing is to convince herself that her unhappiness and lack of opportunity is because of her husband, her children, her "infirmity," or whatever the case may be. A variation of this game is "The reason I'm so fouled up now is that I had an unhappy childhood."

A husband, on the other hand, may be acting out the game called "Alcoholic," which as we all know, consists of falling under the spell of Demon Rum . . . and the spell is so severe that everyone in the family is trying to save him, even to the point of seeking the help of a "psychiatrist"—someone whose business it is to "release the spell" and save the person when everyone else has given up! (In the meantime, of course, the husband's role in the game called Alcoholic is that he is supposed to keep on drinking!)

Eric Berne wished to emphasize how we invent scripts for others to play in our fairy tale or game. The alcoholic may have learned his script early in life by watching his parents play out the script. He may have noted, for example, how the alcoholic can eschew responsibility, get "to play," squander his money, and engage in various antisocial behaviors because he was under the "spell of demon rum." When a person is under a spell, he cannot help himself. So the child of this alcoholic parent grows up, following a similar life script. But every script needs other characters to play their parts. The child, now an adult, has an uncanny instinct for finding a woman to marry who will play the part that his mother did for his father: alternately, the beautiful princess or fairy godmother who will save him from the spell and then the witch from whom he is running away, since part of the alcoholic script is to complain how his wife nags him. The alcoholic is clever, too, in seeking out friends who are willing to be cast as the characters who will try to save him from his life script.

There is another aspect to this life script, that each person in the alcoholic's drama is willing to participate in the alcoholic's life script because it concurs with some need to take on this role in life. In other words, they also are playing out a life script for themselves. There are no "innocents" in Berne's philosophy.

therapeutic approaches for our games and life-scripts

Several therapies have developed specific methodologies for developing insight into and change of our life scripts. We can start with Berne's transactional analysis described earlier in this book. The tragic events that the persons report in the T.A. groups frequently are analyzed for their fairy-tale or tragic-dramatic components. Or they may be analyzed as the moment-by-moment transactions in terms of the child-ego state, the parent-ego state, and the adult-ego state. William Glasser's reality therapy, also discussed previously, emphasizes enabling the person to change his or her lifescript (as a "failure") step by step, by accomplishing specific related goals, and so to devise another kind of role for himself or herself.

Jacob Moreno and Psychodrama[9]

Another approach to understanding and gaining insight into one's "drama" is through psychodrama, devised by Jacob Moreno. Moreno presented to persons in his small groups various real-life conflicts and problems of everyday life: adult-adolescent conflict, mother and mother-in-law problems, conflicts with authority, and marriage conflicts. The participants each would take one of the roles in these situations and act out the drama in nonconstructive ways and then in constructive, problem-solving ways. As the participants became more relaxed and freer to improvise their roles, Moreno would have them devise more personal situations, like those of the participants. After the psychodrama, the participants then would discuss how the person (whose problem it was) handled the situation and make suggestions for more constructive interaction, specifically how not to get caught up in the overly emotional dynamics of the situation. The psychodrama then might be repeated with the main actor trying to handle the situation more objectively.

Assertiveness Training[10]

The psychodrama approach was prominent in the fifties and sixties, and we have not heard much about it recently. But it did reappear in the seventies in a different form, with the growth of assertiveness training. In this, the participants act out for the group their responses to certain situations, how they approach other persons or make known their needs. After doing so, the other members of the group appraise the performance and suggest ways of becoming more self-assertive in the manner discussed in chapter 9 on language. The essential elements of assertiveness training include identifying what one wants, learning to communicate those wants, going after those wants, and thereby winning the respect of others and also respect for oneself. The assertiveness therapist sets up situations in which the person has to confront situations that we sometimes would like to avoid but that occur over and over again: giving honest reactions to others when asked; taking something back to a store for an exchange; asking for a raise; not being pushed out of line by someone else; criticizing one's spouse or colleague in a constructive manner; or refusing a friend's request for help because of lack of time. The therapist and person act out the situation, and the person receives feedback on his or her performance by both the therapist and the other participants. The person is coached by the members in how to improve his or her performance and then repeats the scene. The therapist and the other participants may even model the desired behaviors. The person practices the situation again and again until he or she feels comfortable with the new behavior, thus increasing the likelihood of using it in the real-life situation.

Fritz Perls: Owning One's Projections

Fritz Perls, whom we encountered in previous chapters, used psychodrama of another type, one similar to his noninterpretative dream therapy. Perls's essential thesis is that the "world," as each of us knows it, does not really exist, that our reality is really an extension of ourselves and that we devise ways of projecting our beliefs, our anxieties, and our conflicts on to others. We view the world through our own intrapersonal structure and thus create our own "messes." There is nothing very new about this thesis. What was new in Perls's approach was how he enabled people to get in touch with their projections. Perls accomplished this by having persons assume every role in their conflict, just as he had them act out every symbol of the dream experience. When we act out the various roles of our interpersonal conflicts, we get in touch with how our intrapersonal dynamics are projected onto the world. We then begin to "own" our own thoughts, feelings, and beliefs and no longer project them on to others. It is not some "terrible person," some "sonovabitch boss," some externalized malevolent force who is preventing us from advancing, it is *we* ourselves.

mythic forces and themes: carl jung

There are far more noble themes of human existence than those we find in fairy tales with their simple hopes for personal achievement, material gain, and happy endings. These are the themes of human evolution and personality development. Carl Jung, who was fascinated by these great mythic themes, called our attention to their appearance throughout world literature and art and how they work within us, whether we acknowledge them or not.

Jung, like Freud, accepted the conscious and unconscious elements of the mind, but, whereas Freud viewed the unconscious as a kind of "repository" for repressed, aggressive drives, Jung believed that we also have within us a *collective* unconscious.[11] The collective unconscious, according to Jung, contains not one's personal history, but a kind psychic-emotional history of humankind. As we mentioned earlier, taking the human fetus as an analogy, Jung pointed out that in the mother's womb, the developing human body undergoes the phylogenetic history of the human race. Just as our bodies have evolved over millions of years so too, according to Jung, has our human personality evolved psychologically, and we carry this psychological evolution in our collective unconscious.

Jung viewed this collective unconscious as more than a repository of primitive human consciousness. If understood and acknowledged, the collective unconscious can be a source of great inner wisdom and creativity. Although our primitive forebears may not have developed our modern consciousness with its sophisticated levels of reasoning, they had a wisdom mostly lost to us, a wisdom that we can call "intuition," which animals and primitive societies retain. We have mostly lost our link to the natural forces of the universe. We seek to dominate the elements, and thus we alienate ourselves more and more from the "participation mystique" of the primitive consciousness. Rather than deny these forces within ourselves, Jung urged that we seek to reestablish a connection with these mythic elements of our racial unconscious.

One way to connect with these mythical elements within us, and thus to regain our psychic wisdom, according to Jung, is to become aware of the archetypes within us. We already have discussed several of the archetypes in our discussions of the *Anima, Animus*, and so on. We now shall examine a few more.

The Wisdom of the Wise Ones

The archetypes discussed in earlier chapters are aspects of ourselves that we tend to deny or repress and that consequently manifest themselves into our consciousness through our dreams. But, say the Jungians, there also are other archetypes buried deep within us that are not necessarily denied aspects of our personal self but that represent the evolution of the human race. What is significant about these archetypes is that they represent various types of wisdom we can tap if we are willing to recognize their existence and their power. Four that we shall discuss here are the Wise Old Man, the Wise Old Woman, the Wise Child, and the Trickster. Remember that they are not subpersonalities of ourselves (as are the Shadow and the Anima-Animus) but rather, are symbolic personifications of the accumulated inheritence of human consciousness.

THE WISE OLD MAN.   As the human race developed, it was natural for people to consult the oldest representatives of the tribe, those that had lived the longest and had experienced many of the problems that are part of human life. They frequently had certain invested status and acted as tribal elders and teachers. Their various manifestations are known to us today as the medicine men, the witch doctors, Hebrew rabbis or prophets, Greek seers (such as Tiresias in the story of Oedipus), shamans, or the Mexican *brujos*. Sometimes they appeared magically like Merlin in the King Arthur legend, and sometimes they seemed divine, such as the half-historical, half-legendary Pythagorus of the Greeks, the Moses of the Hebrews, and even Father Time, symbolic of the wisdom of eternity. When these types of archetypes appear in our dreams, say the Jungians, we are communicating with our own wisdom, but with that special kind of wisdom that comes from the rational observations of the lives of men and women without judgment and with compassion. Students in our classes frequently report dreams in which the Wise Old Man is personified as a deceased relative, such as a father, grandfather, or beloved uncle and who seems to comfort them in their confusion and distress. Students say that this person often counseled them and supported them as they were growing up and needed help.

THE WISE OLD WOMAN.   The Wise Old Woman archetype is the female counterpart of the Wise Old Man. She has, however, a special character all of her own. The Wise Old Man seems to be the counselor, the adviser, the judge of rational human decision; but the Wise Old Woman is in touch with the "irrational," with the mysteries of life. She can contact the spirits, talk with oracles (as in the Oedipus myth), consult the runes, read the "cards" of one's fortune, and predict the future. She may appear in dreams or tales as a witch, as a fairy godmother, or as the grandmother in "Sleeping Beauty." She also may appear as a serpent, as the goddess of wisdom (for example, Athena), or even as a peasant woman or matchmaker (as in the play *Fiddler on the Roof*). Whereas the Wise Old Man embodies wisdom, the Wise Old Woman embodies intuition, omens, and other mysterious aspects of life.

THE WISE CHILD.   The positive aspect of the child archetype is the Wise Child or Hero-Child. He also is an aspect of our higher self because of his wisdom. But his wisdom is different from that of the Wise Old Ones. His wisdom comes not from years of experience as with the Wise Old Man, nor is it the wisdom of intuition and the irrational as it is with the Wise Old Woman. It is rather the wisdom born of goodness and purity, innocence and sweetness—the wisdom

Beauty and the Beast
*should be read by every
pretty girl who places
too high a value on
good looks*.

perhaps we all possessed when we were young and idealistic, and which is diminished every time we succumb to the dog-eat-dog credo.

This archetype is personified in the Christ Child and also in the cherubim of popular conception. He is a hero in his infancy, strong or supernaturally wise, though his strength does not rely on brute force but is of yielding gentleness and that which comes of love. He is Cupid, or Love; he also is the pure and innocent Sir Galahad (a mature man in body but with the sweetness of a child). He is the child that the Elf King takes with him into the Land of the Dead. He is also Huckleberry Finn who helps a slave escape from an immoral society. He is Tiny Tim of Dickens's *A Christmas Carol* and the other boy-heroes Dickens wrote about: Oliver Twist, David Copperfield, and Pip. In contemporary literature he is Holden Caulfield of Salinger's *Catcher in the Rye,* whose obscene language hides a heart wounded by the falseness of contemporary society. He is incarnated yet again in Antoine de Saint Exupéry's *The Little Prince* and perhaps now again in the hero of Richard Bach's *Jonathan Livingston Seagull.* The Wise Child is explicitly portrayed in Rudyard Kipling's Mowgli, a young boy who is reared in the jungle by wolves and so lives by the purity of primeval mores.

424

The Wise Child is a powerful archetype.

The child in all of us is wise simply because he represents those ideals and standards which we knew to be true when we were young—the capacity for sweetness and idealism we may have since lost. The Christmas season remains one of the truly holy days even in our culture, perhaps because Christmas celebrates those ideals of loving-kindness, charity, and hope that we perhaps believed in when we were young but are afraid to acknowledge now except during this season. The Wise Child often appears in our dreams, and when he does, the dreamer is being asked to look at some new dimension of himself that may be growing within.

THE CHILD AS "TRICKSTER". Our nature is dual, say the Jungians. If there is a sweet, wise, loving child archetype, then there must also be an opposite: one that manifests itself as a mischievous devil, a trickster who outwits society by ingenuity and wile. The Trickster also is part of our human nature and is that fun-loving, spontaneous prankster so well known in folklore and fairy tale. He is aptly represented in "Til Eulenspiegel's Merry Pranks." He appears also as Bre'er Rabbit or other animals of folklore: the fox or beaver in Amerindian legends or as the babbling, witless monkeys in Kipling's story of Mowgli, the Wolf-Boy. The Trickster has made his appearance in our times as the eternal circus clown, as Charlie Chaplin's tramp who mocks pomposity and hypocrisy—or even as the Marx brothers whose antics made the world seem both hilarious and insane.

The Trickster pops up, too, as the leprechaun, the troll, the sprite; or as a juggler, or an acrobat, as in medieval tales. He can also be Jack of "Jack and the Beanstalk" in his more sympathetic form.

The popularity of contemporary comic strips is partly due to the appeal of such figures, who allow the "child" in us to come out. Daily

we see how superior to the serious adult world with its dishonest nice-
ties and nastinesses is the more direct world of "Peanuts," "Dennis
the Menace," and "Pogo."

A Therapeutic Approach for Expanding Consciousness: "Mind Games" and Creative Fantasy

Personality theorists have devised methods for getting in touch with
these archetypal processes and integrating them into one's developing personality. These techniques are varied, but they generally require persons to make themselves comfortable, close their eyes, and
get into a state of relaxed attention. They then are told to visualize or
imagine, say, "his" Wise Old Man, or "her" Wise Old Woman.

The authors have done this with students in class, and these journeys of the imagination have never failed to produce interesting results, often astonishing insights into the person's problem and even
possible solutions. Often in these "controlled imaginations" persons
are able to get in touch with deeper levels of themselves and to discover the reasons for their present problems simply by encountering
some of their archetype figures. For example, one young woman saw
the Wise Old Man in flowing white robes with a long white beard and
using a cane to walk. When she asked him, "How can I find happiness?" he replied: "Do not worry about tomorrow but rather think of
what you are blessed with today." This girl suffers from an incurable
and fatal blood disease, and so the words of her Wise Old Man were
particularly relevant.

It matters little whether there are archetypes or not; what is relevant is that when these persons were willing to ask themselves significant questions and to listen to that "still, small voice" within them,
they received valid answers. They learned to listen to themselves in
the same way that Rogers's clients learned to listen to themselves
and to get in touch with their own "center of growth." We always
respect the direct, candid responses our students share with us, and
we share a few of their experiences with you.

A Young Man: How can I learn to stop procrastinating?
Answer: Do things now!
A Young Woman: How can I find love?
Answer: By loving others.
A Young Man: How can I stop finding fault and being critical?
Answer: By recognizing the faults within yourself.
A Young Woman: How can I discover what I want to do as a vocation?
Answer: By paying attention to what interests you.

Mythic Themes and Human Motivations

We will recognize the great mythic themes in great works of art. We will feel stirred by something deep within us and for which, perhaps, we have no name. Are we, like Ulysses, being called upon to do some thing we do not want to do but which must be done, nevertheless? Or is it that we, like Jason after the Golden Fleece, or Galahad after the Holy Grail, are on a quest for something higher than ourselves? Does the figure of that great prophet-leader, Moses, appeal because we, too, wish to free not one person from suffering, but an entire nation and to lead them from bondage?

Take, for example, the story of Krishna and Arjuna in the Bhaga-vad-Gita, that classic Hindu myth. The manifest content of that story involves a young prince who must fight a battle to regain his rightful throne. He is accompanied by his charioteer, Krishna, and the story takes the form of a dialogue between Krishna and Arjuna on the eve of a great battle. Arjuna is overwhelmed and saddened by the realization that his enemies are his own friends and relatives. At that moment, Krishna reveals himself to be the Supreme Manifestation of the Lord. Throughout the dialogue, Krishna advises, encourages, and teaches Arjuna the meaning of the battle. At one level, the story of Arjuna is the story of humankind, in which the battlefield is life itself with its rivalries and power struggles. Arjuna's enemies are the forces of the world which he must conquer if he is to attain salvation (his rightful place as a prince).

But according to some interpreters, the story of Krishna and Arjuna can be seen from another perspective as individual man's struggle to develop a higher stage of consciousness (what we have been calling personality integration). Arjuna and Krishna are then not two separate beings, but two aspects of man himself, a polarity exist-ing in each person—and the chariot stands for the physical body which the soul inhabits. On that level of meaning, Arjuna may be thought of as the personal soul or consciousness and Krishna as the supreme consciousness which all men share and which is our higher nature. The battlefield is still reality, but the battle is not an ex-ternal war between good and evil. It has been transformed into a struggle of *inner* reality in which each person attempts to overcome the seductive enemies within himself: slothfulness, anger, pride, and the desire to gossip, to slander, to indulge one's passions, etc. Psychol-ogists in the West might describe this struggle as an attempt to over-come our neurotic defending mechanisms and our past conditionings which prevent us from understanding our rightful place in the evolve-ment of consciousness.

Jung's investigations into myths also led him to believe that myths represent the choices and stages of a person's development throughout his life. He said that our task as adults is for each of us to learn what his or her myth is, to get in touch with it, and to learn from it what we need to know about ourselves.

How do we get to know the personal myth we live out? By studying mythology, Jung said by becoming "religious," and by allowing ourselves to be taught by primitive cultures, by the world's great literature, and by experience. What we each need is to be concerned with the myth that is alive in ourself and to recognize the great archetypes that are a part of our collective unconscious! What kinds of myths do we live out? Well, for one thing, each person is working out the life situation he or she was born into.

For example, if the person is a young man, his particular myth at this stage of his life may be to seek his identity apart from his parents. In that case, he may begin to see himself as a kind of heroic Saint George whose mission is to rescue a maiden, or a princess, from a dragon (a future hostile parent-in-law) who is trying to isolate and hang on to her. On the other hand, his myth may be that of Robin Hood and his band of merry outlaws—a theme that is becoming more and more apparent in our present society. As Robin Hood, the young male adult is then outwitting, or "ripping off" the "Establishment." And he derives his psychological support, as with the original Robin Hood, from the "peasants," or common people, who tacitly approve of his exploits because he acts out what they themselves would like to do, but dare not. Robin Hood's enemy is the sheriff of Nottingham—a corrupt, venal, and totally callous "police official" who does exactly what the king wants. Notice that this fable has already gone beyond the world of childhood. Robin doesn't fight directly with the king; he fights mainly with his minister, and other established functionaries of society, who administer the king's laws. He therefore clearly symbolizes a young man, an adult who supports himself and who is no longer beholden to his parents for his survival, though he fights his father's rule.

We find much the same kind of myth acted out in religious literature. Consider, for example, the Bible story of Lucifer's revolt against God's rule. This myth is spoken of first in a book which recounts the beginnings of Western religion. It is, therefore, already a *sacred* myth, having to do with some of our most unconscious motivations to challenge and to rebel. So we ask you not to be put off by the "quaintness" of some of these stories. Someone who has experienced the truth of Saint George and the Dragon, or of Robin and the Sheriff of Nottingham, or the Satanic conflict, may be actually fighting the powerful hold of his parent-in-law on his young wife, or asserting his right to live on the basis of sharing and help, or asserting his right to be listened to, no matter what! These remain some of the eternal problems in human personality development. And, as Jung says, we can either admit that these kinds of crises exist and live them out (and through), or we can try to deny that archetypal situations exist—although they will motivate us still, except that we will not be aware of them.

Jason, who steals the Golden Fleece, and Oedipus and Arjuna—who were all princes—may seem to be the kind of overpowering personalities next to which our own, more mundane personalities seem to shrink in size and significance. But one should not be put off by these apparent differences: to every person—you and me and the person down the street—is given the opportunity for the same epic struggle, the same adventures and crises, once we take upon ourselves our personal search for integration of personality. If that search is not fostered in childhood by one's parents and family, then each individual is going to have to "get on with it" on his own, with or without his family's blessing—that's all there is to it.

applications and coping techniques

1. Explore the Meaning of Your Favorite Fairy Tales, Myths, and Stories.

Those of you who wish to pursue the themes underlying your motivations, either past or present, can recollect those fairy tales, myths, and stories that were significant to you. It is a great insight into one's own functioning, just as it is to discover the meaning of one's dreams. It is a method of personality integration. Sometimes, too, these stories and myths will have one or more common themes which you can discern by comparing them, just as you can learn to pick up the threads of dreams through your dream journal.

You also will find that literature and art will have more meaning for you. If they do not seem to be applicable to your personal life, at least they will enable you to comprehend the evolution of human psychology. You will understand, too, the significance of the psychological crises of our age and time.

2. Learn to Discern the Fairy-Tale Elements of Human Psychology from the Mythic Elements that Shape and Mold Us.

Fairy tales represent simplistic thinking with their emphasis on personal gain, materialistic accomplishments, and happy endings. This kind of simplistic attitude will condemn us to await a "fairy godmother" or a "Santa Claus" to reward us for "being good." If our lives are to be changed, they must be changed by us. Change requires transformation and transfiguration of our personality in our current living. It requires examination of our personal values and explorations into the meaning of our lives. These are the great mythic themes and getting in touch with our own themes advances our process of personality integration.

3. Give Your Children or Children with Whom You Work the Rich Heritage of Fairy Tales and Folklore.

Bruno Bettelheim and other personality theorists stressed the innate wisdom of folklore and fairy tales. These stories, primitive and simple as they are, reflect the child's consciouness and speak to the child in terms he or she can understand. They deal with the confusions and problems of good and evil, despair and joy, crime and retribution, and the inconstant world of the child's experiencing. Certain stories will have more meaning to the child than others do, and he or she will want those stories repeated over and over. You may be bored reading them, but if you change one word or sentence, the child will stop and correct you. It is the repetition of the story, in the same way over and over again, that catharsizes and heals the anxieties and guilt of the child's own private fantasies and gives him or her hope for the future.

4. Relate Your Fairy Tales and Mythic Themes to Your Dreams and Waking Experiences.

As you become better at unlocking your unconscious and at bringing underlying themes into your consciousness, you will discover correlations between your dreams and your underlying mythic themes. More and more of the elements of your existence will fall into place and have meaning. You will begin to discover that what is happening to you is not accidental. Life will no longer be a world of accidental disconnection. Events will become connected. Your functioning will become more integrated, and you will discover that you can transcend your present limitations and personality "traps."

5. Analyze Your Own "Traps" and Interpersonal Difficulties.

Is there a continuing situation in your life that seems to repeat itself? Are you a sucker for a certain kind of person or do you get bested in certain situations? Then perhaps you had better analyze your life script or game that you may be unconsciously playing out. It is not easy to discover life games and scripts, but one clue is that you seem to get stuck in the same situation time and again. You think you have learned a lesson only to discover that you have fallen for the same old con game again. At this point, you will know that it is not an accidental situation. There is something that is drawing a certain type of person toward you. More specifically, you are setting up a condition in which you are going to be bested. If such is the case, you can talk it over with people whom you know and trust and who have been doing some work on themselves as well. Other people can often spot the traps we are in better than we can.

Of course, insight into one's life script or life game is only half the problem. Changing your behavior or your expectations is the other half. For this, you may want to join an assertiveness group, a transactional group, or a consciousness raising group, particularly if you cannot seem to rewrite your own script by yourself.

6. Enter Into and Become Conscious of Your Inner Wisdom.

One may, if one chooses, join a group which uses mind games and fantasy trips. They doubtlessly are valuable experiences when led by an experienced person.

We can learn to listen to that voice within us if we simply allow ourselves to ask the deep and abiding questions of our ongoing consciousness. We need only sit back quietly and conjure up in our imagination any archetype that we wish, or even any person whom we consider a wise being. We need then to ask that significant question and, above all, to listen to the answer. It is a kind of meditation, one that has been practiced by physicists, mathematicians, novelists, and most creative people. It is an axiom of science that a well-stated question may contain much of the answer. One physicist has told us that he frequently conjures up Einstein in his imagination when he comes across something he is having difficulty solving. Abraham Maslow freely confessed that as he was writing his research on self-actualizing persons, he wrote for an invisible audience, among whom was Thomas Jefferson.

7. Be Wary of Falling for Someone Else's "Drama."

As you become more integrated, you will discern the games and life scripts going on all about you. The more clearly we see our own life situations, the less we are taken in by the drama of other persons. But until that time we ask you to remember that no adult is innocent, even if the script they have written for themselves seems innocent. We all have listened to one side of a marital problem and come away convinced that the spouse is the cause of that mess, only to discover that the other side of the story is equally as convincing. Remember that in any situation everybody has a piece of the truth, and everyone also is part of the problem. But the point is that you can easily be caught up in someone else's game or script, if you are not careful to avoid it. You should be most careful when you are with a person who is telling you a sad tale. All your sympathies and compassion will be stirred. In fact, the more heart wrenching it is, the more we urge caution! It is precisely these persons who are expert in involving others in their "dramas." Before getting caught into their scripts, (that is, their pleas for help) we urge you to be noncommital until you give yourself time and privacy to think it over. We are not speaking of life and death situations, but those we all have experienced when a person we know has involved us in their sordid personal lives or business machinations.

the conscious self: explorations in phenomenology

centering ourselves: transcending personal crisis

Life is composed of both the Light and the Dark.

I. Introduction: The Light and the Dark

A. *Jung and the great archetypal themes*
B. *Are we a death-denying society?*

II. The Acceptance of Death: Elisabeth Kubler-Ross

A. *Denial and isolation*
B. *Anger*
C. *Bargaining*
D. *Depression*
E. *Acceptance*

III. For the Critically Ill Patient and the Family: Some Practical Suggestions

A. *Develop a loving but impersonal awareness of the patient's needs*
B. *Be prepared for surprising emotional reactions in yourself and in other family members*
C. *Encourage the patient's physical recovery*
D. *Provide emotional support*
E. *Relate creatively to the critically ill or disabled person*
F. *Encourage and promote the person's strengths and capabilities*

IV. Unexpected Death: Suicide

A. *The crime of suicide*
B. *Suicide in other eras and societies*
C. *Exonerating the suicide*
D. *Why does suicide affect us so deeply?*
E. *Statistics on suicide*
F. *Working through our feelings after suicide: a therapeutic session*

V. Learning to Survive: Death and Divorce

A. *The stages of grief and recovery*
  1. *The stage of shock*
  2. *The stage of suffering*
  3. *The stage of recovery*

B. Divorce as a kind of dying

C. Reintegrating oneself into society after death and divorce

D. Differences in status between the formerly married woman and the formerly married man

E. Divorce and children

F. Chances for a successful remarriage

G. Coping techniques for the formerly married person
   1. Encourage new friendships
   2. Organize groups of people for social events
   3. As it seems indicated, renew your old friendships
   4. Confide in only one or (at the outside) two persons
   5. To all other persons maintain a strong external appearance
   6. Do constructive work

VI. Applications and Coping Techniques

introduction: the light and the dark

Life is a matter of sun and shadow, times of even, easy living followed by times of intense crisis. But no matter how earnestly we have coped with everyday existence, no matter that we have become highly integrated and self-sustaining personalities, to all of us shall come the darker moments of living.

When we are young, we do not concern ourselves with the shadow side of life. But, eventually, into all our lives will come those moments of pain and anguish that seem to darken our whole existence, that make us wonder what life is all about, and that calls into question everything we have worked and struggled so hard to achieve and to acquire. We may contemplate giving up, running away from it all, or we may even toy with the idea of suicide. Even the strongest and most successful of us will have moments of disillusionment and "astonishment of heart."

As a people, we seem to do well as long as we are working hard at living; that is, pursuing our goals, organizing our lives, balancing our endless tasks, and relating to others in a variety of social contexts at home and in our offices. Our psychological mode works best when our occupation is busy-ness, when our tempo is activity, and when all signals are "go!" As a people, we seem to be able to surmount the small problems and obstacles encountered on our way to achievement and acquisition. We do not do as well in the "darker" moments.

We must not be hard on ourselves for this lag in our development as a people. As a nation, we were born only two hundred years ago; we do not yet have a sense of history. But we are arriving at a more mature consciousness, and we now are ready to deal with the shadow side of life. We are beginning to find ways of coping with shock and trauma. Eventually, we may even come to understand times of crisis as part of the process.

Jung and the Great Archetypal Themes

Carl Jung insisted time and again that how we live our lives is how we confront the great *archetypal themes* of human existence.[1] Be careful not to confuse the concept of *archetypal themes* with another of his

439

concepts, the *archetypes* of human personality. Although the two concepts are related, they are not synonymous.

We already discussed the various archetypes that form the basis of Jung's theory of racial unconsciousness. We examined, for example, the *Persona*, the *Shadow*, the *Anima*, and the *Animus*. Archetypes are buried deep within our *unconscious* and represent the hidden aspects of our "public" personalities. Archetypal themes, on the other hand, pertain to the realities of *our everyday conscious existence*, and have been called "the human condition."[2] Some of the great archetypal themes are conception and birth, existence and nonexistence, joy and suffering, love and hate, crisis and resolution, death and sorrow, and (finally) transcendence and rebirth.

Archetypal themes are not simply the domain of philosophers and psychologists but are reflected in every aspect of human society. They are the sum and substance of our literature, art, architecture, and religions. They are reflected in our social customs, cultural mores and taboos, value systems, and education. How we deal with these ideas forms the basis of our legal system and our government. Of all these themes, the most significant may be the theme of death.

Are We a Death-Denying Society?

Some writers have said that Americans are unable to deal with death; that, in some ways, the concepts of old age, sickness, poverty, and dying are taboo subjects in our society.[3] These writers have said that we hide these aspects of human existence from our awareness by herding the old, the sick, and the infirm into hospitals or convalescent homes, and nowhere is this more true than in how we deal with the dying. These writers have contrasted our "American way of death"[4] with how other cultures have integrated this aspect of human existence.

Elisabeth Kübler-Ross described the death of a farmer in her country of birth, Switzerland, as she remembered it.[5] The old man had had a fall, and when it became evident that he would not survive, he finished his life in a most beautiful and graceful manner. He took care of the financial legalities of his small estate. He had long talks with various members of the family about the affairs of the farm and the house. His neighbors and friends visited him during his fairly long illness and made their farewells toward the end. His family were with him during his last moments. He received the last rites and died in dignity and peace. The funeral and burial were moving tributes to the man's life and achievements. In contrast, said Robert Neale, we isolate the old and dying. (Robert Neale is a psychologist who has worked in pastoral counseling.) Often we send them away to hospitals or rest homes literally to die. We try to hide the facts of the illness from the person and sometimes from the rest of the family and friends. We "protect" our children from having to witness the reality of growing old and dying. We send letters and cards for a "speedy recovery" even when there is no such possibility. When the person eventually dies, funeral attendance is small and attendance at the burial is even smaller. Such events as "laying out" the corpse or gathering at communal meals are passing out of popular custom. Often, the only way we know that someone has died is by the appearance of a small paragraph (in tiny print) in the local newspaper in the obituaries section. At the funeral, we endeavor to "prettify" the corpse and make remarks about "how natural" the deceased appears. At the burial, or afterwards in our visits to the family, we shy away from dealing with the essential grief and loss the family members must be feeling and, instead, talk about mundane and inconsequential things like the weather and the political situation.[6]

Yet, despite our denial of death, said Geoffrey Gorer, we are preoccupied with it. We buy murder mysteries as light, escapist literature; we crowd the movie houses which show murder and violence; we turn on our televisions to similar programs; and we buy newspapers in order to read about crime and death. Our lust and fascination, he asserted, is pornographic. Sexual pornography, he explained, is a way of fulfilling a sexual need without actually being involved in the act. Likewise, our pornographic attitudes toward death are the result of consciously denying death and of viewing it vicariously and furtively through literature and the public media.[7]

the acceptance of death: elisabeth kübler-ross

Our willingness to deal at all openly with death is a recent phenomenon, only within the last decade. The person who has led this significant breakthrough is a psychiatrist, Elisabeth Kübler-Ross, who has done more to help us face the issues of death and dying than any other one person today. She has achieved this breakthrough, not only by her books and articles, but also by traveling throughout the country lecturing to colleges and universities, running workshops for the medical profession and for professionals and paraprofessionals in psychology, counseling, education, sociology, and so on. She has made films to use as teaching aids and has helped create courses for graduates and undergraduates all over the United States.

Her most famous book, *On Death and Dying*,[8] describes vividly how long and arduously she had to work before hospitals would allow her even to talk with patients with terminal illnesses. Her efforts to achieve acceptance of death as a proper study for research and for therapy were often sabotaged by hospital staffs. Physicians and nurses felt a need to "protect" their patients and tended to cling to the belief that, by and large, it was better not to deal directly with the patients concerning their illness. In a hospital full of patients, she often would be told there currently was no one "dying." Even if there were, the medical staff often were obstinate in their opinion that the patients would not be able or not want to talk about it.

But Kübler-Ross found that the patients did welcome the opportunity to talk. It came, for many of them, as a relief to have someone to listen to them, willing to discuss their wants, needs, and wishes. It was therapeutic to have an end to the make-believe that frequently surrounds the terminally-ill patient.[9] Kübler-Ross was willing to come and see them and help them work through their feelings, fears, and concerns when everyone else seemed to want to avoid any mention of the significant issue — their impending death.

Let it not be thought that Kübler-Ross rushed in and told the person that he or she was going to die. On the contrary, she was there not to inform the person about anything but rather, to discover what the person needed — needed to know, needed to understand, needed to have confirmed, or needed to have answered. Kübler-Ross simply asked the patient, "How sick are you?" In that way, the patient was able to tell Kübler-Ross exactly what he or she knew, suspected, or wanted to know. Sometimes, the patient turned out to be very sure that he or she was mortally ill, and it came as a blessed relief for that person to know one person, at least, who was willing to talk about death. Kübler-Ross learned to wait patiently, interview after interview, until the person was able to come to a calm acceptance (and understanding) of his or her own death. Our approach to death, like our approach to life, is individual, but as the result of her clinical observations, Kübler-Ross came to believe that most of us go through definite stages in coping with death. Specifically, she named the five stages 1) denial and isolation, 2) anger, 3) bargaining, 4) depression, and finally, 5) acceptance. The reader is asked to remember (even as we describe these five stages) that the person or therapist working with the dying patient keep alert to the person's individual qualities, strengths, limitations, background, and circumstances which will differ many times significantly.

Denial and Isolation

When a person is genuinely unaware of the seriousness of his or her condition and confronts the possibility of death for the first time, the typical reaction is *shock and denial*. "No, not me!" "I can't have cancer!" "Couldn't there be a mistake?" "Are you sure you have *my* x-rays?" "I just can't believe it. I just can't believe it."

Denial, or at least partial denial, is experienced by almost all patients in the beginning of their awareness or at some point in their illness. Anyone of us can deal with pain and threat just so long, and then we need to have moments of protection against that pain and shock: that is exactly what the stage of denial accomplishes. It acts as a buffer against the pain of realization until such time as the person can accept it more honestly.

Denial may also be present within the family, and sometimes, even the physician denies the eventuality of death. It has been suggested that the physicians's desire to extend life is a part of his or her own denial system. After all, the job of the physician is to get people well; death may appear as a failure rather than as a natural part of the life-and-death process.

Anger

Eventually, however, the patient begins to confront directly the reality of the illness, and when that happens, the most common reaction is anger. "Why me?" "Why does it have to happen to me now before . . ." "If there really is a God, why does He let this happen?" The person may lash out at the spouse, at the physician and at nurses attending him or her. The rage may be direct or it may be indirect: irritation and complaints at not being treated well, dislike of hospital food, or endless demands on the family members. At this stage, meetings with the family become very painful, since they do not know how to react to the irritation of the patient toward them. They do not understand the anger, and neither does the patient. What the patient is experiencing is helplessness against a cruel fate, and a sense of weakness, impotence, futility—the inability to fight back. When we are hurt and cornered, we lash out in anger at others.

Actually, rage is one of the better symptoms in the patient's process. Anger is energy. The patient is mobilizing his or her available resources to fight against the helplessness of the situation. The challenge now is to enable the patient to utilize and direct that angry energy in a useful and constructive manner. There is no magic formula for how that may be done. Kübler-Ross gave one example that seemed to fit the characteristics of one of her patients. Her patient was a businessman who was used to being in charge. Now he found himself at the mercy of others who told him when to eat, when to take his medicine, and woke him up in the middle of the night to check his vital signs. He now was under the control of a dozen other human beings. It was such a reversal of his previous existence that he took it out on his wife when she came to visit him, simply because she was the only person subordinate to himself and that he could snap at without retribution. After some discussions with Kübler-Ross, the wife decided on a plan of action. She no longer just popped in to see her husband but, instead, would telephone him in the morning and ask when it would be convenient for her to come by. Her husband, who had been used to arranging his own appointment schedule at work, consulted his own schedule for the day (lab examinations, physical therapy appointment, etc) and together they decided when would be the best time for her visit. When she did come, he was calmer and less irritable. After a while, the wife would take notes over the phone on what he needed, what office or home management papers he wanted her to bring, and her visits became something like those of a secretary. This particular man had a great need to adjust his affairs, both at home and in the office. Such an arrangement would not work for everybody, but there is certainly much that can be learned from this anecdote. The most basic lesson is to direct the energy of this anger into some constructive activity. Each person can be encouraged to participate in the process in some way or other. Patients can be encouraged to make requests they may feel somewhat reticent to make. They can be encouraged to say what they would like to do or whom they would like to see.

Bargaining

Eventually, the patient realizes that all the anger in the world will not extend life. At this point, the stage of bargaining may begin. As children, we frequently bargain with our parents, with Santa Claus, or with God. "If I am good and do my schoolwork and dishes every night, perhaps I can. . . ." So too does the patient begin to bargain unconsciously with God, the universe, the physicians, or whomever, as death becomes imminent. It is as if the person is reasoning: "If God has decided to take me from this earth and does not respond to my angry demands, perhaps He will react more favorably if I ask nicely."

The bargaining comes in many forms. Kübler-Ross told of an opera singer who had cancer of the jaw. She pleaded for "just one more performance." Kübler-Ross arranged a performance for the hospital staff and other members of the therapeutic community, including the patients on the ward.

Another woman wanted "just enough time" to see her son get married, which was scheduled just a few months away. The hospital staff and the family saw to it that the woman sustained her strength for the next few weeks, took her to the wedding, and remained with her through the ceremony. She looked radiant and the wedding ceremony was a happy event for everyone. The hospital staff thought they had enabled the woman to become more realistic about her illness, but the first words the woman uttered when she got back to the hospital was "Don't forget I have another son."

Depression

There comes a time, however, when the patient begins to realize that bargaining is not going to work forever. Energies begin to wane; operations exhaust emotional and physical strength. Parts of the body may have had to be removed. The patient is becoming weaker and less able to take care of even the most minimal functions. This is one of the most critical stages of all since patients begin to be aware that hospital bills are adding up and become more and more distressed at being burdens to their family. In order to cover the costs of medical and hospital costs, they may have to sell valuable possessions. It is natural for depression to occur.

Unfortunately, the depression often carries with it indifference to bodily appearance and a lack of desire to sustain relationships with those nearest and dearest. They may become withdrawn and listless, and seem uninterested in maintaining contact with those who have come to visit. This stage makes it difficult for family members who are trying to support them emotionally and physically.

Kübler-Ross warned specifically against trying to cheer the patient at this time. Telling the person how good he or she looks and trying to cheer up the person is *our* desire, not the patient's. The patient has come to realize that the end of life is coming. It is better to let the patient express the sorrow and the sense of ultimate loss. It is his or her way of "working through" or "processing" what is happening. Despite the pain and the suffering of this stage, it also has its benefits. The patient is beginning to accept death more realistically than ever before. Allowing expression of the natural sorrow and grief of one's death will enable that realization to come more easily. One of the helpful things we can do for the patient is to say how much the patient has meant to us, how loved he or she has been, and what we will always treasure in our shared experiences. On first reading this suggestion, you may feel that you could never do that. We hasten to assure you that, at times of crisis, we frequently are able to express those things we might never otherwise. The nearness of death seems to allow us to put aside our natural reserve and to open our hearts to those that we care for deeply.

Acceptance

Despite the suffering, the pain, the anger, and the depression of the previous stages, there comes a time when almost all patients enter a calm and almost luminous stage of acceptance. It does not come easily nor does it come to all dying persons. It comes to those who are willing to work through their feelings and who have the support of the hospital staff and their family and friends. If we do not leave patients isolated and alone so that they feel rejected, they will begin to contemplate their approaching end with a certain degree of expectation and peace. The patient's sleep becomes easier, as Kübler-Ross described it, like that of a newborn child. The patient seems to be withdrawing from the world, but it is a withdrawal different from that associated with the stage of depression: in Kübler-Ross's words, it is more like "the final rest before the long journey." The patient needs time for solitude. The time of activity and crisis are over, and the patient is preparing for the end in a contemplative manner. There are very few personal concerns or wasted emotions. Frivolous emotions (such as irritation, resentment, or anger) seem to belong to a world the patient is now leaving. The patient's communications seem to take on a nobility never before evinced. At the great existential moment, the universal archetypal themes come to the fore: we are willing to speak more openly of the meaning of life and death. The patient may no longer see death as a cruel fate or as the Great Avenger but as a welcome friend or as "going home." We others must be willing to step onto this level of communication if we wish to remain in touch with the patient toward the end.

for the critically ill patient and the family: some practical suggestions

Even when a critically ill person may not be terminally ill, an extended illness or disability can bring much emotional and physical stress to both the patient and the family. We may feel a sense of helplessness, not sure what we can do to help the patient and the rest of the family get through the time of stress. We, like the patient, may experience the five stages noted above, even when the patient may recover. "All of us are victims in a crisis!" said Anne Kliman, who worked with families in crisis situations. All the members of a family go through depression, isolation, and desperation. She added that we frequently become so "locked up" in our own thoughts that we stop sharing our grief and anxiety just when we need more than ever to communicate.[10]

446

Our own work with persons in critical situations, as well as with their families, have led us to offer the following coping techniques for families with a critically ill or disabled member. But remember, again, that these ideas are generalizations *only*. All must be evaluated in terms of your particular circumstances and your knowledge of the patient.

Develop a Loving but Impersonal Awareness of the Patient's Needs

Be prepared for outbursts of sorrow, anger, bargaining, and misery, or periods of great courage and fortitude. Furthermore, this pendulum of reactions may swing violently back and forth. There is nothing neat and orderly about our emotional life in times of crisis. But do not, yourself, get caught up in the patient's depression or physical symptoms. Whatever the patient is experiencing, *you do not have to take on his or her symptoms*, a natural tendency in all of us if we love the person. Sometimes, he or she may even feel better seeing that we have picked up their depression or that we are upset. Nor do we have to become martyrs. We need our own strength and energies. We need not take offense or be hurt by the patient's demands. A hospital is, at best, a depressing environment. The patient is given better care than ever before, but the patient is more physically and psychologically assaulted than ever before. Patients are jabbed with needles, awakened for a check of vital signs, given intravenous injections, and sometimes intravenous feedings. They are rolled or pushed hither and yon for x-rays and other laboratory tests. And no matter how beneficial surgery is, it is a physically traumatic shock to the body. It is natural, then, for the patient to experience confusion, helplessness, anger, and you may receive the backlash of all of this. By maintaining equilibrium, you can respond to the patient calmly and empathetically, without picking up the patient's emotions. You are not the person who is "to blame" for the situation. Lend the patient emotional and physical support, of course, but do not be the patient's scapegoat.

Be Prepared for Surprising Emotional Reactions in Yourself and in other Family Members

One of the most difficult aspects of critical illness is the welter of emotions you may experience or that you may witness in other family members. You, too, can experience grief, of course, but you may be surprised and dismayed to discern other less "socially acceptable" emotions in yourself and others. After the first shock of diagnosis and the consequent grief and concern, other kinds of emotions may erupt, particularly as the weeks and months drag on. You may spot elements of anger and irritation that the patient is consuming so much time and energy. Or you may yourself bargain and plead with the universe to "put the patient out of misery." You may find yourself bitter at the mounting expenses of the hospitalization, tests, and medical fees. Then, immediately, you may plunge into despair and guilt for such "unnatural thoughts."

But these are not unnatural thoughts and emotions. They are common, even if most families would be loath to admit their existence. If these feelings can be verbalized, much of this depression and guilt can be released, and the emotional and physical energies of the patient's family can be directed into more constructive channels.

Encourage the Patient's Physical Recovery

For the critically ill person who has a good chance of recovery, the best medicine often is allowing the patient to come home and begin the process of physical self-support and autonomy. The patient may not be able to do much more than go to the bathroom and back, but that is the beginning of recovery. The patient needs to be encouraged to do more, which means we must learn not to overprotect and do too much for the patient. Persons who suffer disabling or crippling diseases can do much more for themselves than is frequently assumed. Part of the patient's physical recovery is psychological recovery, and that entails encouraging the patient *to get up, to get out,* and *to do something.* Even the family member who is going to have to use a wheel chair for the rest of his or her life can do certain household chores: small but significant preparation of meals, answering the telephone and conveying messages, managing the household accounts, babysitting for the older children, or whatever. Many agencies now work with disabled persons toward financial self-support. Family members need to work together for the person's recovery rather than to extend the person's helplessness.

Some advocate bringing the terminally ill patient home so that he or she may die with dignity. That is an admirable suggestion but would depend on the strengths of the family. If the family members discuss the matter and want to do that, they can give no finer gift of love. If the family does not have the cohesion and strength to undertake this project, it is better not to attempt it. In the latter event, it is better to be honest and decide to give the patient emotional support by visiting him or her frequently and lovingly at the hospital.

Provide Emotional Support

In our workshops on critically ill and dying patients, most participants are well aware of the importance of providing emotional support for the patient. What they frequently ask is: How do we do that? The most obvious answer is to stay in touch with the patient. Visit the hospital when you can, and when you cannot, make a telephone call. Nowadays, every hospital room has a phone for the use of their patients and getting a phone call is a pleasant break in the hours and hours of lying there. A personal phone call and a personal visit are much more helpful than flowers and "get well" cards which often are empty demonstrations of concern. Research indicates that instead of providing more emotional support for the critically terminally ill patient, we tend to isolate them from others and to withdraw from them which they soon realize.[11] It is as though we are beginning to mourn them before they are gone. Or perhaps we fear that what they have is catching. One person, who has been suffering from cancer for a number of years, told us that one man she knows refused to accept a glass of water from her out of the absolute conviction that cancer is communicable.

This woman has had eleven years of battling melanoma cancer. She has been in and out of several different hospitals, has had sixteen operations, and has had many of her tissues and muscles cut out and replaced with prosthetic devices. Still, she remains, at fifty years of age, an extraordinarily beautiful and exuberant person. Her plea to the families of persons stricken with illness is to continue *to touch them, to hold them, to caress them, and to hug them.* Said she, there is more to touching than physical contact. A touch transmits emotional strength and spiritual nourishment. When her disease first was diagnosed, she told us, her husband adamantly "refused" to let her go; he fought for her life. So did many of the other family members. They surrounded her with love and emotional support, which, in turn, gave her the strength and will to live. She is a little critical of Kübler-Ross's five stages of death, "If I had 'accepted' death," she says, "I would not be alive today." We asked her if life was worth all the operations, the pain, and the necessity for prosthetic devices. "Oh, yes, to live a little longer with my husband and six children is worth every minute of it."

"Touching" or demonstrative affection is important, but many of us are *not* touchers—that is just not our way. If that is so, there is no sense in trying to become so. But if we have had a touching relationship with the person, we can continue to do so.

For those who are not naturally openly affectionate, there are many other ways "to touch." We can help the patient walk after an operation or when he or she is on the recovery list. Most medical ad-

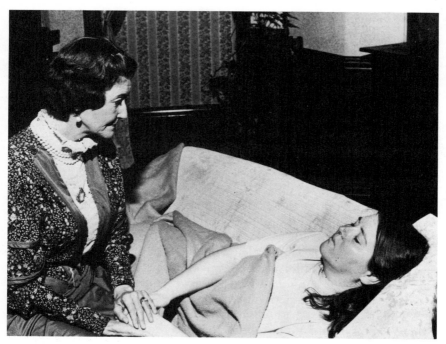

We convey emotional and psychological strength through the sense of touch.

vice urges patients to get back on their feet as soon as possible. When we visit them in the hospital or at home, we can help them to take small walks around the hospital ward or around the house. Physical therapy rooms are crowded, and there are few physical therapists. This small service is of inestimable help in the recovery of the patient. Sometimes, this simple device does not occur to us because we may assume that the patient is too ill or too weak to get out of bed. That may be true, but it does not hurt to find out. If you are willing to provide this help for the patient, do not spring it on the person all at once. The patient may be just as nervous as you are, and getting over the fear of walking is half the problem. On one of your visits or phone calls, tell the patient that the physician has said that it would be good to begin walking around, and ask if he or she is prepared to try. Laugh with the patient when he or she makes a joke about it. You both can admit to being a little afraid. A first walk around the hospital or house will be exhausting for both of you, so do not be surprised if you both collapse at the end. But before you leave, make a date for the next "walk around." Assure the patient it will go a lot easier the next time.

Another type of touching is massage, which is particularly therapeutic for those patients who have suffered a "stroke" or other physically numbing or paralyzing disease. Sometimes the very persons who are least affectionate are those who are able to give the patient a massage. Massage and rubdowns of this sort do many things: they increase the blood flow and circulation to that part of the body; retard atrophy of the muscles and nerves in the afflicted area; prevent development of bedsores; and, at a psychic level, enable the person to stay "in touch" with that part of the body and so to reintegrate body and mind. Another odd effect of rubdowns and massages is the relief from pain that follows.

Relate Creatively to the Critically Ill or Disabled Person

Too often, we tend to dehumanize the critically ill person. We begin to talk of the person in past tense. When we hear of a person who has suffered a heart attack or a stroke, we hear people say, "Oh, what a shame, he was such a nice person" as if he had already died. Hospital staffs tend to talk about the person in terms of the illness or diseased organ: "Check on the bladder patient in Room 246" or "The paraplegic on the fourth floor needs his medicine." They do not intend to dehumanize the patient, but the press of time leads to short cuts in language. We need, therefore, to remember the lesson of general semantics. The way we speak of critically ill or disabled persons will affect our attitude toward them and ultimately our behavior toward them. If we speak of them as objects, we eventually will think of and treat them as objects. Patients are quick to pick up our attitudes toward them. They need our faith and our belief in them as persons who have a chance for recovery and more creative life.

Sometimes our attitudes toward critically ill or long-term recovery patients are reflected in how we visit them in the hospital or at home. We may wear subdued clothing and long faces and talk in sepulchral tones. Without suggesting that visitors to the hospital room be dressed as if going out "on the town," we do urge you to have a cheerful countenance and wear clothes you would normally wear on a normal visit. Instead of bringing flowers (which tends to turn the sick person's room into something akin to a funeral parlor), we can bring items that relate to the person's family, interests, business, or hobbies: news from home, pictures, photographs, or appropriate reading material. We can bring things that the person can use for his or her stay in the hospital: a pair of comfortable slippers or bed socks, or a bed jacket or shawl.

One of the chief concerns that people express in our workshops on the seriously ill or disabled patient is what to talk about with the patient. "I never know what to say," said one lady," and then I ask inane things like 'how is the hospital food?' which is really silly since most institutional food tends to be dreary." Another participant in our workshops admitted that he once said to a patient who had had several operations that he was "looking just fine." He added, ruefully, "I wanted to bite my tongue off when I realized how hollow that sentence was." These kinds of statements reflect our inadequacy in relating to the hospitalized or disabled person. It may reflect also our uneasiness in unintentionally bringing up subjects that might be "hurtful" to the patient. What we need to do is to call on our own creative talents, skills, and competencies and bring them to the patient's bedside or wheelchair. What that will be depends on you and the situation (what the patient can and cannot do), and, of course, on the patient's own personality and interests.

If the patient enjoys reading but is unable to do so, and you are good at reading aloud, you and the patient may consider what book you could read aloud at your visits. A professor in our institution suffered a detachment of the retina first in one eye and then in the other. He underwent surgery in both eyes and for a considerable time was virtually blind. The other teachers at the school organized reading sessions; the hospital room became a gathering place for his friends and associates, and lively discussions and forums followed the reading sessions. We need to caution the reader to make sure not only that the reading material is of interest to the patient, but also to keep alert to signs of fatigue or boredom by the patient. There are times when patients need to rest and be alone after the excitement of visitors.

Encourage and Promote the Person's Strengths and Capabilities

When we treat an invalid as an invalid, he or she becomes more invalided. That is one of the many aspects of the self-fulfilling prophecy. When we do too much for the invalided or aged person, we actually are hastening the aging process. Sometimes we make decisions for a person who is quite capable of lucid and rational thought. We treat invalids sometimes, as if their minds are gone. Sometimes, this may very well be so, particularly when there has been some brain damage. Being hospitalized virtually reduces the person to infancy when even the vital life processes must be taken care of (with use of bedpan) spoon feeding, and so forth. But we tend to regard the patient as more helpless than he or she really is.

We need to think of the patient as having many strengths which we need to encourage, particularly in making decisions. A woman we know suffered a fairly minimal "stroke." Upon recovery she was able to walk, speak, and function as well as she had before, from her friends' point of view. Physically, she seemed to be just fine. Psychologically, however, she had deteriorated considerably. She developed a phobia about going out and stayed close to her small apartment, and she dreaded going to sleep at night. In working with her family, we discovered that they thought she had developed a fear of dying, which, under the circumstances, was natural. When we talked to the person, however, she expressed a different concern. "It's not dying I'm afraid of," she said firmly, "I've lived a good life and my children are married and settled down with families. It's being struck down by another stroke that I'm afraid of. I would hate to be helpless and dependent on my children. I don't want my life extended and I don't want to be a burden to them. What if I can't walk or talk or do anything—what then?" she moaned miserably. We asked her if she had told this to her family. She said she had tried but their answers were something like, "Oh, Ma, don't talk that way; you're going to live a long healthy life yet." She looked at us and said desperately, "They just won't listen to me!"

This woman had always led an independent life. She had always been a strong and emotionally stable person. Her worst dread was suffering another stroke which would leave her paralyzed and dependent on others. She was encouraged to make known her desires and fears, should such an event happen. Her desires were very simple. She did not want her life extended so we had her sign a document to that effect (which was duly witnessed). There were certain articles in her house that she wanted to go to certain people, so we had her write these bequests down for her attorney. She wanted to donate a small specialized library on birds to the local college, so we checked with the library and discovered that they would be only too glad to get them. The books were boxed and taken over, and the library sent the woman a letter of thanks and appreciation.

As the result of seeing some of her simple requests put into action, she was finally able to talk with her son about her fears of being helplessly dependent on them in case of another stroke. He assured her that there was enough insurance money that they could provide her with a part-time attendant and that they would not be "burdened" by such an event. She has not suffered another stroke as of this writing, and her phobias have dissolved. She carries in her wallet a set of instructions of what to do if she suffers a stroke on the street, which includes the name of her hospital and physician, and the telephone numbers of her son and daughter who live at some distance from her. She sleeps much more peacefully at night, and her entire appearance has taken on more vibrancy and contentment.

Patients who must rest at home much of the day or who are confined to a bed or wheelchair will feel much more a part of the family if we assign some jobs to them that they can do. We should not be too concerned if a task may exhaust their energies. There is nothing as psychologically satisfying as knowing that you have put your best effort into something.

unexpected death: suicide

When an aged person dies, there seems something natural about it. We take solace that the person has led a long and useful life. It seems in the natural order of things for a person to die after the biblical "three score years and ten." We may also be somewhat heartened if a person manages to reach the eighties with all faculties intact. We harbor a secret hope that we may do the same.

If an adult is "cut down" in middle adulthood, we may grieve a little more, but (even so) we will be comforted if we know that the person's children are well into their adult years and are self-sufficient, if the widow has financial security, or that the surviving spouse may find someone else with whom to share the remaining years. If dying has been a long, painful, and sorrowful process, we may see the end as merciful.

There are other kinds of deaths, however, which are not as easily understood and accepted, and which are difficult to work through. Furthermore, the closer we are to the person who has died, the more tortured we feel and the more difficult the event is "to process." These deaths seem to us particularly tragic because they are unexpected, because they are violent, and because they happen to those whose lives have just begun and who seem to have been struck down by a cruel and remorseless fate. We are left, after the grief, the burial and the mourning, with a sense that their lives were futile, after all. These deaths include the person who takes his or her own life, the person who dies as the result of an accident, and the untimely death of a young child. In these situations, it is *we* who are the victims and who need the healing. It is we who need to learn how to pick up the pieces of life and reconstruct our life process.

The Crime of Suicide

Death by suicide is, even today, one of our deep cultural taboos. Even our language suggests that a crime has been committed. We say that a person "took his own life" or that she "committed suicide." In the

Judeo-Christian tradition, suicide carries a stigma that it is somehow an act against God and nature. The medieval church considered suicide as the unforgivable sin since no repentance was possible between the act and the death of the person. For centuries, the bodies of suicides were desecrated by being pulled through the streets by horses, buried at crossroads where traffic would trample on their graves, and sometimes a stake was put through their hearts (as a final insult) so that their ghosts would not return to haunt the countryside. Until 1882, the bodies of suicides could not be buried by day but had to be taken to their final resting place in the dead of night.

Suicide in Other Eras and Societies

Suicide has not been as dishonorable and odious in other societies as it still is in ours. In many societies, suicide has been an honorable resolution to a difficult and/or shameful situation. Zeno, the Greek stoic, recommended suicide if one's physical condition prevented one from functioning as an effective human being. Better to die an honorable death than to live in misery and helplessly dependent on others. Seneca, a Roman philosopher, admitted that although he would relish old age if he were functioning in body and mind, he would rather leave this world than live on blind, crippled, and of no use to anyone. The Japanese and Chinese both have had a long tradition of an honorable death by suicide. The Japanese *kamikaze* pilots of World War II were considered heroes and martyrs for their country. Even the early Christians had to be warned against voluntary martyrdom in the early Roman circuses.[12]

Exonerating the Suicide

Although suicide has been an ancient and acceptable choice for the person in other cultures and eras, modern Western society still regards suicide as immoral, a desecration of everything our society holds sacred. The parents, spouse, and children of the suicide victim suffer the consequences of these attitudes. Those closest to the suicide torture themselves with guilt that they did not take the suicide's unhappiness seriously enough or that they could have prevented the death. The parents of the suicide may live with the secret dread that the person's soul may burn forever for this "unpardonable act." The parents may assume the guilt of the suicidal act, that in some way they must have damaged the child since he or she was unable to cope with the stresses of life. Children whose parents have committed suicide frequently have unexpressed and even unrealized anger and resentment at being deserted by the parent who committed suicide. Or they may suffer the remorse of never having had a chance to tell them how much he or she was needed and loved. All of those close to the suicide may still remember angry words exchanged, arguments left unresolved, and acts committed in rage or despair. We tend to blame ourselves for any of the unhappiness in the suicide's life.

All these reactions, while understandable, deny one essential fact, that the responsibility for intentionally taking one's life belongs to no one but the person involved. We do not need to castigate the person for the act; nor do we need to castigate ourselves. Karl Barth, the Christian theologian, said that if there is a kind and loving God (as we do, indeed, preach), then this God will not condemn a soul for a death-by-self. If there is forgiveness for sins at all, there must be forgiveness for suicide.[13] We need a new theological understanding of suicide so that those who loved the person may not agonize for the rest of their lives.

We also need a new psychological understanding, so that those who have been closest to the suicide need not suffer from endless and needless guilt and remorse. Never before in history has so much care and concern been given to the upbringing of children. Yet, suicide in the twentieth century is not declining but is on the rise.[14] Furthermore, the very countries who have the highest affluence and most liberated environments are those that report the highest rate of suicide. Suicide in the United States has turned sharply upward since 1950, at precisely the time in our history in which there has been more affluence and more possibility for self-improvement and self-achievement.[15] We have too long blamed suicide on parental upbringing and need now to look to other factors. Some writers have said that since we live in a time of stress and change, the more vulnerable persons in our society will tend to "go under," in which case we need to blame our society for the increase in suicide (if we need to blame at all). Others have said that we have not considered inheritance and gene structure, that some persons are simply born unable to tolerate the stresses of living. The fact that we are saving more and more babies at birth, babies that would have died in previous times or perhaps would have been left to die because of their "sickly" physical bodies, has brought an increase in the number of persons who are physically weak and handicapped by birth defects. It also is possible that we are saving more babies who are psychologically "weaker." Suicide might better be considered the index of our modern pressures than as the end result of poor parental upbringing.

Why Does Suicide Affect Us So Deeply?

Suicide, by its very nature, seems to strike terror and anguish into our innermost being. We are haunted for months and years afterwards and ask ourselves such questions as "Why did he do it?" or "What was so terrible in her life, that she had to end it?" We like to have reasons and answers and not one is sufficient. Even when there is a suicide note, we know that what is written on the suicide note does not sufficiently explain a person wanting to put an end to life, the very thing that most of us hold dearer than all else. We suspect that even the suicide did not know all the reasons for this ultimate act. We know only that the person must have been plunged into such depths of despair that death seemed preferable to life. The survivors go over and over in their minds all the details of their interactions with the person: "Could it have been prevented?" "Did he seem all right when we last saw him?" "Did anyone ever hear her talk of committing suicide?" We may think to ourselves: if only we had listened more or paid more attention; if only we had answered that last letter; if only we had returned the telephone call. . . . if only. . . .

Why is death by suicide so haunting? Robert Neale has written cogently on the underlying reasons for our reactions and trauma.[16] Suicide, he explained, is an affront to what we consider to be good and viable. It is a rejection of our values. The suicide has passed judgment on us and found us wanting. He or she has cast off all that is prized by us. It is as though he or she has said, "What you find delightful, I find intolerable." Is that person wrong? Or are we? Neale asserted that even psychiatrists and psychologists do not understand the phenomenon of suicide, that labeling the person "neurotic" or "insane" is not an explanation, but a nonexplanation.

Neale suggested that suicide is an attack, yes, but an attack to right what is wrong. The suicide is trying to make an end of a bad start and to begin again. The suicide recognizes that life is a matter of birth, life, death, and rebirth (the great archetypal themes) and is trying to speed up the process. The suicide is unwilling to continue a living death, so he or she is choosing another existence. It is an attempt at affirmation. It is an act of radical transformation of the body, mind, and spirit. It may even be an act of faith.

What then is *wrong* with suicide? What is wrong, said Neale, is that it is too literal an act. All of us are transforming ourselves throughout our lives. Sometimes our personality transformation is a radical one as the result of personal crisis, but this transformation is part of the process of living. The suicide has mistaken radical transformation of the *personality* for a transformation of the *body*. The suicide does not understand that the process cannot be hurried. The suicide has recognized the need to begin again, but at the ultimate moment of despair, he or she saw only one way to begin again and that was to come to an end. This was not an attack on God, as much as an end of a life mediated by Satan. We need to understand the suicide as wanting to start again. And the need to begin again is occurring within more and more people in our society.

Statistics on Suicide

We do not know how many people take their own lives. A very conservative estimate is that there are 25,000 suicides in our country every year. If we accept this figure, then at least 60 persons are dying by their own hand every day. But these figures are far from accurate, for suicide is frequently covered up by ministers, magistrates, and coroners. When Ernest Hemingway shot himself with a rifle, his wife originally reported the death as a "hunting accident." Many of the reported "hunting accidents" may actually be suicides of persons who did not want their families to suffer the guilt and opprobrium that follows. Besides the number of actual suicides that go unreported are the large number of *attempted* suicides that go unreported. Friends, physicians, and family engage in a conspiracy of silence to protect the person and to protect the family.

In consideration of all these facts, 25,000 suicides a year is an extremely deceiving figure. A more realistic figure may be upwards of 60,000 every year, and some have said that the figure may be closer to 100,000. If that is so, then suicide is tenth on the scale of killers in the United States alone. We now can begin to get a realistic view of suicide. It is not a rare and occasional offense against God and humankind but one of the more common paths to death. It is time we take suicide out of "the closet" and learn to understand it for what it is — one of the "separate paths"[17] to nonexistence, as one team of writers put it.

Working through Our Feelings after Suicide: A Therapeutic Session

How do the survivors of suicide heal their agony and ease their burden of guilt and self-recrimination? They do it, first, by remembering the huge number of suicides and attempted suicides and realizing that it is far more common than we have been led to believe. That being so, the survivors need not berate themselves personally. Suicide is a societal problem! We can recognize that the burden of living became so great for the person that he or she believed that they could not manage one more moment of pain. For that, they need not be condemned. At least that person chose to take his or her own life and not the life of another. We can cherish the brighter moments we shared with the person and not condemn ourselves mercilessly for the darker moments of conflict. We can forgive the person that act of suicide, for it is in that forgiveness that we also can forgive ourselves. If we are unable to resolve our grief by ourselves, we can seek therapy to help us resolve the unfinished work of mourning and grief. We have included an actual transcription of a person who worked through and resolved the suicide of his father which had occurred many years before. This young man was a student and had come to us to get over his depression and inability to do his school work. He was very intelligent and recognized that his personal situation had become critical. During therapy he referred to the death of his father which had left him so bereft. The transcription follows.

DAVE: I was just thinking about my father, for a minute.

O'CONNELL: What about your father?

DAVE: Nothing much. He died when I was young. I didn't know him very well. It seems strange to be thinking of him right now. I hardly ever do.

O'CONNELL: Are you aware of what you are doing with your hands?

DAVE: (Looking at his hands) Oh, this? This is just a habit I have.

O'CONNELL: Your hands are speaking.

DAVE: You know, now that I come to think of it, my father used to do that. It's one of the memories that I have of him. He was away a lot of the time on business so I didn't get to know him very well. But I remember sometimes sitting next to him when he was home and watching him turn this ring around. . . . Hmmmm!

O'CONNELL: What's going on now?

DAVE: It just occurred to me that I wear this ring on the same hand he did. I used to wish that ring was mine and now I've got one like it. Not exactly like it, but close enough. (Silence)

O'CONNELL: What's going on now?

DAVE: I just feel sad all of a sudden. I'd forgotten this, but I used to play a game about my father after he died. I used to pretend he was still alive, that he was just off somewhere on business. And he would come back some day.

I guess I miss him. Or I miss the fact I never had a father like other kids. There would be these father-and-son things, you know, like Cub Scout dinners and things, and I would either show up with my mother or not go at all. I used to hate going with my mother. It was embarrassing. But she didn't know. I just used to tell her they were dumb things I'd rather not go to at all. *(Silence)*

O'CONNELL: What's going on now?

DAVE: I was thinking about my mother. How dumb she always was. She used to think I didn't care whether my father died or not. She used to tell me that all the time.

O'CONNELL: Do you know how come she thought that?

DAVE: Sure I do! You see, my father didn't just die—he killed himself. It was pretty awful. I was just a kid, nine years old, but I was the oldest. When it happened, there were a lot of people. I mean afterward. I had just come home from school, and there was my mother crying and the neighbors and the police and even some photographers shooting pictures. I don't remember exactly, but anyway my uncle called me over and told me what had happened. I couldn't believe it, I just couldn't believe it and then I started to cry. But he said I shouldn't cry because that would upset Mom. What a goddamn bastard! Anyway, he said I was to be a big man and all that, and I'd have to be the man in the family now and not to let my Mom see me crying because that would upset her even more. So I didn't cry. Not once. Not then. Not at the funeral. Not ever. So Mom came to the conclusion that I didn't have any feelings about my father.

O'CONNELL: But you did have feelings.

DAVE: You bet I did. *(He is suddenly holding his head and the tears are coming down quietly.)* I feel pretty stupid crying after all these years.

O'CONNELL: You have a right to cry. Everyone has the right to cry.

DAVE: Yeah. You know I really did miss my Dad. I guess I never realized how much. *(He cries now still quietly)* Why does a person commit suicide? How does he do it, I mean? I can't imagine it. I can't even imagine it. *(He cries some more)* I feel a little better now.

O'CONNELL: You look a little better. But what are your hands saying now?

DAVE: Oh, I'm twisting the ring again.

O'CONNELL: Something is still unfinished, evidently.

DAVE: Isn't it just a habit?

O'CONNELL: Nothing is ever "just." Would you be willing to take another step?

DAVE: What?

O'CONNELL: You've finally cried for your father. Are you willing to bury him now?

DAVE: I have to get used to that idea. . . . Yeah, I guess so. What do I have to do?

O'CONNELL: Put your father over there. Do you want him alive or dead?

DAVE: Alive. O.K. He's on the chair.*

O'CONNELL: All right, what do you want to say to him now?

DAVE: I guess I gotta say goodbye to you, Dad. I never really knew you to begin with. You never got to know me either. *(Turns to therapist)* Is that all?

O'CONNELL: Are you ready to say goodbye? Have you said everything you've wanted to say?

DAVE: I guess I want to tell him it wasn't right to do what he did.

O'CONNELL: Tell him, now.

DAVE: You know, it wasn't right to do that, Dad. It was just not right. Mom needed you. I needed you. And Tina and Betta needed you. God, I needed you so much. *(Breaks down now into real weeping and sobbing)* Every kid needs a dad. *(Weeps some more)* I guess I've said it all.

O'CONNELL: Can you still see your father in the chair?

DAVE: Yeah.

O'CONNELL: How does he seem to you?

DAVE: Kind of sad.

O'CONNELL: Does he say anything to you?

DAVE: I guess he says he's sorry.

O'CONNELL: Do you want to say anything back?

DAVE: Yeah, I'd like to tell him it's all right. I made out all right.

O'CONNELL: Go ahead.

DAVE: It's O.K. I've made out all right. I'm going to keep making it. I guess that's it.

---

*It should be noted that this young man was used to the visualizing methods of gestalt therapy.

O'CONNELL: How does he seem to you now?

DAVE: He's not there anymore. He's really gone.

O'CONNELL: Can you say farewell?

DAVE: Sure I can. Goodbye, Dad. I don't have to keep you alive anymore.

Saying goodbye and saying hello are opposite sides of the process which is your living. To be able to say hello to a new personal involvement is, in some measure, directly related to our willingness to say goodbye when a death or separation occurs. When we fail to say goodbye to what is past, gone, completed, and finished, we interrupt and interfere with our ongoing energies. Rather than being expressive, then, we become depressive—turned in on ourselves and the past— and so we are less available to those persons who may cross our paths and who can touch our hearts.

The process of saying goodbye sometimes requires anger. More frequently, it requires the necessary tears that were at first held back, the final words that were not then spoken. When people allow themselves to live these events through, there comes the finality of understanding that the lost one, the one who left, no longer has to be mourned—all that was unspoken or unsaid, undone and unfinished is now resolved . . . *Consumata est.* And with this understanding the person knows relief: the slow filling up of expressive energy which revitalizes the organism and his or her present life forces.

learning to survive: death and divorce

When a person dies, and we bury him or her, only part of the task of the bereaved has been accomplished. The funeral and the burial are helpful in that they are the last remnants of the ancient "rites of passage"[18] that allow the family and the community to recognize the person's transition from the state of life to the state of afterlife. But our funeral and burial rites are pitifully inadequate to catharsize the grief we feel. Even the Catholic viaticum (which contains the element of blessing the person on his or her way to the other side) does not have its former solemnity and grandeur. After the funeral and after the condolences have been expressed, those who have been nearest and dearest to the person are left to manage their grief alone just at the time they need emotional support. It is only *after* the crisis is past that the real grief and suffering and mourning begins.[19] Moreover, in our society, we are supposed to be strong, courageous, and industrious. The mourner is supposed to grieve silently, keep up appearances, and get back into the swing of things as soon as possible.

In earlier days, the widow, widower, and family wore black clothes or a black arm band for an extended period of time (a year was minimal) and were expected to lead quiet lives during this period of mourning. We regard this practice as unduly harsh on the family, but there was an advantage to it that our socially liberated society may have overlooked. The grieving family may have welcomed that time to withdraw from the world and from having to keep up appearances or to continue the social game while heart was heavy and spirit still oppressed. It was a method of healing for the survivors. We seem to lack a method for that kind of healing at the present time. Yet it is a situation all of us will encounter in our lifetime. In the following section, we will discuss some of the ways of coping with grief and of learning how to survive both the death of a loved one and separation and divorce.

The Stages of Grief and Recovery

In a small book entitled *Up from Grief,* Bernadine Kreis, who lost her mother, father, and husband in quick succession, described her own experience of grief and recovery, along with the experiences of over 500 persons who also went through the process of grief and recovery.[20] As the result of her investigations, she concluded that grief and recovery have three stages, which, if understood, can be helpful to those of us who have experienced or will experience the mourning process. Like the stages of dying, these three stages must not be thought of as a series of discrete steps but as overlapping trends in the process toward recovery.

1. THE STAGE OF SHOCK.   Kreis emphasized that the real process of mourning does not come at the moment of death, nor even at the time of the funeral and burial rites. These events are part of the stage of shock. Even when the death has been long expected, when the actual moment of death arrives, our bodies and psyches still react with shock. This has been expressed by the survivors as: "I knew she was going to die but knowing it in advance somehow didn't make her death any easier to bear or understand."

Kreis explained that the state of shock is a protective device to enable us to manage the grim events that must be endured at the time of death. Shock numbs the pain and postpones the suffering so that we can get through what has to be done: notifying various friends and members of the family, arranging for funeral and burial, the endless bills, and sometimes feeding and caring for relatives who have come a long distance to attend the funeral.

In the state of shock, the persons who have been closest to the deceased may find themselves perplexed by confused and ambiguous feelings: wanting company but wanting also to be alone, feelings of being half-dead and half-alive, wanting (perhaps) to be buried with the person who died but experiencing also anger at the person for dying. In our state of shock, we may distort reality, blame ourselves for not having done more, and regret the unkind things we said or the things we meant to do but did not. We may act out our shock by rebelling against society. Kreis described a widow who wore a red hat to the funeral. When her family expressed surprise, she insisted that her husband loved to see her in red. She told Kreis that later she realized that the red hat had been a symbol of defiance and anger, anger toward the fate that had made her a widow. Another example of such rebellion is beautifully described by Caitlin Thomas (widow of the poet, Dylan Thomas) in her autobiography, *Leftover Life to Kill*,[21] when she threw herself at the husbands of her friends in defiance of the social mores of the small Welsh village that had been their home.

During the stage of shock, not only will the survivors go through psychological changes, but frequently their appearance will undergo a change. Since they may eat little and lose weight, they may look haggard. If the stage of shock is severe, the person may not attend to external appearances as before, and the person's countenance may take on a somewhat "wild" or "vacant" look. Shock alienates us from ourselves, from our feelings, and from our thoughts. It follows then that we may even feel somewhat deranged but, fortunately, this stage generally does not last long.

2. THE STAGE OF SUFFERING.   It may take some weeks for the shock to wear off. The signal that this is happening is, surprisingly enough, that the amount of pain and grief will begin to *increase*. For that reason, Kreis called the next phase the stage of suffering. Kreis drew the analogy from medicine: when our bodies have received a deep physical wound and enter a state of shock, it is not until after the shock wears off that we begin to feel the pain. Likewise, said Kreis, the real suffering and pain of grief does not begin until the state of psychological shock begins to lift.

The stage of suffering is a significant part of the road to recovery, but it is a long and lonely part of the journey. It is at this time that the house seems empty, and life seems to have lost its meaning and purpose. The most difficult hours, said Kreis, are those we spend with our loved one, twilight and evening. Weekends may seem desperately

The refusal to "let go" of the deceased and to continue to mourn, saps the psychic energy of the person which prevents living in the present.

long. In the stage of shock, one had a protective barrier for the pain and grief. One's actions were mechanical and automatic. In the stage of suffering, one no longer has a buffer against pain and loneliness. The funeral and burial are long past; the thank-you notes have been written; and the legal details have been taken care of. Now our life is our own, but we are not sure what to do with it. We still are mourning, but we know that others do not want to be bothered with our suffering, so we put on that "face to meet the faces that we meet." We pretend a cheerful exterior to hide our vulnerability.

3. THE STAGE OF RECOVERY. The first sign that the stage of suffering is ending and that the stage of recovery is beginning is that we begin to worry about our future, what we can do with our lives, and

what is going to happen to us. We begin to wonder about the choices available to us and the kinds of changes we need to make in order to reconstruct our life in our new circumstances. Shall we sell the house and move to a smaller one? Shall we go back to work or shall we seek a new job? Shall we try to get back into our previous social activities or would the people and things that we used to do together be too painful to do alone? One begins to realize that one has the rest of life to confront, and it is a little frightening.

Kreis warns us specifically to be careful about acting on our first impulses. They may turn out to have been destructive or dangerous choices. One such example is from the authors' experience. A woman we know who was going through the stage of recovery, took her old photograph albums and souvenirs and burned them. Although such an action may shock most of us, her explanation was that she was trying to confront the fact that her past life was dead. As a part of this desire, she decided to burn the things that would hold her to her past. It was a method of radical transformation for her. Would she do it again? she was asked. Probably not, was her answer.

Another aspect of recovery to keep in mind is that moments of pain, loneliness, and suffering will return time and again just when we think we have gotten through the worst of it. The road to recovery, even at this stage, is a forward-and-back affair, sometimes two steps forward and one back. We may, for example, find ourselves reliving memories of happier times. We may have dialogues with the loved one who still lives in our memory. We may be seduced into imagining the past was happier than it was, since we tend to remember happy times and forget the more painful ones.

But eventually, there will come that moment of truth, that what has been can never be again. We must go on with the process of living.

Divorce as a Kind of Dying

No matter how terrible and unhappy a marriage has been, divorce can be experienced as a kind of "dying." Certainly, one part of our existence is over. No matter how much stress there may have been in the marriage, separating ourselves from our spouse has the same characteristics (in kind if not degree) as separation by death. In this instance, we may grieve for our life that was but is no more, for our spoiled hopes and dreams, for the end of our illusions of a happy ending, or perhaps, even, our loss of innocence and childhood faith. Although the divorce may have ended the most painful relationship we ever had, it also ended the most intimate relationship we ever had.

The divorced person experiences the same kinds of readjustments as a widow or widower. Both widows and divorced women have the same kinds of vulnerabilities and problems so that the coping methods discussed below can be applied to both. The widower and the divorced man also have similar problems and will be discussed together. Let us call these persons the formerly married.

Reintegrating Oneself into Society after Death and Divorce

Divorce occurs at all levels of marriage: marriages of only a few months or not quite a year, marriages of a few years, marriages of nine, ten, or twelve years, and even marriages of twenty or thirty years. The facts are that more and more people are getting divorced at all ages so that there are many persons returning to the social and business scene who formerly were married and now are single again. Reintegrating oneself back into society is difficult for both the divorced and the widowed person. The older the person is, the more difficult it tends to be. Nevertheless, there are some coping methods which can help the formerly married person construct a new life.

Differences in Status between the Formerly Married Woman and the Formerly Married Man

In our society, divorced and widowed women have a more ambiguous social status than divorced or widowed men do. Although the formerly married woman may be interested in male companionship rather than in sexual engagement, the men who approach her may be looking for a primarily sexual, casual emotional relationship. As one recently divorced woman in her early thirties expressed it, "I'm good enough to go to bed with, but I'm not good enough to marry." If the formerly married woman is content to have only a sexual relationship, she has less of a problem than does the woman who hopes to create another home-family relationship. Sometimes the formerly married woman discovers that invitations to social affairs are few, since her friends do not know how to invite her to parties or do not know any eligible men. The formerly married woman discovers that she is a kind of fifth wheel in an essentially man-woman social scene.

Formerly married men also have problems, although of a different kind. They are besieged with invitations to fill in at a party or to be introduced to another woman. Mel Krantzler, author of *Creative*

Divorce[22] and now a divorce counselor, admitted that the formerly married man may enjoy the sexual freedom that is now confronting him and may even "play the field" as he never did when he was young. But, said Krantzler, for a man in his thirties, forties, or fifties, womanizing can get boring, and the formerly married man begins to realize, soon enough, the emptiness of chasing sexual partners, which also requires a lot of creative energy. After a while, the formerly married man longs to settle down, but he too needs a time for healing. If the formerly married woman sees herself as a convenient sexual object for the exploitive male, the formerly married man, said Krantzler, seems to be expected to play the part of a sexually aggressive and exploitive male by the women he approaches.

Divorce and Children

If the couple has had children, the woman and man have distinctive problems in relating to them and caring for them. The formerly married woman now may have the burden of caring for all the children's needs which were once somewhat shared by her husband. Although the woman may be able to act as a parental guide for her daughters, it becomes increasingly difficult for her to relate to her sons as they get older, and frequently, they become unmanageable, particularly if she has gone back to work. The formerly married woman may resent the differences in the relationship her children have with her as compared to that of her husband. She has the odious tasks, it seems to her, to see to their physical needs such as taking them to the dentist, doctor, school counselors, and she must be the disciplinarian, which they increasingly resent as they get older. It seems to her that when the children are with their father, his associations with them are on the order of a holiday and entertainment, since the children frequently come back talking about going to the movies, the zoo or to a restaurant. She wishes she could relate to them similarly, but her job as a parent seems to boil down to supervising their homework, telling them to clean their rooms and to do their chores, or nagging them about coming in at night and checking their whereabouts.

Added to these problems are the hostile feelings her children may have toward anyone she may be seeing. Some divorced women have told us that they see no choice but to postpone marriage until the children are older—so opposed and jealous are the children of her private life. Yet, she cannot help but notice that the children do not

Children often resent the parent's new romantic
interest.

seem to have the same prohibitions toward the women whom their
father may be seeing or with whom he may even be living. The double standard raises its ugly head even here.

Although the divorced woman may see the father's role as envi-
able, he too has problems relating to his children, although they are
much different. The divorced father may be concerned that his interactions with his children are somewhat artificial. In the beginning, it
was fun to take them to the movies, to have a hamburger, or to the park
for a picnic. After a while, however, he begins to run out of things that
they can do together and the "holidays" take on a more enforced gaity
than actual "fun." He worries also that perhaps his value to his child-

ren has less to do with any real affection they have for him as much as what they can get out of him. Although they may relate casually to a woman that he brings into the picture, their acceptance of her is usually not much more than tolerance of a person they view as a necessary intruder in their relationship with their father. They may not openly resist her presence, but they do not relate to her as "one of them" as their father had hoped.

If the father remarries, his relationship to his children may actually worsen, particularly if the woman he has married has children of her own. No matter how hard the woman may work to establish rapport with her husband's children, she will inevitably fall into the trap of "stepmother" since children love to dramatize this archetypal role. No matter how fair she tries to be with them, the first minute she must side with her own children in any squabble, she will hear the inevitable accusations that she always "sticks up" for her own children. Children are natural fairy-tale writers, story tellers, and actors, and it will salve their bruised feelings to cast her in the "wicked stepmother" role.

Chances for a Successful Remarriage

We have painted a rather dismal picture for the social and family scene of the formerly married. Nevertheless, there is a brighter side. Second marriages usually tend to be happier overall than first marriages. Many reasons have been given for this. First, the remarried persons have a sense of acquiring back what they have lost: love, sex, home, stability, and status. Also, much has been added that puts more excitement into one's life: the relationship to the new spouse's friends, the spouse's own interests to be learned and shared, and companionship on holidays. The burdens of living alone have been eased by sharing the various tasks of maintaining a household.[23]

There is another reason for the more enduring quality of second marriages. Some of the romantic illusions about marriage have dissolved, allowing both partners to approach marriage on a much more realistic basis. Both partners are more adult in that they realize that marriage is not perfect but a relationship of give and take. Both partners are more willing to resolve conflicts and know better how to compromise opposing points of view.

A third reason is that both have more experience in self-management as the result of their first marriage. Both are more aware how money can become a major problem, and both have had experience with budgeting or the lack of it.

Finally, both want the marriage to work, and that implies less temptation to engage in extramarital affairs that might endanger their new marriage. Despite the frictions of stepchildren, they are wiser parents.

Furthermore, there may be less need to worry about the effects of divorce in our society. Under the management of anthropologist Paul Bohannan, a research team did not discover any undue differences between children whose parents were divorced as compared to children whose parents have not been divorced. Their grades in school are just as good, their relationship to their new parents seem to be as good as any relationship between the generations, and they seem to be just about as happy.[24]

Coping Techniques for the Formerly Married Person

Kreiss advised the unmarried person to face up honestly to his or her situation after widowhood or divorce. The going will be rough but the road to recovery requires adventuring into the unknown. Even if some of the advice given here turns out to be a negative experience, all your experiences, good or bad, are information and data for yourself to understand, analyze, and to influence your new life.

1. ENCOURAGE NEW FRIENDSHIPS. Be willing to issue invitations to new people of both sexes to go places and do things. Whether because of death or because of a painful marriage and divorce, the formerly married person may tend to feel hesitant about establishing new relationships with either sex. One may feel vulnerable and expect rejection. That kind of attitude may become a self-fulfilling prophecy. Rather, one must assume that although some people may reject the bid for friendship, others will respond if one goes about it in the right way. Decide whom you would like to get to know better and discover their interests. If one of their interests coincides with yours, invite them to that kind of an event. Or it may be that you might like to learn a new interest, in which case you can frankly ask them to initiate you into that activity. The point here is that friendships are easier to develop when approached through a common task or recreation.

2. ORGANIZE GROUPS OF PEOPLE FOR SOCIAL EVENTS. Kreis suggested that groups make easier reintegration. These groups may enjoy athletic events, theater parties, or political action groups. The formerly married person has more freedom in social relationships within task or activity-oriented groups.

3. AS IT SEEMS INDICATED, RENEW YOUR OLD FRIENDSHIPS. In your new status, it may be difficult to relate to old friends since they and you may both be nervous about your new situations. You may

feel that they were friends more of your spouse than yourself. There may be many couples who feel a conflict of loyalty and are afraid to relate to either one or the other partner for fear of causing resentment in both persons. Or they may simply not know how to relate to a formerly married person whom they have known as one of a couple. Do not feel pressured to come to definite decisions about their relationship to you; that is, do not cut them off. If you sense any reserve between you and them, let the relationship simmer on the back burner, so to speak, until you have reintegrated yourself back into society as an independent person. Your new image will make it easier for them to relate to you, and in the meantime, a little time may enable them to work through their reassessment of you.

4. CONFIDE IN ONLY ONE OR (AT THE OUTSIDE) TWO PERSONS.   Real friendship is a rare thing. Most people are only vaguely interested in us. If we insist on dredging up all our miseries and unhappinesses to casual friends, we soon will find ourselves without any. Choose rather, those one or two persons to whom you can release those sad feelings that come to all of us occasionally. But even here, be circumspect. Do not make your troubles the *raison d'être* of your friendship. Allow them to talk of their problems and when they do so, be warm and receptive. We all need confidants, but having a close personal friend on this order is a two-way street. Even if your friend seems happily married, that person too may have problems and would welcome a chance to discuss them.

5. TO ALL OTHER PERSONS, MAINTAIN A STRONG EXTERNAL APPEARANCE.   Even if you must pretend, put your best foot forward in the social and business arena. A down-in-the-mouth look will not attract the people you want to attract. Furthermore, if you act confident, the confidence will come. This is not a magic formula; it is a formula based on behavioral psychology, John Dewey's theory of learn-by-doing, and the best principles of self-management as set down by rational-emotive therapists, reality therapists, and many other theoreticians and practitioners.

6. DO CONSTRUCTIVE WORK.   No matter how menial a job it may be, working gives us a sense of achievement and self-worth. To that extent, the formerly married man has an advantage over the formerly married woman who did not work before the separation by death or divorce. For a person who has not held a job in a long time, this prospect may be frightening. One may not know what one can do. One may not even be able to find a job because of lack of experience. One may not know the politics of the world of work. All of these problems can be remedied, however, although it may take some time.

For example, there are many positions available for which only a little education may be necessary. Consult your local community college or adult education center to learn about courses that will make you readily employable. If you are older, you may be fearful about finding a job at mid-life. But again, your approach will count for a lot. Simply advise your prospective employer, in a calm and detached manner, that you are at a transition point in your life and that you are looking for a long-term position, with a possible chance for advancement and salary increase. You may tell him or her also that you are willing to become more competent in needed areas by going to school in the evenings. Such an approach cannot help but impress a prospective employer.

One thing is certain. Events do not happen by chance; you have to get out there and make them happen.

applications and coping techniques

We have been able to discuss only a few of the crises that occur in human existence; namely, death, critical illness and disability, suicide, and divorce. There are many other kinds of crises which, though they occur more infrequently, can happen from time to time to any of us. Our house may burn down with all our possessions. We may incur problems with the law, and although we pay the price, we find that society has stigmatized us so that we cannot easily find lawful employment. We may be vulnerable to alcoholism and, as a consequence lose our personal possessions and alienate our loved ones. We may have been orphaned at an early age. We may become disabled with a chronic disease, blindness, or deafness. What generally will enable us to survive these traumas and to process these events in our ongoing integration of personality?

1. REMEMBER THAT ALL OF US WILL SUFFER TRAUMA OF ONE SORT OR ANOTHER.   Frequently, persons who have suffered a traumatic event tend to express openly or to themselves, "Why did it happen to me?" "Why did God choose to make me suffer?" "Why did Fate single me out?" These thoughts and feelings have an animistic quality about them, as if vengeful spirits have lain in wait to hurt or destroy us. This is not the case. We all will die. Some persons have said that we are born just to die. The fact that our parents or our spouse or our child died earlier than we expected does not mean that a vengeful deity has thrown a lightning bolt at us in particular. The fact that one or the other of us has been crippled, has succumbed to a disabling disease, or has lost all our possessions does not mean that we have been singled out in some way for this dreadful fate. There is not a man

or woman in the world who has not suffered cruelly from at least one tragic event. The Old Testament states: "It rains on the just and unjust alike." You are not the only one upon whom tragedy and trauma has been visited. It is part of the human condition.

2. "PROCESS" THE SUFFERING WITH ALL THE AVAILABLE RESOURCES YOU CAN MUSTER.   To deny the pain and suffering that tragedy and trauma incur is to bring on worse consequences. Denying our suffering may only "psychosomaticize" the pain which may cause physical sickness, necessitate surgery, or result in emotional breakdown. Allow yourself to feel the pain and to work through the suffering. It is better to express it than to repress it only to have it emerge as a crippling physical or emotional disease. Allow your friends to help you, at least those who genuinely desire to do so. Use your community agencies and resources. There are many types of crisis and rehabilitation centers for various problems. To name only a few: centers for rape and crisis disaster victims, alcohol and drug abuse, vocational rehabilitation, unmarried pregnant women and girls, and child and spouse abuse.

3. PART OF THE RECOVERY AND REHABILITATION REQUIRES LETTING GO OF THE SUFFERING ITSELF.   Rehabilitation and recovery will not come about without your determined attitude to work it through. There is no "magic pill" we can take that will transform our lives. It is a matter of will power and self-determination. Eventually, there must come an end to tears and private pain. Suffering something through is cathartic, but there comes a point at which suffering can become destructive. We may hold on to grief and mourning as a kind of escape or excuse to resign from active life. Somewhere along the line, we need to draw up a plan for our lives, as Levinson would put it, to create a new life structure for ourselves. Tears may catharsize emotion; they do not rebuild. For that, we need to adopt a realistic, practical attitude.

4. LEARNING TO SAY GOODBYE AND HELLO.   The process of redesigning our life and creating a new life structure requires saying goodbye: goodbye to our past, goodbye to our previous life structure, and goodbye to previous hopes and aspirations. Life itself is a constant process of beginnings and endings. We say goodbye to our childhood when we enter adulthood. We say goodbye to our old home when we move away to a new city for advancement. We process these small endings (even "dyings" if you will) so that we can make ready for what is to come.

Tragedy and trauma can be likened to leave-taking, but a leave-taking that was unexpected, violent, and overwhelming. Yet without the leave taking, we cannot prepare for the future. It may be a grim leave taking, to be sure, but not until we have said goodbye can we say a genuine hello to what is to come.

5. LEARN TO USE YOUR PERSONAL EXPERIENCES FOR YOUR OWN GROWTH AND CREATIVITY.   It is not enough simply to survive and work through the critical events of life. Every experience we have, joyous or sorrowful, has a lesson to teach. Wisdom is not a given; it is the end process of all our experiences, if we are willing to learn from them. If may even be that we can learn more from painful experiences than we can from more positive ones. Great writers often were unhappy as children but used their unhappiness toward creation of their literature. Many famous people have been orphaned early in life, and it seems to have given them the understanding that they had only themselves on whom to rely. We can use our suffering to our benefit or to our detriment.

the choice is always ours:
toward higher levels of personality integration

Highly integrated persons have had the courage to be themselves. Original and creative, they have illumined our lives and enabled humankind to evolve.

I. The Memorable Originals: "Persons in Process"

II. Historical Development of Personality Theory
A. The study of the sick and neurotic
B. The study of the "average" personality
C. The study of "persons in process"
D. The study of the highly integrated and creative personality

III. Four Processes in Personality Integration
A. The continual development of one's intellectual or cognitive function
   1. Highly integrated persons are willing to strive all their lives toward further intellectual insights
   2. Highly integrated persons are more willing to perceive the world accurately
   3. Highly integrated persons are more willing to perceive themselves accurately
B. The steady unfolding and enrichment of one's emotional repertory
   1. Highly integrated persons allow themselves to stay open to emotional experiences
   2. Highly integrated persons pursue their inner lives with diligence
   3. Highly integrated persons attend the here-and-now
C. The striving to direct one's destiny
   1. Highly integrated persons are more willing to be themselves
   2. Highly integrated persons are more willing to make decisions and to take responsibility for their lives
D. The quest to relate oneself to one's world
   1. Highly integrated persons are self-governing
   2. Highly integrated persons have a commitment to the growth of others
   3. Transcending self

IV. Viktor Frankl: The Spiritual Dimension

the memorable originals: "persons in process"

The memorable persons in history always have been originals. Think of some of the names that excite us: Albert Einstein, Marie Curie, Pablo Picasso, Georgia O'Keefe, George Sand, Joan of Arc, Abelard and Heloise, Shakespeare, Emily Dickinson, Gandhi, Theresa of Avila, Michelangelo, Freud, Florence Nightingale, Socrates, Darwin, Abraham Lincoln, Bach, Beethoven, Golda Meir, Albert Schweitzer, the Bronte sisters—the list is long. These persons light up the history of humankind like stars in the sky. We always are struck by their originality of thinking, the depth of their feelings, and their unique way of being. As artists, they perceived the world in ways that the rest of us could rediscover its archetypal images and forms. As philosophers, they formulated new ideas. As musicians, they made us aware of sound and of silence and brought together harmonies that stir the soul. As social scientists and reformers, they risked their lives and reputations for their visions of humankind, and how men and women may live together. As scientists, they were ruthless in their fight against superstition, dogma, and ignorance.

They were men and women of spirit and passion. They dedicated their lives to self-awareness and to the greater awareness of us all. In Carl Rogers's phrase, they were "persons in process"—humankind evolving—and by their example and works, we too evolved with them.

We do not expect you to become a Socrates, a Gandhi, or a Marie Curie. They are the giants of civilization. Each of us, however, can evolve in our own existence and further our personality integration to higher levels of awareness and creativity. We, too, can be "persons in process." The *raison d'être* of humanistic psychology is to enhance that process. The humanist asserts that we do not have to lock ourselves into patterns of adjustment that are uncreative for us, or destructive to society. Never before in history have we had the freedom to become ourselves. But freedom *to be* and freedom *to become* require a commitment to personality integration that is not for the faint hearted. It requires courage and strength, not the external kind of courage and strength found on the battlefield but an internal strength that enables us to look into ourselves and to take responsibility for our lives. To know ourselves (as the Greeks said three thousand years ago) is to understand humankind.

In this last chapter, we shall examine the most creative, integrated, fully-functioning, and self-actualizing persons in society. We shall try to understand the processes that enabled them to achieve their goals and to become unique personalities. Finally, we shall attempt to discover some ways in which we can become more integrated and more creative within ourselves and in relation to the larger community.

It is good to hold up these memorable originals as models of personality integration, but in one respect these men and women are idealized concepts: there is something of the folk hero in each of them. We know the heights that they attained, and we are awed by their courage to be what they could be. But folk heroes are one-dimensional personalities: it is the grand and transcendent qualities in them that are emphasized; we lose those other aspects of them that are forgotten in the course of time, the human frailties that are characteristic of us all. Beethoven and Michelangelo achieved heights of grandeur in music and art, but their tempers and depressions also were monumental. Albert Einstein has become something of the archetypal Wise Old Man, but in everyday life, he was a shy and retiring individual who seemed somehow lost in the everyday world of human affairs. Albert Schweitzer seemed to many to be a living saint, but visitors who traveled to Lambarené, Africa, sometimes reported that he was one of the most uncompromising and authoritarian personalities that they had ever come across. What we are saying is that even the great originals had their weaknesses and limitations. What lifted them beyond the average, however, what thrust them beyond their limitations, was their *dynamic process,* and it is that process that we shall study.

historical development of personality theory

An understanding of the process of personality integration must come not from legends or folk heroes but from the scientific observation of real persons in their human totality. It must come by observing these persons in a variety of circumstances, not only by what they said about themselves and by what they did when they were at the peak of their achievements, but also what they did under stress, and when they had setbacks and obstacles. We need to understand how they managed to break through the confusions and difficulties with which we all are beset. It has only been in the last century that we have begun to do that and only in that last several decades that we have begun to approach the study of the truly healthy, integrated, and creative personality.

1. The Study of the Sick and the Neurotic.

As the reader will remember, the first scientific approach to the study of personality began in the nineteenth century, when physicians began to study the mentally deranged and insane, as they were called then. As these pioneering physicians discovered, mental patients were different from most of humankind, sometimes, only in the degree of depression or confusion. They discovered, too, that with care and proper treatment, some of these mental patients could begin to find themselves again and return to live and work in society.

This was a great step forward in the scientific understanding of emotional problems, since before that the insane were thought to be somehow different, "touched by the Gods," perhaps, or "the instrument of the Devil." If deranged persons could be considered not terribly different from most of us, psychiatrists reasoned, then by observing them they could discover the underlying dynamics of human personality. After all, the patients were in the hospital. They could be studied, tested, observed, analyzed, and discussed in their day-to-day unfoldment.[1]

There was one major difficulty with this approach. The personality theorists who studied the "sick" and the "neurotic" individuals of our time tended to derive their hypotheses of the "healthy," "creative," or "integrated," personality from their observations of "unhealthy," "uncreative," or "dis-integrated" persons. Such an approach is inferential rather than observational. It is rather like saying because men are *this* way (aggressive, dominant, athletic), then women must be *that* way (docile, submissive, unathletic), a method that we now know to have all kinds of logical and scientific fallacies. Yet, this was the kind of personality theorizing that prevailed for many years.

2. The Study of the "Average" Personality.

A step in the right direction came when psychologists and sociologists began to study large groups of people to discover how they function in various circumstances. They studied school children from kindergarten right up through high school, college, and beyond. They began to study babies in nursery schools and in hospitals. They studied workers in their place of work, consumers and what induces them to buy this or that product, broad segments of our population to determine what made "farmers" or "suburbanites" or "auto workers" vote for this presidential candidate or that gubernatorial nomination. They began to study public opinion and what influences it. In short, they were looking for another ideal concept: Mr. and Mrs. "average" person.[2]

We can give credit to American psychologists for this approach. They were seeking to understand our American personality as different from the European tradition of personality functioning, which rested on many assumptions of caste and class. They knew that what a person is depends as much on environment as on genetic inheritance. They were determined to provide their fellow citizens with the best educational and working milieu so that all Americans could pursue life, liberty, and happiness as they chose. In the course of this approach, they developed what is called the "statistical" approach to human personality which helped us to understand broad categories of people.

The major problem with this approach was its tendency to reduce human personality to broad generalizations of personality functioning. It lost sight of the individual. If the "average" *this* or *that* did not behave according to the statistical model, we tended to think that there was something "abnormal" or "maladjusted" about that individual. We sought to "adjust" him or her to the societal "norm." What had happened, in brief, is that we had confused the word "norm" with "normal." We did not realize that society evolves and that personality functioning evolves with it. Our understanding of how men and women may live together on this planet still is in process.

What is good and viable for one generation may not be good and viable for another. We rediscovered this in the late sixties and early seventies. As a result, we are more aware of human differences and human individualities.

3. The Study of "Persons in Process."

The next step in understanding of the evolution of personality came when the American psychologist, Carl Rogers, began to study persons who were attempting to discover more viable and creative ways to live and work.[3] Carl Rogers is a psychotherapist who believed that all of us have within us a "center of growth." He believed that if we can get in touch with this "center," that we will discover what is truly right, energizing, rewarding, and consonant with our individual personality patternings. Rogers observed his own clients and listened to what they discovered as they moved forward in their own growth process. Later, he observed and listened to persons in group therapy and in encounter groups as they reported their experiences with each other. His contributions helped us understand how people change in the course of therapy: how they experience themselves, and how they interact with others when they seem to be only "partly functioning," and then when they are "more fully functioning" persons.

Rogers's method was a kind of "before" and "after" photograph of human personality. He helped us to understand that personality is a matter of *process*. He emphasized that no one, not even the person in therapy, can predict the limits of human potential.

4. The Study of the Highly Integrated and Creative Personality.

In the fifties, American psychology took another step forward when it began to study human functioning at its "highest" level. The most famous of these studies is that by Abraham Maslow.[4] Maslow, another American psychologist who seems to us to have been one of the true originals, studied what he called highly "self-actualizing" persons: those who apparently can live according to their beliefs throughout most of their lives and can achieve their life goals and ambitions despite the exigencies of fate and fortune. Maslow considered his subjects to be among the healthiest types of personality in our society and chose his subjects from friends and acquaintances as well as from public and historical personalities. Maslow's findings helped to affirm Rogers's belief that truly integrated and creative persons do not "just happen" but are the result of their own endeavors to become all that they can be. Their highly self-actualizing process came as a result of self-study, insight, uncompromising discipline, and self-development.

Maslow's research was not the only such study, nor was it the first of its kind. Others have studied the human personality at its highest level and have reported their findings of highly successful executives, the intellectually gifted, the highly creative artist or physicist, and the like. These studies have enabled us to understand how human personality can transcend limitations and obstacles. The research findings in these areas of personality development are many, but we shall try to summarize the observations and conclusions from these diverse sources. There are some difficulties in such a task. Each personality theorist has his or her own particular point of view and methodology. Some persons study the therapeutic process while others study persons who have already received recognition in their respective fields.

Still others study very different kinds of personalities: artists, executives, the gifted, scientists, or whatever. Next, the terminology may differ from one study to another. Carl Jung described what he called the "individuated" man; Carl Rogers called his subjects "fully-functioning persons"; Maslow studied the "self-actualizing" person (see Box A). We begin with the assumption that all of these social scientists describe some aspect of what we call the highly integrated person.

Box A

INVESTIGATOR	SUBJECTS
T. W. Adorno	low-authoritarian persons
F. Barron	"creative" persons
S. Freud	functioning persons
J. P. Guilford	"creative" artists and engineers
Karen Horney	"self-realized" persons
Carl Jung	"individuated" persons
D. W. MacKinnon	"creative" persons
A. Maslow	"self-actualizing" persons
D. C. McClelland	"successful" executive
S. L. Pressey	"geniuses"
Anne Roe	"artists"
C. Rogers	"fully-functioning" persons
M. Rokeach	"open-minded" persons
L. M. Terman	"gifted" persons
C. W. Taylor	"creative" scientists and artists

four processes in personality integration

Throughout all these studies, four areas of competence appear in the subjects, four processes basic to all of us but which seem to be particularly well developed and articulated in the highly integrated person. These processes are components of that larger process described in chapter 1 and that we identify with human existence itself. The four processes are *psychological* (as distinct from physiological) and include:

1. The continual development of one's *intellectual* or *cognitive* function.
2. The steady unfolding and enrichment of one's *emotional* repertory.
3. The determination to direct one's own destiny.
4. The quest to relate oneself to one's world.

The Continual Development of One's Intellectual or Cognitive Function

The first process of personality integration is the continuing desire of human beings to perceive their own world; to understand the physical properties of everything they see and hear, and to make some kind of sense out of their experiences. The baby, said the American psychologist William James, is a "blooming, booming confusion of sights and sounds." This baby will spend the rest of its days on earth putting these sights and sounds together to form significant events. It is an urge that dominates the consciousness in many and subtle ways. It expresses itself in six-week-old infants as they learn to follow with interest the objects and the persons in their visual field. When the child grows to a point of self-locomotion, this urge takes the form of exploring its environment, even to biting and tasting the things it encounters. Feeling, tasting, and touching with fingers and mouth are the baby's primitive methods for learning about things. The child is discovering if things are hard, soft, or good to eat, or if something can be dropped, thrown, kicked or sat on, or whether something is light or heavy, or hot or cold. All of these events are the beginnings of its knowledge of the world.

It is because of their total absorption in wanting to know and classify the phenomena of their world that four-year-olds ask their "why," "where," and "how" questions: Why is the fire hot? Why does Daddy go to the office? Why do I have to go to sleep? Where does the sun go at night? How did I get to be born? Growing children are bombarded with events that they want to understand, and they spend many years in school learning about their world.

This basic process has been identified by many names. It has been called the "intellectual function" and the "thinking process." It has been seen as a "curiosity trait," a "sensoriperceptual modal function," "problem solving," "decision making," "creativity," and the "ability to analyze and synthesize." Individual success in developing this process is what is supposedly measured in tests of intellectual functioning (IQ tests).

This same *need to know* is manifested in the scientist's urge to investigate the universe, in the newspaper reporter's determination "to uncover the facts," in the scholar's research into ancient civilizations, and in the philosopher's continuing search into the nature of goodness, truth, and beauty. It is the same underlying process behind your own search for answers to such questions as "Who am I?" What is life?" and "What shall I do with my life?" It is also the impulse behind the student's quest for knowledge, and it is society's attempts to help us answer these questions for ourselves that are, at least ideally, the sum and substance of education.[5]

A. HIGHLY INTEGRATED PERSONS ARE WILLING TO STRIVE ALL THEIR LIVES TOWARD FURTHER INTELLECTUAL INSIGHTS. Most persons seem to settle down into routine living. Their sense of interest in those issues which do not touch their small, everyday world seems to fade. Reading books becomes a thing of the past and is replaced by the hypnotism of television, for example, or the quick scanning of newspaper headlines. In contrast, highly integrated persons, said Maslow, never seem to lose their drive for learning about new things or their desire to delve more deeply into those things already familiar to them.

Not only do integrated persons want to know about things, they also want to learn how events are related to each other. Donald Mac-Kinnon, who has spent his life studying what he calls "highly creative" people, describes them as "very open to experiences." They always are seeking to understand information that comes to them through their sensory experiences. The hallmark of these persons, he said is their intense *perceiving* attitude. When faced with an almost overwhelming amount of information and experience, they constantly are on the alert to discover similarity in these thousands of bits of information. They are able to discover relationships because they are adept at scanning their thoughts and their past experiences to absorb what now is coming to them.[6] Another psychologist, Frank Barron, added that they do not accept the "as is-ness" of things, the simple and oversimplified answer for why things are as they are. They are persons who are willing to topple the accepted social explanations and to discover more comprehensive explanations.[7] In short, their thinking is radical.

It is not easy to make a breakthrough in thinking. Copernicus was willing to lose his head rather than to deny the truth of his own perceptions. Descartes' grand achievement was his declaration that he must be free to think for himself, even if that meant rejecting the authority of his teachers, his parents, his friends, even his church.[8] Freud and Darwin both were aware that their revolutionary theories might result in public condemnation.

Before we become too awed by the intellectual courage of the highly integrated person, we must remind ourselves that all of us are capable of becoming more self-determining in our assessment of "reality." In fact, it is a process that all of us have experienced, at one time or another, when we have been willing to diverge from popular opinion, when we have been willing to take exception to what others think, and when we have, in brief, dared to be different and to express that difference. It is not easy, by any means, to stand up and say what we think is right when others tell us that we are wrong. But when we have done so, we know that satisfaction of having made our own decisions.

It is very difficult to keep from sliding into an easy acceptance of traditional thought, attitudes, and beliefs. It is easy to get stuck in a rigid perceptual set, even for promising scholars, scientists, and artists. Lawrence S. Kubie, who studied the creative process for many years, wrote:

There are scientists and engineers who produce brilliantly as students, and even through their graduate years of study, but then collapse. There are gifted investigators who turn out one or two creative achievements early in their careers, but thereafter are never productive again.

Kubie related this "freezing" of one's intellectual capacities to an "inflexibility of spirit and psychology." Creativity demands the willingness to hold open one's perception of reality, the continual willingness to look at a thing in many ways and from more than one point of view, the constant contemplation of a thing or event to gain new perspectives. Kubie concluded that flexibility is synonymous with health since it allows us the freedom to learn through experience and the freedom to make changes within and without. The noncreative person and the neurotic person, said Kubie, has frozen his or her behavior into "unaltering, repetitive and insatiable patterns." He went on to say:

We see examples of such frozen behavior in all creative fields. In painting, we see it in men of worldwide reputations, men who after passing through some inner convulsion of the spirit start on a new "period," dominated perhaps by a new color or by a new subject matter, or a new way of applying the paint, or a new way of stressing outlines, or a new way of distorting proportions, each such innovation becoming as rigid as the work of the earlier periods . . .[9]

Remaining flexible in one's thinking and behavior requires a certain humility of spirit; that is, integrated persons understand that there are no permanent answers, that no matter how diligently they may have pursued an idea, a question, or a task, they have only scratched the surface of what there is to know.

Abraham Maslow discovered this sense of humility among his "self-actualizing" subjects. Despite their profound learning, they knew that their knowledge was only a little of what there was to be known. They knew that their achievements were only a small step in the process of human understanding of the world. They saw themselves as life-long students and still were (even those in their sixties and seventies) concerned with the same basic issues and eternal questions that interested them as students. Maslow regarded them as philosophers, still willing and eager to learn from anyone, if they sensed that person had something to teach them. They also were more involved in the process of intellectual learning and insight than in the discoveries and achievements of that process. It is the search that delights the highly integrated person.[10]

B. HIGHLY INTEGRATED PERSONS ARE MORE WILLING TO PERCEIVE THE WORLD ACCURATELY.   Over and over we have emphasized that we do not see the world as it really is. What we experience as "reality" or "truth" is a combination of many factors: our sensory awareness (or blindness), sensitivity (or insensitivity) to others, prejudices (prejudgments), past experiences, fears and angers, and hopes and fantasies. All of these conspire to prevent us from perceiving accurately. Our understanding of events, things, and persons are seen "as through a glass darkly," a mirror that is fogged by our emotions and our defensive attitudes. The more "neurotic" we are, the less able we are to assess a situation clearly, while the "psychotic" lives in a world clearly removed from reality.

When we say that our world view is distorted by our prejudicial attitudes, we are speaking not just of prejudice toward persons different from us in race, creed, or color. These are the obvious prejudices. Rather, we are speaking of all those small, subtle attitudes to which we have been conditioned or that we have acquired without realizing it.

Our needs and deprivations further influence our perceptions: poor children overestimate the size of common coins, and hungry persons will see candy, cake, and ice cream in clouds and other amorphous shapes. Juries will tend to believe an attractive, well dressed witness over a grubby witness.

None of us, then, perceives the world with absolute accuracy. The studies of highly creative persons, however, indicate that they are more able to see the world "as it really is" than the rest of us can. Maslow's healthy subjects could, in fact, describe the personalities of other persons with remarkable insight. Furthermore, they could see behind the masks and facades of personalities and were especially good at detecting the spurious and the phony.

What enables highly integrated persons to be as perceptive as they are? First, they are far less judgmental about what they observe in others and in the world. Since they do not have to judge what they observe, they are more detached and "scientific" in their conclusions. When we place extreme value judgments on our observations, we already are so emotionally involved that we cannot be good observers and reporters.

Second, highly integrated persons are not as blinded by external appearances or stereotypic thinking as the rest of us are. They can accept the opinions of the fat person as being potentially as valid as those of the well-proportioned individual.

Third, highly integrated persons are more able to stay in the "here and now"—that is, they are able to disattach themselves from past preconceptions so as to assess the current situation. Many of us, as we go about our daily work, are faced with the same situations over and over. The fact that we have dealt with these situations *in the past* tends to cause us to deal with the same situations in the future in the same way. We may keep treating our twelve-year-old son (now on the brink of adolescence) just as we treated him when he was, say, four years old, which infuriates him. What we need to do is to realize the changes in the growth and competence of our children from year to year, which is very difficult when we see them every day. But integrated persons are able to do just that. How we learn to do that, said Maslow, is by our willingness to break with past habits of stereotypic thinking, no matter how well those habits have served us in the past. This process of "emptying the mind," as it is called by Zen masters, is helpful in overcoming obstacles[11] and in making transitions from one life cycle to another.

Finally, being highly intergrated is a matter of dissolving (insofar as we are able) our ego defenses so that we can hear what others are saying to us and to heed the facts at our disposal. Again, it is humility that reminds us that we do not know everything there is to know, no matter how learned or respected we have become in our professional or social milieu. We recognize that no matter what our standing, experience, or reputation is, others may have "a piece of the truth." This lack of ego is what distinguishes the wise person from the egotist about whom others say: "It's no use trying to tell him anything. He thinks he knows it all."

C. HIGHLY INTEGRATED PERSONS ARE MORE WILLING TO PERCEIVE THEMSELVES ACCURATELY. Hand in hand with the ability to perceive others more accurately is the ability to perceive oneself with a high degree of accuracy—that is, more objectively. Maslow's subjects did not deny their own shortcomings, even as they sought to overcome their limitations. Although they did not dwell on their imperfections, they were not impressed by their achievements. MacKinnon and his associates, studying the highly creative person, reported that their subjects were extremely candid about themselves and exhibited an extraordinary lack of defensiveness. They could speak with equal frankness about their abilities and their problems. Not only were they willing to reveal thoughts and feelings of the sort that others might prefer to keep to themselves, but they also showed no need for false modesty when discussing their strengths and abilities.

Most of us seem to wear a mask, a public face, or a public personality quite different from what we think ourselves to be. This public image is what we would like to be, it is our best self-concept. Carl Jung called this mask our *Persona*, which he contrasted to our *Shadow*, which is what we dislike about ourselves and which we keep hidden from others. But, said Jung, when we split ourselves off from this other side of ourselves, we deny ourselves one-half of our personal energy and creativity. It is not easy to stay in touch with the Shadow aspect, said Jung, but social scientists who have investigated the extremely creative individual are convinced that these persons are far more in touch with that side of themselves than the average person is. Creative writers, scientists, and artists, are more willing to look at the darker aspects of self and to delve into their creative unconscious. They do not deny their fantasies as much; they are more apt to remember their dreams; and they see themselves more completely for what they are. They are persons willing to see in themselves what others are afraid to see or are embarrassed by, or are ashamed to admit. Because highly integrated people are willing to do that, they have less "split" in their personalities and thus are more "integrated."[12] It is just because highly integrated persons are willing to see themselves accurately that they are better able to see the world and others more accurately. Because they know themselves and their own human frailties, they do not project their negative feelings and negative thoughts onto others. Their insights into themselves then provide them with more complete insights into others. They have self-knowledge, and thus they have knowledge of others.

The Steady Unfolding and Enrichment of One's Emotional Repertory

Perhaps nothing is as basic to human beings as their emotional selves. Very quickly, even before babies can distinguish the shapes and sounds of their environment, they can express fear, frustration, or anger. Little by little, they are able to express delight, joy, and pleasure. But in babies, these are very primitive emotions and do not have the same degree of subtlety as they have in adult human beings. Adults are capable of richer and more complex emotional experiences. Children are capable of self-love and love of a parent who treats them kindly but they are largely incapable of empathy for another individual. They also are incapable of altruistic love until they reach a certain age. Adults, on the other hand, can be so intensely loving of parents, spouse, and children, that they can sacrifice their own happiness to take care of their loved ones. Children can enjoy a pretty flower or a sunset for a few moments; it is the adult who is capable of awe, ecstasy, and thanksgiving.

Our emotional repertory increases with age until we can respond to the complexities of the composer's harmonies, a Gothic cathedral poetry and song, and the immensity of the physical universe. Our ability to experience the numerous qualities of love is a manifestation of our growth as individuals. We may be more able to express our emotions spontaneously as children, but it is not until we reach adulthood that we can experience the deepest and richest emotions: human compassion and universal loving kindness. But not all of us reach that level.

Some of us seem to close off emotional experiences. Perhaps we have experienced too many disappointments, shocks, or sorrows. Or maybe we have become jaded with sophistication and overstimulation. Perhaps we have developed such a low threshold for pain that we block out emotions of all kinds to avoid being hurt or being disappointed yet again. Whatever the reason, it is true that some of us prefer to live within a narrow range of emotional existence. These people seem to say: "Life may be drab, but it is at least safer this way. I may not experience as many of the depths and heights that life can offer, but at least I have less bother, chaos, and unwelcome surprises."

Furthermore, age can diminish those energies that once stirred us to extremes of feeling and emotion. For example, older people sometimes begin to shy away from activities that exhaust their energies so that they can cope more adequately with the slowing down of their energies that comes with increasing years. But even young people, as they situate themselves comfortably in their personal and vocational lives, lose what spontaneity they had in childhood. Other demands seem to crowd it out. ("What a lovely day to go birdwatching or for a swim — but the baby has to go to the pediatrician.") We cannot enjoy the rose garden if we worry about having to pull weeds in the future. Our realization that we have to pay bills this evening can prevent us from enjoying the whole day. So little by little we close ourselves off to the moments of joy and excitement by refusing to allow them to happen.

Highly integrated persons, however, seem to avoid the trap of emotional rigidity or coldness. They do this, evidently, in very definite ways. One is by pursuing new experiences and emotional understanding of these experiences.

HIGHLY INTEGRATED PERSONS ALLOW THEMSELVES TO STAY OPEN TO EMOTIONAL EXPERIENCES.   Being willing to allow oneself to experience one's own feelings entails also the willingness to experience many complex — even conflicting — emotions. We are taught as children, for example, that we should love our parents, and as parents that we should love our children — no matter what. Yet it seems obvious that when children are spanked or otherwise disciplined by their parents, they can momentarily have feelings of anger or resentment, even hatred. Likewise, when parents face for the hundredth time yet another instance of a child's tricks and manipulations, it is a relief for them to realize it is occasionally appropriate for them not to love their child, especially since they are in fact now furious with him or her.

After counseling, Rogers's subjects discovered that it is natural to feel love, anger, frustration, and confusion, all at the same time, toward another human being. With this discovery, they felt much less confused since they were not repressing or denying their emotions.

Rogers also discovered that his clients became more "fluid and changeable," less in need of arriving at fixed conclusions or retreating into static emotional states. This loosening and broadening of their emotional personality structure may be compared with findings in studies of the authoritarian personality in which a high degree of rigidity in thinking and behavior is exhibited and the person tends to experience a narrow spectrum of emotions. For such persons, the world remains dichotomized into good or bad, right or wrong, evil or virtue, or masculine or feminine. This type of thinking is called *either-or thinking* and is the cause of much emotional and intellectual heartache. A person may say to himself or herself, "Either I am right and he is wrong or he is right and I am wrong." Such "either-or" thinking leads to feelings of failure, feelings of superiority, hard feelings, inaccurate perceptions, and the like. Rogers's subjects, in comparison, show a "middle ground" in their personalities and much less of a need to come to fixed conclusions of right or wrong or good or bad.

Finally, highly integrated persons are willing to accept all the experiences life has to offer. They are willing to endure those moments of fear, grief, disappointment, shock, and sorrow because they know that life is a constant processing of the entire emotional spectrum. "When you pick up a stick," says a Zen proverb, "you pick up both ends of it." Even when it seems that the painful moments come more frequently than the moments of extreme contentment, highly integrated persons seem able to accept that fact expressed so well in the title of one of Robert Frost's poems: "Happiness Makes Up in Height for What It Lacks in Length."

HIGHLY INTEGRATED PERSONS PURSUE THEIR INNER LIVES WITH DILIGENCE. In the preface to his autobiography, *Memories, Dreams, and Reflections,*[13] Carl Jung warned the reader that the book would be a revelation of his *inner* life (his memories, dreams, and reflections) because, he explained, it is only his internal life that had meaning for him. Although he had known many great statesmen, writers, scientists, and artists and had treated them for their crisis transitions, these encounters were not the essential aspect of his life, nor did he consider the honors that came to him important. What was important was his *interior life,* and it was precisely his inner life that he chose to reveal.

This statement reflects precisely the attitude of the highly integrated person, for it is *his* or *her* inner life that is valued: one's thoughts, meditations, ideas, projects, inspirations, and aspirations. Highly integrated persons observe the external world to learn more about it but always to further the growth and expansion of their internal understanding and awareness. They are in touch with their "center of growth" and are not as liable to get caught up in the distractions of the sensate life. They are inner-oriented.

So at ease are highly integrated and creative personalities with their inner selves and "Shadow selves" that they are able to get in touch with those parts of themselves from which many of us shy away.

Studies of creative artists, engineers, and scientists have revealed that these persons (all men, incidentally) were able to allow themselves a range of interests and emotions still thought at the time of the study to be "feminine" in the American culture, to allow themselves to express the feminine or emotional side of their nature more readily than less creative individuals were. Studies of creative women, on the other hand, revealed them to have more "masculine" interests and to be unafraid of expressing themselves in serious ways.

Highly integrated persons study their feelings and thoughts for enjoyment, for inspiration, and for solutions to perplexing problems. Many deep interpersonal relationships take much time and energy, and Maslow's subjects preferred to devote this time and energy to their inner world and their own growth, and they needed a respite from everyday relationships. Maslow's subjects showed much need for such time and privacy. Not only did they pursue their inner lives intensely, but many of them also reported deep mystical experiences—what Maslow called "peak experiences":

. . . feelings of limitless horizons opening up to the vision, the feeling of being simultaneously more powerful and also more helpless than one ever was before, the feeling of great ecstasy and wonder and awe, the loss of placing in time and space with, finally, the conviction that something extremely important and valuable had happened, so that the subject is to some extent transformed and strengthened even in his daily life by such experiences.[14]

Being willing to attend to one's inner life means being willing to get in touch with one's dreams and to learn to understand them. It also means the willingness to spend some time each day in meditation or reflection and the desire to become more self-analytic and self-knowledgeable.

HIGHLY INTEGRATED PERSONS ATTEND THE HERE-AND-NOW. The ability to enjoy the moment (to let go of the past and avoid preoccupation with the future) was called by Frederick Perls (and other existential therapists) as "being in the here-and-now." Being in the here-and-now includes enjoyment of the senses, and Perls was well aware that many persons in our society have closed off much of their sensory functions. Perls's intuition of the sensory deficit in the "adjusted" person of our time is reflected also in Maslow's research findings with his self-actualizing subjects. Maslow called his self-actualizing subjects "good animals"—that is, they allowed themselves full enjoyment of their physical senses: they ate well, slept well, played well, were able to derive strong satisfaction from loving, sexual contact, and generally were able to "count their blessings." In regard to their ability to appreciate what they had, Maslow commented:

> I have also become convinced that getting used to our blessings is one of the most important nonevil generators of human evil, tragedy and suffering. What we take for granted we undervalue and we are therefore too apt to sell a valuable birthright for a mess of potage, leaving behind regret, remorse, and a lowering of self-esteem. Wives, husbands, children, friends are unfortunately more apt to be loved and appreciated after they have died than while they are still available. Something similar is true for psychological health, for political freedoms, for economic wellbeing; we learn their true value after we have lost them. . . .
> . . . My studies of low grumbles, high grumbles, and meta-grumbles all show that life could be vastly improved if we would count our blessings as self-actualizing people can and do and if they could retain their constant sense of good fortune and gratitude for it.[15]

Gratitude—a key ingredient in living in the here-and-now—means being able to thank someone honestly; it is the understanding that none of us has achieved our present level of functioning without considerable help from others. It is sadly amusing to listen to a young student, when asked who has helped him attain his accomplishments, reply (with innocence): "No one!" And in our time, we seem to have lost the capacity for giving thanks for one's good fortune, or for expressing appreciation to specific people who have helped us on the way. As Maslow said, we have grown "used to our blessings"!

Being in the here-and-now, being "good physical animals," and being "in touch with our bodies" are sources of creative inspiration. We are at our most basic level, a biological "energy transformer." It is at this level that we receive the data and information we need to operate at the many levels of personality: physical, emotional, and intellectual. We receive continual bombardment of unconscious, preconscious, and conscious signals from our bones, muscles, joints, tendons, skin, apertures, and all the internal organs of our body pertaining to ingestion, digestion, egestion, respiration, and metabolism. The more we are in touch with these signals, the better we operate at the many levels of human functioning. Yet we know that some people have eliminated many of these data from their ongoing experience of themselves. They operate at a reduced level of sensory awareness; they have "deadened" themselves, so to speak, to their bodily feelings.

Most of us are aware that artists, poets, and sculptors allow themselves to experience their living, breathing, and sensing selves to an extraordinary degree. Musicians also seem in touch with their internal rhythms and harmonies, and athletes have a sense of their bodily coordinates to a remarkable degree. But studies of creative persons in all areas, including physicists and mathematicians, reveal that they remain in touch with their bodily selves. This bodily self may even be the inspiration for people's technological achievements, said Herbert Gutman, who studied the creative process itself.[16]

Consider, said Gutman, the basic tools of our society. How was it that humankind invented the lever, the hammer, or the chisel? It may be, he answered, that these tools are simply analogues of bodily dexterity. In early times, "scientists" observed their bodily capabilities and extended them. The hammer is an extended, heavier, and harder arm and fist. Nails and teeth probably were the forerunners of saws, chisels, screwdrivers, and awls. In the last analysis, tools are extensions of ourselves and perform essentially those actions that our bodies perform: pushing, pulling, sliding, rotating. Even the action of springs is exemplified by us when we jump. Stethoscopes and radar are really the extension of our ears; microscopes and telescopes extend our near and far vision. The computer resembles the "on-off" firing of neurons in our nervous system.

What may be applied to tools also can be applied to machines. Machines are simply hands and legs duplicated several times over. We have only two hands but a machine can have many. We have two legs; a machine can have two wheels (as in a bicycle) constantly in revolution; three wheels (as in a wheel barrow); four wheels (as in a car); many more (as in a truck); or simply one continuous wheel (as in a tractor). The creative scientist and inventor have improved on their bodies because they are in touch with their bodies.

Our bodies are our physical vehicles for autonomy, but they also are our inspiration for psychological and intellectual invention and progress. To be in touch with our physical selves is one of the ways to be in touch with our creative wellsprings.

The Striving to Direct One's Destiny

We can never be completely in control of our environment or our destiny. We are born into a society not of our choosing, and we shall assuredly die when the fates will it. There are powers and events over which we have little or no influence: the death of loved ones, natural catastrophes, accidents, and all the chance events of the natural world.

In our own lives we have more control, although not complete control. No matter how hard we work to achieve position, esteem, security, family ties, prestige, and honor, no matter how carefully we work to make a success of our careers and interpersonal environment, there always is the possibility that our dreams and plans may go awry. What we thought we built as strongly as a castle may be toppled like a house of cards. What we thought was secure and firm as a rock may turn out to have been built on sand. No matter how we pursue our dreams of glory and romance, they may turn out to be always the mirage that retreats farther and farther into the distance. There is, then, a reality to the Greek gods' allusion to the capriciousness of fortune.

The fates notwithstanding, there has been a remarkable agreement among the studies of highly creative or highly integrated persons that they are determined, insofar as they are able, to direct their own destinies and to achieve their designated ends. Whether they are called "mature," "fully-functioning," "self-actualizing," "individuated," "healthy," or whatever, on this one point all the researchers and theorists agree: that these persons seek to control their lives, pursue their dreams, and master their environments. The integrated person, like John Philip Henley, is determined to be "the master of his fate and the captain of his," no matter what the contingencies of life.

Maslow called his self-actualizing subjects "self-starters." They do not wait for "Santa Claus" to reward them; they are not "waiting for Godot" to tell them what to do. They decide what they want to do and chart their life course toward those goals. In short, they take responsibility for their own lives.

Studies of highly self-actualizing persons reveal that they were not docile schoolchildren or college students. Indeed, the indications are that they were sometimes so independent that they may have seemed rebellious or somewhat aggressive in their behavior. As adults, they still may make us slightly uncomfortable because they are not satisfied with the status quo. They may rock the boat a little and bring to our attention the facts of life that we really do not wish to see. They sometimes may seem to be rude or abrupt in their interpersonal relationships, not because they want to be impolite or inconsiderate, but because they are more absorbed in the task to be done than in being liked. Furthermore, their originality and unconventional apperceptions of the world may make them seem eccentric and restless, driven by inner forces and so less attentive to social amenities. Although they may exude a magnetic charisma or be well liked, they are not overly concerned with public opinion, and they do not court popularity. Consequently, they may appear to be overly domineering and brusque.

HIGHLY INTEGRATED PERSONS ARE MORE WILLING TO BE THEMSELVES.   Carl Rogers called this the willingness "to be that self which one truly is." As Rogers' subjects progressed through therapy, they began to lose their fear of showing themselves as they felt themselves to be. They allowed the "real me" to show outside, even if that "real me" should prove to be less acceptable to others. Interestingly enough, the very reverse was true: Rogers' subjects discovered that their real personalities were as acceptable, if not more acceptable to others. Why is the real self generally more acceptable to others? Because it is just that—real. It is the authentic side of the person, and no

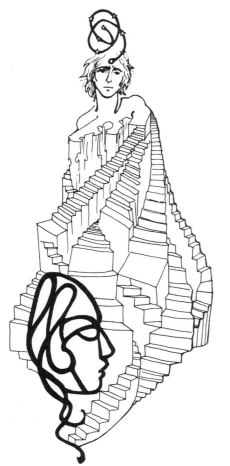

Highly integrated persons pursue their inner experiences.

matter how attractive or charming the *Persona* may be, nothing wins our respect and admiration as much as authenticity and openness.

To become oneself, Rogers explained, requires giving up earlier notions of what others want us to be. Furthermore, it requires giving up one's own unrealistic or overidealized image of oneself—what psychologists call the "self-concept." Rogers's subjects began to feel free of their own list of "shoulds" and "oughts": what they *should* do and *should* be like.

HIGHLY INTEGRATED PERSONS ARE MORE WILLING TO MAKE DECISIONS AND TO TAKE RESPONSIBILITY FOR THEIR LIVES. As Rogers's subjects gradually moved away from the endless demands of others and of themselves, they moved toward following their own desires. In doing so, they became more like Maslow's subjects again, for Maslow's subjects were self-structured and self-determining. In fact, Maslow's subjects exhibited decidedly unconventional thinking and action in private life, although they could assume the cloak of convention when it suited them. They were not wild-eyed bohemians and rebels. On the contrary, they realized their unconventionality might be confusing to others and preferred to dress in conventional garb, speak in a conventional manner, and work in a conventional way so that they could go about the routine, day-to-day tasks of working with others in slow, quiet, undramatic ways and thus achieve real progress rather than call attention to themselves.

When Rogers's clients moved away from pleasing others and toward pleasing themselves, they did not in any way turn into hedonists or thrill seekers. On the contrary, they were more willing to be self-governing and to take responsibility for their own lives and their own mistakes.

Likewise, Maslow's subjects were highly motivated to stake out their own objectives, accepting responsibility for mistakes. We all have known persons who blame society, their parents, or other external factors for their current unhappiness. Maslow's subjects, highly "actualizing" as they were, also found themselves occasionally in unhappy straits. But they did not blame others for their circumstances. They could be foolish, even stupid at times, but their willingness to admit their foolishness and their stupidity (and to learn from the experience) was one of the marks of their creativity and wisdom. They did not suffer any longer than necessary from their mistakes and follies, nor did they indulge themselves in endless remorse, shame, or guilt. They were willing to see their shortcomings realistically, but they attempted to learn from their mistakes and stupidities and to go on from there.

One of the principal obstacles in the way of many persons' progress is the fixation on past misfortunes. This particular difficulty frequently comes up in therapy. In seeking to blame some event or person in their childhood (one parent or both, one's teachers, or "society") for the mess in their lives, such persons fail to see that the "blaming game" is a dead end, a vicious circle that leads nowhere except to more of the same. More important, it prevents persons from taking responsibility for their present actions and direction—until they see that they are thinking in a (vicious) circle.

Great men, as Maslow pointed out, seem to be no less vulnerable to bad breaks and injustices than are the rest of us. What matters is how they overcome such difficulties; it is this quality which distinguishes them. Maslow's subjects knew how to remain stable in the face of life's contingencies. They, too, experienced anxiety, guilt, shame, sorrow, and grief, but they did not allow themselves to get trapped in self-pity and self-blame or in blaming others.

It often has been suggested that a certain amount of pain and anxiety are necessary for developing one's personality beyond a certain point. Indeed, it does appear that pain and anxiety can be useful to us in many ways. For example, suffering can act as a warning that all is not well with us. It can become a signal to reexamine one's present situation, a motivation to grow and change, an inspiration for achievement—if only we know how to use these experiences. As is well known, such events and happenings can become the route by which we discover compassion and empathy for others, or an incentive to pursue knowledge and justice. Creative individuals seem to know how to turn their suffering to constructive use. It is as if they are able to recycle the raw data of their experiences with minimum shame, sorrow, guilt, or conflict. Somehow they then can transcend to another level of their personality on which the "larger view" of life becomes possible. We know surely that this kind of personality transformation is possible. We know much less about how to set this process in motion.

The Quest to Relate Oneself to One's World

At the end of chapter 1 we discussed the possible trap of the growth model. You will recall that the trap in the adjustment model was conforming to other people's standards. The possible trap in the growth model, we said, was unbridled hedonism—self-interest to the extent of exploiting, manipulating, or even hurting others. Actually, we added, the trap is possible only if self-growth is misunderstood as "me *first*, *last*, and *always*" and if *liberty* is misinterpreted to mean *license*. The highly integrated person does not fall into this trap.

HIGHLY INTEGRATED PERSONS ARE SELF-GOVERNING. Rogers

was well aware that self-interest and trusting one's own perceptions can become a handy excuse for unbridled egotism. He therefore raised an essential point when he asked: does such self-direction lead to cruelty or exploitation of others? Rogers's reply: when the person becomes more self-functioning, he also becomes more socialized; at that point he does not need to have someone else control him or inhibit his aggressive impulses — *he is in control* of his impulses, and therefore of himself. Moreover, he does not become less sensitive to others in his environment, he becomes *more* sensitive, *more* accepting of others in the world — and of himself as well.

HIGHLY INTEGRATED PERSONS HAVE A COMMITMENT TO THE GROWTH OF OTHERS.   Maslow's research findings are similar. His subjects had a deep and abiding feeling of identification with others, a general feeling of loving kindness, a genuine desire to help the human race. (In other walks of life, in other times, Maslow said, they may have been called "people of God.") He found them to be highly ethical, and they often had a sense of mission — what might be described as a call or a vocation to serve others.

This kind of steady love of mankind (even when we recognize that individual persons may disappoint us) the Romans called *caritas*, which may be loosely translated as "charity." *Caritas* is said to be the dominant quality of personality in the great saints and reformers of the world. John the Evangelist's last teaching, it is said, was "Love one another!" Jesus of Nazareth's teaching to "Love your neighbor as yourself" is still remembered. It may well be that *caritas* — "charity," what we today call love and compassion — is a powerful force in transcending the personal difficulties and suffering of our individual lives and of attaining peace and certainty. It does seem at any rate to be the mark of certain *originals* — namely, those persons who are remembered for their "love of humankind." Today we might describe these people as loving persons.

Relating to one's world and becoming involved with it can be expressed in many vocations. It may be as a prophet or a priest, or it may be as a diplomat. It may be as a reformer whose life is dedicated to sounding out the facts of life that people need to hear and few want to hear. One thing seems sure: either each of us walks the path on his or her own feet, or the adventure that we call life and growth of personality does not happen.

TRANSCENDING SELF.   Our twentieth century is a remarkable time, even as it has been a time of turbulence, stress, and change. To borrow from Charles Dickens: we live in the best of times and the worst of times. This we know, assuredly, from the demands that are being placed upon each of us, seemingly with ever-increasing frequency. But whatever else it is, life in the late twentieth century is an adventure, and a great part of this adventure is the great change taking place in the consciousness of people. We are beginning to understand ourselves as perhaps no other generations have ever done. Though we struggle and stumble with our new awareness, there seems to be a strength and hope in all our confusion, our excesses, and our search for what can be possible. We are heeding the ancient Greek dictum to "know thyself."

We also are accepting the knowledge (and the responsibility) that we ourselves are the creators and the destroyers of our own persons and, to an even greater extent, of our species and our total planetary environment. We are beginning to rid ourselves of the fallacies and dangers of looking to higher authorities for our salvation, and we also are beginning to give up the belief that "outer" authorities can tell us what to do and how to live our lives. We are beginning to get in touch with what it means to be free, to become aware of our choices, and to think of making changes in our society and ourselves that we want to make. Most important of all, we are beginning to acknowledge and understand that change in the world, our shared world, begins with change in ourselves; that, for example, violence in oneself breeds, in turn, violence in the world at large. In the extended world of plants, trees, air, and water, that kind of consciousness is called *ecological* thinking. In the realm of psychology and individual personality development, which is what we have been discussing, it is becoming an integrated, individuated, authentic person. It is becoming a person who is interested in self-growth but also in advancing the consciousness of others. It is, in the last analysis, the recognition that we all must survive together on this planet. It is a commitment to transcend the self.

viktor frankl: the spiritual dimension

In 1942, a thirty-seven year old neurologist from Vienna was taken from his home and with fifteen hundred other prisoners was taken to the infamous Nazi concentration camp, the death camp known as Auschwitz. His name was Viktor Frankl, and he recorded his experiences for us in a small autobiography, *Man's Search for Meaning*.[17] Every member of his family was destroyed by the Holocaust. He was stripped of all his possessions and when he sought to save just one, a manuscript that would have been his first book, the reaction of a fellow prisoner made Frankl realize that he had arrived at the depths of all possible existence and that his former life was unalterably eradicated; that, in fact, his continued existence had no meaning to anyone but himself. For some time, Frankl was not sure that his life had meaning even for himself, such was the suffering, filth, and horror that he saw all about him.

What saved him, said Frankl, what gave him the will to survive was the discovery of a piece of paper in the clothing of a dead Jew, which contained the prayer sacred to all Jews, the *Shema Yisrael:* it is difficult to put into English the meaning of this small prayer, but it is (in its contextual meaning) a prayer and a call to life.

Frankl returned from Auschwitz, convinced that there is something more to the process of living than pursuing personal happiness, something which inspires the human psyche in even the darkest moments and which gives it the will and purpose to go on. He developed a therapy called *logotherapy,* which is based on the importance of meaning to human existence. Indeed, without meaning, the pursuit of happiness may not even be possible.

Frankl believed that without transcendent values and meaning in our life, we develop what he called *noogenic* neurosis, a state of apathy, aimlessness, and boredom. Frankl considered this state a condition of our times. We have lost traditional conventions, values, and meanings, he said, which accounts for our widespread pursuit of pleasure for its own sake and which must ultimately leave us unsatisfied and empty. Like Jung, Frankl believed that life without purpose and meaning is a nonlife. Like Jung, Frankl affirmed the need for spiritual values, a concept difficult to define because it implies the transcendence of human egotism. Given the freedom that we have, Frankl stressed the responsibility of each human being to choose a life with meaning outside the self. It is not a matter so much of *how* we live but *why* we live that leads to a creative life. We can suffer any ordeal, if there is a self-transcending purpose to our living, if we can give ourselves to something more than self. No person may choose that meaning for us. Meaning is derived by each of us according to what we learn from our experiences, the wisdom we garner from our suffering, and the creations we give to the world. Frankl believed that those who find meaning in life reach the state of self-transcendence, the ultimate state of being for the truly healthy, creative person.

There are three ways to establish meaning for ourselves, said Frankl. These three ways are three fundamental systems of value: creative values, experiental values, and attitudinal values.

Creative values are realizing oneself through creative and productive work, a work which we know gives something to other human beings as well as to ourselves. We may not finish this work, but, said Frankl, an unfinished symphony may be among the most beautiful. Work which helps us to forget "the self" gives joy to our life.

The second value is the experiential value, which is surrendering ourselves to the beauty of nature or art. We may not have experiential fulfillment very often, since it is apt to be the peaks of human existence, but when it comes, we must be ready to perceive it and absorb it.

The third value is our attitudinal values, which are how we respond to and use the darker moments of existence. We are not inundated by suffering, but rather we allow pain and suffering to ennoble the spirit and psyche, to become aware, even as we experience pain, loneliness, and death, that it is by loving others that we receive love. In this facet of his philosophy, a Jewish psychiatrist echoed the prayer of Francis of Assisi: "Let me not so much seek to be loved, as to love."

We, who face the ecological crises of the last decades of the twentieth century, have before us the opportunity to find meaning in our lives as never before. There is much work for us to do toward the preservation of peace on this earth and the survival of the planet for those who who come after us. It is the continuing struggle, said Frankl, that gives excitement and purpose to our lives. There are many ways to work for that ecological peace. What changes that each of us works for must be our individual choice.

chapter 1 footnotes

1. A book typical of this approach is by James W. Bridges, *Psychology, Normal and Abnormal* (New York: D. Appleton and Co., 1930).
2. Sinclair Lewis, *Main Street* (New York: Harcourt Brace Jovanovich, Inc., 1950).
3. Laura Z. Hobson, *Gentleman's Agreement* (New York: Dell Publishing Co., Inc., 1946).
4. Vance Packard, *The Pyramid Climbers* (New York: McGraw-Hill Book Company, 1962). Also by the same author, *The Status Seekers* (New York: David McKay, Inc., 1959).
5. John Steinbeck, *Grapes of Wrath* (New York: The Viking Press, 1939).
6. David Riesman, *A Lonely Crowd: A Study of the Changing American Character*, rev. ed. (New Haven, Conn.: Yale University Press, 1969).
7. Ronald D. Laing, *The Politics of Experience* (New York: Pantheon Books, Inc., 1967).
8. Lawrence K. Frank, "Society as the Patient" in *Dimensions of Social Psychology*, ed., W. Edgar Vinacke and others (Glenview, Ill.: Scott, Foresman & Company, 1964), pp. 50–53.
9. Karl Menninger, *The Crime of Punishment*, (New York: The Viking Press, 1968).
10. Paul W. Barkley and David W. Seckler, *Economic Growth and Environmental Decay* (New York: Harcourt Brace Jovanovich, Inc. 1972).
11. There are many excellent studies on this subject including: Allison Davis and others, *Deep South: A Social Anthropological Study of Caste and Class* (Chicago: University of Chicago Press, 1941).
    John Dollard, *Caste and Class in a Southern Town* (New Haven, Conn.: Yale University Press, 1937).
    W. Lloyd Warner and others, *Social Class in America* (Chicago: Science Research Institutes, 1949).
12. Michael Harrington, *The Other America: Poverty in the United States* (New York: Macmillan Publishing Co., Inc., 1963).
13. Robert N. Butler, *Why Survive: Being Old in America* (New York: Harper & Row, Publishers, Inc., 1975).
14. Abraham H. Maslow, *The Farther Reaches of Human Nature* (New York: The Viking Press, 1971).
15. David Riesman and Nathan Glazer, *Faces in the Crowd* (New Haven, Conn.: Yale University Press, 1952).
16. Abraham H. Maslow, *Motivation and Personality*, 2nd ed. (New York: Harper & Row, Publishers, Inc., 1954), pp. 171–74.
17. R. Buckminster Fuller, *Approaching the Benign Environment* (Riverside, N.J.: Macmillan Publishing Co., Inc., 1970).
18. Carl R. Rogers, "Toward a Modern Approach to Values: The Valuing Process in the Mature Person" in *Person to Person: The Problem of Being*

Human, ed., Carl Rogers and Barry Stevens (New York: Pocket Books, 1971), pp. 19–20.

19. Elisabeth Kübler-Ross, *Death: the Final Stage of Growth* (Englewood Cliffs, N.J.: Prentice-Hall, Inc., 1975).

20. Thomas Szasz, *The Myth of Mental Illness* (New York: Harper & Row, Publishers, Inc., 1961).

21. Ronald D. Laing, *The Politics of Experience*, (New York: Pantheon Books, Inc., 1967).

22. William James, *The Principles of Psychology* (New York: Dover Publications, Inc., 1950).

23. Hannah Green, *I Never Promised You a Rose-Garden* (New York: Holt, Rinehart & Winston, 1964).

24. Sigmund Freud, *The Ego and the Id* (London: Hogarth Press, 1935).

25. Sigmund Freud, *An Outline of Psycho-Analysis* (New York: W. W. Norton & Co., Inc., 1949).

26. Sigmund Freud: *Civilization and Its Discontents* (New York: W. W. Norton & Co., Inc., 1962).

27. N. R. F. Maier, *Frustrations: A Study of Behavior without a Goal* (New York: McGraw-Hill Book Company, 1949).

28. Carl G. Jung, *Memories, Dreams, Reflections* (New York: Pantheon Books, Inc., 1961).

29. Carl G. Jung, *Modern Man in Search of a Soul* (New York: Harcourt Brace Jovanovich, Inc., 1955).

30. Mary Renault, *The King Must Die* (New York: Pantheon Books, 1958).

31. Erik Erikson, *Childhood and Society*, 2nd ed. (New York: W. W. Norton and Co., Inc., 1950).

32. There have been many studies of the effect of long-term institutionalism on babies and children. Some of the classic studies are: Sally Provence and Rose C. Lipton, *Infants in Institutions* (New York: International University Press, 1963). John Bowlby, "Observations of Older Children Who Were Deprived in Infancy," in *Outside Readings in Psychology*, ed., Eugene L. Hartley and Ruth E. Hartley (New York: Thomas Y. Crowell Company, Publishers, 1957), pp. 378–91.

33. William James, *The Principles of Psychology* (New York: Dover Publications, Inc., 1950).

34. Daniel J. Levinson with Charlotte N. Darrow, Edward B. Klein, Maria H. Levinson, and Braxton McKee, *The Seasons of a Man's Life* (New York: Alfred A. Knopf, Inc., 1978).

35. Gail Sheehy, *Passages* (New York: E. P. Dutton & Co., Inc., 1976).

36. Carl G. Jung, "The Relations between the Ego and the Unconscious" in *Collected Works*, Volume 7: *Two Essays on Analytical Psychology* (New York: Bollingen Series XX, 1953).

chapter 2 footnotes

1. Abraham H. Maslow, *Motivation and Personality*, 2nd ed. (New York: Harper & Row, Publishers, Inc., 1954).

2. Walter B. Cannon, *Bodily Changes in Pain, Hunger, Fear, and Rage*, rev. ed. (New York: Appleton-Century-Crofts, 1929).

3. Clark L. Hull, *Principles of Behavior* (New York: Appleton-Century-Crofts, 1943).

4. Desmond Morris, *The Naked Ape* (New York: McGraw-Hill, Book Company, 1967).

5. Robert W. White, ed., *The Study of Lives* (New York: Atherton Press, 1963).

6. Alfred Adler, *What Life Should Mean to You* (New York: G. P. Putnam's Sons, 1931).

7. Eduard Spranger, *Types of Men: The Psychology and Ethics of Personality* (New York: Johnson Reprint Corp., 1928).

8. Gordon W. Allport, Phillip E. Vernon, and Gardner Lindzey, *Study of Values*, 3rd ed. (Boston: The Riverside Press, 1951).

9. Gordon W. Allport, *Becoming: Basic Considerations for a Psychology of Personality* (New Haven, Conn., Yale University Press, 1955).

10. Carl G. Jung, *Psychological Types or the Psychology of Individuation* (New York: Harcourt Brace Jovanovich, Inc., 1924).

11. Carl G. Jung, *Memories, Dreams, Reflections* (New York: Vintage Books, 1961).

12. Carl G. Jung, *Psychological Types or The Psychology of Individuation* (New York: Harcourt Brace Jovanovich, Inc., 1924).

13. William H. Sheldon, S. S. Stevens, and W. B. Tucker, *The Varieties of Human Physique* (New York: Harper & Row, Publishers, Inc., 1940).

14. Anne Anastasi, *Psychological Testing*, 3rd ed. (New York: Macmillan Publishing Co., Inc., 1968).

15. Roger J. Williams, *Biochemical Individuality: The Basis for the Genetotrophic Concept* (Austin: University of Texas Press, 1969).

16. Erving Goffman, *Stigma: Notes on the Management of "Spoiled Identity"* (Englewood Cliffs, N.J.: Prentice-Hall, Inc., 1963).

17. Robert Rosenthal and Lenore Jackson, *Pygmalion in the Classroom* (New York: Holt, Rinehart & Winston, 1968).

18. Janet D. Elashoff and Richard E. Snow, *Pygmalion Reconsidered* (Worthington, Ohio: Charles A. Jones, 1971).

19. Wendell Johnson, *Stuttering and What You Can Do about It* (Danville, Ill.: Interstate, 1966).

20. Nancy Bayley and R. Tuddenham, "Adolescent Changes in Body Build," in *43rd Yearbook, National Society for the Study of Education* (1949), pp. 33–55.

21. Mary C. Jones and Nancy Bayley, "Physical Maturing Among Boys as Related to Behavior," in *Journal of Educational Psychology*, 41 (March, 1950), pp. 129–48.

22. Leon J. Kamin, "Heredity, Intelligence, Politics and Psychology," N. J. Block and Gerald Dworkin, eds., in *The I. Q. Controversy* (New York: Pantheon Books, 1976).

23. Jerome Kagan and Howard Moss, *Birth to Maturity: A Study in Psychological Development* (New York: John Wiley & Sons, Inc., 1962).

24. Sigmund Freud, *An Outline of Psychoanalysis* (New York: W. W. Norton & Co., Inc., 1949).

25. Brian Sutton-Smith and B. G. Rosenberg, *The Sibling* (New York: Holt, Rinehart & Winston, 1970).

26. Irving D. Harris, *The Promised Seed* (Riverside, N.J.: Macmillan Publishing Co., Inc., 1964).

27. Alfred Adler, *Understanding Human Nature* (New York: Fawcett Books, 1959).

28. Lillian Belmont and Francis A. Marolla, "Birth Order, Family Size, and Intelligence," in *Science*, 182 (Dec., 1973), pp. 1096–1101.
29. Jonathan R. Warren, "Birth Order and Social Behavior," in *Psychological Bulletin*, 65, (Jan., 1966), pp. 38–49.
30. Simone De Beauvoir, *The Second Sex* (Westminster, Md.: Random House, Inc., 1974).
31. E. E. Maccoby and C. N. Jacklin, *Psychology of Sex Differences* (Stanford, Calif.: Stanford University Press, 1966).
32. Anne Anastasi, *Individual Differences* (New York: John Wiley & Sons, Inc., 1965).
33. Jerome Kagan, *Change and Continuity in Infancy*, (New York: John Wiley & Sons, Inc., 1965).
34. Donald W. MacKinnon, "What Makes a Person Creative?" in *Contemporary Readings in General Psychology*, 2nd ed., ed., Robert S. Daniel (Boston: Houghton Mifflin Company, 1965), pp. 153–57.
35. Brian Sutton-Smith and B. G. Rosenberg, *The Sibling* (New York: Holt, Rinehart & Winston, 1970).
36. Margaret Mead, *Coming of Age in Samoa* (New York: William Morrow & Co., Inc., 1929).
37. Geoffrey Gorer, *Sex and Marriage in England Today* (New York: Humanities Press, Inc., 1971).

chapter 3 footnotes

1. John Dollard and Neal E. Miller, "What Is a Neurosis?" in *Basic Contributions to Psychology: Readings*, ed., Robert L. Wrenn (Belmont, Calif.: Wadsworth Publishing Co., Inc., 1966), pp. 206–11.
2. David C. McClelland, J. W. Atkinson, R. A. Clark, and E. A. Lowell, *The Achievement Motive* (New York: Appleton-Century-Crofts, 1953).
3. "Angst," *Time*, March 31, 1961, p. 46.
4. Condensed from Vincent F. O'Connell and April O'Connell *Choice and Change*, (Englewood Cliffs, N.J.: Prentice-Hall, Inc., 1974), pp. 55–63.
5. Nathan Azrin, "Pain and Aggression" in *Readings in Psychology Today*, (Del Mar, Calif.: CRM Books, 1967), pp. 114–21.
6. William H. Grier and Price M. Cobbs, *Black Rage* (New York: Basic Books, Inc., Publishers, 1961).
7. Robert R. Sears, E. E. Maccoby, and H. Levin, *Patterns of Child Rearing* (New York: Harper & Row, Publishers, Inc., 1957).
8. Sigmund Freud, *A General Introduction to Psychoanalysis* (New York: Liverwright Publishing Corp., 1935).
9. Wilder Penfield and Herbert Jasper, *Epilepsy and the Functional Anatomy of the Human Brain* (Boston: Little, Brown & Company, 1954).
10. Sigmund Freud, *The Psychopathology of Everyday Life*, Volume 6 (London: Hogarth, 1952), pp. 1–310.
11. John M. Darley and Bibb Latane, "When Will People Help in a Crisis?" in *Readings in Psychology Today* (Del Mar, Calif.: CRM Books, 1967), pp. 428–33.
12. Eric Berne, *Games People Play* (New York: Grove Press, Inc., 1964).
13. Frederick S. Perls, *Egos Hunger and Aggression* (New York: Random House, Inc., 1969).

14. Everett Shostrom, *Man the Manipulator* (New York: Bantam Books, Inc., 1968).
15. Anna Freud, *Ego and the Mechanisms of Defense* (New York: International University Press, 1967).
16. Jerome L. Singer, *The Inner World of Daydreaming* (New York: Harper & Row, Publishers, Inc., 1975).
17. Ronald Laing, *Knots* (New York: Random House, Inc., 1972).
18. Paul Tillich, *Courage To Be* (New Haven, Conn.: Yale University Press, 1952).
19. Erich Fromm, *Escape From Freedom* (New York: Holt, Rinehart & Winston, 1963).
20. James Kettle, *EST Experience* (New York: Zebra, 1976).
21. Karen Horney, *The Collected Works of Karen Horney*, Volume 2 (New York: W. W. Norton & Co., Inc., 1942), p. 65.
22. Arthur Koestler, *Act of Creation* (Riverside, N.J.: Macmillan Publishing Co. Inc., 1964).

chapter 4 footnotes

1. Hans Zinsser, *Rats, Lice and History* (Boston: Little, Brown & Company, 1935).
2. Edwin G. Boring, *A History of Experimental Psychology*, 2nd ed. (New York: Appleton-Century-Crofts, 1950).
3. Morton Kelsey, *Healing and Christianity* (New York: Harper & Row, Publishers, Inc., 1976).
4. Norman R. F. Maier, *Psychology in Industrial Organizations*, 4th ed. (Boston: Houghton Mifflin Company, 1973).
5. Karl Menninger, "Man Against Himself," in *General Psychology: Selected Readings*, ed., Joseph F. Perez (New York: Van Nostrand Reinhold Company, 1967).
6. Franz Alexander, *Psychosomatic Medicine* (New York: W. W. Norton & Co., Inc., 1963).
7. Flanders Dunbar, *Mind and Body: Psychosomatic Medicine*, rev. ed. (Westminster, Md.: Random House, Inc., 1955.)
8. Walter B. Cannon, *The Wisdom of the Body*, 2nd. ed. (New York: W. W. Norton & Co., Inc., 1963).
9. Hans Selye, *The Stress of Life* (New York: McGraw-Hill Book Company, 1956).
10. Thomas H. Holmes and Richard H. Rahe, "The Social Readjustment Rating Scale," in *Journal of Psychosomatic Research*, 11 (August, 1967), pp. 213–17.
11. Thomas H. Holmes and T. Stephenson Holmes, "Short-term Intrusions into the Life Style Routine," in *Journal of Psychosomatic Research*, 14 (June, 1976) pp. 121–32.
12. Sol Levine and Norman A. Scotch, eds., *Social Stress* (Chicago: Aldine Publishing Company, 1970).
13. Joseph Brady, R. Porter, D. Conrad, and J. Mason, "Avoidance Behavior and the Development of Gastroduodenal Ulcers," in *Journal of the Experimental Analysis of Behavior*, 1 (Jan/Feb, 1958), pp. 69–72.

14. Sidney Cobb and Robert Rose, "Hypertension, Peptic Ulcers, and Diabetes in Air-Traffic Controllers," in *Journal of the American Medical Association*, 224 (April, 1973) pp. 489–492.

15. Isaac Berenblum, *Cancer Research Today* (Elmsford, New York: Pergamon Press, Inc., 1967).

16. Harold G. Wolff, "A Concept of Disease in Man," in *Psychosomatic Medicine*, 24 (Jan-Feb, 1962), pp. 25–30.

17. Meyer Friedman and Ray H. Rosenman, *Type A Behavior and Your Heart* (New York: Alfred A. Knopf, 1974).

18. Herbert Basedow, *The Australian Aboriginal* (New York: AMS Press, Inc., 1977).

19. J. M. Sawrey and C. W. Telford, *Psychology of Adjustment* (Boston: Allyn & Bacon, Inc., 1971).

20. Ethel Shanas, *The Health of Older People: A Social Survey* (Cambridge, Mass.: Harvard University Press, 1962) and Robert N. Butler, *Why Survive?* (New York: Harper & Row, Publishers, 1975) p. 260.

chapter 5 footnotes

1. Ivan Pavlov, *Conditioned Reflexes* (New York: Dover Publications, Inc., 1960), p. 26.

2. Gordon W. Allport, *The Nature of Prejudice* (Reading, Mass.: Addison-Wesley Publishing Co., Inc., 1954).

3. Carl I. Hovland, "The Generalization of Conditioned Responses," in *Journal of General Psychology*, 17 (July-Oct, 1937), pp. 125–48.

4. John B. Watson with Rosalie R. Watson (New York: W. W. Norton & Co., Inc., 1928).

5. B. F. Skinner, *The Behavior of Organisms* (New York: Appleton-Century-Crofts, 1938).

6. Colin Wilson, "Existential Psychology: A Novelist's Approach," in *Challenges of Humanistic Psychology*, ed., J. F. T. Bugental (New York: McGraw-Hill Book Company, 1967).

7. Keller Breland and Marian Breland, *Animal Behavior* (New York: The Macmillan Company, 1966).

8. Florence R. Harris and others, "Effects of Adult Social Reinforcement on Child Behavior," in *The Causes of Behavior*, Volume II, 2nd ed., eds., J. F. Rosenblith and W. Allensmith (Boston: Allyn & Bacon, Inc., 1966), pp. 99–106.

9. "Thirty-Year Follow Up: Counseling Fails," *Science News*, November 26, 1977, p. 357.

10. Lyle E. Bourne and Bruce R. Ekstrand, Psychology: Its Meaning & Principles, 2nd ed. (New York: Holt, Rinehart & Winston, 1976).

11. Edmund Jacobson, *Progressive Relaxation*, 2nd ed. (Chicago: University of Chicago Press, 1938).

12. Frederick Perls and others, *Gestalt Therapy* (New York: Dell Publishing Co., Inc., 1951).

13. Joseph Wolpe, *Psychotherapy by Reciprocal Inhibition* (Stanford, Calif.: Stanford University Press, 1958).

chapter 6 footnotes

1. Wilhelm Reich, *Character Analysis* (New York: Farrar, Strauss & Giroux, Inc., 1949).
2. Frederick S. Perls, personal communication, 1963.
3. Abraham H. Maslow, *Toward a Psychology of Being*, 2nd ed. (New York: Van Nostrand Reinhold Company, 1968).
4. Stanley Keleman, *Your Body Speaks Its Mind* (New York: Simon & Schuster, Inc., 1975).
5. Walter B. Cannon, *The Wisdom of the Body*, 2nd ed. (New York: W. W. Norton & Co., Inc., 1963).
6. Hans Selye, *The Stress of Life* (New York: McGraw-Hill Book Company, 1956).
7. Alexander Lowen, *The Betrayal of the Body* (New York: McGraw-Hill Book Company, 1956).
8. Frederick S. Perls and others, *Gestalt Therapy: Excitement and Growth in the Human Personality* (New York: Dell Publishing Co., Inc., 1951).
9. Y. C. Tsang, "Hunger Motivation in Gastrectomized Rats," in *Journal of Comparative Psychology*, 26 (Jan. 1938), pp. 1–17.
10. Frances M. Lappe, *Diet for a Small Planet* (New York: Ballentine Books, Inc., 1971).
11. Harmon Bro: *High Play: Turning on without Drugs* (New York: Coward, McCann & Geoghegan, Inc., 1971).
12. Norman Cameron, *Personality Development and Psychopathology*, (Boston: Houghton Mifflin Company, 1963).
13. Irving L. Janis, *Psychological Stress* (New York: John Wiley & Sons, Inc., 1958).
14. James L. McCary, *McCary's Human Sexuality*, 3rd ed. (New York: Van Nostrand Reinhold Company, 1968).
15. Aldous Huxley, *Ape and Essence* (New York: Harper & Row, Publishers, Inc., 1972).
16. Donald S. Marshall and Robert C. Suggs, eds., *Human Sexual Behavior* (New York: Basic Books, Inc., Publishers, 1971).
17. Frank A. Beach, ed., *Sex and Behavior* (New York: John Wiley & Sons, Inc., 1965).
18. A. C. Kinsey and others, *Sexual Behavior in the Human Male*, (Philadelphia: W. B. Saunders Co., 1948).
    A. C. Kinsey and others, *Sexual Behavior in the Human Female* (Philadelphia: W. B. Saunders Company, 1953).
19. Clellan S. Ford and Frank A. Beach, *Patterns of Sexual Behavior* (New York: Harper & Row, Publishers, Inc., 1951).
20. Robert E. Ornstein, *The Psychology of Consciousness*, 2nd. ed. (New York: Harcourt Brace Jovanovich, Inc., 1977).
21. Swami Prabhavananda and Christopher Isherwood, *How to Know God: The Yoga Aphorisms of Patanjali* (New York: Harper & Brothers, 1953).
22. C. Eisdorfer and M. P. Lawton, eds., *The Psychology of Adult Aging* (Washington, D.C.: American Psychological Association, 1971).
23. Claudio Naranjo and Robert E. Ornstein, *On the Psychology of Meditation* (New York: The Viking Press, 1971).
24. Desmond Dunne, *Yoga* (New York: Funk & Wagnalls, Inc., 1953).

25. Ernest E. Wood, *Practical Yoga* (North Hollywood, Calif.: Wilshire Book Co., 1972), p. 116.
26. Bernard Gunther: *Sense Relaxation below Your Mind* (New York: Collier Books, 1968).
27. Evelyn Underhill, *Practical Mysticism* (London: J. M. Dent & Sons, 1914).
28. Charles C. Tart, *Altered States of Consciousness* (New York: John Wiley & Sons, Inc., 1969).
29. Denise Denniston and Peter McWilliams, *The TM Book* (Allan Park, Mich.: Veremonger Press, 1975).
30. B. K. Anand, G. S. Chhina, and B. Singh, "Some Aspects of Electroencephalographic Studies in Yogis," in *Psychology and Life*, 9th ed., Philip G. Zimbardo and Floyd L. Ruch, eds. (Glenview, Illinois: Scott, Foresman and Company, 1977) p. 304.
31. Jack Forem, *Transcendental Meditation* (New York: E. P. Dutton Co., Inc., 1973).

chapter 7 footnotes

1. G. C. Davison and John M. Neale, *Abnormal Psychology: An Experimental Clinical Approach* (New York: John Wiley & Sons, Inc., 1974).
2. William Shakespeare, *Macbeth*, act 5, sc. 1, lines 56–58.
3. Martin E. Seligman: *Helplessness: On Depression, Development and Death* (San Francisco: W. H. Freeman & Company Publishers, 1975).
4. Emile Durkheim, *Suicide* (Riverside, N.J.: The Free Press, 1951).
5. Earle A. Grollman, *Suicide* (Boston: Beacon Press, 1971).
6. J. C. Coleman, *Abnormal Psychology and Modern Life*, 5th ed. (Glenview, Ill.: Scott, Foresman & Company, 1976).
7. R. A. Woodruff, Jr., D. N. Goodwin, and S. B. Guze, *Psychiatric Diagnosis* (New York: Oxford University Press, Inc., 1974).
8. Alexander Lowen, *Betrayal of the Body* (London: Collier-Macmillan, 1967).
9. C. H. Thigpen and H. Cleckley, *The Three Faces of Eve* (New York: McGraw-Hill Book Company, 1957).
10. Flora Rheta Schreiber, *Sybil* (Chicago: Henry Regnery, 1973).
11. Hervey Cleckley, *The Mask of Sanity*, 4th ed. (St. Louis: C. V. Mosby Co, 1964).
12. I Samuel, 16:14–23.
13. G. Zilboorg and G. W. Henry, *A History of Medical Psychology* (New York: W. W. Norton & Co., Inc., 1941).
14. Harry S. Sullivan, *The Interpersonal Theory of Psychiatry*, ed., S. Penry and M. S. Gowel (New York: W. W. Norton & Co., Inc., 1953).
15. Carl Rogers, *Client-Centered Therapy* (Boston: Houghton Mifflin Company, 1951).
16. Eric Berne, *Transactional Analysis in Psychotherapy* (New York: Grove Press, Inc., 1961).
17. Thomas Harris, *I'm O.K.—You're O.K.* (New York: Harper & Row, Publishers, Inc., 1969).

18. Frederick S. Perls, *Gestalt Therapy Verbatim*, ed., John A. Stevens (Lafayette, Calif.: Real People Press, 1967).
19. Frederick Perls, *In and Out of the Garbage Pail* (Lafayette, California: Real People Press, 1967).
20. Lowell H. Storms, "Implosive Therapy: An Alternative to Systematic Desensitization" in *Modern Therapies*, eds., Virginia Binder and others (Englewood Cliffs, N.J.: Prentice-Hall, Inc., 1976).
21. Thomas G. Stamfl and Donald J. Lewis "Essentials of Implosive Therapy," in *Journal of Abnormal Psychology*, 72 (Dec. 1967), pp. 496–503.
22. Stuart Chase, *Tyranny of Words* (New York: Harcourt Brace Jovanovich, Inc., 1966).
23. Albert Ellis, *Humanistic Psychotherapy: The Rational-Emotive Approach* (New York: McGraw Hill Book Company, 1974).
24. William Glasser, *Reality Therapy* (New York: Harper & Row, Publishers, Inc., 1967).
25. George Bach and Peter Wyden, *Intimate Enemy: How to Fight Fair in Love and Marriage* (New York: William Morrow & Co., Inc., 1969).
26. Ira Progoff, *At a Journal Workshop: The Basic Text and Guide for Using the Intensive Journal* (New York: Dialogue House, 1975).
27. Roberto Assagioli, *The Act of Will* (New York: The Viking Press, 1973).
28. Edith Kramer, *Art Therapy in a Children's Community* (New York: Schocken Books, Inc., 1977).
29. Everett Shostrom, "Let the Buyer Beware" in *Psychology Today*, 2, no. 12 (May, 1969), pp. 38–40.

chapter 8 footnotes

1. David Cooper, *The Death of the Family* (New York: Vintage Books: Random House, Inc., 1970).
2. *Ruth:* 1:11.
3. Humphrey D. Kitto, *The Greeks* (New York: Penguin Books, 1950).
4. Suetonius Tranquillus, C. *Lives of the Twelve Caesars*, tr. Philemon Holland (New York: E. P. Dutton Co., 1923).
5. Morton Hunt, *The Natural History of Love* (New York: Alfred A. Knopf, Inc., 1959).
6. Paramahansa Yogananda, *Autobiography of a Yogi* (Los Angeles: Self-Realization Fellowship, 1972).
7. Albert Ellis, *The Art and Science of Love* (New York: Lyle Stuart, 1960).
8. Jean-Pierre Hallet, *Pygmy Kitabu* (New York: Random House, Inc., 1973).
9. James L. McCary, *McCary's Human Sexuality*, 3rd ed. (New York: Random House, Inc., 1973).
10. R. R. Bell, "Female Sexuality as Related to Levels of Education," in *Sex and Behavior*, (November 1971), pp. 8–14.
11. M. F. Demartino, "How Women Want Men to Make Love," in *Sexology*, 45 (October, 1978), pp. 4–7.
12. A. C. Kinsey, W. B. Pomeroy, and C. E. Martin, *Sexual Behavior in the Human Male* (Philadelphia: W. B. Saunders Company, 1948).
13. William H. Masters and Virginia E. Johnson, *The Pleasure Bond* (Boston: Little, Brown & Company, 1970).

14. R. Zick, L. A. Peplau, and C. Hill, quoted in *The Psychology of Being Human*, ed., E. B. McNeil (San Francisco: Canfield Press, 1977).
15. Frank Cox, *Human Intimacy: Marriage, the Family and Its Meaning* (St. Paul: West Publishing Co., 1978).
16. Rollo May, *Love and Will* (New York: W. W. Norton & Co., Inc., 1969).
17. Alan Watts, *Nature, Man and Woman* (Westminster, Md.: Random House, Inc., 1970).
18. James L. McCary, *McCary's Human Sexuality*, 3rd ed. (New York: Van Nostrand Reinhold Company, 1978).
19. William H. Masters and Virginia E. Johnson, *The Pleasure Bond* (Boston: Little, Brown & Company, 1970).
20. Robert O. Blood, Jr. and Donald W. Wolfe, *Husbands and Wives: The Dynamics of Family Living* (New York: The Free Press, 1965).
21. E. Van Den Haag, "Love and Marriage?" in *Love, Marriage, Family: A Developmental Approach*, ed., M. E. Lasswell and T. E. Lasswell (Glenview, Ill.: Scott, Foresman & Company, 1973).
22. E. Walster, E. Berscheid, and G. W. Walster, "New Directions in Equity Research," in *Journal of Personality and Social Psychology*, 25 (February, 1973), pp. 151–76.
23. Jean Piaget, *Genetic Epistemology* (New York: Columbia University Press, 1970).
24. Carl Rogers, *Client-Centered Therapy* (Boston: Houghton Mifflin Company, 1951).
25. George Bach and Peter Wyden, *Intimate Enemy: How to Fight Fair in Love and Marriage* (New York: William Morrow & Co., Inc., 1969).
26. James L. McCary, *McCary's Human Sexuality*, 3rd ed. (New York: Van Nostrand Reinhold Company, 1978).
27. William H. Masters and Virginia E. Johnson, *The Pleasure Bond* (Boston: Little, Brown & Company, 1970), p. 253.
28. A. C. Kinsey, W. B. Pomeroy, and C. E. Martin, *Sexual Behavior in the Human Male* (Philadelphia: W. B. Saunders Company, 1948). Also, A. C. Kinsey, W. B. Pomeroy, C. E. Martin, and P. H. Gebhard, *Sexual Behavior in the Human Female* (Philadelphia: W. B. Saunders Company, 1953).
29. Morton Hunt, *Sexual Behavior in the Seventies* (Chicago: Playboy Press, 1974).
30. I. L. Reiss, "Toward a Sociology of the Heterosexual Love Relationship" in *Love, Marriage, Family: A Developmental Approach*, ed., M. E. Lasswell and T. E. Lasswell (Glenview, Ill.: Scott, Foresman & Company, 1973).
31. Morton Hunt, *Sexual Behaviors in the Seventies* (Chicago: Playboy Press, 1974).
32. Robert N. Butler, *Why Survive? Being Old in America* (New York: Harper & Row, Publishers, Inc., 1975).
33. J. C. Haughey, "The Commune-Child of the 1970's," in *Intimate Life Styles: Marriage and Its Alternatives*, ed., J. O. De Lora and J. R. DeLora (Pacific Palisades, Calif.: Goodyear, 1975).
34. James Leslie McCary, *Freedom and Growth in Marriages* (Santa Barbara, Calif.: Hamilton Publishing, 1975).
35. John F. Cuber and Peggy B. Harroff, *The Significant Americans* (New York: Appleton-Century-Crofts, 1965).

chapter 9 footnotes

1. Alfred Korzybski, *Science and Sanity,* 4th ed. (Lakeville, Conn.: Institute of General Semantics, 1958).
2. Irving Lee and Laura Lee, *Handling Barriers in Communication* (Lakeville, Conn.: Institute of General Semantics, 1968).
3. Ralph G. Nichols and Leonard A. Stevens, *Are You Listening?* (New York: McGraw-Hill Book Company, 1957).
4. Donald E. Bird, in *Are You Listening?* by R. G. Nichols and L. A. Stevens (New York: McGraw-Hill Book Company, 1957).
5. Wendell Johnson, *Your Most Enchanted Listener* (New York: Harper & Row, Publishers, Inc., 1956).
6. Harvey Goldstein, "Reading and Listening Comprehension Rates At Various Controlled Rates," in *Contributions to Education, no. 821* (New York: Bureau of Publications, Teachers College, Columbia University, 1940).
7. Carl Rogers, *Client-Centered Counseling* (Boston: Houghton Mifflin Company, 1951).
8. Eric Berne, *The Games People Play* (New York: Grove Press, Inc., 1964).
9. Carl Jung, *Collected Works: Archetypes and the Collective Unconscious* (New York: Bollingen Series, 1959).
10. Randall Harrison, "Nonverbal Communications: Exploration into Time, Space, Action and Object," in *Dimensions in Communication*, ed., J. H. Campbell and H. W. Hepler (Belmont, Calif.: Wadsworth Publishing Co., Inc., 1965) p. 161.
11. E. T. Hall, *The Silent Language* (Garden City, N.Y.: Doubleday & Co., Inc., 1959).
12. Mark L. Knapp, *Nonverbal Communication in Human Interaction* (New York: Holt, Rinehart & Winston, 1972).
13. Albert E. Scheflen, *Body Language and Social Order* (Englewood Cliffs, N.J.: Prentice-Hall, Inc., 1973).
14. Seymour Fisher, *Body Consciousness* (Englewood Cliffs, N.J.: Prentice-Hall, Inc., 1973).
15. W. Wolff, *The Expression of Personality* (New York: Harper, 1943).
16. Robert Ardrey, *The Territorial Imperative* (New York: Atheneum Publishers, 1966).
17. Seonaid Robertson, *Rosegarden and Labyrinth: A Study in Art Education* (London: Routledge and Kegan Paul, 1963).
18. Michael Argyle, *Social Interaction* (New York: Atherton Press, 1969).
19. E. T. Hall, *The Hidden Dimension* (Garden City, N.Y.: Doubleday & Co., Inc., 1966).
20. A. F. Kinzel, "Towards an Understanding of Violence," in *Attitudes*, 1, no. 1 (1969).
21. Michael Argyle, *Social Interaction* (New York: Atherton Press, 1969).

chapter 10 footnotes

1. Sigmund Freud, *The Interpretation of Dreams* (New York: Avon Books, 1965), p. xxv.
2. Charles Dickens, *A Christmas Carol.*
3. *Book of Job.*

4. Genesis 40, 41.
5. I Kings:3.
6. Matthew 1:20.
7. Matthew 2:12.
8. Matthew 2:13.
9. Matthew 2:19-20.
10. Matthew 27:6.
11. Norman McKenzie, *Dreams and Dreaming* (New York: Vanguard Press, 1965).
12. "The Babylonian Talmud," in *The World of Dreams*, ed., R. Woods, tr. A. Cohen (New York: Random House, Inc., 1947), p. 123.
13. Norman McKenzie, *Dreams and Dreaming* (New York: Vanguard Press, 1965).
14. Sigmund Freud, *Introductory Lectures on Psychoanalysis* (London: Hogarth Press, 1961), p. 171.
15. Sigmund Freud, *Introductory Lectures on Psychoanalysis* (London: Hogarth Press, 1961), pp. 344–45.
16. Carl G. Jung, *Memories, Dreams, Reflections* (New York: Pantheon Books, Inc., 1963), pp. 168–69.
17. Carl G. Jung, *Memories, Dreams, Reflections* (New York: Pantheon Books, Inc., 1963), p. xiv.
18. Carl C. Jung, *Collected Papers* (London: Balliere, Tindall and Cox), pp. xiii-xiv.
19. Carl G. Jung, *Man and His Symbols* (Garden City, N.Y.: Doubleday & Co., Inc., 1964), p. 85.
20. Carl G. Jung, "Two Essays on Analytical Psychology," in *Collected Papers,* Volume 7 (Princeton, N.J.: Princeton University Press, 1959).
21. Carl G. Jung, "The Archetypes and the Collective Unconscious," in *Collected Works*, Volume 9 (Princeton, N.J.: Princeton University Press, 1959).
22. T. S. Eliot, *The Love Song of J. Alfred Prufrock.*
23. David Foulkes, *The Psychology of Sleep* (New York: Charles Scribners' Sons, 1966).
24. A. Nathaniel Kleitman, *Sleep and Wakefulness*, 2nd ed. (Chicago: University of Chicago Press, 1963).
25. Calvin S. Hall, *The Meaning of Dreams* (New York: McGraw-Hill Book Company, 1966).

chapter 11 footnotes

1. Sigmund Freud, *Totem and Taboo* (New York: Norton Library, 1952).
2. Erich Fromm, *The Forgotten Language* (New York: Grove Press, Inc., 1957).
3. Bruno Bettelheim, *The Uses of Enchantment* (New York: Alfred A. Knopf, Inc., 1976).
4. Michael Hornyansky, "The Truth of Fables" in *Only Connect: Readings in Children's Literature*, ed., Sheila Egoff and others (Toronto, Canada: Oxford University Press, Ltd., 1969), pp. 121–32.
5. Jean Piaget, *The Origins of Intelligence in Children* (New York: International University Press, 1952).

6. Jean Piaget, *The Moral Judgment of the Child* (Glencoe, Ill.: The Free Press, 1948).
7. Lawrence Kohlberg, "Development of Moral Character and Moral Ideology," in *Review of Child Development Research*, Volume 1, eds., M. S. Hoffman and L. W. Hoffman (New York: Russell Sage Foundation, 1964), pp. 383–431.
8. Eric Berne, *Games People Play* (New York: Grove Press, Inc., 1964).
9. J. L. Moreno, *The First Psychodramatic Family* (New York: Beacon House, 1964).
10. Herbert Fensterheim and Jean Baer, *Don't Say Yes When You Want to Say No* (New York: Dell Publishing Co., Inc., 1975).
11. Carl G. Jung, "The Archetypes and the Collective Unconscious," Volume 9: *The Collected Works of C. G. Jung* (Princeton, N.J.: Princeton University Press, 1959).

chapter 12 footnotes

1. Carl G. Jung, *Collected Works, Psychology and Alchemy*, Volume 12, (New York: Bollingen Series, 1953).
2. Hannah Arendt, *The Human Condition* (Chicago: University of Chicago Press, 1970).
3. Franze Borkenau, "The Concept of Death" in *Death and Identity,* ed., Robert Fulton (New York: John Wiley & Sons, Inc., 1965), pp. 42–56.
4. Jessica Mitford, *The American Way of Death* (New York: Simon & Schuster, Inc., 1963).
5. Elisabeth Kübler-Ross, *On Death and Dying* (Riverside, N.J.: Macmillan Publishing Co., Inc., 1970).
6. Robert E. Neale, *The Art of Dying* (New York: Harper & Row, Publishers, Inc., 1971).
7. Geoffrey Gorer, *Death, Grief and Mourning* (New York: Doubleday & Co., Inc., 1967).
8. Elisabeth Kübler-Ross, *On Death and Dying* (Riverside, N.J.: Macmillan Publishing Co., Inc., 1970).
9. Barney G. Glaser and Anselm L. Strauss, *Awareness of Dying* (Chicago: Aldine Publishing Co., 1965).
10. Anne Kliman, *Psychological First Aid for Recovery and Growth* (New York: Holt, Rinehart & Winston, 1978).
11. Barney G. Glaser and Anselm L. Strauss, *Time for Dying* (Chicago: Aldine Publishing Co., 1965).
12. Norman L. Faberow, "The Cultural History of Suicide," in *Separate Paths* by Linnea Pearson (New York: Harper & Row, Publishers, Inc., 1977).
13. Karl Barth, *Ethics* (New York: Macmillan Paperbacks, 1965).
14. Linnea Pearson, *Separate Paths* (New York: Harper & Row, Publishers, Inc., 1977).
15. Edwin Schneidman, *The Psychology of Suicide* (New York: Science House, 1970).
16. Robert E. Neale, *The Art of Dying* (New York: Harper & Row, Publishers, Inc., 1971).

17. Linnea Pearson, *Separate Paths* (New York: Harper & Row, Publishers, Inc.,1977).
18. Arnold vanGennep, *The Rites of Passage* (Chicago: University of Chicago Press, 1960).
19. Edwin S. Shneidman, *Death of a Man* (The New York Times Book Co.: Quadrangle Press, 1973).
20. Bernadine Kreis, *Up From Grief* (New York: The Seabury Press, 1969).
21. Caitlin Thomas, *Left-over Life to Kill* (Boston: Little, Brown & Company, 1957).
22. Mel Krantzler, *Creative Divorce* (Philadelphia: J. B. Lippencott Company, 1973).
23. Morton Hunt and Bernice Hunt, *The Divorce Experience* (New York: McGraw Hill Book Company, 1977).
24. Paul Bohannan, "Stepfathers and the Mental Health of Their Children." Unpublished report to the National Institute of Mental Health, U.S. Dept. of Health, Education, and Welfare, December, 1975 in *The Divorce Experience*, by Morton Hunt and Bernice Hunt (New York: McGraw Hill Book Company, 1977).

chapter 13 footnotes

1. Edwin G. Boring, *A History of Experimental Psychology*, 2nd ed. (New York: Appleton-Century-Crofts, 1950).
2. Anne Anastasi, *Psychological Testing*, 2nd ed. (New York: Macmillan Company, 1961).
3. Carl R. Rogers, *Client-Centered Therapy* (Boston: Houghton Mifflin Company, 1951).
4. Abraham Maslow, *Motivation and Personality* (New York: Harper & Row, Publishers, Inc., 1954).
5. Lawrence Kohlberg, *Development of Moral Character and Moral Ideology, Review of Child Development Research*, Volume I, eds., M. S. Hoffman and L. W. Hoffman (New York: Russell Sage Foundation, 1964), pp. 383–431.
6. Donald W. MacKinnon, "What Makes a Person Creative?" in *Contemporary Readings in General Psychology*, 2nd ed., ed., Robert S. Daniel (Boston: Houghton Mifflin Company, 1965) pp. 153–57.
7. Frank Barron, "The Needs for Order and Disorder as Motives in Creative Activity" in *Scientific Creativity: Its Recognition and Development*, eds., Calvin W. Taylor and Frank Barron (New York: Wiley & Sons, Inc., 1963) pp. 157–158.
8. Rene Descartes, *Discourse on Method*, tr. Lawrence J. Lafleur (Indianapolis, Ind.: Bobbs-Merrill Company, Inc., 1960).
9. Lawrence S. Kubie, "Blocks to Creativity" in *Explorations in Creativity*, eds., Ross L. Mooney and Taher A. Razik (New York: Harper & Row, Publishers, Inc. 1967) pp. 33–42.
10. Abraham Maslow, *Motivation and Being* (New York: Harper & Row, Publishers, 1954).
11. D. T. Suzuki, *Zen Buddhism, Selected Writings of D.T. Suzuki*, ed., William Barrett (Garden City, N.Y.: Doubleday Anchor Books, 1956).

12. Carl Jung, "Approaching the Unconscious" in *Man and His Symbols,* ed. Carl G. Jung and others (Garden City, New York: Doubleday, 1964) pp. 18–103.
13. Carl G. Jung, *Memories, Dreams, Reflections,* ed., Aniela Jaffe (New York: Random House, Pantheon Books, Inc., 1961).
14. Abraham Maslow, *Motivation and Personality* (New York: Harper & Row, Publishers, Inc., 1954) p. 164.
15. Maslow, *Ibid.,* pp. 163–164.
16. Herbert Gutman, "The Biological Roots of Creativity" in *Explorations in Creativity,* eds., Ross L. Mooney and Taher A. Razik (New York: Harper & Row, Publishers, Inc., 1967) pp. 3–32.
17. Viktor Frankl, *Man's Search for Meaning: An Introduction to Logotherapy* (Boston: Beacon Press, 1962).

glossary

Note: The following glossary defines words and terms as they are used in this book, rather than as they would be defined by a standard dictionary. If the term you are seeking is not here, check the index.

abnormal: Behavior that deviates from the standard or average. Although the word is supposed to apply to deviation at both ends of the scale, the word has generally come to mean the negative extreme as in low intellectual functioning or schizophrenic behavior.

abstraction: A concept or idea that is not rooted in concrete objects. Frequently, abstractions are ideals such as *freedom, justice, happiness*, or psychological constructs such as *intelligence, mental health,* and *personality integration.* An abstraction cannot be seen, touched, tasted, or in any other manner made tangible. Therefore, when we deal in abstractions we are always in danger of abstruseness and miscommunication.

accident proneness: The tendency to have more than the average number of accidents. Accident proneness occurs more often with persons suffering from chronic emotional problems than with those who have a more stable personality structure. The former are more tense and therefore less aware of their environment and of the objects in it. We can all also be accident prone from time to time as the result of acute environmental stress.

acute: Sudden, sharp, and critical, demanding immediate attention as compared to *chronic*. One may suffer from chronic headaches as a matter of course, but an acute appendix attack will send one to a hospital.

addiction: Reliance on anything to the point of dependence where one feels physically or psychologically depressed without it. Common addictions are alcohol, cigarettes, marijuana, and coffee. Less recognized addictions may be excitement (according to Hans Selye), reading, movies, and even sex can become an addiction.

adjustment psychology: The psychological thrust of the first half of the twentieth century (roughly) in which the person was expected to adjust to problematic situations in contrast to the humanistic thrust. See *humanistic psychology.*

adolescence: In human beings, the period from puberty to early adulthood, roughly from the early teens to the early twenties.

Aesop's Fables: A series of short stories by a Greek named Aesop. In these stories, written down almost 2,000 years ago, animals act like humans similar to the Uncle Remus stories or nursery stories in which human foibles are revealed.

affect: The emotional state of the person as contrasted to the intellectual or cognitive function.

altered state of consciousness: A distinctive change in one's perception of the universe and/or one's self-awareness. An ASC can be induced in many ways: drugs, starvation, sensory deprivation, meditation, sensory stimulation, religous experiences, etc.

ambivalence: The existence of contradictory feelings toward a given situation. Individuals may be confused by their ambivalent feelings toward a loved one until one understands that one may love someone, but also have angry, resentful, and other alienating feelings for that person.

amnesia: Loss of memory concerning oneself and one's life. Amnesia can be partial or total.

anal character: According to Freud, a personality patterning which is characterized by obstinacy, excessive orderliness, and stinginess.

animism: Primitive cause-and-effect explanations of natural events. Common phenomena such as lightning, accidents, sickness, and famine are attributed to malicious spirits or angry gods that must be placated.

Animus-Anima: According to Jung, the Anima represents the feminine polarity in a man's personality and is his inspiration and creativity when he allows himself to get in touch with it. The Animus is the unconscious male component in a woman's personality and represents her intellectual and creative aspect.

antagonistic behaviors: Those behaviors which cannot normally occur at the same time. Wolpe uses antagonistic behaviors to de-condition a person's fears. If a person can stay relaxed while visualizing a feared object or event, the phobia will extinguish since fear cannot exist in a state of relaxation.

anxiety: Generalized feelings of apprehension, dread, and uneasiness often having to do with future events and anticipation of disaster. Anxiety differs from fear in that the latter is associated with a specific object or event while anxiety is a diffuse emotion seemingly unconnected to specific situations. See also *global anxiety* and *social anxiety*.

anxiety neurosis: An emotional state which results in physiological symptoms. Among many others, these symptoms can be "queasy" stomach, insomnia, headaches, tics, alcoholism and drug abuse, excessive smoking, overeating, etc. See also *character neurosis*.

apathy: Listlessness, indifference. One of the consequences of overwhelming frustration.

Archetype: A Jungian concept that refers to the autonomous forces in the collective or racial unconscious. These Archetypes represent the psychological development of the human race, and are frequently expressed in art, religious symbolism, literature, mythology, and dreams. See also, the *Wise Old Man, Wise Old Woman, Wise Child, Trickster, Shadow,* and *mandala*.

Archetypal themes: These are the great themes of "the human condition." Among these themes are birth, life, suffering, death, rebirth, transcendence, and transfiguration. These themes are also the themes of art, religion, literature, philosophy, and existential psychology.

asanas: The stretching postures of Hatha Yoga.

assumptions: These are inferences about observed events. Assumptions are dangerous in that one may interpret a situation quite wrongly.

asthma: A condition characterized by wheezing, difficulty in breathing, and a feeling that one is about to suffocate. It has long been associated with overprotection and "smother" love.

attitude: One's feelings or ideas about certain events or persons. Generally speaking, one's attitudes are unconscious and unexamined, but they influence our behavior to an enormous degree.

autogenic training: Learning to control one's physiological responses through concentration or meditation. Example; learning to relieve oneself of headache by imagining one's head getting cooler and one's arms and hands receiving the heat.

autonomy: Erikson's term for the second life-stage in which children learn to stand on their own two feet and perform the basic functions of eating, defecating, walking, etc. by themselves.

basic needs: In Maslow's theory of personality, these are the physiological needs of water, food, air, etc.

behavior: Any response made by a person or other organism which can be observed and measured.

behavior modification: This is therapeutic change through an adaptation of operant conditioning. Behavioral therapists do not seek causative explanations for abnormal behavior. They seek to discover those events which are reinforcing the negative behavior, and once having identified them, to remove them. At the same time, desirable behaviors are reinforced until the person or child is responding in a more constructive manner.

behavior therapies: Therapies which aim not just at insight, but at change. Includes Wolpe's de-conditioning therapy of phobia, rational-emotive therapy, reality therapy, and implosive therapy.

behavioral predispositions: Characteristics of neonates which seem to be innate or inborn.

benign: A state of being nonmalignant; harmless; kindly.

Bhagavad-Gita: An ancient Hindu religious epic which recounts the story of Arjuna and Krishna. It is an allegory of human struggle and personality development.

bias: A tendency to lean toward an opinion; sometimes synonymous with prejudicial thinking.

bioenergetics: Therapeutic treatment that focuses on body posture and body language. Bioenergetic therapists believe that our character is revealed in our body language and that change in our posture will have feedback on our character. They often use physical exercise to "break through" body armor.

biofeedback: A technique in which biological signals, such as heart rate, electroencephalographic activity, or blood pressure are converted to visual or auditory signals so that persons become aware of them (i.e. biological signals are "fed back" to the subject).

"blaming" game: The tendency to blame others for our misfortunes. "You are responsible for what has happened to me." We tend to blame our parents, our spouses, our children, our race, or ethnic background for our problems. The blaming game is dissolved when we use the concept that we are responsible for our own lives.

bodily awareness: An acceptance and appreciation of one's body with all one's feelings and functions. Maslow noted that highly self-actualizing persons have good bodily awareness, or as he said, they are "good animals." In contrast, many persons are cut off from their feelings as, for example, schizoid personalities.

catharsis: A psychoanalytic term indicating the release of repressed emotions and "forgotten" thoughts through dreams, drama, literature, and other creative expressions.

catatonic: A reaction in which the person's energy level drops to minimal activity. The person tends to be negative, rigid, withdrawn, and sometimes remains in the same position for hours, even days.

celibacy: The state of existence in which the person voluntarily foregoes sexual activity.

chakras: Hindu philosophy postulates the existence of seven energy centers along the spinal cord corresponding roughly to the major ductless glands. Meditation is supposed to open these centers and in so doing, raise the person to a higher level of consciousness.

channeling of emotions: Although the human being is capable of a rich repertory of emotions, some tend to use only a narrow spectrum of this repertory. When the individual is under excessive stress, he or she will tend to channel anxiety into those emotions or defense mechanisms which provide the most emotional support.

character armor: A Reichian concept which postulates that defense mechanisms are not only psychologically evident, they can be seen on the physical body as hardening or "armoring" of areas of the torso and head. As a result these "rings" are more vulnerable to dysfunctioning and disease.

character neurosis: As contrasted to the anxiety neurosis, the character neurosis (according to Reich) does not result in uncomfortable or painful symptoms, but rather in no symptoms at all; in fact, the person cuts himself off from bodily awareness. See *character armor.*

chauvinism: An unexamined belief that one's country, ideology, and beliefs are superior to others.

chronic: Describes a condition that exists over a long period of time as contrasted to acute. See also *acute.*

classical conditioning: Another name for Pavlovian conditioning or stimulus substitution conditioning.

client-centered therapy: A system of psychotherapy which is based on the belief that the client himself can solve his own problems if a warm, safe climate of trust has been established.

cognitive function: Called also the intellectual function, or thinking.

coitus: Sexual intercourse.

coitus interruptus: A form of birth control in which the man withdraws from the woman before climax is reached.

collective objects: A Freudian concept which states that in dreaming, one object or person can stand for many objects or persons. A soldier, for example, might represent an entire army.

collective unconscious: According to Jung, the human race retains in its memory archetypes of previous generations and civilizations. See also *Archetype, Shadow, Animus-Anima, Wise Old Man, Wise Old Woman, Wise Child* and *Trickster.*

compensation: A fairly benign defense mechanism in which the person performs well in one area to make up for a deficiency in another.

compensatory function: Jung believed that the person seeks to be a balanced organism. If he is weak in one function, he or she will tend to become stronger by finding a person strong in that function. See also the four *functions: intuitive; sensing; thinking; feeling.*

compulsive personality: One that is excessively orderly, rigid, and pedantic. Such persons often have to perform certain acts in rigid ways in order to allay excessive anxiety.

condensation: As used by Freud to describe dream symbols, it is the fusing of two or more objects, words, or persons. *Norekdal,* for example, is the condensation of two names: *Nora* and *Ekdal.*

conditioned response (CR):   A response aroused by a conditioned stimulus. A learned behavior.

conditioned stimulus (CS):   A neutral stimulus which, when paired with an unconditioned stimulus, eventually arouses a response (CR) similar to the unconditioned response.

conditioning therapies: Therapies which treat the symptoms and do not depend on causal factors. Since neurosis is considered to be poor habits (inappropriate responses), the treatment is to extinguish the poor responses and replace them with more constructive responses.

conscience: According to Freud, our super-ego, or all the voices of our society when we are young, which are introjected.

consciousness: That state of awareness when we experience ourselves as "I."

conversion hysteria: Psychological repression which takes the form of a physical symptom such as psychological deafness, psychological blindness, psychological paralysis, etc.

coping: The attempts of the individual to manage one's life problems.

correlation: The relationship of two variables or events.

creative fantasy: The therapeutic technique to increase creativity by having the person imagine or visualize certain images.

cross-era transitions: Levinson's term to indicate the major passages and turning points of our lives.

daydream: A dream-like fantasy while awake.

defense mechanisms: The many ways we avoid feeling pain, anxiety, loss of self-esteem, etc.

delusions: Unreal beliefs.

denial: Defense mechanism in which the person rejects the reality of actual events. Example: a mother of a dead child may plead with people to help get her child to a hospital in spite of evidence that the child is, in fact, dead.

depression.   The feeling of being "down," helpless, and apathetic. The person experiences a low level of energy and may even cease much of the normal everyday activity.

developmental task: Erikson's concept of the competencies the person needs to master at every major life stage.

deviant behavior: Any behavior not shared by most of the persons in one's society or peer group.

disassociation: Feelings of unreality which are attributed to the splitting off of unacceptable emotions and thoughts.

displacment: As related to dreams, the transference of strong emotions to relatively neutral symbols.

doctrine of specific etiology: The theory that a specific disease is caused by one germ, bacillus, or virus and no other.

"double-bind": A communication that contains two messages that are contradictory and that result in feelings of confusion or impotence in the receiver of that communication.

double standard: The attitude that suggests that what is appropriate for one sex is not appropriate for the other.

dream work: Freud postulated that the dreamer translates unacceptable wishes and feelings into disguised dream symbols.

dynamics: Pertaining to the underlying motivations of behavior, particularly "unconscious" behavior.

ectomorph: According to Sheldon's physical classifications, a person who is "all skin and bones" and prefers intellectual activities.

ego: Latin for "I" or the conscious aspect of personality.

ego integrity: The life task, according to Erikson, of old age.

ego strength: The amount of psychic energy a person has to cope with life problems. A person with minimal ego strength will tend to "break down" over problems that will not affect one with more ego strength.

either-or thinking: Thinking which tends to be categorical, judgmental, and stereotypic. Examples: good/bad; right/wrong; virtue/vice, etc. Such thinking tends to limit a person's ability to perceive reality clearly since he or she rejects the infinite possibilities between these two extremes.

Electra complex: A Freudian concept indicating excessive or highly sexualized affections between a father and his daughter. Incest is possible but not implied in this term.

enculturation: The process by which societies, institutions, and other groups mold, shape, and otherwise influence human personality.

endomorph: The Sheldon classification in which the person's muscular structure predominates the physique, resulting in someone who is physically active and "always on the go."

epistemology: That branch of philosophy that studies *how* we know what we know.

Era: Levinson's term for the four great ages of human existence: Youth, Early Adulthood, Middle Adulthood, Later Adulthood.

etc.: The symbol used by general semanticists to indicate all the variables that may exist but are not accounted for.

existential psychology: The school of psychology that deals with the person's inner experiences as compared to behaviorism (which focuses on observable overt behaviors), or psychodynamics (which focuses on unconscious motivations).

extravert: A term used by Jung to describe the person whose primary orientation is focused on the outside world and on interactions with others. See also *introvert*.

fallacy: An erroneous belief.

fantasy: 1) A daydream; 2) sometimes used as a therapeutic approach designed to stimulate creativity.

feeling function: One of Jung's four functions in which emotions predominate. See also *thinking, intuitive,* and *sensing* functions.

figure-ground relationship: Perls' term to indicate the influence of past experiences on "here-and-now" perceptions.

fixation: Stereotypic behaviors that indicate a neurotic adaptation to certain events. A person may be fixated in one or more areas but be very flexible and creative in others.

folklore: Stories that have been handed down through generations.

fratricide: The killing of one's brother, as in the story of Cain and Abel. One of society's taboos.

free association: The so-called "talking cure" invented by Freud wherein a person relates his "stream of consciousness" thoughts and feelings without attempting to censure or edit them.

fully-functioning: Rogers' term for the person who is operating at top efficiency and creativity.

general semantics: A branch of linguistics that attempts to increase clear communication between persons.

generalized responses: Behaviors which are similar to conditioned responses and aroused by similar, but not the original, conditioned stimuli. Example: after Albert was conditioned to fear a white rat, he exhibited generalized responses of fear (but not as intensely) to other white, furry objects such as a muff, a rabbit, a white fur-coat.

genocide: The destruction of a whole tribe, nation, or race.

geriatrics: The study of the psychology and problems of old age and of ways to assist the elderly.

global anxiety: Anxiety that has to do with the destruction of the planet and survival of the human race.

"going negative": Jacobson's term for a state of extreme relaxation.

growth group: Any group which assembles for the purpose of increasing effective behavior and creativity.

hallucination: A visual or other sensory experience which is not shared by others, and which is the result of many factors as, for example, alcohol, hallucinogenic drugs, hypnosis, extreme fatigue, illness, etc.

hedonism: The philosophic point of view that one's life goals should be aimed at pleasurable sense experiences, eptomized as, "Eat, drink, and be merry for tomorrow you may die." In psychology, hedonism can be correlated with Freud's *pleasure-pain principle.*

here-and-now: Focus on the immediate situation. In Gestalt therapy the person is encouraged to focus on his/her present feelings and emotions rather than dredge up past material.

heredity: The transmission of physical and psychological characteristics through genetic material.

heterosexuality: A sexual preference for the opposite sex.

homeostasis: Referring to the changes the body goes through in order to adapt to changes in the environment and maintain the equilibrium of the body. For example, in hot weather the organism sweats, which lowers body temperature.

homosexuality: A sexual preference for members of the same sex.

hormones: Substances produced by the

endocrine glands and released into the blood stream which then act upon body organs or other glands.

humanism: A philosophy that asserts the dignity and worth of men and women and their capacity for self-realization.

humanistic psychology: The philosophic thrust to emphasize the growth potential of men and women and their ability to make free choices about the goals of life.

hypochondria: Excessive concern for one's health, often without evidence that there is anything "really" wrong. This term should be clearly distinguished from the term *malingering* which implies that the person is pretending sickness but knows that he or she is not really sick.

hysteria: A condition in which emotional conflicts are converted to physical symptoms such as hysterical paralysis, blindness, deafness, amnesia, etc.

id: Formulated by Freud, it is a concept that describes the deepest unconscious aspect of human personality; the pleasure-oriented, lustful and narcissistic being that is born into this world.

identity: Erikson's term for the adolescent life-task. The young person's need to find an identity that is distinct from parents and family.

impotent: Pertaining to lack of ability, strength, or power. Used many times as the inability to perform sexually.

incest: Sexual relations between persons of close blood ties. Incest is a strong taboo throughout most civilizations and cultures.

individual differences: The specifically unique characteristics that distinguish one person from another. Humanistic psychology emphasizes the recognition and value of these differences between people.

individuation: Carl Jung's term for the process by which the person emerges psychologically from group, or tribal, or mass consciousness to become a unique and wholly creative person.

industry: The major life-task of the school child, as formulated by Erik Erikson: in our society, the ability to read, write, and compute.

initiative: As formulated by Erikson, the task of the preschooler which includes the acquisition of the principles of time, space, planning, and cooperation with others.

innate: Unlearned; inborn.

intimacy: Erikson's term for the life-task of early adulthood. Sharing ourselves with others physically and psychologically.

introjection: The adoption of attitudes and values which may not be consistent with one's personality type.

introspection: The process of self-analysis and self-examination.

introvert: Jung's term for the person who focuses on inner thoughts and feelings rather than on the actions of others. See also *extravert*.

intuitive function: One of Jung's four functions by which we sense what is not presently self-evident; the ability to imagine future possibilities and to make lightning swift solutions to problems.

Krishna: The Hindu god representing supreme consciousness.

latency period: According to Freud, the period from about 6 years to puberty when the sexual drive is relatively quiescent.

latent dreams: The disguised or hidden

meaning of the symbols of the dream.

libido: The instinctual drive for sexual expression.

life crisis units: The relative amount of emotional impact of any given event.

life "script": The way we program our lives and manipulate others into acting out our life expectations, goals, and even disappointments.

life style: As defined by Alfred Adler, it is the underlying motif or life theme of our individual existence. One person's life style may reflect his obsession with power; another person may be acting out the hero myth; still another may be attempting to assuage some real or imaginary guilt over and over again.

magical thinking: Primitive cause-and-effect thinking typical of childhood and animistic religions.

malingering: The act of feigning sickness as, for example, the little girl who complains of feeling sick so she won't have to go to school.

mandala: Generally, a quadrilateral or circular figure which is used as a meditative guide in Tibetan (Tantric) and other religious and philosophic studies; a way of altering consciousness.

manic-depressive psychosis: A kind of personality patterning characterized by extreme mood swings from depression to elation and vice versa.

marker events: Levinson's term for those events which accompany transitional phases of our lives. Examples: divorce, sickness, change of job, death.

masturbation: The manipulation of one's own sexual organs to achieve orgasm.

matricide: The killing of one's mother which is a strong societal taboo in most civilizations and religions.

meditation: The calming of body and mind so as to achieve a higher level of consciousness. It is also used as a way of treating certain physical ailments such as high blood pressure, hypertension, tension headaches, etc.

mesomorph: Sheldon's term for the muscular person who is very active and always "on the go."

monogamy: One man-one woman bonding in a marriage-type relationship as compared to other relationships such as polygamy, group marriage, homosexuality, etc.

myth: A story, tale, fable, or epic which attempts to explain natural phenomena and the human condition.

narcissim: The need to seek pleasure in oneself. The term is taken from the Greek myth in which the beautiful Narcissus fell in love with his own image reflected in a pool. Narcissistic persons are, essentially, self-absorbed and unaware of the needs of others.

needs: The basic requirements for survival and adequate living.

neonate: The infant from birth to two weeks.

neurasthenia: A 19th century term to describe a state of chronic physical and psychological lethargy.

neurosis: A mental, emotional, or behavioral disorder. Specifically, it is the inability to cope with a given event(s) except by fixated, unconscious, and stereotypic responses. See also *fixation*.

neutral stimulus: Any stimulus which does not arouse a conditioned or unconditioned response. After pairing with an unconditioned stimulus, the NS becomes a conditioned stimulus arousing a specific conditioned response.

nomadism: A defense mechanism in

which the person is unable to maintain a stable life situation. He may become a hobo, change jobs frequently, or even switch from one sexual partner to another in an attempt to find "happiness" or "peace of mind."

norm: Behaviors typical of a specific group or population.

normal: In psychiatry or psychology, it implies freedom from a debilitating disorder. Growth psychologists are becoming more wary of using this term.

numinous: Indicates the presence of the supernatural, the mystical, the aesthetic, or the spiritual.

obsession: A thought which occurs over and over. All of us have experienced obsessional thoughts such as a song which "keeps playing" over and over in our heads.

obsessive-compulsive reaction: A "neurotic" reaction in which the person is subject to recurring thoughts and seems compelled to repeat certain behaviors. Lady Macbeth's handwashing ritual is a classic example.

Oedipus complex: The term Freud used to represent excessive attachment of a son to his mother.

operant conditioning: A type of learning (conditioning) which depends on the prior behaviors of the organism. These emitted responses are reinforced (or not reinforced) which has the effect of increasing (or decreasing) the frequency of these behaviors.

oral stage: According to Freud, the first psychosexual stage of development. The baby finds erotic pleasure in activities involving the mouth such as sucking and eating.

orgasm: The emotional and physical climax of the sexual act.

overcompensation: The attempt to make up for an actual or perceived inferiority in one area by becoming outstanding in another.

overconformity: A term employed to describe a lack of originality and initiative.

"own" or "owning": A term employed by Fritz Perls which involves the person becoming aware of his own projections.

pain-attack response: The response of animals to pain in which they attack other animals or even inanimate objects in the vicinity.

paranoid: Pertaining to the tendency toward delusional thoughts, particularly the idea that certain people are out to harm one.

patricide: The killing of one's father, considered by most societies as taboo.

patterning: An arrangement of the parts that form a characteristic and unified impression to the observer.

Pavlovian conditioning: See classical conditioning.

"peak" experiences": Maslow's term for the experience that has been variously labeled "the mystic experience," "satori," "Zen," "enlightenment," "cosmic consciousness," etc.

perceptual defense: A defensive mechanism by which a person screens out disagreeable perceptions.

Persona: The mask worn by the ancient Greek and Roman actor to indicate his role in the play. In Jungian psychology, the Persona refers to the "public face" we put on in front of others and that we frequently believe ourselves to be. See also *Shadow*.

personal anxiety: Concern about one's personal survival such as how to pay the bills, concern over one's children, etc.

personality integration: The process or

processes by which a person coordinates his mental, emotional, physical, and sociological experiences toward a unified pattern of goal-striving behaviors.

phallic stage: Freud's term to indicate a sexually mature person's development.

phobia: An exaggerated fear of something which renders that person helpless to deal with the event in an objective and rational manner.

pleasure-pain principle: Freud's doctrine to indicate that the infant is governed by hedonistic instincts. Ordinarily, the pleasure-pain principle is mediated by the superego, but the psychopathic or sociopathic personality is still largely dominated by the desire to please the self regardless of the rights or feelings of others.

polarities: Jung believed the human personality is made up of oppositional forces (male/female; material/spiritual; Anima/Animus). The task of personality integration is to reconcile and harmonize these polarities.

polygamy: Male/female bonding involving one man with two or more women.

process: The individual way each of us integrates our experiences toward purposeful action and further growth. Each person's process is unique and expressive of the self. Personality integration is learning to understand and value one's own "process" as distinct from others, and to attune to that process.

proprioceptors: Cell receptors in the muscles of the body which convey information to the central nervous system (CNS) about our internal physiology.

psychoanalysis: The therapy originated by Freud which sought to alleviate the person's suffering from neurosis by bringing unconscious (repressed) material into consciousness through free association and dream analysis.

psychosomatic illness: A term used for any physical illness in which part of the etiology of the disease is caused by stress.

Pygmalion effect: The manner in which our perceptions of a person will tend to influence that person's behavior.

racial unconscious: Jung's term to indicate another type of memory besides our personal memory. The racial or collective unconscious extends back to the progenitors of our species, and unites us with the rest of humankind.

"real me": Carl Rogers's term for the experience people have when they take off their "masks" (see Persona) and be and talk as themselves.

reality principle: Freud's term for the way the *id* (which is governed by the pleasure-pain principle) is mediated by the forces of society and "socialized" into a civilized being. See also, *id* and *pleasure-pain principle*.

receptors: Structures which are sensitive to certain kinds of energies and which transmit these energies to the central nervous system.

reciprocal inhibition: The principle by which Wolpe enables phobic patients to overcome their fears. Wolpe teaches the person to extinguish anxiety responses by inducing deep relaxation in the person and then has the person imagine the feared object or event. Wolpe reasons that anxiety and relaxation cannot exist at the same time.

reflex: An unlearned, involuntary response to a stimulus.

regression: A defense mechanism which

is a type of "forgetting." Regression differs significantly from forgetting in that forgetting is a passive decay of unimportant material while regression is an active submerging into the unconscious of painful or guilt-producing thoughts, feelings, memories, etc.

scape-goating: The act of taking out one's unhappiness or frustration on others in destructive ways.

self-esteem: One's perception of self.

self-revealment: Allowing one's inner thoughts and feelings known to others.

sensing function: Jung's term to indicate that part of self involved with physical reality: the dimensions of space and geography. A good sensor can describe and map his physical environment with a good deal of accuracy. See also *thinking, intuitive function, feeling.*

sensory awareness: The ability of the person to be in touch with one's body and its physiological reactions to internal and external stimuli.

Shadow: The Archetypal opposite of the *Persona*. The Shadow is that part of ourselves that we dislike, disown, and deny. See also *Persona.*

shaping behavior: An application of operant conditioning in which the desired behavior is reinforced and the undesirable behavior is nonreinforced.

sibling: Term used to indicate any brother or sister relationship.

sibling rivalry: The natural competition of brothers and sisters for their parents' affection.

social anxiety: Concern for the welfare of others and for living up to the expectations of others.

spontaneous recovery: The sudden reappearance of a supposedly extinguished behavior.

stereotypic behavior: Any act which is repetitive and "fixated." See also *fixation.*

stress: Any event in the environment which produces "wear and tear" on the organism. Excessive stress produces psychosomatic illness.

sublimation: Directing "lower" infantile and aggressive impulses into more socially acceptable outlets.

subliminal: Below conscious awareness.

superego: That part of the human personality that functions as the "voices of our society;" Freud's term for "conscience."

symbol: An image or object or activity which stands for something else. A flag is simply a piece of cloth but as a symbol, it has inspired people to go to battle and to die.

syndrome: A set of symptoms that appear together.

taboo: Acts which are profoundly repugnant to any society as, for example, incest and matricide.

tactile: Pertaining to the sense of touch.

Tao: An Eastern philosophy of life which stresses the ebb and flow of existence.

therapy: Any form of treatment which can be considered healing.

thinking: The cognitive or rational decision-making part of our consciousness.

tranquilizer: Any drug which calms the bodymind.

transcend: To rise above one's present limits; to go beyond one's present world view to a more comprehensive state.

trauma: An injurious event, whether physical or psychological.

Trickster: An Archetype which polarizes the mischievous and spontaneous aspects of human personality. See also *Wise Child*.

unconditioned stimulus (US): Any physical event which arouses an unconditioned response (innate, reflexive-type behavior).

unconditioned responses (UCR): Any unlearned, reflexive type behavior.

unconscious: That part of human functioning of which we are unaware.

valid: Founded on fact; capable of being verified.

variable: Any factor which brings about an observable event.

wisdom of the body: An instinctive sense which maintains the body's homeostasis and health.

Wise Child: The Archetype which personifies the wisdom of innocence, idealism, and spontaneity. See also *Trickster*.

Wise Old Man: The Archetype which represents the wisdom of the masculine personality; i.e., logic, reason, the experience of observing human nature; The Wise Old Man is the counselor, the prophet, the Medicine Man, the Shaman, etc.

Wise Old Woman: The Archetype which represents feminine wisdom; i.e., intuition, hunches, foresight, clairvoyance, etc. Examples: the gypsy, the sybil, the oracle, the high priestess, etc.

Yin-Yang: The oppositional forces of the universe. See *Tao*.

yoga: Any Eastern technique for personality integration such as meditation, asanas, service to others, etc.

Zen: The Japanese form of Buddhism which is characterized by lightning-quick flashes of transcendence.

index